8

D0893396

WITHDRAWN

Revolution
and Convention
in Modern Poetry

811.09
St 24 r

Revolution and Convention in Modern Poetry

Studies in

Ezra Pound, T. S. Eliot, Wallace Stevens,
Edwin Arlington Robinson, and Yvor Winters

Donald E. Stanford

Newark: University of Delaware Press
London and Toronto: Associated University Presses

© 1983 by Associated University Presses, Inc.

Associated University Presses, Inc.
4 Cornwall Drive
East Brunswick, N.J. 08816

Associated University Presses Ltd
27 Chancery Lane
London WC2A 1NF, England

Associated University Presses
2133 Royal Windsor Drive
Unit 1
Mississauga, Ontario
Canada L5J 1K5

Library of Congress Cataloging in Publication Data

Stanford, Donald E., 1913—
  Revolution and convention in modern poetry.

  Bibliography: p.
  Includes index.
  1. American poetry—20th century—History and criticism. I. Title.
PS324.S66 1982   811'.52'09   81–50342
ISBN 0–87413–197–9   AACR2

Printed in the United States of America

For Maryanna

CAT Jun28'83

82·6860

Contents

A Prefatory Note

In this volume I attempt to assess the literary value of the experimentalist or revolutionary movement in Anglo-American poetry (which began shortly after Ezra Pound's arrival in London in 1908) by comparing the work of its two most influential poets, Pound and T. S. Eliot, with that of Edwin Arlington Robinson, who was never affected by the poetic revolution, and Yvor Winters, who at first wrote under the influence of the experimentalist poets Pound and William Carlos Williams and then reacted against this influence and became a counter-revolutionist in principle and in practice. Wallace Stevens, who perhaps had the greatest talent of the five poets here studied, stands at the center of the group, for he wrote several great poems, including "Sunday Morning," "Of Heaven Considered as a Tomb," and "On the Manner of Addressing Clouds," in conventional blank verse. But he was deeply affected by the poetic revolution, and he wrote several fine poems, such as "Domination of Black" and "The Snow Man," in the cadenced, concrete, free-verse manner of the imagists.

My conclusion is that the revolutionary movement will pass into history as an interesting, provocative, and sometimes brilliant deviation from the main line of poetry in English written since the sixteenth century and that the major work in this century (with the partial exception of Stevens) has been accomplished by those poets who were not participating (in their mature period) in the poetic revolution. I have in mind especially William Butler Yeats, Thomas Hardy, Robert Bridges, Robinson, Robert Frost, Winters, and perhaps a few others. Such an opinion would not have been given a hearing thirty years ago, but increasing distance has lent increasing disenchantment with the eccentricities of the revolutionary generation, and my conclusions do not appear as absurd as they would have had they been published several decades earlier. I ask the reader to suspend judgment until he has read the book.

I have chosen only five poets to illustrate my thesis. I wished to write a short book rather than a long one. I chose Pound and Eliot because of their profound influence on the first half of the twentieth century. Stevens had to be included because of the literary importance of a few of his poems. I have long considered Robinson to be one of the best of the conventional poets. Winters, because he wrote brilliant poems as an experimentalist and (in my opinion) very important poems as a writer in conventional forms, was also a natural choice.

I hope that this will not be considered to be merely a thesis-ridden book. All of these writers wrote "difficult" poetry. In my discussion of the individual poems I have attempted to clarify the author's intentions when I thought it possible to do so. And I hope I have communicated the enthusiasm I feel for certain poems by Robinson, Winters, and Stevens which have been overlooked by most critics.

Acknowledgments

I wish to express my thanks to the following publishers and individuals who have granted me permission to quote passages from the writings of the five authors who are the subject of this book:

New Directions for quotations from the following: Ezra Pound, *Collected Early Poems.* Copyright © 1976 by the Trustees of the Ezra Pound Literary Property Trust. All Rights Reserved Ezra Pound, *Personae.* Copyright 1926 by Ezra Pound. *The Cantos* of Ezra Pound. Copyright © 1976 by the Estate of Ezra Pound.

Excerpts from T. S. Eliot's *Collected Poems 1909–1962, Selected Essays,* and *Selected Prose of T. S. Eliot* edited by Frank Kermode are reprinted by permission of Harcourt Brace Jovanovich, Inc., copyright 1932, 1936 by Harcourt Brace Jovanovich, Inc.; copyright © 1960, 1963, 1964 by T. S. Eliot, copyright © 1975 by Valerie Eliot.

From *The Palm at the End of the Mind: Selected Poems and a Play,* edited by Holly Stevens. Copyright © 1971 by Holly Stevens. Reprinted by permission of Alfred A. Knopf, Inc.

From *Letters of Wallace Stevens,* edited by Holly Stevens. Copyright © 1966 by Holly Stevens. Reprinted by permission of Alfred A. Knopf, Inc.

From *The Necessary Angel,* by Wallace Stevens. Copyright 1951 by Wallace Stevens. Reprinted by permission of Alfred A. Knopf, Inc.

Excerpts from the poetry of Edwin Arlington Robinson are reprinted with permission of Macmillan Publishing Co., Inc. from the *Collected Poems of Edwin Arlington Robinson.* Copyright 1915, 1916, 1920, 1921 by Edwin Arlington Robinson, renewed 1943, 1944, 1948, 1949 by Ruth Nivison. Copyright 1925 by Edwin Arlington Robinson, renewed 1953 by Ruth Nivison and Barbara R. Holt.

Also from Edwin Arlington Robinson, *The Children of the Night* (New York: Charles Scribner's Sons, 1897). Reprinted with the permission of Charles Scribner's Sons. From Edwin Arlington Robinson, *The Town down the River* (New York: Charles Scribner's Sons, 1910). Reprinted with the permission of Charles Scribner's Sons.

Excerpts from *The Collected Poems of Yvor Winters,* copyright 1980 by Alan Swallow/Ohio University Press, 1980, are reprinted with the permission of the Ohio University Press, Athens.

Excerpts from Yvor Winters, *Collected Poems of Yvor Winters.* Copyright 1943 by New Directions Publishing Corporation. Reprinted by permission of New Directions.

That part of the chapter on Robinson which deals with "The Wandering Jew" was first published in *Tulane Studies in English,* and I wish to thank its editor, Donald Pizer, for permission to reprint it here.

In addition, I wish to thank the staffs of the Louisiana State University Library, the British Library, and the Bodleian Library for their ever-courteous assistance. I am grateful for grants awarded me by the Graduate Research Council of Louisiana State University which enabled me to spend several summers of study and writing in this country and abroad. I am especially grateful to my wife for her never-tiring assistance in preparing the manuscript of this book.

Revolution
and Convention
in Modern Poetry

Ezra Pound

1

Ezra Pound

(1885–1972)

Ezra Pound was "more responsible for XX century revolution in poetry than any other individual."
                                                             T. S. Eliot

The revolution in modern poetry, as Eliot and many others have noted, began in 1908 when Ezra Pound settled in London. Within a few years he became a dominant figure in the London literary scene, where he was discovering and promoting the then unknown talents of such writers as James Joyce, T. S. Eliot, H. D., Marianne Moore, William Carlos Williams, and others. He provided much of the poetic theory behind the poetry of these revolutionists, and he himself was soon engaged in writing what he correctly termed "revolutionist" poetry. Yet Pound's work *as an original poet* is disappointing for reasons which I hope will emerge from this chapter. His career as a translator is another matter. His "translations" (or imitations or paraphrases or adaptations, whatever one wishes to call them), although controversial, have been widely and justly praised.

In his very earliest poetry Pound was extremely eclectic and imitative. As he proceeded, he began to formulate a body of poetic theory which he put into practice in his own work, and he attempted to develop his own poetic style. His poetic theories, like his early style, were not original, being derived from sources as diverse as T. E. Hulme, Dante, Remy de Gourmont, Flaubert, Ernest Fenollosa and the Chinese ideogram, the Pre-Raphaelites, James Joyce, and the empirical scientific method which stresses observation of particulars—to mention a few. He developed his basic theories fairly early in his career and he was consistent in his employment of them. But they contained the seeds of distintegration: excessive emphasis on visual experience, on sensations, and almost complete disregard of conceptual experience; a theory of the structure of a poem which led to extreme looseness, obscurantism, overallusiveness, and an excessive use of quotations. As for his style—he went from a too obvious imitation of the Celtic Twilight Yeats, Browning, and the Pre-Raphaelites in his earliest verse to what can only be called "no style at all" in the last of the *Cantos.* It is ironic then, that the poet who made originality—"Make It New"—his catch phrase may in future years be most highly respected for his free translations of foreign poets. A major cause of his failure as a stylist was this fact: Pound, early in his career, spent a good deal of time trying to master the techniques of Provençal, French, Italian, Latin, Greek, Anglo-Saxon, Japanese, and Chinese poets, but he made little attempt to master the techniques of poetry in English since the sixteenth century. Yet of course English was the medium of his own poetry. He overlooked the simple principle that if one is to write successful poetry in English, one should give priority to the study of English rather than foreign verse. Yet Pound shows an appalling ignorance of English poetry from the Renaissance to the mid-nineteenth century — that is, up to but not including the Pre-Raphaelites, and not including Browning. Although he mastered the intricacies of Arnaut Daniel's sestina and other complicated Provençal forms, he had little appreciation of what has been accomplished and can still be accomplished in blank verse and in all the various kinds of rhymed iambic verse.

Pound was supposed to have said that he owed it to English poetry to become acquainted with William Butler Yeats in order to reform the Irish poet's style, and Pound also wrote a very early poem attacking the crepuscular school of poetry entitled "Revolt, against the Crepuscular Spirit in Modern Poetry," published in the first edition of *Personae* (1909). Yet at the same time Pound was himself imitating Yeats's Celtic Twilight style. N. Christoph de Nagy lists twenty-five poems published by 1911 or earlier as "reminiscent of the poetry of the 'Nineties and, in particular, of the young W. B. Yeats."[1] "Song" from *Exultations*, "Laudantes," and "Nel Biancheggiar" with its lines:

> "Her" dreaming fingers lay between the tunes,
> As when the living music swoons

(all on Nagy's list) are pure Celtic Twilight. And in addition to these poems, phrases like "The soft dim cloud of her hair" in "Fair Helen" and "I praise dim hair" from "Sestina for Ysolt," which also show, as Nagy points out, the influence of the Pre-Raphaelites and Swinburne, are reminiscent of Yeats as well.

It was natural that Pound, who from the very beginning of his career was fascinated by the Middle Ages, should also be influenced by and attempt to imitate the styles of that school of Victorian poets which turned to the Middle Ages for its inspiration in painting and in poetry — the Pre-Raphaelites. In his later *Hugh Selwyn Mauberley* (1920) Pound, in "Yeux Glauques," recalls brilliantly but ambiguously his early admiration for Swinburne, Rossetti, Burne-Jones, and others of the school, but in defending them against the attacks of the more prudish Victorian critics he at times seems to be making fun of them. He appears to be unsure of his own tastes. Be that as it may, there are a number of early poems which are obviously Pre-Raphaelite or Swinburnean. Nagy lists fifteen poems,[2] pointing out in particular that "Ballad Rosalind" and "Oltre la Torre: Rolando" are imitations of William Morris's ballads, and he also calls attention to the fact that the decorative representation of the ideal woman in "The Blessed Damozel" and elsewhere as well as the ideal woman herself — usually of slender figure and golden hair — had considerable impact on Pound. Indeed, this ideal woman — the Pre-Raphaelite "stunner" — haunted

Anglo-American literature for almost a century, particularly in the poetry of Yeats and Wallace Stevens, as well as in Pound,[3] as did the dreamlike transcendental world she inhabited. Yet even in this matter Pound is not consistent. Foreshadowing his later ironic attitude toward the Pre-Raphaelites in "Yeux Glauques," he parodies Rossetti in his early poem "Nicotine." And he tries to bring the heavenly "Blessed Damozel" back to earth in his "Donzella Beata." As for Swinburne, Pound praised him in "Salve O Pontifex," and we find echoes of Swinburne's style in Pound's "Aux Belles de Londres," "Ballad for Gloom," and elsewhere.

A more fortunate influence on the very early Pound was Robert Browning. In "Mesmerism," suggested by Browning's poem of the same title, Pound addresses Browning thus:

> Here's to you, old Hippety-Hop o' the accents
> True to the Truth's sake and crafty dissector,
> You grabbed at the gold sure. . . .

The poem, partly parody and partly praise, is written in Browning's jocular style. Browning's dramatic monologue, his interest in unusual and abnormal personalities, and his psychological insights also exerted their influence on a number of Pound's early poems, including "Fifine Answers" and "Piere Vidal Old."[4] And as Nagy has demonstrated, Pound's masks (*personae*) were probably derived from a combination of Browning and Yeats.

The Troubadours

When Pound arrived in London in 1908 he had a number of things on his mind; one of the most urgent was his desire to re-create for English readers the poetry of the troubadours, which he had been studying since his undergraduate days at Hamilton College where he learned Provençal under William Pierce Shepherd. "Na Audiart," inspired by Bertran de Born's "Borrowed Lady" poem, had already appeared in *A Lume Spento* (1908). In his four other volumes of verse subsequent to *A Lume Spento* and prior to the imagist *Ripostes* (1912),[5] he published a number of poems inspired by the troubadours and their period, which fall into two categories—those derived from a specific text in Provençal (and these range from almost literal translations to very free adaptations) and those which have no discernible relation to a specific Provençal poem but make use of the personality of a troubadour poet as a mask or *persona*. This second group of poems shows the aforementioned influence of Browning, and they frequently remind the reader of Browning's dramatic monologues. Many of these experiments are unsuccessful, and in fact Pound eventually rejected most of them in his own selection for the later *Personae* (1926), which contained all the early verse he wished to preserve. Yet the young Idaho-born American in his self-imposed exile abroad deserves our sympathetic respect at this stage of his career, for he was undertaking an extremely difficult task—to make the complicated verse forms of these medieval poets, not to mention their complex social system, relevant to early-twentieth-century London. There are two main reasons for the failure of most (but not all!) of the troubadour poems: the remoteness of the period Pound was trying to re-create and, more important, the incongruous mélange of styles Pound had acquired at this time—a mixture, as we have seen, of Browning, Swinburne, the Pre-Raphaelites, the early Yeats, and the fin de siècle decadence of the nineties. And frequently Pound made it worse by deliberately employing archaic locutions which were designed to give a medieval flavor to the verse but instead usually made it artificial and awkward.

One of the most successful of the "translations"—one fairly close to its anonymous Provençal source, "En un vergier sotz fuella d'albespi"—is "Alba Innominata," which Pound considered the best of the troubadour *albas*. The first three stanzas as they appear in *Exultations* (1909) read:

> In a garden where the whitethorn spreads her leaves
> My Lady hath her love lain close beside her,
> Till the warder cries the dawn—Ah dawn that grieves!
> Ah God! Ah God! That dawn should come so soon!
>
> "Please God that night, dear night should never cease,
> Nor that my love should parted be from me,
> Nor watch cry 'Dawn'—Ah dawn that slayeth peace!
> Ah God! Ah God! That dawn should come so soon!
>
> "Fair friend and sweet, thy lips! Our lips again!
> Lo, in the meadow there the birds give song!
> Ours be the love and Jealousy's the pain!
> Ah God! Ah God! That dawn should come so soon!

Stuart McDougal in his detailed analysis of this *alba*[6] points out that Pound in using the language of Dowson and of the nineties, as in the line

> Fair friend and sweet, the lips! Our lips again!

emphasizes the physical nature of the passion much more than does the original Provençal, where this line reads in a literal translation:

> Beautiful gentle friend, let us kiss, you and I.

He also states that the languid, Dowson-like expressions "Ah dawn that grieves" and "Ah dawn that slayeth peace" have no basis in the Provençal text. This kind of misrepresentation of Provençal sources is typical in the early Pound, but it was inevitable in a young poet brought up on the verse of the middle and late nineteenth century without sufficient time to develop a style of his own. Donald Davie has coined a good term for this early style; he calls it "translatorese" (with specific reference to Pound's later "Homage to Sextus Propertius"), and he demonstrates in *Ezra Pound: Poet as Sculptor* that much of

Pound's pre-*Cantos* poetry was written in it—original verse as well as adaptations. Yet, to return to the "Alba Innominata," it remains, I think, one of Pound's better early poems, with a unity of tone and effect rare in Pound and, in spite of the diction, with some of the freshness and loveliness of the medieval dawn poem. Perhaps one reason for its relative success is the stanza form and rhyme scheme, which is simpler in the original than that of most troubadour poems and which Pound further simplified in his translation.

Pound himself found this early translation inadequate, rejecting it in his later *Personae* and substituting a new version first published in the *Little Review* in 1919 as "Vergier" in the *Langue d'Oc* series. The first three stanzas now read as follows:

> In orchard under the hawthorne
> She has her lover till morn,
> Till the traist man cry out to warn
> Them. God how swift the night,
> > And day comes on.
>
> O Plasmatour, that thou end not the night,
> Nor take my belovèd from my sight,
> Nor I, nor tower-man, look on daylight,
> 'Fore God, How swift the night,
> > And day comes on.
>
> "Lovely thou art, to hold me close and kisst,
> Now cry the birds out, in the meadow mist,
> Despite the cuckold, do thou as thou list,
> So swiftly goes the night
> > And day comes on."

Pound has got rid of the Dowson languor; the diction is crisper and clearer than in the 1909 version; yet some poeticisms remain and such words as *traist* and *Plasmatour* are perhaps too recherché. Furthermore, in his reaction against the dreamlike rhythms of the first version, Pound has made his new rhythms too choppy, as in the unfortunate runover at the end of line three of the opening stanza. Judged simply as a poem in English, the earlier *alba* is better.

The other most nearly successful translation is the well-known "Planh for the Young English King," a nearly literal version of Bertran de Born's lament written on the occasion of the death of Prince Henry Plantagenet, elder brother of Richard the Lion-Hearted, with whom Bertran had usually sided in the fratricidal strife of the sons of Henry II. Henry Plantagenet was called the "Young English King" because he had been crowned during the lifetime of his father, Henry II, to assure him of his succession to the throne. The poem begins:

> If all the grief and woe and bitterness,
> All dolour, ill and every evil chance
> That ever came upon this grieving world
> Were set together they would seem but light
> Against the death of the young English King.

The style is fairly direct and simple throughout the poem, although a few archaic expressions are employed to give what Pound thought would be a twelfth-century tone. As we have seen, Pound is vulnerable to adverse criticism — indeed he later criticized himself — for his archaic diction; yet in this poem, I think, it is not obtrusive. Indeed, it bothers me less than the absolutely dead epithets and clichés so abundant in the translations and imitations of Dryden and Pope.

As in the "Alba Innominata," the stanza structure and rhyme scheme of the "Planh" are relatively simple. As an example of a more complicated stanza and of the difficulties Pound faced as a translator and imitator of Provençal verse, consider the quotation below from Arnaut Daniel's canzon which Pound entitled "Glamour and Indigo." The original "Doutz brais e critz" ("Sweet clamor and cries") was considered by Pound to be the most beautiful of all the surviving poems of Pound's favorite troubadour. I quote the fourth and fifth stanzas, first in Pound's prose translation as it appears in *The Spirit of Romance* (1910)[7]:

> May God, the Chosen, by whom were absolved the sins of the blind Longinus, wish if it please him, that I and my lady lie within one chamber where we shall make a rich covenant, whereon great joy attendeth; where, with laughter and caresses, she shall disclose to me her fair body, with the glamour of the lamplight about it.

> The flowering bough with the flowerets in bud, which the birds make tremble with their beaks, was never more fresh (than she); wherefore I would not wish to have Rome without her, nor all Jerusalem, but altogether, with hands joined I render me to her, for in loving her the king from beyond Dover would have honour, or he to whom are Estela and Pampeluna.

In his verse translation of these lines,[8] Pound employed the rhyme scheme of the original, *cobla estrampa* abcdefg. No line rhymes within the stanza, but each stanza rhymes with the one which precedes it. Thus we have in a six-stanza poem the necessity of five rhymes for each line of the initial stanza. Furthermore, the first half line of each stanza is rhymed with that of the preceding stanza. There is, then, an obvious and sometimes awkward searching for rhymes; yet these two stanzas are fairly successful, especially when we consider the technical difficulties:

> God who did tax
>   not Longus' sin, respected
> That blind centurion beneath the spikes
> And him forgave, grant that we two shall lie
> Within one room, and seal therein our pact,
> Yes, that she kiss me in the half-light, leaning
> To me, and laugh and strip and stand forth in the lustre
> Where lamp-light with light limb but half engages.

> The flowers wax
>   with buds but half perfected;
> Tremble on twig that shakes when the bird strikes —
> But not more fresh than she! No empery,
> Though Rome and Palestine were one compact,

Would lure me from her; and with hands convening
I give me to her. And if kings could muster
In homage similar, you'd count them sages.

To see what Pound can do with this versification but with more or less original
subject matter, we turn to "Canzon: Of Incense" (first published in 1910), which
begins:

I

Thy gracious ways,
                    O Lady of my heart, have
O'er all my thought their golden glamour cast;
As amber torch-flames, where strange men-at-arms
Tread softly 'neath the damask shield of night,
Rise from the flowing steel in part reflected,
So on my mailed thought that with thee goeth,
Though dark the way, a golden glamour falleth.

II

The censer sways
                    And glowing coals some art have
To free what frankincense before held fast
Till all the summer of the eastern farms
Doth dim the sense, and dream up through the light,
As memory, by new-born love corrected—
With savour such as only new love knoweth—
Through swift dim ways the hidden pasts recalleth.

The subject, praise of a beautiful woman, is Pre-Raphaelite in its sensuousness,
and lines 3 through 5 of the first stanza might be descriptive of a Pre-Raphaelite
picture. The sensuousness is glamorized, idealized, and refined to the point of
mysticism, or at least such may have been Pound's intention. But as the poem
proceeds the style becomes soft and diffuse like that of the early Yeats. Pound
himself rejected the poem, but Eliot, against Pound's objections, included it in
his edition of Pound's *Selected Poems,* perhaps because he felt the complication
of the stanza form made the poem interesting.

In "Sestina: Altaforte" (frequently and justifiably anthologized) Pound
employs a form invented by Arnaut Daniel, the sestina, a mask or persona
derived from the troubadour Bertran de Born, and a style reminiscent of
Browning in "Soliloquy of the Spanish Cloister" and elsewhere, together with
subject matter that is partly original, yet partly derivative from Bertran's battle
poems. The result is curious and interesting. Here are the first three stanzas:

I

Damn it all! all this our South stinks peace.
You whoreson dog, Papiols, come! Let's to music!
I have no life save when the swords clash.
But ah! when I see the standards gold, vair, purple, opposing
And the broad fields beneath them turn crimson,
Then howl my heart nigh mad with rejoicing.

II

In hot summer have I great rejoicing
When the tempests kill the earth's foul peace,
And the lightnings from black heav'n flash crimson,
And the fierce thunders roar me their music
And the winds shriek through the clouds mad, opposing,
And through all the riven skies God's swords clash.

III

Hell grant soon we hear again the swords clash!
And the shrill neighs of destriers in battle rejoicing,
Spiked breast to spiked breast opposing!
Better one hour's stour than a year's peace
With fat boards, bawds, wine and frail music!
Bah! there's no wine like the blood's crimson!

The material for Pound's poem is taken from two or more poems by Bertran and rewritten in the boisterous style of Browning. Pound gives us some of his source material in his verse and prose translations of Bertran's battle verse in *The Spirit of Romance* (1910).[9] One stanza, in which Bertran is speaking, begins:

"When I see spread through the gardens
The standards yellow and indigo and blue
The cries of the horses are sweet to me
And the bruit the jongleurs make sounding from tent to bivouac
The trumpets and horns and shrill clarions."

And a stanza from another war poem reads:

"I tell you that I find no such savour in eating butter and sleeping, as when I hear cried 'On them!' and from both sides hear horses neighing through their head-guards, and hear shouted 'To Aid! To Aid!' and see small and great falling into fosses, and on the grass, and see the dead with lance truncheons, the pennants still on them, a-piercing their sides."

Born's original poem is obviously superior to the Pound-Browning re-creation. Detail such as the lance truncheons with the pennants still on them piercing the corpses is vivid and authentic. The Pound-Browning line:

Bah! there's no wine like the blood's crimson!

is sheer poeticism. Browning is not one of the best influences on Pound (although a better influence than Swinburne and the early Yeats), but in "Sestina: Altaforte" the spirit of the troubadour poet does come through in spite of Browning. Bertran was in fact the kind of man Browning admired and is here presented in a style influenced by, but on the whole superior to, that of Browning himself.

Pound also wrote a series of poems in which he uses a troubadour poet as a mask or *persona*. The material is taken from biographical fact and legend. In the structure of the poem Pound makes no attempt to re-create the Provençal stanza forms. A good example of this kind of early Poundian poem is "Piere Vidal Old."

Peire Vidal, as his name is usually spelled, who flourished from 1180 to 1205, was a widely traveled troubadour, soldier, and braggart. According to his own accounts he was fearless in warfare and a great seducer of women. Some of his more extravagant poems may be parodies of himself or of contemporary troubadours, but Pound in "Piere Vidal Old" treats his subject seriously. As Pound explains in a prefatory statement, the poem deals with one of Vidal's most eccentric alleged exploits. For love of Loba (She-Wolf) of Penautier, he himself ran mad as a wolf, was hunted with dogs, captured, and brought to the dwelling of the aforesaid she-wolf where he was gently treated and made welcome by the lady and her lord. In his eccentricity he reminds us of a number of Browning's characters, and as he speaks his monologue we are reminded of Browning's monologues, particularly in the final stanza, yet no reader would mistake it for a poem by Browning. The style at times is closer to Rossetti and the Pre-Raphaelites than to Browning, and in the last two lines of the moving second stanza, the style can only be described as Pound's own early idiom at its best. The second stanza reads:

> Behold me, Vidal, that was fool of fools!
> Swift as the king wolf was I and as strong
> When tall stags fled me through the alder brakes,
> And every jongleur knew me in his song,
> And the hounds fled and the deer fled
> And none fled over long.

The poem is more in the nature of a complaint or, as Nagy correctly describes it, "an outcry" against old age and the ravages of time than it is a dramatic monologue. As Vidal looks back on his youthful prowess and bitterly complains about his present weakness—

> Behold me shrivelled as an old oak's trunk
> And made men's mock'ry in my rotten sadness!

—I am reminded of Frost's macabre "The Pauper Witch of Grafton" who in a monologue laments the loss of her sexual prowess. The stanza form is not that of any known Provençal stanzaic structure, and in spite of some of the imitative language, the poem as a whole is an original creation and probably one of the best of Pound's pre-imagist poems.[10]

Pound's Theory of Poetry

While operating under the heterogeneous influences we have noted and while trying to re-create the troubadours for twentieth-century London, Pound began to develop his theory of poetry, at first implicitly in his poems, sometimes stated in his poems, and then explicitly in his prose. In his earliest poems we find Pound expressing (as we would expect) highly eclectic and inconsistent theories.[11] At one moment, in "Grace before Song," he prays that his poems be

As drops that dream and gleam and falling catch the sun

—that is, that they be nothing but pure poetry in the Paterian sense. But in his "Revolt against the Crepuscular Spirit in Modern Poetry" he states exactly the opposite, that poetry should be a call to action. There is a similar inconsistency in his early admiration for Walt Whitman, who praised democratic America en masse, and Pound's notion, expressed in "The Flame" and elsewhere, that the poet is by his very nature alienated and isolated from normal society—a mystic and a transcendentalist. Similarly in "In Durance" (dated 1907) Pound states that

I am homesick after mine own kind,

his "own kind" being an early Yeatsian aesthete striving in a crude commercial society for transcendent beauty.

By 1911, when he began publishing his essays in the *New Age*, under the title "I Gather the Limbs of Osiris," Pound (as his title suggests) was making an attempt to pull his heterogeneous ideas about poetry together, and in these essays a few dominant notions emerge which (although Pound's phrasing of them changed somewhat) were to dominate Pound for the rest of his life. Of great importance was his concept of the "luminous detail," first described in the *New Age*, December 7, 1911, in his "A Rather Dull Introduction" to the Osiris series in which he formulates "the method of Luminous Detail, a method most vigorously hostile to the prevailing mode of today."[12] He considers the mode of his time to be that of multitudinous detail and the mode of the past to be that of generalization. He goes on to say, "The artist seeks out the luminous detail and presents it. He does not comment. His work remains the permanent basis of psychology and metaphysics. . . . A few dozen facts of this nature give us the intelligence of a period."[13] These luminous details "govern knowledge" as a "switchboard governs the electric current."[14] As Thomas H. Jackson has demonstrated, this notion has affinities with the Pre-Raphaelite and Paterian "charged moment."[15] It also has affinities, I would like to point out, with Joyce's theory of epiphanies,[16] with Pound's theory of the image as an intellectual and emotional complex in an instant of time, and with the later theory of Eliot's objective correlative. Pound's early statements about the luminous detail are also the basis of the theory and method of the *Cantos*, which were considered by Pound himself at one time to be his major life work. The *Cantos* are a series a luminous details giving us the intelligence of a period. The poet has nothing to do with ideas or with generalizations. It is the job of the poet—Guido Cavalcanti for example—to render *emotions* precisely.[17] From Pater to Eliot the basic theory is identical although phrased somewhat differently by each writer. In Pound's case, in the later *Cantos* particularly, we find the theory carried to its illogical conclusion. Rational structure, evaluation of experience, understanding—all are sacrificed to presenting, in a short poem, the luminous detail and in a long poem a series of luminous details. The method led in Pound's final *Cantos* and in Joyce's last work to almost complete obscurantism.

The theory of the luminous detail led directly (with some assistance from T.E. Hulme) to Pound's famous doctrine of imagism, or *imagisme* as Pound named it when he started the movement by sending a few of his friend Hilda Doolittle's poems from a British Museum tearoom to Harriet Monroe of *Poetry.*

Before going on to imagism, however, let us note Pound's concept of *virtu.* "It is the artist's business to find his own virtu."[18] *Virtu,* as Pound defines it, is the distinctive characteristic of the individual's soul. The great artist (Pound cites four — Homer, Dante, Chaucer, and Shakespeare) expresses his *virtu,* his individual genius, in a few poems only. Nagy relates this idea to Dante's *ingenium.*[19] The concept of *virtu,* of excellence, was of course a commonplace of the Renaissance. As Pound defines and uses the term, it seems to be more closely related to Hopkins's romantic doctrine of individualism, *inscape* — that which makes something different from anything else. For Hopkins (who also was influenced by the Pre-Raphaelites) the job of the poet is to express his individual experience in inscapes. For Pound the poet expresses his *virtu* in luminous details.

The history of imagism has been written, rewritten, and thoroughly documented. Although Pound later denied it, T. E. Hulme probably exerted considerable influence on Pound during the early formative period of the movement. As I have written elsewhere,[21] Hulme's major concepts and attitudes are basically romantic, in spite of the fact that he called himself a classicist. Like Emerson and Sandburg, he had little respect for the past: "I have no reverence for tradition. . . . I am of course in favor of the complete destruction of all verse more than twenty years old."[22] The new, so-called classical verse which he thought would prevail in this century would be the product of fancy rather than of the imagination. Each poem would consist of an image or series of images presented in noniambic cadenced rhythms with little or no paraphrasable content, with little or no commentary, with no clear statement. "Never, never, never a simple statement. It has no effect." The poem, according to Hulme, should be original, concrete, unique, a product of the poet's intuition rather than his reason. The method of composing a poem of more than a few lines is to select from "a certain landscape . . . certain images which, put into juxtaposition in separate lines, seem to suggest and evoke the state he feels. To this piling up and juxtaposition of distinct images in different lines, one can find a fanciful analogy in music."[23] These quotations are from Hulme's "Lecture on Modern Poetry," which was probably delivered as early as 1908, the year of Pound's arrival in London, several years before Pound was publishing his doctrine of luminous detail and the image, and several years before he was formulating his theoretical doctrine with specific reference to the associational structure of the *Cantos,* which he explained to Yeats had a musical structure similar to a Bach fugue.[24] Hulme was immersed in the aesthetic theories of Wilhelm Worringer and in the philosophy of Henri Bergson at the time he was prophesying the future of twentieth-century poetry.[25] To repeat: in spite of Hulme's claim to being a classicist, his "Lecture on Modern Poetry" appears to me to be a minor manifesto of the romantic movement. In any event, whoever was first in theory, the poetic theories of the early Pound and of Hulme have very close affinities. And it was Pound who put the theories into practice, although Hulme wrote a few minor poems to illustrate his doctrine.

Pound's manifesto, "A Few Don'ts by an Imagiste," as it appeared in *Poetry* in 1913, would have occasioned no surprise to the reader of "I Gather the Limbs of Osiris" two years earlier. The imagist doctrine as set forth by Pound here and elsewhere may be summarized as follows—in diction to avoid abstract language, stereotyped "poetic" language, ornamental language, and an overuse of adjectives. *Le mot juste*, the exact word, must be found. In rhythm, the iambic foot should be replaced by the cadence of unrhymed "free verse" so that each poem will have an entirely unique rhythm. Imagery and concentration are the essence of poetry. The image is defined as "that which presents an intellectual and emotional complex in an instant of time." There should be absolute freedom of subject matter. The poem should suggest rather than state.

The immediate result of these theories was a much-needed revitalizing of poetic diction, a new sense of freedom, even permissiveness, in the choice of subject matter, and highly interesting experiments with complex rhythms outside the scansion systems of conventional poetry. Brilliant (but, I think, minor) poems were written in "free verse" by H. D., William Carlos Williams, Wallace Stevens, Mina Loy, Marianne Moore, and Ezra Pound. However, the long-term result was unfortunate. The poetry of the imagist revolution became increasingly obscure and irrational as it was practiced by Pound and others. A kind of freeze set the techniques of all the above mentioned poets except Stevens, so that they never developed beyond the limitations of their early work. And there was a widespread neglect of the efficacy of conventional rhythms to express modern subject matter and an equally widespread neglect of what American and English poets had accomplished before the twentieth-century revolution, although this was offset somewhat by the erudition of Eliot and his admiration for the metaphysical poets.

Pound himself wrote several beautiful poems during his imagist phase, and in some respects he never outgrew imagism, although, as a result of a quarrel with Amy Lowell, he abandoned doctrinaire imagism and for a very brief time became a "vorticist," together with his friend Wyndham Lewis, who edited the short-lived magazine *Blast*. Vorticism was of some importance in the paintings of Lewis. In poetry it was simply a rephrasing of the doctrine of the image with emphasis on the supposed emotional energy concentrated in and liberated by the image or vortex. It was imagism set in motion.

A word here is necessary concerning Pound's so-called ideogrammatic method. Very soon after Pound began publishing the Osiris series of essays with its theory of luminous details in the *New Age*, he met in London the widow of Ernest Fenollosa. She sent him the Fenollosa manuscripts in 1913, the same year that Pound began the imagist movement in *Poetry* with the poems of H. D. The Fenollosa manuscripts contained poems in Chinese ideograms with English transliterations, as well as indications of the Japanese sound of each ideogram (Japanese because Fenollosa was living in Japan and working with

Japanese scholars) and also Japanese Noh plays and an essay on the Chinese ideogram as a medium for poetry. From Pound's study of the Fenollosa manuscripts came Pound's *Cathay* (1915), a collection of loose translations and adaptations of Chinese poems; *Noh, or Accomplishment* (1916); *Certain Noble Plays of Japan* (1916); and *The Chinese Written Character as a Medium for Poetry* (1919), this last an essay by Fenollosa edited and perhaps in part rewritten by Pound. In the year 1913, then, Pound was reformulating his theory of luminous details and calling it imagism, and at the same time he was becoming interested in Fenollosa's transliterations and discussion of the ideogram as a medium for poetry. Pound soon discovered that what Fenollosa had been saying prior to 1908 (the year of his death) about the nature of poetry had close affinities with his own theory, which he had formulated under the influence of T. E. Hulme. Pound said of Fenollosa's essay "We have not a bare philological discussion, but a study of the fundamentals of all aesthetics."[26] Fenollosa stressed the concreteness and dramatic qualities of the ideogram. He said that Chinese "brings language close to *things*, and in its strong reliance upon verbs it erects all speech into a kind of dramatic poetry,"[27] and he illustrated as follows: "In Chinese the chief verb for 'is' not only means actively 'to have,' but shows by its derivation that it expresses something even more concrete, namely, 'to snatch from the moon with the hand.' Here the baldest symbol of prosaic analysis is transformed by magic into a splendid flash of concrete poetry."[28] The flash of dramatic concreteness was exactly what Pound was looking for in the image and, a bit later, in the *vortex*. He therefore adopted what he called the ideogrammatic method of writing poetry as part of his own creed. "Luminous detail," "image," "vortex," and "ideogram" — all mean about the same thing in Pound's aesthetic. It is interesting to note in passing that Pound, in finding a structure for his poems, opted for a loose association of "images" and abandoned logical structure, which had been used since the Middle Ages, and that Fenollosa too condemned logic as medieval and "discredited."

Fenollosa's analysis of the Chinese ideogram has been frequently challenged. It has been argued that he overemphasized its concreteness — that the ideogram for the modern Chinese reader is just as abstract as most English words — that the concrete origins of Chinese ideograms have been long forgotten. There is also the possibility that Pound may have rewritten Fenollosa's essay to correspond to his own ideas. Regardless of all this, Fenollosa's concept of the ideogram as it appears in the essay published by Pound has marked affinities with Pound's own theories and in fact seems to have reinforced Pound's theories.

To go back to Pound's imagist phase for a moment, Pound's "The Return" is a typical imagist poem, and with Wallace Stevens's "The Snow Man," H. D.'s "Orchard," and W. C. Williams's "On the Road to the Contagious Hospital," it represents the high point of the movement. Pound felt that a poem should suggest rather than state and that what it suggests should have a certain complexity. It is not surprising, then, that there have been various interpretations of "The Return":

See, they return; ah, see the tentative

Movements, and the slow feet,
The trouble in the pace
and the uncertain
Wavering!

See, they return, one, and by one,
With fear, as half-awakened;
As if the snow should hesitate
And murmur in the wind,
            and half turn back;
These were the "Wing'd-with-Awe,"
Inviolable.

Gods of the winged shoe!
With them the silver hounds
            sniffing the trace of air!

Haie! Haie!
      These were the swift to harry;
These the keen-scented;
These were the souls of blood.

Slow on the leash,
            pallid the leash-men!

One should not fail to notice the completely successful rhythms throughout, but particularly the tentative wavering cadence of the first stanza, the fine and completely appropriate simile of the snow in the second stanza, and the beautifully realized feeling of doubt and possible defeat following in the wake of past glory. What is the poem about? Those who are returning may be soldiers or hunters but I think the suggestion that they are pagan gods who are slowly and tentatively returning to modern literature through the efforts of poets like Pound and H. D. may be close to Pound's intention. Pound himself said of the poem that it "has a complicated sort of significance like Mr. Epstein's Sun God."[29]

From imagism and vorticism Pound proceeded, under the partial influence of the quatrains of Théophile Gautier, to write his farewell to London, a series of poems entitled *Hugh Selwyn Mauberley,* published in 1920. The poem is closer to conventional verse than Pound's imagist poetry. In a few instances the iambic foot and slant rhymes are handled with skill. Eliot considered *Mauberley* to be one of the finest poems in English in the twentieth century. Nevertheless, there are typical Poundian difficulties: obscurity, excessive allusions, and, particularly in the final section, an indefensible looseness of structure. *Mauberley* is in fact a conglomerate of separate poems written in various styles. Several of the individual poems are successful, but the work as a whole is not. Besides the looseness of structure there is also an indecisiveness of attitude toward his subject matter and, indeed, an ambiguity concerning the protagonist Mauberley. Who is he? In the first poems he appears to be Pound or a mask for Pound. But in part 2, entitled "Mauberley," he appears to be a sterile aesthete who ends his life on a tropical isle, whereas Pound himself went off to France and then to Italy and became involved, more or less, in politics and economics. Perhaps in part 2 he represents what Pound might have become. Throughout part 1, which has by far the best writing in the series, Pound seems to be indulging in Laforguian romantic irony directed at himself, but he also seems to be blaming his environment, his social milieu, for his lack of success more than himself—that is, the vulgarities of twentieth-century London. Yet, in contrasting his contemporary London with that of the Pre-Raphaelites (whom Pound admired as a young man) and with the decadents of the nineties (who also influenced the early Pound), he seems to be treating them with more irony than approbation. There is, then (as in the *Cantos*, the earliest of which Pound had recently completed), no satisfactory evaluation of himself or of his milieu. There is rather a series of impressions or scenes, ironically described, of the contemporary poet and of literary life in London from the mid-Victorians to 1920. In his cleverly written portrait of the Pre-Raphaelites entitled "Yeux Glauques" he describes Elizabeth Siddal, the revered model and wife of Dante Gabriel Rossetti, as she appears as the beggar maid in Burne-Jones's painting in the Tate gallery entitled *King Cophetua and the Beggar Maid*:

> The Burne-Jones cartons
> Have preserved her eyes;
> Still, at the Tate, they teach
> Cophetua to rhapsodize;
>
> Thin like brook-water,
> With a vacant gaze.

The last two lines quoted are marvelously accurate, and the rhythm of the quatrain is masterfully handled. But what is Pound up to here? Is he praising the Pre-Raphaelites or is he ironically rejecting what was once a major influence on his early work? There is a similar problem in his attitude toward the decadents:

> For two hours he talked of Gallifet;
> Of Dowson; of the Rhymers' Club;
> Told me how Johnson (Lionel) died
> By falling from a high stool in a pub . . .
>
> But showed no trace of alcohol
> At the autopsy, privately performed—
> Tissue preserved—the pure mind
> Arose toward Newman as the whiskey warmed.
>
> Dowson found harlots cheaper than hotels. . . .

Pound wrote an appreciative preface in 1914 to a collection of Johnson's poems, and he seems to be praising Dowson in his early "In Tempore Senectutis," which has the subtitle "An Anti-stave for Dowson." But what is his attitude in this poem? It is difficult to say whether or not he is repudiating the decadents.

When we consider the long final effort of Pound's career, the *Cantos*, the problem of point of view, of the attitude of the author toward his material, is ever present. The problem rises directly from his poetic method—the presentation of his material as a series of luminous details which will supposedly give us a sudden subtle insight into a historical situation or a period. As early as 1915 Pound, while explaining vorticism in the *New Age*, wrote, "The Vorticist is expressing his complex consciousness.... To be civilized is to have swift apperception of the complicated life of today; it is to have a subtle and instantaneous apperception of it, such as savages and wild animals have of the necessities and dangers of the forest."[30] Will there be any principles, any method by which this series of luminous details can be organized? Pound goes on to say, in the same *New Age* article, "The musical conception of form....that you can select materials of form from the forms before you, that you can recombine and recolour them and 'organize' them into a new form—this conception, this state of mental activity, brings with it joy and refreshment." It is interesting to note that Pound puts the word *organize* in quotes, as if he were embarrassed by it. Years later in "A Packet for Ezra Pound," which Yeats dates March and October 1928, Pound is speaking the same way about the structure of the *Cantos.* Yeats records the conversation with Pound in Rapallo in which they are discussing Pound's first twenty-seven cantos, and Yeats says, "I have often found there brightly printed kings, queens, knaves, but have never discovered why all the saints could not be dealt out in some quite different order."[31] That is, Yeats, like so many early readers of Pound, admired the luminous details but could not discover an overall principle of structure, or for that matter any final purpose or meaning in the *Cantos.* Pound replied that eventually the *Cantos* would have a structure like a Bach fugue. "There will be no plot, no chronicle of events, no logic of discourse, but two themes, the Descent into Hades from Homer, a Metamorphosis from Ovid, and mixed with these, medieval or modern historical characters." And he goes on to speak of the "dream association of words and images, a poem in which there is nothing that can be taken out and reasoned over, nothing that is not a part of the poem itself." It is a clear statement of Pound's intentions and in principle does not go beyond his remarks in the *New Age* article thirteen years earlier. The *Cantos* will be a composition of luminous details organized like a fugue in which two major themes will be stated and repeated in various ways and minor details added. Pound rejects the traditional methods of organizing a poem: narrative ("no plot"), chronological ("no chronicle of events"), logical ("no logic of discourse"). He uses instead the procedure of "dream association" and the analogy of music. In a poem of medium length such as Eliot's *The Waste Land* or the *Four Quartets*, the employment of motifs repeated with variations may be a fairly successful, although inefficient, way of organizing a poem. But this method is impossible with a poem of over 750 pages and over 100 cantos in length.[32] Of course the original intention of two major themes—a descent into Hades and a Metamorphosis from Ovid—broke down over the years, as did the analogy with a Bach fugue. We are left with a mass of luminous details which, according to Pound himself, should not be extracted from the poem and reasoned over. But because the structure broke down, the only thing one can do with the *Cantos* is to extract details or sections of details—such as the *Pisan Cantos* or the Malatesta cantos—look up the historical background and try to make some sense of them. And this often leads to failure because (as in the John Adams series) Pound does not clearly indicate his point of view. The famous canto against usury (number 45), in which Pound does make his attitude clear, is an exception. In his 1928 conversation with Yeats he said, to repeat, that there would be in his poem "nothing that can be taken out and reasoned over." He is being consistent here with his musical analogy. One can appreciate a Bach fugue as a whole without reasoning over the details, although one should be able to recognize themes and variations. But Pound's *Cantos* of over 750 pages cannot be so appreciated.

Pound, then, as he said himself toward the end of his life, "botched it." There is no structure or overall purpose in the *Cantos*, although heroic attempts have been made to find unity or at least principles of unity in them. Because there is such a mass of material, these various "structures" are always partially successful. The critic (who is in fact imposing his own structure on the *Cantos*) can always find some details here and there to substantiate his argument. But he always has to leave outside his system more material than he puts into it. Each of these structures appears to me to be more the creative work of an individual critic than the demonstrable intention of Pound. For example Daniel D. Pearlman in *The Barb of Time* (New York, 1969) gives us a well-organized discussion of the *Cantos* derived from his theory that Pound intended a modern *Divine Comedy*. Thus Cantos 1–30 are his *Inferno* and the tone is despair; 31–71 are his *Purgatorio* and the tone is hope; 74–109 are his *Paradiso*, which express his cosmic consciousness in which Pound identifies himself with the processes of nature. Within this overall structure Pearlman finds certain groups, such as the Chinese cantos (52–61), which demonstrate that Confucian philosophy is universally applicable to the social condition of man, and others, such as the John Adams group (62–71), which represent Confucianism in practice in the West. Undoubtedly, his classification of these smaller groups is correct and represents Pound's intention, although the interpretation of Pound's attitude toward much of the subject matter of each group is open to question. As for the overall structure of this modern *Divine Comedy*—I doubt that it can be convincingly demonstrated. As a simple example, what is Canto 13 (which is about Confucius and does *not* maintain a tone of despair) doing in the *Inferno* section? Why isn't it in the *Purgatorio* section and within the Chinese group?

The Malatesta cantos (8–11) may be used to demonstrate the weakness of Pound's method, although almost any other group of cantos—the Jefferson-Adams series, for example—could be used as well. The background material for the Malatesta group is fascinating. The protagonist is Sigismondo Malatesta (1417–68). He was a patron of the arts and a professional soldier who fought in the wars between the city-states of Italy—sometimes on one side, sometimes on another. The Malatestas who rose to prominence in Italy in the thirteenth century were a violent, passionate lot. The famous story of Paolo and Francesca, described by Dante, was a Malatesta family quarrel. Francesca, married to Giovanni Malatesta, had a love affair with Giovanni's brother Paolo. Giovanni murdered both of them. Pound's hero Sigismondo had the Malatesta temperament. He had three wives—Ginevra d'Este, Polissena Sforza, and Isotta degli Atti. The first two died by poison, probably administered by Sigismondo. He was, however, passionately in love with his third wife, Isotta, and built the Tempio at Rimini in her honor. Among his enemies was Pope Pius II, whose troops he fought. He eventually lost all of his possessions except Rimini. He was excommunicated in 1460 and he was sentenced by the Pope to be burned alive in Rome, but he declined to appear for the sentence and he was burned instead in effigy on the steps of St. Peter's.

He was a formidable character, typical of his time and place. Browning could have done an entertaining dramatic monologue on him. But in Pound's cantos he, his associates, and the historical context are presented in such a confused collage of fragmentary details that even the most devoted Pound aficionado can get little out of them in a first reading. If the aficionado goes to the standard books on Malatesta and his period or to some of Pound's sources, if he looks up the references in the *Index to the Cantos*, he will be able to get something out of the mélange, if he bothers to reread it, but he will get more understanding of Malatesta and his period, and probably a profounder emotional response to the Malatesta story, by simply reading Pound's sources, such as Edward Hutton's *Sigismondo Pandolpho Malatesta, Lord of Rimini: A Study of a Fifteenth Century Italian Despot* (London, 1900), and forgetting the *Cantos*. The sources are superior to the poem. This is a harsh judgment; therefore, let me defend it with an illustration. The warfare between the city-states of fifteenth-century Italy, such as Naples, Siena, Milan, Rimini, Venice, Florence, was extremely complex, with alliances being constantly broken and reformed so that an ally one year might be an enemy the next. Malatesta's relation to these shifting alliances was also complex, for he frequently changed his loyalty from one city to another. Malatesta's political and military exploits are very difficult to follow even when described in the plainest of expository prose. In Pound's cantos we have neither expository poetry nor prose but a series of fragmentary quotations from various historical documents, sometimes interspersed with comments by Pound. What Malatesta is doing at any given moment is almost impossible to make out.

One of Pound's favorite devices is to quote from letters. In Canto 9 we have the following excerpt from a letter without any explanation:

> First: Ten slabs best red, seven by 15, by one third,
> Eight ditto, good red, 15 by three by one,
> Six of same, 15 by one by one.
> Eight columns 15 by three and one third
>   etc.... with carriage, danars 151.

I would like to suggest that this is not poetry of a very high order. Hugh Kenner, however, approves of this device, saying in his *The Pound Era:* "Hence the Malatesta Cantos, the American Cantos, The Sienese Bank Cantos conserve the vigor of actual documents to convey a *senso morale* and a purpose. (p. 428)" Pound in fact is guilty of the error of excessive specificity. Mere factual items regardless of their source have little or no poetic value. But Kenner, to demonstrate the "vigor of actual documents" cites Pound's excerpt from another letter in the same canto:

> the aliofants [elephants] aren't yet here and one
> can't get the measurements for the cornice to the
> columns that are to rest on the aliofants

and he shows a picture of the "aliofants" in the Tempio at Rimini on the opposite page.[33] The "aliofants" as they appear in the picture are very charming animals, but our emotional and aesthetic response to them comes from looking at the picture and not from Pound's quotation with its unusual spelling of *elephants*.

Pound's method, to refer to a famous dictum by Samuel Johnson, is not merely to number the streaks of the tulip, but to present a confused, innumerable collage of streaks, so that we are left with nothing but the streaks, and the tulip disappears.

Of all the groups of cantos, *The Pisan Cantos,* 74–84, are the most famous. They were published as a book in 1948 and awarded the Bollingen prize as the best book of poems by an American poet for that year. The award was attacked by Robert Hillyer in a series of articles during the summer of 1949 in the *Saturday Review* under the title of "The Fruits of Treason." Hillyer asked some embarrassing questions. Pound had been declared insane and had escaped a trial for treason. (Charges of treason had been brought against him as a result of his pro-Mussolini and anti-American radio broadcasts from Italy during American participation in World War II.) Hillyer's main argument was that Pound was either insane or a traitor and that an award was not appropriate in either case. Hillyer's attack was broad enough — for it included a charge against the so-called New Critics, some of whom had taken Pound's poetry seriously — to arouse not only Pound's friends but also a number of poets and critics who felt that Hillyer's charges were politically motivated and had nothing to do with the quality of the poetry in *The Pisan Cantos*. Others came to the defense of Hillyer, and bitter exchanges were published in the magazines. Thus the book achieved a *succès de scandale,* and in the furor the question of the value of the poetry itself was overlooked.

Because of the circumstances of their composition — Pound was arrested near Rapallo and thrown into an American concentration camp near Pisa, where he lived and composed his poetry under intolerable conditions — a good deal of sympathy for Pound was aroused, particularly after the passions of the war had subsided. Furthermore, in the widely anthologized Canto 81, Pound displayed a new humility and (at least for those who admired the *Cantos*), the broken poet who had aimed so high in both literature and politics achieved a kind of tragic dignity. Also, this canto had more unity and coherence and somewhat less obscurity than most of Pound's late verse and it might be expected that this Pisan theme — the fall of a poet whose life had been spent in the search for beauty — would unify and render less obscure the other cantos in the group.

But as we examine the *Pisan Cantos* three decades or so after the event, we find in them most of the same flaws—deriving directly from Pound's method—which we found in the preceding cantos: wide-ranging allusiveness extending now to Chinese as well as to Greek, Latin, and a dozen other literatures, a complete incoherence of texture with a few beautiful images juxtaposed to rags of meaningless (meaningless unless researched and annotated) bits of conversation, and remembered events of significance only to Pound. For example, consider two quotations chosen at random, the first from Canto 74:

> nor Charlie Sung's money on loan from anonimo
> that is, we suppose Charlie had some
> and in India the rate down to 18 per hundred
> but the local loan lice provided from imported bankers
> so the total interest sweated out of the Indian farmers
>   rose in Churchillian grandeur
> as when, and plus when, he returned to the putrid gold standard
> as was about 1925   Oh my England
> that free speech without free radio speech is as zero
>   and but one point needed for Stalin
> you need not, i.e. need not take over the means of production;
> money to signify work done, inside a system
>   and measured and wanted.

The passage is comprehensible. Pound is expressing his paranoid obsession with the chief evil of capitalism—interest, which he considers usury as in Canto 45. But the quality of the poetry is certainly negligible. And now the second quotation, from Canto 77:

> —niggers comin' over the obstacle fence
>   as in the insets at the Schifanoja
> (del Cossa) to scale, 10,000 gibbet-iform posts supporting
>   barbed wire
> "St. Louis Till" as Green called him. Latin!
>   "I studied latin" said perhaps his smaller companion.
> "Hey Snag, what's in the bibl'?
>   what are the books of the bibl'?
> Name 'em! don't bullshit me!"
>   "Hobo Williams, the queen of them all"
> "Hey/Crawford, come over here/"

The poetry in this passage is also not of a very high order, and there are several obscure private allusions. And what is one to make of Canto 75, which consists of seven lines of verse (one exclamation, one question, and an incomplete sentence) and a musical score of two pages from a piece for the lute by Francesco da Milano? Pearlman quotes Clark Emery in defense of this canto, which "comments upon...the durability (recurrent vigor) of the excellent."[34] Surely no technique for achieving excellence in verse has been devised which is easier to accomplish than this—to reprint verbatim a musical score which one admires! It is Pound's method carried to its reductio ad absurdum—a method defended by

Pearlman with reference to a passage in canto 74.[35] "Pound is justifying the general poetic method he has employed throughout the *Cantos*, the inductive, intuitional, *ideogrammic* method of trusting to an accumulation of concrete particulars rather than to abstract, logical statement as the way of presenting the truth of things." (We see the same practice in some of William Carlos Williams's longer poems where he quotes verbatim letters written to him by admirers.) This is the end of the road which Pound began with his theory of luminous details, formulated before World War I—a poetry of accumulated particulars thrown together without any principle of structure except that of random reverie. They may be fragments composed by the poet himself and therefore of some original literary value—or they may be fragments of art, of music, of almost anything. Their sole value lies in their juxtaposition, and the juxtaposition in the late cantos often appears to be as haphazard and meaningless as the musical compositions of John Cage which are "organized" by pure chance. It is difficult to understand how a number of critics have accepted Pound's irresponsible method without demur.

I should like to examine two cantos in which it seems to me Pound achieves some limited success in spite of his method—the widely admired Canto 81 of the Pisan group and Canto 49, which was supposed to have been one of Pound's favorites.

Number 81 opens with these first three lines:

> Zeus lies in Ceres' bosom
> Taishan is attended of loves
>   under Cythera, before sunrise[.]

According to Pearlman these lines are "prelusive of the mystic union that is shortly to take place between Pound and Nature conceived of as love."[36] Pearlman points out that Cythera (among other things) is the moon and nature and is identified with love, Aphrodite. Such was probably Pound's intention, and thus the lines have structural and thematic significance and echo those lines in Canto 1 where Aphrodite was first introduced as a major symbol. Also, they anticipate the striking passage later on in Canto 81 in which Pound achieves mystical union with what Pearlman calls "love that is the center of the universe."[37]

But with line 4, Pound begins one of those tiresome digressive passages of purely personal reference which have no significance until one has checked the *Index to the Cantos*, and even then the significance is trifling. Furthermore, the lines in themselves have no value as poetry:

> and he said: Hay aquí mucho catolicismo—(sounded catoli*th*ismo)
>   y muy poco reliHion"
> and he said: Yo creo que los reyes desparacen"
> That was Padre Jose Elizondo
>   in 1906 and in 1917
> or about 1917
>   and Dolores said: Come pan, nino," eat bread me lad
> Sargent had painted her

> before he descended
> (i.e. if he descended
>   but in those days he did thumb sketches,
> impressions of the Velasquez in the Museo del Prado
> and books cost a peseta.

If we look up Jose Elizondo in the *Index* we discover that he was a Spanish priest who helped Pound get a photostat of the Cavalcanti manuscripts in the Escorial, Madrid. If we look up Dolores we draw a blank. Sargent is sufficiently well known without looking up, but no one has explained why his possible descent occurs within an unclosed parenthesis. If Pound intended a joke to indicate the uncertainty of the descent or its depth, it is a feeble one. The only possible defense of these lines is that Pound is simply recalling in the degrading circumstances of the prison-camp scenes from a past life and a more fortunate time, but this kind of incoherent recall makes for tiresome poetry. There are many such lines of reminiscence, including references to T. S. Eliot and George Santayana. Occasionally in these references to individuals Pound is successful, as in his remarkable and justifiably famous minature portrait of Henry James in Canto 7:

> And the great domed head, *con gli occhi onesti e tardi*
> Moves before me, phantom with weighted motion,
> *Grave incessu,* drinking the tone of things,
> And the old voice lifts itself
>   weaving an endless sentence.

There is no portrait so good as this in Canto 81. Eventually, in canto 81, we reach the passage marked *libretto*, which begins with the widely admired but (it seems to me) rather conventional imitation of the style of 17th-century love poetry and includes the refrain

> *Lawes and Jenkyns guard thy rest*
> *Dolmetsch ever be thy guest,*

and then occurs the mystical moment of the eyes of Aphrodite:

> there came new subtlety of eyes into my tent,
> whether of spirit or hypostasis....

The mystical union is followed by the comment

> What thou lovest well remains,
>   the rest is dross.

The entire scene is one of the most moving in the *Cantos.* Pearlman considers it "the visionary climax of the Pisan *Cantos.*"[38]

The famous and frequently anthologized final passage of Canto 81, "Pull down thy vanity," is quite acceptable as didactic poetry and probably would have been attacked as "moralistic" if it had been written by anyone but Pound. The passage has unity and coherence within itself—it can stand as an independent poem—and because of the personal tragedy of Pound and the circumstances of its composition, it has poignancy and pathos. The final lines, expressing Pound's lifelong search for beauty, are particularly touching. But it is not great poetry. The style in fact is not even distinguished, and the repetition of phrase is somewhat too rhetorical.

The primary source of Canto 49, "the Seven Lakes Canto," is a series of Chinese paintings in a seventeenth-century manuscript once owned by Pound's father, then Pound himself, and now by Princess Mary de Rachewiltz, who supplied photographs of the paintings and the accompanying Japanese and Chinese poems to Daniel Pearlman, who published them in the appendix of his *The Barb of Time*. Pearlman's analysis of this canto is the best to date. The Chinese and Japanese poems which describe aspects of the pictures must also be considered sources of Pound's poem; however, the canto appears to be first of all a response to the visual effect of the pictures and therefore it belongs to that large group of poems which owe their origin to the visual arts, one of which I would like to compare with Pound's poem. T. Sturge Moore, a friend of Yeats and an acquaintance of Pound, wrote a fine, although almost totally forgotten, poem entitled "From Titian's 'Bacchanal' in the Prado at Madrid." Titian's painting is fairly well known. It is still hanging in the Prado, and reproductions are available. The pictures which inspired Pound's canto are in a unique manuscript — only one known copy is extant — and it is only by the fortunate courtesy of Princess Rachewiltz that the pictures are now available. I think this difference in sources indicates the comparative solipsism of Pound's method. A poem about a picture is best understood and appreciated if the picture or a copy of it is available. However, there are more important differences between the poems themselves, as well as a few similarities. Although both poets describe the picture or pictures, both go beyond mere description and find in their response to pictorial art philosophical significance and (in Pound's case) ethical and political significance. The most striking similarity is that both poems have their emotional climaxes in mystical moments of absolute stillness, of transcendental peace in which all of life's complexities are resolved. It is the stillness of the Chinese jar which Eliot refers to in "Burnt Norton" — the stillness of God at the center of the world. But the poetic procedures of the revolutionist Pound and the traditionalist T. Sturge Moore are quite different. Moore focuses on a single picture and on a single figure in the picture, the bacchante, who lies asleep, or rather in a mystical trance of absolute silence, of union with the god Bacchus, while the revelers dance and carouse in orgy around her — and not only the revelers but the entire background of nature which joins in the dance of which she is still the unmoved center:

> This noisy crew still haunts thee; — but unheard
> They sing, and birds are singing; thou dost sleep;
> These dance, carouse, and pledge each other's joy;
> Slowly the tree tops, in the wind's embrace,
> Dance too; lush branches and gay vestures float,
> Float, wave and rustle, sighing to the wind;
> But thou art still; thou sleepest, art divine.

Throughout the poem, until the final few lines, Moore is writing with his eye on the picture—the descriptive details of the poem are in the picture. In the final lines Moore looks forward in time and imagines the revelers as abandoning the dreaming bacchante. Alone, she transcends her union with the god Bacchus and is joined with the divine spirit of the universe, which in several poems Moore personifies as Silence and which in this poem, on the mythological level, is Persephone. Her attributes in this poem are perfect beauty and perfect peace:

> She then, for ever and for aye, will take thee
> To her deep dwelling and unechoing halls;
> How could she leave thee? she who owns them all
> Owns all the stars, whose beauty is complete,
> Whose joy is perfect, and whose home is peace;
> While all their duty is to shine for love.

Pound in canto 49 is, like Moore, attempting to use a picture or series of pictures to define a similar kind of spiritual experience, which he describes in a single line as "The fourth; the dimension of stillness." (The *fourth* is probably taken from the popular phrase used to describe one aspect of Einstein's relativity theory—"the *fourth* dimension.") Yet because of his fragmentary method, Pound comes out with a poem weaker and thinner than Moore's.

The first line of Pound's Canto 49 reads:

> For the seven lakes, and by no man these verses.

Pearlman thinks that the phrase *no man* refers to the supposed anonymity of the manuscript poems and that it also refers to Odysseus, who gave his name as *No Man* to the drunken Cyclops. Pound is thinking of himself as an impersonal, ego-less Odysseus encountering a barbaric modern world inhabited by Cyclopes. This is considerable interpretive weight to put on a phrase of two words; however, the *Cantos* invite such desperate reaching for meaning.

The first 32 lines are descriptive details derived from the poems and the pictures of the Chinese manuscript. The verses are at times quite lovely, representing Pound in one of his more successful lyrical moments. However, the texture of the verse is rather fragile and diffuse, and the descriptive detail lacks focus. It is difficult, for example, to tell how many pictures Pound is describing. The reader does not get a unified coherent scene, clearly visualized, as he does from Moore's poem. There is, as Pearlman demonstrates, a development of sorts, from the storm scene in stanza 1 to the scenes of relative calm in stanzas 2 and 3. These lines from stanza 2 are typical of the style of the first section of the poem:

> Behind the hill the monk's bell
> borne on the wind.
> Sail passed here in April; may return in October
> Boat fades in silver; slowly;
> Sun blaze alone on the river.

According to Pearlman the sail refers to the Confucian ship of state in harmony with the world and the sun represents mind and intelligence—but again this may be reaching for a meaning.

Lines 32 – 33 are a statement of the political and economic significance Pound wished to imply in the preceding descriptive passage:

> State by creating riches shd. thereby get into debt?
> This is infamy; this is Geryon.

We see here Pound repeating the obsessive hatred of capitalism and usury which is the main subject of Canto 45 and which is recurrent throughout the *Cantos*. Geryon, the guardian of the eighth circle of hell in Dante's *Inferno*, is a symbol (for both Dante and Pound) of fraud and usury. The idealized Confucian society implicit in the descriptive detail of the first part of the poem cannot exist if Geryon is master, but the implication is that the Confucian state has power over Geryon and the other "wild beasts" mentioned in the last line of the canto. There are, incidentally, toward the end of the canto four lines of transliterated Japanese from one of the manuscript poems which, various commentators inform us, give a picture of stillness at the center of the flux, but they will mean nothing to the reader not familiar with Japanese and without a commentary handy. There are further references to healthy and harmonious labor in the Confucian state, after which the poem ends:

> The fourth; the dimension of stillness.
> And the power over wild beasts.

The essence of the poem — "the dimension of stillness" — achieved by the individual living in an integrated and harmonious state is in a flat statement without much poetic power or value. And yet this poem, according to Pearlman, is supposed to be the emotional center and climax of all 107 cantos. In fact, it consists of about 40 lines of rather lovely impressionistic verse which are given significance by three or four lines of flat prosaic statement. The poem, although somewhat more unified and coherent than most of Pound's cantos, lacks the power and precision of a poem like Moore's "From Titian's 'Bacchanal'" which is organized by conventional methods. The weakness of Pound's poem may be in part a failure of talent; it certainly demonstrates a failure of method.

It is probable, then, that as an original poet, Pound's place in literary history will be that of a minor writer of short impressionistic poems. The method of "luminous detail" which he formulated early in his career and retained until the end — under different labels and phrases — prevented his becoming a major poet, even if he had had the talent to be one.

T.S. Eliot

2
T. S. Eliot
(1888–1965)

> *Poetry is a superior amusement.*
> T. S. Eliot (1928)

I
Poetic Theory

As one works one's way through the reviews and essays of Eliot's entire career, two things become evident. When Eliot comments on individual authors he is usually sensitive, acute, and perceptive, and this is particularly true when he deals with poets and with dramatists who write plays in verse. Eliot is an excellent ad hoc critic. I am thinking especially of the essays on the metaphysical poets and on certain Elizabethan and Jacobean playwrights in which he calls attention with almost unfailing taste to the merits of passages of verse, and sometimes of entire poems or plays, which were not well known at the time he was writing his early essays. He displays the same critical tact in dealing with better-known poets such as Donne and Marvell, and if his discussion of some of these poets seems old hat to us today it is because two generations of readers have made Eliot's appreciation of metaphysical poets their own. Eliot changed the taste of intelligent readers of poetry for half a century.[1] After 1920 almost everyone could quote by memory the metaphysical poets at some length. Very few dared to read Shelley after Eliot's critique of "To a Skylark" in his essay on Crashaw,[2] and who could take Byron seriously after Eliot got through with him? "We have come to expect poetry to be something very concentrated," Eliot said, "something distilled; but if Byron had distilled his verse, there would have been nothing whatever left."[3]

On the other hand, although he was addicted to making dogmatic general statements about the nature of poetry, Eliot never did set forth a comprehensive or comprehensible theory of poetry, nor was it his intention to do so. He remarked in one of his later essays that "my own theorizing has been epiphenomenal of my tastes."[4] Nevertheless, his theories about poetry, such as his famous definition of poetry as "objective correlative," have been taken very seriously, and this has been unfortunate, for as a theorist Eliot was a failure, an assertion which can be easily demonstrated. There is hardly a general statement of his about poetry that he did not repudiate, qualify beyond recognition, or directly contradict—consciously or unconsciously. The seminal essay on the subject is Yvor Winters's "T. S. Eliot: The Illusion of Reaction," published over thirty-five years ago in the *Kenyon Review*.[5] Others, more recently, have noted the same problem.[6] Eliot himself admitted his inconsistency in "The Music of Poetry" (1942) when he wrote:

> I can never re-read any of my own prose writings without acute embarrassment: I shirk the task, and consequently may not take account of all the assertions to which I have at one time or another committed myself; I may often repeat what I have said before, and I may often contradict myself.[7]

I do not wish to repeat at length what has already been said on this subject, but I would like briefly to call attention to one of Eliot's most famous pronouncements—the criterion of "impersonality" of the poet and his poem, which has its best-known formulation in "Tradition and the Individual Talent" (1919):

> The progress of an artist is a continued self-sacrifice, a continual extinction of personality. There remains to define this process of depersonalization.[8]

And Eliot proceeds to define it by comparing the mind of the poet to a shred of platinum which as a catalytic agent may bring about a new combination of gases but itself remains unchanged. So the mind of the true poet (as distinct from the bad romantic poet who expresses his own emotions and is himself changed by his creative act) will remain unchanged as he brings about a new combination of emotions and feelings to produce the "objective correlative" which is the poem. "The more completely separate in him [the true poet] will be the man who suffers and the mind which creates." The doctrine is substantiated by other remarks in the same essay such as "the difference between art and the event is always absolute" and "Impressions and experiences which are important for the man may take no place in the poetry" and finally, towards the end of the essay: "Poetry is not a turning loose of emotion but an escape from emotion; it is not the expression of personality, but an escape from personality." This doctrine resulted in *The Waste Land,* which as we know now is a highly personal, autobiographical poem in disguise. The doctrine is widely considered to be Eliot's main achievement as a critic and theoretician, but of course he did not stick to it. In his essay on Yeats (1940) we find to our astonishment (that is, if we are taking Eliot seriously) that Eliot is downgrading the early poems of Yeats because they do not often enough give "that sense of a unique personality which makes one sit up in excitement and eagerness to learn more about the author's mind and feelings." Here the criterion of a successful poet seems to be his ability to express a unique personality, a difficult assignment for a shred of platinum. We have in fact a complete reversal of Eliot's earlier doctrine of impersonality, and suddenly Eliot seems to realize this and we discover him in a moment of embarrassment:

> I have in early essays, extolled what I called impersonality in art, and it may seem that, in giving as a reason for the superiority of Yeats's later work the

greater expression of personality in it, I am contradicting myself. It may be that I expressed myself badly, or that I had only an adolescent grasp of that idea [Eliot was over thirty years old when he wrote "Tradition and the Individual Talent"] — as I can never bear to re-read my own prose writings, I am willing to leave the point unsettled — but I think now, at least, that the truth of the matter is as follows. There are two forms of impersonality: that which is natural to the mere skilful craftsman, and that which is more and more achieved by the maturing artist. The first is that of what I have called the "anthology piece," of a lyric by Lovelace and Suckling, or of Campion, a finer poet than either. The second impersonality is that of the poet who, out of intense and personal experience, is able to express a general truth; retaining all the particularity of his experience, to make of it a general symbol.[9]

We now have two kinds of impersonal poetry — the first the result of good technique, the second the result of intense personal experience — but it is very doubtful if anyone could distinguish between the second kind of "impersonal" poem and any successful, well-written "personal" poem. Into which category would we put Yeats's "Prayer for My Daughter"? And we may wonder in passing whether Eliot would consider Yeats's later poetry "romantic" or "classic." He was careful to distinguish between these two terms when he called himself a "classicist" in the twenties. But perhaps this question is an unfair one, for Eliot later repudiated the distinction between these terms also. Eliot, however, did not wait until 1940 (the date of his essay on Yeats) to contradict his notion of "impersonality" as a criterion for good poetry. As early as 1931 he was praising Tourneur for revealing his personality in his plays: "Yet in no plays by any minor Elizabethan is a more positive personality revealed than in *The Revenger's Tragedy.*"[10] A year later he was praising Ford for "the distinct personal rhythm in blank verse which could be no one's but his alone,"[11] and in the same essay he praises Shakespeare's plays because they are "united by one significant, consistent, and developing personality."[12] And again in "What Is Minor Poetry" (1944) in comparing Herbert's poetry with Herrick's, Eliot says that Herrick's verses are inferior to Herbert's because "the personality expressed in them is less unusual."[13] But we can go back even further than this. In his essay on Massinger which appeared in *The Sacred Wood* (1920), the same volume which contained "Tradition and the Individual Talent," he wrote:

Marlowe's and Jonson's comedies were the transformation of a personality into a personal work of art, their lifetime's work, long or short. Massinger is not simply a smaller personality: his personality hardly exists. He did not, out of his own personality, build a world of art, as Shakespeare and Marlowe and Jonson built.[14]

The fact is that Eliot was championing both a personal and an impersonal art at the same time.

I have commented at some length on Eliot's extolling of "impersonal" poetry because it is generally considered his central doctrine. But one may mention in passing a few other contradictions and inconsistencies. At one point in his career he attempted to bring order into his theory of poetry by announcing himself to be a classicist, but as I have shown elsewhere, even as he wrote these words in

1927 for the *Criterion*, his classicism was spurious.[15] In "The Perfect Critic" (1920), which must have been a seminal essay for the New Criticism, with its praise of Coleridge and its pronouncement that the only job of a critic was to elucidate, Eliot says that Coleridge "was perhaps the greatest of English critics," but at about the same time he was saying in "Hamlet and His Problems" (1919) that Coleridge was "that most dangerous type of critic: the critic with a mind which is naturally of the creative order, but exercises itself in criticism instead," and he calls Coleridge's critical evaluation of the play *Hamlet* "the most misleading kind possible."[16] Did Eliot really believe that Coleridge was perhaps one of the greatest of English critics but that he had a most dangerous type of mind and wrote misleading criticism? In "The Perfect Critic" Eliot states that "in matters of great importance the critic must not coerce, and he must not make judgments of worse and better. He must simply elucidate: the reader will form the correct judgment for himself." This statement helped give rise to a whole group of critics who did nothing but elucidate and were later satirized by Eliot as the "lemon squeezer type of critic."[17] But Eliot did not stay long with this pronouncement. He made many judgments of worse and better in the very volume (*The Sacred Wood*) in which "The Perfect Critic" appeared. And also in the same volume he was saying at approximately the same time that "*qua* work of art, the work of art cannot be interpreted; there is nothing to interpret; we can only criticize it according to standards, in comparison to other works of art."[18] This is the exact opposite of the previous statement unless one can work out a subtle distinction between "elucidate" and "interpret" and between "judgments of worse and better" and "criticize according to certain standards." In his introductory lecture (1932) to *The Use of Poetry and the Use of Criticism*,[19] he said, "The rudiment of criticism is the ability to select a good poem and reject a bad poem; and its most severe test is of its ability to select a good *new* poem." I think most of us would agree—but this statement is a complete reversal of his former position.

There is also the problem of what Eliot meant by autotelic art. "I have assumed as axiomatic that a creation, a work of art, is autotelic," he wrote in "The Function of Criticism" (1923).[20] By "autotelic" he seems to be saying that a work of art, a poem for example, is about itself and not about something else, not about "life" for instance. And this statement is consistent with several others—"But the difference between art and the event is always absolute" and "Impressions and experiences which are important for the man may take no place in the poetry." The poet endeavors to "express feelings which are not in actual emotions at all"; the "emotion of art is impersonal"; a poem gives us "a new art emotion." These quotations from "Tradition and the Individual Talent" seem to be asserting that the divorce between art and life is complete. And see also these comments (1917) on Jean de Bosschère, whom he praises for his "obstinate refusal to adulterate his poetic emotions with ordinary human emotions. Instead of refining ordinary human emotions (and I do not mean tepid human emotions, but human however intense—in the crude living state) he aims direct at emotions of art."[21] Eliot's apparent contempt for human emotions at this early stage in his career is very revealing. The poem, the objective correlative, to repeat, is autotelic, about itself only, and provides an aesthetic experience different from anything in life. There is little room in this theory for poetry with ethical content or for poetry as a criticism of life. It was Shakespeare's business, he said, "to express the greatest emotional intensity of his time, based on whatever his time happened to think."[22] But Eliot also expressed an opposite view in his essay "Religion and Literature" (1935), in which he said that Christian readers should "scrutinize their reading, especially of works of imagination, with explicit ethical and theological standards. The greatness of literature cannot be determined solely by literary standards."[23] How one can scrutinize an autotelic objective correlative which is solely about itself and judge it by ethical and theological standards and at the same time *not* make a judgment about it as to better or worse (see above) is difficult to explain. The same difficulty arises when in "The Social Function of Poetry" (1945) Eliot says that "poetry may have a deliberate, conscious social purpose."[24]

It is impossible, then, to formulate Eliot's overall theory of poetry. It does not exist except as a jumble of contradictions. However, from time to time Eliot made statements about the nature of poetry which were in fact defenses of or explanations of what he himself as a poet was trying to do. He said in "The Music of Poetry" (1942):

> The poet at the back of his mind, if not as his ostensible purpose, is always trying to defend the kind of poetry he is writing, or to formulate the kind that he wants to write.[25]

And he wrote later in "The Frontiers of Criticism" (1956) "It [my literary criticism] is a by-product of my private poetry workshop; or a prolongation of the thinking that went into the formation of my own verse."[26]

It will be worth our while therefore to consider further several of these theoretical formulations. They will aid us in understanding what, from time to time, Eliot's intentions were as he wrote his poems, and they may help us towards a tentative "final" evaluation of Eliot's verse. We may discover that the failure of some of Eliot's poetry may be traced to unsound theory.

Before doing this, however, I would like to consider briefly the relationship between Ezra Pound and Eliot, for in some respects Eliot was a protégé of Pound, and some of Eliot's theory can be traced directly to Pound.

The marked difference in personality between the reticent and reserved Eliot and the flamboyant Pound and their widely divergent careers from the mid-twenties on have obscured their basic similarities of poetic theory and practice, as well as the historical fact that the older Pound had direct and precise influence on certain works of his younger friend and a more general and pervasive influence on his entire career. Eliot's essays on Dante (1920, 1929, and 1950) all owe something to Pound's seminal essay on Dante in *The Spirit of Romance* (1910). *The Waste Land* (dedicated to Pound) owes as much to the technique of the *Cantos* as it does to Joyce's *Ulysses,* which is considerable. If Eliot had been unfamiliar with the early *Cantos* and with *Ulysses* as it appeared in magazine form and in manuscript, he would have written a very different poem. Also, the fact that Eliot allowed Pound to cut the original version drastically (thus making it even more like the *Cantos* in structure) is indicative of the influence Pound was having on him at this stage in Eliot's career. Eliot, besides paying tribute to Pound in conversation, in letters, and in various articles, wrote a number of essays praising Pound's work,[27] and some of his statements are high praise indeed. In 1934, long after their personal relationship had cooled, Eliot said that Pound was "probably the most important living poet in our language."[28] He thought the early *Cantos* and *Hugh Selwyn Mauberley* to be among the finest achievements of Western civilization in the twentieth century.

They met for the first time in London in September 1914;[29] Eliot had read at Harvard some of Pound's earliest published verse (*Exultations*, 1909, and *Personae*, 1909). As far as we know, Pound had read nothing of Eliot's, although Eliot had published verse in the *Harvard Advocate*. Shortly after this meeting, Eliot sent Pound "The Love Song of J. Alfred Prufrock." Pound was impressed and succeeded in getting Harriet Monroe to accept it for *Poetry*, where it appeared after considerable delay and vacillation on the part of Miss Monroe. The most important literary relationship of the century was under way. Its first stage lasted until the end of 1922 (the year of the publication of *The Waste Land*), and after that the personal friendship fell off somewhat, partly because Pound was living on the continent and Eliot was in London, partly because Eliot could not put up with Pound's economic obsessions or his materialistic philosophy, and for that reason he sometimes denied him access to the *Criterion*. Pound took to occasional sharpshooting at Eliot and his growing reputation. Nevertheless, Eliot's admiration for Pound's poetry continued; he praised it until the end of his career, and he helped Pound on certain critical occasions, notably in getting him discharged from St. Elizabeth's hospital. But at first the relationship was pretty much a case of the older poet aiding the younger. The story has been told and often retold of how Pound was instrumental in getting Eliot's early poetry into print,[30] including "Prufrock," "Portrait of a Lady," "Preludes," and "Rhapsody on a Windy Night." Pound arranged for and paid the printing bill for Eliot's first volume of verse, and he was involved in negotiations for the publishing of later volumes, including *The Waste Land*. And of course he did his best to help Eliot financially, procuring for him the job of assistant editor on the *Egoist* and later attempting to arrange a fund which would make Eliot independent of his job at the bank. The enthusiasm of Pound for Eliot's work naturally had its effect on the younger writer's theory and practice. It was Pound who called Eliot's attention to the excellence of Gautier's quatrains, an event which changed Eliot's style, temporarily at least, and resulted in Eliot's employing the quatrain stanza in his second volume, notably the Sweeney poems, "The Hippopotamus," "Burbank with a Baedeker," and "Whispers of Immortality." Pound even claimed the credit for introducing Eliot to the woman who was the model for Grishkin! The direct, specific influence of Pound in matters of style ended with Pound's revision of *The Waste Land*; however, Eliot in his statement of poetic theory owes more to Pound than has previously been noted. Indeed, Gallup stresses the *differences* in theory between Pound and Eliot, but he draws his examples of Eliot's theory from fairly late essays, and I think somewhat exaggerates the differences.[31]

There is, for example, a direct relationship between Pound's famous theory of the image and Eliot's objective correlative. Although many sources have been suggested for the objective correlative, including Plato, Donne, Byron, Coleridge, Washington Allston, Nietzsche, Husserl, Pater, Hegel, F. H. Bradley, Poe, and Pound, I venture to suggest that if Pound had not attempted to formulate his theories of the image and the vortex, Eliot would not have phrased his notion of the objective correlative as he did. Although Poe had exactly formulated the objective correlative years before Eliot and Pound, I am inclined to think that Pound (who was closest to home as it were) was the primary source.[32] Donald Davie has said that Eliot's theory is the mirror-image of Pound's, and so it is. Pound said that an image is "an emotional and intellectual complex in an instant of time," and he believed that a successful poem should present one or more of such images. Pound also said that "poetry is a sort of inspired mathematics, which gives us equations. . . for the human emotion." This idea of *equivalence* is implicit in Eliot's objective *correlative,* which he formulated as follows in "Hamlet and His Problems" (1919):

> The only way of expressing emotion in the form of art is by finding an "objective correlative"; in other words, a set of objects, a situation, a chain of events which shall be the formula of that *particular* emotion; such that when the external facts, which must terminate in sensory experience, are given, the emotion is immediately evoked.[33]

He rephrased the notion more briefly in "The Possibility of a Poetic Drama" (1920):

> Permanent literature is always a presentation: either a presentation of thought, or a presentation of feeling by a statement of events in human action or objects in the external world.[34]

And he stated the same idea again in his essay on Lancelot Andrewes (1926) when he said of Donne, "He is constantly finding an object which shall be adequate to his feelings."[35] But here *Donne is being criticized for using the objective correlative!* For Eliot goes on to imply that Andrewes is superior because he "is wholly absorbed in the object and therefore responds with the adequate emotion." That is, Andrewes reverses the process by beginning with the object and responding to it with the appropriate emotion. It is a typical Eliot inconsistency.[36] But to return to Eliot's original definition and method. Eliot believed that a successful poem should present one or more objective correlatives. Pound starts with sensory data to communicate his feeling. Eliot starts with a feeling and finds the sensory data with which to communicate it. The result in practice if one follows either theory is the same — emphasis on sensory data to communicate feeling; poetry (in a poem of any length) becomes a series of sensory data, often without logical transition, certainly without the use of abstract language or simple statement — that is, we get the *Cantos* and *The Waste Land.*

Let us note again in both Pound and Eliot the suddenness with which the emotion is transmitted—"an instant of time" (Pound) and "the emotion is immediately evoked" (Eliot). It seems that by providing "sensory experience" poetic feeling is almost automatically evoked. Eugene England made a cogent comment on this method of writing when he remarked that "the trouble with the notion of the objective correlative is that it leaves out the mind and language."[37] That is, the response to poetry is *completely emotional*, and language should merely provide transmission of sensory data and therefore be as *transparent* as possible. Eliot praised the opening scene of *Hamlet* for its transparency, certain lines in Dante for their translucency; and in an unpublished lecture (1933) said he wished to "write poetry which should be essentially bare bones, or poetry so transparent that we should not see the poetry, but that which we are meant to see through the poetry," And both F. O. Matthiessen and Frank Kermode believe that when Eliot goes on to say he had written "forty of fifty original lines" of this kind he was referring to (among others) the lines about the water thrush in *The Waste Land,* which he told Ford Madox Ford were the only *good* lines in that poem.[38] The water-dripping song reads in part:

> If there were water
> And no rock
> If there were rock
> And also water
> And water
> A spring
> A pool among the rock
> If there were the sound of water only
> Not the cicada
> And dry grass singing
> But sound of water over a rock
> Where the hermit-thrush sings in the pine trees
> Drip drop drip drop drop drop drop
> But there is no water

This passage is, I think, a successful achievement of Eliot's intention to produce a transparent objective correlative, particularly in the penultimate line quoted. It is the kind of poetry which may be produced, according to Eliot, by "language in a healthy state." "Language in a healthy state," he said in his essay on Swinburne, "is so close to the object that the two are identified."[39] He has succeeded in almost eliminating mind, in almost eliminating language, and in the process (although it may not have been his intention) of almost eliminating feeling. But it is an extremely thin, limited, and primitive kind of writing (the kind of thing, incidentally, which Hemingway was sometimes trying to do in prose). It is the kind of verse which might appeal to the nonintellectual, illiterate audience which Eliot at one time said he wanted. "I myself should like an audience which could neither read nor write."[40]

The *mythic method* is another famous theoretical statement by Eliot. It owes something to Joyce, but more, I think, to Pound. Eliot said in his 1923 review of *Ulysses:*

In using the myth, in manipulating a continuous parallel between contemporaneity and antiquity, Mr. Joyce is pursuing a method which others must pursue after him. . . . It is simply a way of controlling, of ordering, of giving a shape and a significance to the immense panorama of futility and anarchy which is contemporary history. . . . Instead of narrative method, we may now use the mythic method.[41]

Eliot gives Yeats the credit for discovering the method. Pound is not mentioned, nor is *The Waste Land*. And yet the mythic method as defined here is an exact description of the method by which Pound tried to organize the *Cantos* (of which a number were in print or manuscript at the time of this essay) and by which Pound-Eliot tried to organize *The Waste Land*. The "continuous parallel between contemporaneity and antiquity" was a device by which Pound and Eliot attempted to bring order and significance to a series of seemingly unrelated images or objective correlatives.

I would like next to consider another interesting affinity between Pound and Eliot — their common interest in the "charged moment," which in the case of Pound goes back, as we have seen, to the Pre-Raphaelites. Frank Kermode in the introduction to his selection of essays by Eliot, *Selected Prose of T. S. Eliot,* discusses an important and fascinating letter which Eliot wrote to Stephen Spender in May 1935. Eliot in commenting on what he considered the proper response of a critic (or presumably any intelligent, sensitive reader) to poetry said, "You don't really criticize any author to whom you have never surrendered yourself. . . . Even just the bewildering minute counts; you have to give yourself up, and then recover yourself."[42] Kermode calls attention to the fact that Eliot is referring to a line in Tourneur's *The Revenger's Tragedy* which Eliot quotes with admiration in his essay on Tourneur and also in "Tradition and the Individual Talent":

> Are lordships sold to maintain ladyships
> For the poor benefit of a bewildering minute?

(Actually, Tourneur probably wrote "bewitching minute," but Eliot preferred the probable printer's error as giving the richer meaning.) Kermode rightly calls "the bewildering minute" a description of sexual surrender and equates it with the famous lines from *The Waste Land*:

> . . . blood shaking my heart
> The awful daring of a moment's surrender.

The appropriate response to poetry, Eliot seems to be saying, is similar to the sexual orgasm, a brief and intense and bewildering surrender, and presumably the best poetry is that which gives the most intense (and by necessity brief) pleasure or *frisson*. There are other passages in Eliot which emphasize this function of poetry:

> The experience of a poem is the experience both of a moment and a lifetime. It is very much like our intense experience of other human beings. There is a first, or an early moment which is unique, of shock and surprise, even of terror (*Ego dominus tuus*), a moment which can never be forgotten.[43]

it was his [Shakespeare's] business to express the greatest emotional intensity of his time, based on whatever his time happened to think.[44]

Clear visual images are given much more intensity by having a meaning—we do not need to know what the meaning is.[45]

where you have "imitations of life" on the stage, with speech, the only standard that we can allow is the standard of the work of art, aiming at the same intensity at which poetry and the other forms aim.[46]

Intensity as the criterion of true poetry has a definite affinity with A. E. Housman's famous definition of poetry which Eliot cites with approval in the published version of his eighth Norton Lecture:

...I could no more define poetry than a terrier can define a rat...we both recognised the object by the symptoms which it provokes in us. One of these symptoms was described in connexion with another object by Eliphaz the Temanite: "A spirit passed before my face: the hair of my flesh stood up." Experience has taught me, when I am shaving of a morning, to keep watch over my thoughts, because if a line of poetry strays into my memory, my skin bristles so that the razor ceases to act. This particular symptom is accompanied by a shiver down the spine.[47]

Housman's statement is more discreetly phrased than Kermode's account of Eliot's equivalence of poetic response with sexual surrender, but the idea is the same. The greatest poetry is that which causes intense, automatic, subrational, "bewildering" excitement in "an instant of time." It is an attitude toward poetry which we would expect to find in the romantic tradition but not in the classic tradition which emphasizes (here I use Eliot's own words) "dignity, reason, and order." In the classic tradition we expect a response to poetry much less emotional than Eliot's. The mind of the poet is not "bewildered" by a classical poem. His emotions are refined and his mind clarified. The response to classical poetry is fully conscious and not subconscious. Meaning is not disregarded (Eliot said, "As for the meaning of the *Cantos* that never worries me, and I don't think I care")[48] but rather meaning motivates the appropriate emotion. Yet Eliot during the 1920s was calling himself a classicist, and he is still considered to be so by many today.

Kermode also says of the lines we have been considering, "it is a characteristic 'surrender.' We are here, I think, contemplating an aspect not only of Eliot's critical, but of his poetic genius." Kermode considers this surrender of a "bewildering minute" a positive good. "Without the first moment there is nothing worth having."[49] Eliot's source (Tourneur), of course, did not consider the "bewildering minute" a positive good. His line reads, "For the poor benefit of a bewildering minute." Nor did Eliot when he was lecturing at the university of Virginia on the benefits of Christian orthodoxy the year before he wrote the letter to Spender: "It is in fact in moments of moral and spiritual struggle depending upon spiritual sanctions, rather than in those 'bewildering minutes' in which we are all very much alive that men and women come nearest to being real."[50] The obviously contradictory attitude toward the benefits of the "bewildering minute" is characteristic of Eliot.

If by poetic genius Kermode means that it was Eliot's intention to provide the reader of his poems with a series of "charged moments" or "bewildering minutes" to which the reader may surrender, then I think the statement is correct. If he means that Eliot in the act of creation has himself such moments of intense excitement, then either he is wrong or (more likely) he is right and Eliot is simply being inconsistent again. For Eliot has told us in his famous passage that the mind in the act of creation should be completely unmoved and unchanged by what it creates — "like the God of the creation...indifferent" in Joyce's phrase, or like a shred of platinum according to Eliot's analogy.

Let us consider for a moment Eliot's catalytic agent:

> The analogy was that of the catalyst. When the two gases previously mentioned are mixed in the presence of a filament of platinum, they form sulphurous acid. This combination takes place only if the platinum is present; nevertheless the newly formed acid contains no trace of platinum, and the platinum itself is apparently unaffected; has remained inert, neutral, and unchanged. The mind of the poet is the shred of platinum.[51]

I think here that Eliot may have been more influenced by Joyce than by Pound, for it was Joyce who said, through his persona, Stephen Dedalus:

> The personality of the artist, at first a cry or a cadence or a mood and then a fluid and lambent narrative, finally refines itself out of existence, impersonalises itself, so to speak. The esthetic image in the dramatic form is life purified in and reprojected from the human imagination. The mystery of esthetic like that of material creation is accomplished. The artist, like the God of the creation, remains within or behind or beyond or above his handiwork, invisible, refined out of existence, indifferent, paring his fingernails.[52]

Portrait of the Artist as a Young Man was first published in complete book form in 1916, about three years before Eliot wrote "Tradition and the Individual Talent." (Eliot was also undoubtedly familiar with the earlier partial serialization in the *Egoist*.) Eliot's theory of the impersonal poet as stated and restated in various essays obviously owes a good deal to this passage by Joyce.

Eliot's analogy is completely unsatisfactory, as anyone who has written poetry knows. Every poet of any merit is moved to some extent as he creates his poems. The writing of a poem is not, I venture to say, a game, "a superior amusement" as Eliot called it in 1928,[53] in which the writer fits pieces together as if the poem were a jigsaw puzzle or tries new combinations of material like an experimental chemist. And surely great poets develop and mature in the act of writing their poetry. Eliot was writing much more sensibly when he said, "But maturing as a poet means maturing as the whole man, experiencing new emotions appropriate to one's age, and with the same intensity as the emotions of youth."[54] (Note again the criterion of "intensity.") Of course, this statement is inconsistent with the analogy of the mind of the poet as a shred of platinum. Platinum doesn't mature.

As we read further in Eliot's theoretical statements about the nature of poetry and the act of creating poetry we are more and more impressed with the importance of the mysterious, the magical, the subconscious, the mystical, in a word the *irrational* in Eliot's position. Irrationalism in the poetic theory and practice of a twentieth-century poet should not surprise anyone. The century by and large as far as literature goes has been predominantly irrational. But Eliot, we repeat, was supposed to have set himself against this trend. He called himself a classicist, and for the classicist, reason is supposed to be paramount. Let us consider next Eliot's *auditory imagination*. He defines it in his eassy "The Use of Poetry" (1933):

> the feeling for syllable and rhythm penetrates far below the conscious levels of thought and feeling, invigorating every word; sinks to the most primitive and forgotten, returns to the origin and brings something back, seeks the beginning and the end.[55]

By means of the auditory imagination, then, we employ the subconscious, the subrational, and racial memory to furnish us images and rhythms for our poetry. In the same essay he remarks that certain images "may have symbolic value, but of what we cannot tell, for they come to represent the depths of feeling into which we cannot peer," and in a note he says "the pre-logical mentality persists in civilized man, but becomes available only to or through the poet," and "he who has reached in these matters, a state of greater *purity*, does not bother about understanding." It was in such a state of purity that he read Pound's *Cantos* and said, as previously noted, "As for the meaning of the *Cantos*, that never worries me." And indeed it was Pound himself who first formulated the auditory imagination, although he did not call it that. In "The Chinese Written Character" (1920) Pound said, "Poetry only does consciously what the primitive races did unconsciously. The chief work of literary men in dealing with language, and of poets especially, lies in feeling back along the ancient lines of advance. He must do this so that he may keep his words enriched by all their subtle undertones of meaning."[56] Eliot's auditory imagination is a rephrasing and elaboration of this seminal statement.

Irrationalism, obscurantism, and downright mystification and hocus-pocus are surprisingly frequent in Eliot's literary essays. A few examples must suffice. Eliot frequently said in his essays and in his interviews that a poem may have a multiplicity of meanings, at least one, in fact, for each reader. The meaning of a poem is what it means to the reader. Such an attitude leaves the field wide open for interpretative criticism, although at one time Eliot deplored interpretation. The poem does not, it seems, communicate in the ordinary sense of that word. It stimulates. In "The Frontiers of Criticism" (1956) he said," the meaning is what the poem means to different sensitive readers." But in fairness it must be pointed out that he contradicts himself in the same essay two pages later: "to enjoy a poem under a misunderstanding as to what it is, is to enjoy what is merely a projection of our own mind."[57] However, elsewhere he has stated clearly that he welcomes misunderstanding because it enriches meaning. At his seminar at the University of Chicago he is reported to have said that in his fourth Quartet he had intended the phrase "spectre of a Rose" to refer to the Wars of the Roses and to Sir Thomas Browne's famous "ghost of a Rose" but was delighted when some readers thought it referred to Nijinsky. He went on to say that his intention was to describe Prufrock, in the lines "I grow old," etc., as a young man conscious of growing old but that he also welcomed the interpretation that he was describing an old man who could only wade on the beach and not swim.[58] In commenting on a passage at the rehearsal of *The Cocktail Party*, he is reported to have said that it means whatever it means to the actor or audience. But we are not dependent on journalistic hearsay. Eliot seriously believed in the doctrine of multiplicity of meaning and said so in writing a number of times. In "The Music of Poetry" he wrote: "The reader's interpretation may differ from the author's and be equally valid—it may even be better."[59] And he calls on Shakespeare to support this view: "He [Shakespeare] would simply be astonished and bewildered to discover the endless variety of meanings that his words have contained for different men and women, and for different generations. . . . In the end he would say simply 'I don't know'; and, to *any interpreter* [italics mine] 'Possibly. You may be right.' "[60]

What *should* poetry communicate? Certainly not comprehensible rational meaning, according to Eliot. "Genuine poetry can communicate before it is understood."[61] "Poetry begins, I dare say, with the beating of a drum in the jungle."[62] "It may make us from time to time a little more aware of the deeper, unnamed feelings which form the substratum of our being, to which we rarely penetrate."[63] For the genuine poet is dealing with "dark psychic material," when he writes in what Eliot calls the first voice:

> he is haunted by a demon, a demon against which he feels powerless, because in its first manifestation it has no face, name, nothing; and the words, the poem he makes, are a kind of form of exorcism of this demon. . . . he is going to all that trouble, not in order to communicate with anyone, but to gain relief from acute discomfort.[64]

I believe that this is an accurate description of how much of Eliot's own verse came to him. "Meaning" in the ordinary sense of the word is of minor importance in the kind of poetry which Eliot frequently wrote. He said in "The Use of Poetry,"

> The chief use of the "meaning" of a poem, in the ordinary sense, may be (for here again I am speaking of some kinds of poetry and not all) to satisfy one habit of the reader, to keep his mind diverted and quiet, while the poem does its work upon him; much as the imaginary burglar is always provided with a bit of nice meat for the house-dog.[65]

To keep his mind diverted and quiet! Eliot has said a number of times that it is dangerous for a poet to think. He should not philosophize. He should not generalize:

> A poet who is also a metaphysician, and unites the two activities, is conceivable as an unicorn or wyvern is conceivable. . . but such a poet would be a monster. . . . Such a poet would be two men. It is more convenient to use,

if necessary, the philosophy of other men than to burden oneself with the philosophy of a monstrous brother in one's own bosom. Dante and Lucretius used other men's philosophies cheerfully without bothering too much about verifying them for themselves.[66]

The poet should feel, he should bring up images from his subconscious, but he should not think. Or if a poet does have thoughts, he should have them not as abstractions or generalizations but as sense-perceptions: "certainly many men will admit that their keenest ideas have come to them with the quality of a sense-perception."[67] And in a famous passage he said that the metaphysical poets could "feel their thought as immediately as the odor of a rose." The fear of abstract thought and abstract language—we find it in T. E. Hulme, Pound, Eliot, John Crowe Ransom, William Carlos Williams, to mention a few distinguished poets of our time. Eliot praises Charles-Louis Philippe, the author of *Bubu of Montparnasse*: "He had a gift which is rare enough: the ability not to think, not to generalise. To be able to select, out of personal experience, what is really significant, to be able not to corrupt it by afterthoughts, is as rare as imaginative invention."[68]

One is reminded at this point of some remarks by C. P. Snow:

> There is a syndrome of attitudes in literature, nearly all quite modern, apparently unconnected, which spring from the same root—the romantic conception of the artist, the alienation of the intellectual, the aesthetic of the antinovel, the abdication of the generalizing intellect, the hatred of the scientific-industrial revolution, the prizing of verbal innovation, the desire to contract out of society. This syndrome is seen at its most complete in writers like T. E. Hulme, Joyce or Pound.[69]

To the three writers named one wonders why Snow did not add a fourth, T. S. Eliot, who was a friend of all three and who owed them a great deal. The period from 1910 on has been one of considerable confusion in the arts, and Eliot's theoretical pronouncements such as those quoted above have done little to clarify the situation as far as poetry is concerned. Eliot's theories (regardless of which came first, theory or practice) are directly related to, and descriptive of, a considerable amount of Eliot's poetic practice. In the light of what has been said, we should not be surprised to find a body of verse that is frequently and deliberately obscurantist, that suggests more than it says, that often has little paraphrasable content, that aims at intense emotional effects rather than a just appraisal of human experience, and that achieves its effects by means of highly charged "images" or "objective correlatives" which may be brought together without rationally demonstrable coherence.

II
Laforguian Decadence

In one of Eliot's most frequently quoted comments on his own work, we are told that he began writing his early poems under the influence of Jules Laforgue and the later Elizabethan (he also means Jacobean) dramatists. The influence of

Laforgue is obvious and pervasive, and it has been extensively documented.[70] However, there does not appear to be much influence of the dramatists before "Gerontion" (1919) although Eliot was certainly reading these dramatists and may have been influenced by them in the general way, that is, by their disillusioned decadence. Disillusioned decadence, however, or at least the pretense or mask of disillusioned decadence, also accurately describes much of Laforgue's poetry, and the superficial, rather facile cynicism of the early Eliot seems to me closer to Laforgue than to that of the somber Webster. Eliot's decadent verse is also somewhat different from that of the English decadence of the 1890s. The verbal virtuosity of Eliot (and Laforgue too) is superior to that of Dowson and Lionel Johnson and Wilde. Eliot is never guilty of the softness and clichéd style of Dowson, and in this respect he is even superior to Yeats, that is, to the Yeats of the 1890s who shared some of the weaknesses of that period. The hall mark or *virtu* of the early Eliot derives directly from Laforgue. It is romantic irony, irony directed against the poet or a persona of the poet — brilliant, cynical, shallow, the melancholy pleasantry, the quotable witty phrase:

> I have measured out my life with coffee spoons

the touch of nostalgia that suggests a mysterious profundity:

> My buried life and Paris in the spring.

Eliot's poetry of romantic irony is superbly done — especially so when we remember that Eliot was still in his early twenties when he wrote much of it — but it is in the end a minor accomplishment, lacking true depth and substance. For Eliot's master, after all, was a *very* minor poet. The quality of much of the French poet's verse can be discerned in the opening stanza of Eliot's "Humoresque" (1909/10) composed according to the subtitle "After J. Laforgue":

> One of my marionettes is dead,
> Though not yet tired of the game —
> But weak in body as in head,
> (A jumping-jack has such a frame).[71]

The poem was suggested by the second stanza of "Locutions de Pierrot, xii":

> Encore un de mes pierrots mort;
> Mort d'un chronique orphelinisme;
> C'était un coeur plein de dandyisme
> Lunaire, en un drôle de corps.[72]

Eliot's stanza is trivial and juvenile, like the entire poem, and Eliot fortunately omitted it from his first volume of poems. But the adaptation is no worse than the original.

"Prufrock" is clearly the best poem written under the Laforguian banner. It is a classic example of romantic irony, full of self-pitying disillusionment, for Prufrock is, of course, a persona for Eliot. Beauty, if it is allowed to appear momentarily, is immediately undercut by a violently contrary sentiment:

> I should have been a pair of ragged claws
> Scuttling across the floors of silent seas.

The irony of "Prufrock," as in so much of Laforgue, is supposedly a defense against sentimentality and boredom. Laforgue's irony has been called "a magnesium spark struck out between the halves of a divided personality."[73] And the same can be said of Eliot's

> Let us go then, you and I
> When the evening is spread out against the sky
> Like a patient etherized upon a table.

Laforgue, according to Ramsey, frequently "assumed a role, a mask. . . there is a movement toward dramatization, a tendency having its origin in self awareness and self defense, to exteriorize the lyric emotion."[74] This is also an exact description of Eliot's method in "Prufrock."

There are other Laforguian characteristics of this poem — sordid images from an urban environment "sawdust restaurants with oyster-shells" and a preoccupation with the nerves,

> . . . as if a magic lantern threw the nerves in patterns on a screen.

Arthur Symons in the book that drew Eliot's attention to Laforgue, *The Symbolist Movement in Literature,* said of his poetry, "It is an art of the nerves, this art of Laforgue, and it is what all art would tend towards if we followed our nerves on all their journeys."[75] Symons's comment applies to much of Eliot's early verse. Also, like Laforgue, Eliot showed an early interest in the subconscious, in experiences on the fringe of consciousness, and in submarine and water imagery which is frequently used to illustrate this kind of experience. It is my opinion that the recurrent rain, water, and drowning motifs in Eliot's verse started with Laforgue and with the writing of "Prufrock," the last line of which refers to drowning, rather than with, as has been suggested, the supposed death by drowning of Eliot's intimate Parisian friend Jean Verdenal, who is sometimes considered the original of Phlebas the Phoenician who died by water in both "Dans le Restaurant" and *The Waste Land.*[76]

There are of course verbal similarities in the work of the two poets. Laforgue, like the young Eliot, employed bizarre and exotic language and juxtaposed formal with colloquial diction for shock effect. Both poets were interested in creating special musical effects and in weaving the names and sounds of various musical instruments into their verse. The tinkle of the street piano is heard in the lines of both poets. There are direct verbal echoes and "thefts" of Laforgue's lines in "Prufrock." For example, "When the evening is spread out against the sky/Like a patient etherized upon a table" may have been suggested by

> Un disque safrané, malade, sans rayons
> Qui meurt à l'horizon balayé de cinabre.
> > ("Couchant d'hiver")

The yellow smoke and fog may have been derived from the same poem:

Au gaz jaune et mourant des brumeux boulevards.

"Do I dare/Disturb the universe?" is taken from Laforgue's letter to his sister Marie, in which the French poet describes an evening walk somewhat similar to Prufrock's.[77].

The Laforguian influence, then, on the early Eliot has been established. But one misconception, for which Eliot himself is responsible, remains to be cleared up. Eliot said that he found similarities between Laforgue's technical devices and those of the metaphysical poets.[78] But there is little or no sign of Donne or of the other poets of his school in Eliot's early verse or, for that matter, in Laforgue, none of the toughness of structure nor the brilliantly involved conceits of the English poets. There is, however, some debt to Baudelaire, Mallarmé, and Corbière, but it is very slight compared to the debt to Laforgue.

"Portrait of a Lady" (1910), Eliot's second-best early poem, inspired by a lady whom the poet and his friends, including Conrad Aiken, knew when they were students at Harvard, also owes much to Laforgue. The scene, like that of "Prufrock," is Boston or Cambridge, but the urban imagery owes something to Laforgue's Paris (as it does in "Prufrock"). A number of Laforguian verbal echoes have been identified. "Well! and what if she should die some afternoon" is an echo of "Enfin, si, par un soir elle meurt dans mes livres" from "Autre Complainte de Lord Pierrot,"[79] and also of "Mais voici qu'un beau soir, infortunée à point/Elle meurt!"[80] The musical instruments that play intermittently throughout the poem, the "street piano, mechanical and tired," the "cracked cornets," "the windings of the violins" are similar to the various musical instruments in Laforgue.[81]

Although its style and tone are Laforguian, "Portrait of a Lady" has more structure than the rambling associational poems of the French poet. There are three scenes, each set in a season of the year — winter, with the same smoke and fog we experienced in "Prufrock," spring ("she has a bowl of lilacs in her room"), and fall. In each scene or tableau the young man is in conversation with the older woman who wishes to increase the intimacy of their relationship — to the young man's embarrassment. At the conclusion of each scene the male narrator escapes the oppressive feminine atmosphere to the freedom of the park where he smokes, drinks bock beer, and reads the comics and the sporting page. The tone deepens somewhat in the concluding lines when the poet thinks, "Well! and what if she should die some afternoon," in which event he would not know "what to feel or if I understand."

In both "Prufrock" and "Portrait" the protagonist narrator is in a perplexed, bewildered, and indecisive state of mind. Leonard Unger, A. Walton Litz, and others trace Eliot's indecisive protagonists to Henry James, and particularly to Marcher of "The Beast in the Jungle." Eliot may have been reading James at this early age (1910/11). (Prufrock's phrase "evenings, mornings, afternoons," incidentally, occurs several times in *The Golden Bowl.*) However, the moral paralysis of Eliot's personae is probably more attributable to Laforgue.

It should be noted that while Eliot is satirizing his social milieu in the early poems he is in a way engaging in self-ridicule, for he belongs to the milieu he is satirizing and shares some of the characteristics of the persons satirized. Self-ridicule, but not self-criticism. There is a kind of snobbish satisfaction in being a member of genteel society, Bostonian or otherwise, and sharing in its weaknesses. In spite of its brilliance, the early verse is emotionally and morally feeble—a poetry of alternating exasperated nervous tension and smug complacency.

"La Figlia Que Piange" (The Girl Who Weeps; 1911) seems to have had a special personal significance for Eliot.[82] Several of its lines are hauntingly and unforgettably beautiful. One line was stolen from Laforgue's "Pétition," "Simple et sans foi comme un bonjour" becomes in Eliot's English "Simple and faithless as a smile and shake of the hand." The poem as a whole is superior to anything by Laforgue.

When Eliot was in Europe in 1911 he was advised to look up a stele in an Italian museum which depicted a young girl weeping. He never found it, but he wrote a poem about this weeping girl (nameless, hence the epigraph *O quam te memorem virgo*—O maiden, how may I name thee) whom he never found, in which he imagines the cause of her grief to be a parting from her lover. Eliot seems to be thinking of himself as the lover. The idealized imagined girl with "her hair over her arms and her arms full of flowers" is highly suggestive of Alain-Fournier's princesse lointaine, the dream girl of his novel *Le Grand Meaulnes,* not published until 1913 but probably available to Eliot in manuscript by 1911. But there is a difference, for in Eliot's poem of idealized love and grief we have a touch of Laforguian cynicism not present in Alain-Fournier's story. After all, the lovers in Eliot's poem may have been "simple and faithless." It seems impossible for Eliot to sustain a vision of beauty or fullness of being without destroying it with a cynical remark. Indeed, fullness of being is introduced into Eliot's poetry for the purpose of destroying it to convey a sense of sudden deprivation.

As for the other poems in *Prufrock,* "Rhapsody on a Windy Night" has been singled out for considerable attention. Again, there are verbal echoes of Laforgue, particularly his "Complainte de cette bonne lune" from which Eliot took the line "La lune ne garde aucune rancune" (The moon holds no grudge), modifying Laforgue's original line slightly. Laforgue's "La Première Nuit" probably suggested some of the details of the street scene, particularly the lamps and the prostitutes, and Laforgue's lines

> Dans un album
> Mourait fossile
> Un géranium

perhaps suggested Eliot's two references to geraniums, although the graphic lines

> Every street lamp that I pass
> Beats like a fatalistic drum
> And through the spaces of the dark
> Midnight shakes the memory
> As a madman shakes a dead geranium

owe something to Wilde's "Ballad of Reading Gaol" and a good deal more to Eliot's surrealistic imagination, his talent for motiveless terror. The poem is a successful example of Eliot's doctrine that a poem may achieve intensity of effect through imagery and rhythm with little regard to meaning. The poem is an exercise in pure intensity. However much we admire its brilliance we cannot defend the poem on any rational grounds.

The other poems in *Prufrock,* especially "Preludes" and "Conversation Galante," are also heavily indebted to Laforgue. They are too slight to merit serious attention although because of Eliot's later reputation they have been frequently discussed.

III
Purgation

In Eliot's second volume of verse, *Poems* (1920), there are seven poems in tetrameter quatrains which reveal a tightening up of form under the influence of Gautier and perhaps under the influence of Pound's *Hugh Selwyn Mauberley,* if we can assume that Eliot saw the poem in manuscript. There are four poems in French of uncertain literary merit but of help in charting the progress of Eliot's spiritual development. These were followed by "Ode" in *Ara Vos Prec* (the title of the first British edition of this collection), omitted from the American edition. "Ode," too, is of questionable merit and taste, but it is important biographically and psychologically.

It was Pound himself who turned Eliot's attention to Gautier as a model for tightening up poetry in an age which was beginning to eschew form altogether under the rubric of "free verse" and "imagism." In "Sweeney among the Nightingales" Eliot, within the restrictions of the quatrain, achieves a precision of style quite impossible in the long lax lines of the "Prufrock" period:

> The silent vertebrate in brown
> Contracts and concentrates, withdraws;
> Rachel *née* Rabinovitch
> Tears at the grapes with murderous paws....

On the other hand, because in most instances he is still sticking to his earlier method of communicating feeling by means of contrasting abruptly juxtaposed objective correlatives without explanatory comment, he achieves immediate but meaningless intense emotional effects. For example, after a stanza which is a precise and perfectly comprehensible description of Sweeney we have this:

> The circles of the stormy moon
> Slide westward toward the River Plate,
> Death and the Raven drift above
> And Sweeney guards the hornèd gate.

> Gloomy Orion and the Dog
> Are veiled; and hushed the shrunken seas;

> The person in the Spanish cape
> Tries to sit on Sweeney's knees. . . .

The style continues to be excellent—the quatrains move well, the details are vivid and precise, but to what end? After fifty years of wild-goose chasing after the various mythological connotations of Orion, the Dog, the Raven, the Horned Gate, we can only say that the lines build up an atmosphere of impending doom, and that the solemnity of the first six lines quoted is in violent contrast to the last two lines. And no one knows for sure what the River Plate is doing in that context. The writing is deliberately obscurantist. The poem as a whole presents scenes of violence past and present, the conspiracy against and murder of Agamemnon, the conspiracy against Sweeney, and the past and the present are united in the singing of the nightingales, but Eliot's attitude toward this violence is never clear, nor is it clear why he should be comparing the murder of the Greek hero with the threatened murder of Sweeney. The usual explanation is that he is contrasting the heroic circumstances of the Greek's death with the sordid circumstances of Sweeney's possible demise, but at the end of the poem the nightingales are depicted as singing in both the sordid present and the heroic past. Their function in the poem is obscure.

In "Whispers of Immortality" we meet Grishkin who, we now know, was modeled on a woman introduced by Pound to Eliot to stimulate the Muse, and once meeting her in Eliot's lines (adapted from Gautier)[83] we never forget her:

> Grishkin is nice: her Russian eye
> Is underlined for emphasis;
> Uncorseted, her friendly bust
> Gives promise of pneumatic bliss.

Her friendly bust is in contrast to the "breastless creatures underground" which, according to the first stanza of the poem, obsessed Webster and Donne much as Grishkin obsesses the twentieth-century imagination. We have the same formula as in "Sweeney among the Nightingales"—a series of contrasting scenes vividly perceived. The reader is left to draw his own conclusions, if any. It is basically the same method used by Pound in the *Cantos* except that each luminous detail is more coherently presented than in Pound's work.

"Sweeney Erect" places the vulgar Sweeney and his epileptic bedmate against a stormy natural and mythological background similar to that of "Sweeney among the Nightingales":

> Display me Aeolus above
> Reviewing the insurgent gales
> Which tangle Ariadne's hair
> And swell with haste the perjured sails.
>
> Morning stirs the feet and hands
> (Nausicaa and Polypheme).
> Gesture of orange-outang
> Rises from the sheets in steam.

The mythological backdrop suggests a past culture considerably more elevated than that represented by Sweeney and the vulgar "ladies of the corridor." But the poem has the same weakness as the others involving Sweeney. There is a series of vivid, contrasting pictorial scenes, and that is all. The poem lacks final meaning. Similarly, in "Mr. Eliot's Sunday Morning Service" we have a church scene and a picture of the Umbrian School showing a baptized God where

> . . . through the water pale and thin
> Still shine the unoffending feet

contrasted to a vision of Sweeney who

> . . . shifts from ham to ham
> Stirring the water in his bath.

There is a good deal of subtle allusion to various theological matters, but Eliot's attitude toward Christianity is more complex than clear. In "Burbank with a Baedeker: Bleistein with a Cigar" we see, against a backdrop of once glorious but now decadent Venice, scenes from a beautiful heroic past — Cleopatra on her "shuttered barge" and her love affair with Anthony — contrasted with Burbank's casual affair with Princess Volupine, who has a "meagre, blue-nailed, phthisic hand," and with the twentieth-century Jew Bleistein whose

> . . . lustreless protrusive eye
> Stares from the protozoic slime.

Again, there seems to be no "final cause" (to use Aristotle's and Eliot's terminology) for this poem. And there is a disquieting nastiness in most of the poems in this volume, of which the above lines are a good example. "A Cooking Egg," one of the weakest poems of the lot, presents Pipit, perhaps a former lover of the narrator, amid daguerreotypes and silhouettes of her ancestors, while the narrator reflects on the wreck of their dreams:

> But where is the penny world I bought
> To eat with Pipit behind the screen?

There is nothing left but rubbish, and the "red-eyed scavengers" are brought in to clean it up.

"The Hippopotamus" (1917), probably the first written of the quatrain poems, is in some ways the most successful. There is little doubt of Eliot's intention; the poem is a satire on the "True Church" as it exists in the twentieth century. It has wit, coherence, and unity of effect. It is clearly indebted to Gautier's "L'Hippopotame," but Eliot in this case makes a completely original use of his source material, rather than merely stealing a line or two.

The four poems in French which are interspersed with those in quatrains, although quite different in form from those written under the banner of Gautier (they probably derive from de Bosschère[84]), are nevertheless similar in theme. They are poems of purgation, especially those two which have received the most attention — "Lune de Miel" and "Dans le Restaurant."[85] "Dans le Restaurant" introduces Phlebas, who appears a few years later in *The Waste Land*. The poem depicts an incident in which a shabby waiter forces his unwelcome attention on a diner who narrates the poem (Eliot himself, we may presume). The waiter recalls a childhood incident in which he and a girl find shelter from the rain beneath some dripping willows. He gives her primroses, tickles her to make her laugh, and experiences a moment of power and ecstasy, but only a moment, for his incipient lovemaking is interrupted by a big dog who comes up to them for a romp. The disgusted diner replies "Mais alors, tu as ton vautour!" (Well then, you have your vulture) and "By what right do you pay for experiences as I do?" He gives the waiter ten sous and advises him to go take a bath. (My brief summary does not do justice to the extreme nastiness of the slobbering waiter or to the complexity of the allusive language. For an extended discussion see Arrowsmith's essay cited above.) We now have the usual abrupt Eliotic shift to a contrasting scene without explanation, the death by drowning of a man named Phlebas which appears to be a *memento mori* and a cleansing and purification of the preceding ugliness. It is tempting to believe that this scene (repeated in English in *The Waste Land*) is a reference to the supposed death by drowning of Eliot's Parisian friend Jean Verdenal, to whom the *Prufrock* volume was dedicated, but for reasons mentioned above, this interpretation now seems to be doubtful. The poem seems to be a kind of purgation with unexplained personal connotations. Girls with flowers appear elsewhere in important passages in Eliot's poetry, and there is a memorable line in "Burnt Norton" — "The moment in the arbour where the rain beat" — which suggests the possibility of an experience similar to that of the waiter beneath the dripping willows. The private experience is generalized and mythologized as it were by literary allusions. The vulture recalls the story of Prometheus of classical mythology. The diner and the waiter each had *his* vulture or eagle, but the *vautour* in "Dans le Restaurant" probably derives in part from André Gide's *Le Prométhée mal enchaîné* and Eliot equates it with the Eumenides so prominent in *Family Reunion*. Eliot in his Norton Lecture on Wordsworth and Coleridge (1932) says:

> But Wordsworth had no ghastly shadow at his back, no Eumenides
> to pursue him . . . His inspiration never having been of the
> sudden, fitful and terrifying kind that visited Coleridge. . . . As
> André Gide's Prometheus said. . . "*Il faut avoir un aigle.*" Coleridge
> remained in contact with his eagle.[86]

The central event of "Dans le Restaurant" is an epiphany in which the diner suddenly recognizes a bond between the waiter and himself. They are both in contact with their vulture-eagle "sudden, fitful and terrifying," and this experience distinguishes them from the majority of mankind. Eliot is obviously implying that he too — like the waiter, the diner, and Coleridge — has his vulture. Eliot's identification with Coleridge is clearly indicated at the end of the Norton lectures where Eliot says, "The sad ghost of Coleridge beckons to me from the shadow." And years later, in his lecture delivered in 1955 to the London Conservative Union, Eliot said, "As for Coleridge, he was rather a man of my own type."[87]

Dante, it will be remembered, had his eagle also as the result of an encounter at an early age with the young Beatrice, and like Coleridge he remained in contact with it for the rest of his life. We are not surprised then to find only partially concealed allusions in "Dans le restaurant" to the *Divine Comedy,* the most obvious being that in line 18, "Moi j'avais peur, je l'ai quittée à mi-chemin," where "à mi-chemin" is probably an echo of the first line of the *Divine Comedy,* "Nel mezzo del cammin di nostra vita."[88] These semimystical, semisexual experiences of childhood haunted Eliot throughout his life. They find expression in *The Waste Land,* in *Four Quartets,* and elsewhere.[89]

"Lune de Miel" depicts a scene of more mature sexual experience, and (typically of these poems) the sexual scene is disgusting and repugnant. As in "Dans le Restaurant," there is an abrupt shift to a contrasting scene that suggests purity. It is another poem of purgation. In Ravenna a wretched honeymoon couple smelling of summer sweat, between sheets crawling with bedbugs, spread their knees and scratch their flabby flea-bitten legs, while not far away stands firm and "ascétique" the basilica of Saint Apollinaire in its precise Byzantine outline. In the British edition of the 1920 volume an "Ode" in English which immediately follows the French poems also refers in terms of repugnance to a wedding night; contrasted with a scene of innocence:

> When the bridegroom smoothed his hair
> There was blood upon the bed.
> Morning was already late.
> Children singing in the orchard
> (Io Hymen, Hymenae)
> Succuba eviscerate. . . .

The title of the English edition, *Ara Vos Prec* (Now I pray you), indicates the central theme of most of the poems in this volume. The title comes from Dante's *Purgatorio* 26. 145 – 48. The shade of the Provençal poet Arnaut Daniel, much admired by both Eliot and Pound, is speaking:

> "Now I pray you, by that Goodness which
>   guideth you to the summit of the stairway,
>   be mindful in due time of my pain." Then he
>   hid him in the fire which refines them.

The original, of which the first three lines are Provençal, Daniel's native tongue, reads:

> "Ara vos prec, per aquella valor
>   que vos guida al som de l'escalina,
>   sovegna vos a temps de ma dolor."
> Poi s'ascose nel foco che gli affina.

These lines evidently meant a great deal to Eliot, for he inserted the last one into the concluding passage of *The Waste Land*; he used "Som de l'escalina" as a temporary title for section 3 of *Ash Wednesday*; and he quoted the phrase "Sovegna vos" in section 4 of the same poem. In giving the title *Ara Vos Prec* to this volume, Eliot is by implication comparing himself to Arnaut Daniel and he is indicating that his verses are a kind of expiation and purgation of a good deal of ugly experience. The process of purgation continued through *The Waste Land* period and then for the most part ceased as far as the poems are concerned, excluding the plays. After 1922 we get no more revolting images of broad-bottomed Sweeneys, slobbering waiters, epileptics, or the feet of the daughters of Mrs. Porter. Instead, we have increasing attention given to images like the blue of larkspur, Mary's color, white sails seaward flying, etc. True there are lines describing limbo or purgatory or the dark night of the soul. They often have a somber beauty or even terror; but they do not disgust.

Although "Gerontion" appears first in the 1920 volume, I have reserved it for last because it was probably the last written of this group of poems; it is in a style quite different from the seven poems in quatrains, and it looks forward to Eliot's next phase, the poetry of psychic crisis, as represented by *The Waste Land*. And indeed Eliot once considered using it as a prologue to *The Waste Land* until Pound talked him out of it. The texture of the poem reminds us of a conglomeration of the loose blank verse of late Elizabethan and Jacobean dramatists — Webster, Tourneur, Middleton, Chapman, and others — although much of the poem cannot be described as even loose blank verse, for lines of two beats are interspersed with lines of three, four, or more beats, and the iambic movement as far as scansion is concerned is lost. Nevertheless one has the impression of a soliloquy in Jacobean blank verse being spoken on stage. There are passages of considerable power, and the emotional surge of the verse rises to approach the conclusion of the poem when everything ends in trancelike silence. The central theme is never lost sight of — as it is in *The Waste Land*, if that poem can be said to have a central theme. Gerontion, the little old man, is representative of the modern mind removed from grace. There are a few obscure lines, but not enough to destroy the poem.

"Gerontion" is a web of historical, literary, and philosophical allusions with too many lines filched from Eliot's reading. Lines 1 and 2 are taken with slight rephrasing from A. C. Benson's biography *Edward FitzGerald;* line 17 is from Matthew 12:38; lines 18–19 are extracted from Lancelot Andrewes's *Nativity Sermon;* line 21 is made up of words and phrases from *The Education of Henry Adams,* chapter 18, par. 1; lines 29–30 are adapted from Job 7:6–7; line 55 is a rewrite of a line from Thomas Middleton's *The Changeling;* line 69, "the shuddering bear," is a revision of a line from Chapman's *Bussy d'Ambois.* Thus at least ten lines of this poem can hardly be considered original. Eliot made no excuses for these thefts ("bad poets imitate, good poets steal"), and he has even helped to identify some of the quotations. Incorporating verses by other poets into a new combination was a method he consciously and deliberately followed throughout his career. It is a procedure that one hesitates to praise.

"Gerontion" is a typical Eliot collage, reminding one of Pound's early *Cantos,* which were being written at the same time — a collage of contrasting scenes, epiphanies, and objective correlatives, juxtaposed without comment or transitional phrases. We begin with the little old man, Gerontion (a persona for Eliot, of course), soliloquizing as he is being read to by a boy "waiting for rain." As in *The Waste Land*, rain is symbolic of grace, and the narrator with his shabby life-style is symbolic of the decline of the West. After the description of Gerontion, we are given, with a quotation from Matthew and another from Andrewes's sermon, a suddenly evoked contrasting view of Christ the tiger amid the pagan sensuousness ("depraved May," with connotations of May Day) of springtime. Christ is a tiger because at one time his religion was as strong and vital as that of Bacchus and his leopards, and there may be overtones also of Henry James's "The Beast in the Jungle" and of Blake's tiger — at least Eliot, with his doctrine of multiple meanings, could not object to such an interpretation. Next we have a vision of the Mass, where Christ is eaten, divided, and drunk by Mr. Silvero, Hakagawa, Madame de Tornquist, and Fräulein von Kulp, all of whom are engaged in various unexplained activities. Allen Tate's suggestion that they represent the secularization of the Christian Mass[90] makes as good sense as any. But the scene is still not very satisfactory because of the shadowy nature of the characters who are given proper names and a descriptive phrase or two and actions that can only be partly explained by Tate's hypothesis.

> . . .Fräulein von Kulp
> Who turned in the hall, one hand on the door.

And that is all we know about Fräulein von Kulp. Yvor Winters was right in faulting this scene as an example of pseudo-reference in which the author lays claim to an emotion motivated by a nonexistent plot.[19] Eliot was fond of dropping strange names into his poems as if the name alone could conjure up significance. He does the same thing at the end of "Gerontion" with De Bailhache, Fresca, and Mrs. Cammel. We know now what Fresca meant to Eliot, for there is a long and amusing description of her in the *Ur–Waste Land*, but we had to wait fifty years later, until Valerie Eliot's edition of *The Waste Land*, to discover what was in Eliot's mind.

After the mass scene we return to Gerontion in his "draughty house" as he contemplates the failure of Western man to understand or learn from his own history. These lines are an echo of similar passages in *The Education of Henry Adams*, and of Eliot's reading in current affairs. We know, for example, that the treaty of Versailles was on Eliot's mind in the period in which he wrote "Gerontion" and therefore "contrived corridors" may refer to the Polish corridor.

Next, Christ the tiger "springs in the new year" (we are reminded again of Henry James's "Beast in the Jungle") and the one positive note of the poem is sounded — "Think at last/ We have not reached conclusion. . . ," a suggestion, perhaps, that we may return to a Christian culture — but this hope is immediately rejected by a moving passage beginning "I that was near your heart was removed therefrom" (which can also be read on a personal level as applying to Eliot and his wife). A few lines later we see De Bailhache, Fresca, and Mrs. Cammel "whirled beyond the circuit of the shuddering Bear" in fractured atoms, a white gull disintegrating in the wind, and Gerontion sunk in a sleepy corner. Presumably this is the end of Western civilization. There is no hint of coming rain, of God's grace, as there is at the conclusion of *The Waste Land.*

IV

Psychic Crisis

To me it [The Waste Land] *was only the relief of a*
personal and wholly insignificant grouse against life; it
is just a piece of rhythmical grumbling.

T. S. Eliot

In his lectures *After Strange Gods*, given at the University of Virginia in 1933, Eliot attacks Hardy for being primarily interested in men's emotions. He says:

This extreme emotionalism seems to me a symptom of decadence; it is a cardinal point of faith in a romantic age, to believe that there is something admirable in violent emotion for its own sake.[92]

He does not mention in this lecture that his own theories of poetry which set up *intensity* of emotion as a chief criterion for successful verse contributed considerably to a continuation of the romantic decadence into the twentieth century. He goes on to scrutinize a scene in *Far from the Madding Crowd* in which Bathsheba unscrews Robin's coffin. Eliot says:

it seems to me deliberately faked. . . . the author seems
to be deliberately relieving some emotion of his own at
the expense of his reader.[93]

Now that we know in considerable detail the biographical, psychological, and literary genesis of *The Waste Land,* we are, I think, justified in criticizing Eliot on exactly the same grounds on which Eliot criticized Hardy; indeed, Eliot himself years after the publication of *The Waste Land* so criticized himself when he said of his poem," it was only the relief of a personal and wholly insignificant grouse against life."[94] Nevertheless, this insignificant grouse held captive the imagination of many (although by no means all) of our most distinguished men of letters for over fifty years. A brief recapitulation of the genesis of the poem and an equally brief reexamination of its contents and value would seem to be in order.

The quality of the emotion that Eliot was relieving when he composed *The Waste Land* is graphically described much later in his essay "The Three Voices of Poetry" in which he describes the germination of a poem written in what he calls the first voice (actually, all of the voices of *The Waste Land* are those of Eliot speaking through various masks or personae). Eliot says:

He [the poet] is oppressed by a burden which he must bring to birth in order to obtain relief. Or, to change the figure of speech, he is haunted by a demon, a demon against which he feels powerless because in its first manifestation it has no face, no name, nothing; and the words, the poem he makes, are a kind of form of exorcism of this demon. . . . he is going to all that trouble, not in order to communicate with anyone, but to gain relief from acute discomfort.[95]

And Eliot goes on to say:

> It is likely, of course, that it is in the beginning the pressure of some rude unknown *psychic material* that directs the poet to tell that particular story, to develop that particular situation.[96]

This *dark* psychic material as he calls it elsewhere in the essay may very well be associated with mental breakdown. Indeed, Eliot speaks of the "advantages" of certain kinds of disease in his "The Use of Poetry and the Use of Criticism":

> I know...that some forms of ill-health, debility or anaemia, may...produce an efflux of poetry in a way approaching the condition of automatic writing....To me it seems that...these moments,...are characterized by the sudden lifting of the burden of anxiety and fear which presses upon our daily life so steadily that we are unaware of it.[97]

He expresses the same idea in his essay "The *Pensées* of Pascal":

> some forms of illness are extremely favourable, not only to religious illumination, but to artistic and literary composition.[98]

Under some such conditions of physical distress and mental despair Eliot, it would seem, composed the poem that he eventually called *The Waste Land*, which came to be interpreted by many as the profound prophecy of either the doom of western civilization or of its resurrection, depending on which analyst one is reading. The "*Waste Land* generation" had come into being and Eliot was its spokesman. Almost thirty years after its first publication, Eliot, in his BBC broadcast "Virgil and the Christian World" (1951), almost certainly had himself and *The Waste Land* in mind as well as Virgil when he said:

> A poet may believe that he is expressing only his private experience; his lines may be for him only a means of talking about himself without giving himself away; yet for his readers what he has written may come to be the expression both of their own secret feelings and of the exultation or despair of a generation. He need not know what his poetry will come to mean to others; and a prophet need not understand the meaning of his prophetic utterance.[99]

"A means of talking to himself without giving himself away" — how aptly that describes what we know now to be the many autobiographical passages and the "in" jokes of Eliot's poem which seemed to be expressing "the exultation or despair of a generation." This disguised autobiography was composed (as one critic put it) while Eliot was working his way through a nervous breakdown:

> On Margate sands
> I could connect nothing with nothing.

A just and objective evaluation of the poem must be in accord with certain historical facts.

Eliot for several years had planned to write a fairly long poem, and by the spring of 1921 he had some of it on paper; but by September of that year he was on the verge of nervous collapse brought on by overwork, marital troubles, and worry over his own health as well as that of his wife Vivien. After consulting a nerve specialist who advised complete rest, he took a leave of absence from Lloyd's bank, and later in October he went with his wife to Margate, a resort near London. He composed and revised some of his poem there. After a stay of three weeks he then, on the advice of lady Ottoline Morrell and Julian Huxley, made arrangements with the specialist Dr. Roger Vittoz to go to Lausanne, Switzerland, for treatment. He set out for Lausanne in November, leaving Vivien in Paris to consult her specialist. In December, in Lausanne, he went to work again on his poem—against doctor's orders. He then spent a brief time in Chardonne above Vevey. When he returned to Paris in January of 1922, he had in hand the first draft of a poem of about 1,000 lines entitled "He Do the Police in Different Voices" which he showed to Ezra Pound. The bulk of this poem had been composed in about eight weeks at Margate, Lausanne, and Chardonne, while Eliot was under psychiatric treatment. He wrote to his mother that much of his life went into it, and indeed, besides many references to Eliot's reading in various literatures of the world, there are a number of allusions to Eliot's private life, including his marital and mental problems ("By the waters of Leman I sat down and wept"); his urban life in London; his travels; his sailing off the coast of Massachusetts as a young man; his hasty, almost secret marriage ("The awful daring of a moment's surrender"); snatches of conversation with a Lithuanian girl by the Starnbergersee; the conversation of his cockney charwoman in London, who talked of abortions; bits of dialogue with Vivien, who talked of her nerves as they played chess; "in" jokes such as Madame Sosostris as a disguise for Bertrand Russell—all of this material is presented in a collage of "objective correlatives" or "epiphanies" in various kinds of metrical and nonmetrical verse, juxtaposed without explanation) as first published in the *Criterion* (Eliot added the notes later to fill up the blank pages for the first book edition.)

The poem which Eliot gave to Pound took its title from Dickens's *Our Mutual Friend*, chapter 16, in which the foundling Sloppy is praised as "a beautiful reader of a newspaper. He do the Police in different voices."[100] Eliot's original intention was probably to write a poem focused on London specifically but including the urban scene in general and illustrating the incoherence, the ennui, and the horror of urban life. Perhaps he had Baudelaire's critique of urban life in *Les Fleurs du Mal* in mind. He would do for London what Baudelaire had done for Paris. The police section of the city newspaper was an example of the kind of material he might use. The original manuscript carried an epigraph from Conrad's *Heart of Darkness* in which Kurtz cries out just before his death, "The Horror! the Horror!" Pound talked Eliot out of using it, but this may have been poor judgment on Pound's part. Kurtz is expressing self-loathing just before he dies; he has had a double revelation of evil: of the dark psychic material in himself, the heart of darkness, and of the darkness of the world around him. Self-loathing mixed with contempt of the created world (perhaps coming from the depths of Eliot's Calvinistic heritage) is a major theme in both versions of *The Waste Land* and elsewhere in Eliot's work. It is a theme of "The

Death of St. Narcissus," of "Gerontion" (after such knowledge what forgiveness? — *self*-knowledge as well as knowledge of the created world, that is, history). Eliot makes himself very clear on that point in his preface to Djuna Barnes's *Nightwood* (1937) where he refers to "the still small wailing and whining of humanity," and he says "so far as we attach ourselves to created objects and surrender our wills to temporal ends, we are eaten by the same worm."[101]

Eliot's prototype persona, then, in the original draft of *The Waste Land* is Sloppy who impersonates various characters drawn from the seamy side of London life. Eliot will do likewise. The poet becomes ventriloquist. The original poem is in five parts, each with a title which was retained in the final version. In "The Burial of the Dead" there is an account in the first person of several young men spending an evening "on the town," getting drunk, running into trouble with a cop, racing a taxi-driver, etc. One of them visits a prostitute. The narrator arrives home at dawn. The episode, realistically and authentically drawn, is probably taken from Eliot's student life at Harvard, with overtones from the visit to Nighttown in Joyce's *Ulysses*. The entire episode was canceled, probably by Eliot himself. There are no comments by Pound on the manuscript of this section. There follows next a passage beginning "April is the cruelest month...," retained with a few minor changes (most of them suggested by Pound and most of them improvements), which became part 1 of *The Waste Land*. Part 2, "A Game of Chess," is in its original form substantially the same as the final version. "The Fire Sermon" (part 3) underwent considerable excision and some revision of stylistic detail — most of the changes being suggested by Pound. At the beginning of the original draft there is a passage of over eighty lines describing and satirizing the "white-armed Fresca," a young female who in an earlier age would have been a Magdalen or a street walker but in the twentieth century is a fake intellectual as a result of her immersion in a soapy sea of Symonds, Pater, and Vernon Lee. The passage is coherent, comprehensible, and witty. Pound (perhaps for these reasons) disliked it and persuaded Eliot to omit it. All that was left of Fresca until Mrs. Eliot's edition is her appearance in "Gerontion," where she is whirled beyond the circuit of the shuddering bear. The Fresca episode, in heroic couplets, is an obvious pastiche of Pope, but it is very skilful pastiche and no one in England in the second and third decades of this century was capable of writing better satirical couplets than those devoted to Fresca. This passage also, like the original first section of "The Burial of the Dead," has overtones from Joyce's *Ulysses*, that is, from the Calypso episode. Most of the remainder of "The Fire Sermon" is identical with the final version, but there are a few other small but important changes. After the Fresca episode was abandoned, Eliot wrote new introductory lines for part 3 beginning, "The river's tent is broken..."; he cut a vivid passage of fourteen lines describing the swarming life of London; and with the help of Pound he cut and revised the Tiresias scene, much improving it.

"Death by Water" (part 4) in *He Do the Police* is ninety-two lines long and begins with a passage of eight-three lines which was inspired in part by Dante's description of Ulysses' last voyage in canto 26 of the *Inferno*, a voyage which seems to have been a product of pure imagination on the part of Dante, having no known source in classical literature.[102] Dante's canto seems to have been of especial significance to Eliot, particularly the phrase in the penultimate line, "com' altrui piacque" (as pleased Another). He mentions the Ulysses voyage in at least three essays, first in his essay on Dante published in *The Sacred Wood* (1920):

> And I think that if Mr. Sidgwick had pondered the strange words of Ulysses,
> com' altrui piacque
> he would not have said that the preacher and prophet are lost in the poet.[103]

Eliot returns to the Ulysses *Canto* in his 1929 essay on Dante:

> The story of Ulysses as told by Dante, reads like a straightforward piece of romance, a well-told seaman's yarn;... Tennyson's poem is flat; it has only two dimensions.... We do not need, at first, to know what mountain the mountain was [it was Purgatory] or what the words mean, *as pleased Another*, to feel that Dante's sense has further depths.[104]

And in the essay "In Memoriam" (1936) we hear about Dante's story once more, where Eliot calls it a "condensed and intensely exciting narrative" with "real men talking" and "real events moving" and contrasts it to Tennyson's poem, which merely states an elegiac mood.[105]

It seems to have been Eliot's intention to make the story of a fatal seavoyage as condensed and as intensely exciting as Dante's account of the last voyage of Ulysses, and as realistic with "real men talking," and at the same time to give it the philosophic depth of Dante's canto 26 and to call attention to and contrast it to Tennyson's treatment of the same subject. In the midst of realistic descriptive details of the hardships of Eliot's voyage, where the crew ate biscuits full of weevils and complained of their lot, we have these lines:

> So the crew moaned; the sea with many voices
> Moaned all about us....

This juxtaposition of contrasting moods is an implicitly ironic comment on what Eliot considered to be Tennyson's flat, elegiac poem. And he calls attention to Dante's *Canto* with his final two lines which come after the shipwreck,

> And if *Another* knows, I know I know not
> Who only know that there is no more noise now,

which are the best two lines of Eliot's "Voyage."

There are other literary allusions, as we might expect. As the ship drives on to the white barrier just before the wreck, the reader is reminded of the conclusion of Poe's *The Narrative of Arthur Gordon Pym*. The entire episode appears to me fairly successful in itself and worth preserving. But it does not have the immediate "intensity" of many other passages in *The Waste Land*, and Pound canceled it. There follows after asterisks in the original manuscript a passage of eight lines beginning "Phlebas the Phoenician..." which Pound insisted that Eliot retain. Eliot did so, and it is all that remains of part 4, "Death by Water."

"What the Thunder Said" (part 5) remains in the final version with little change.

It is difficult to visualize and read as a whole the poem that Eliot showed to Pound in Paris, for by necessity it is broken up into many heavily annotated pages in Valerie Eliot's admirable edition. I took the trouble to type up from Mrs. Eliot's edition, unbroken and unannotated, a poem entitled *He Do the Police in Different Voices* which must be a fairly close approximation of the manuscript which Pound encountered in January 1922. (I included the first section of "The Burial of the Dead" which Eliot may have canceled before he showed it to Pound.) The poem as a whole gives an impression quite different from that which confronted the readers of the *Criterion* in October 1922. *He Do the Police* is much less fragmented, much less, in fact, like Pound's *Cantos* than the *Criterion* version. The original poem is a series of episodes and scenes, each scene possessing considerable substance and coherence, each scene spoken by a different voice; these scenes are interspersed with brief "flashes" of considerable intensity, of a kind of visionary or hallucinatory quality, such as the vision of the Church of Magnus Martyr, or the "bats with baby faces in the violet light," or the crowd of shades from Dante's *Inferno* flowing over London Bridge. There are four narrative sections— the night on the town, the adventures of Fresca, the seduction of the typist, and the fatal seavoyage— each fairly long, unified, and comprehensible. In addition there are two fairly long "static" scenes which appear to be comments on two levels of London "society"— the description of the lady in the boudoir which opens "A Game of Chess" and the monologue by a cockney woman in the pub.

When Pound got through with the poem there was left a collocation of "luminous moments"— some of them of memorable intensity— without coherence and without very much paraphrasable content if one sticks to what is said in the poem without reference to literary parallels or Eliot's notes. There is no question, however, that Pound in revising *He Do the Police* was very sensitive to qualities of style. Every passage he cut was of relatively low intensity— or as he would have said, *dull.* And Pound cut few if any passages in which there was implicit (though never fully realized) a mythological framework. The Jessie Weston and *Golden Bough* material was retained.

The final version of *The Waste Land* has no demonstrable organization beyond what has been called "a music of ideas," which turns out to be variations on a few basic themes or motifs. *The Waste Land,* section by section, does not develop. It repeats. This procedure, with its analogy to music, might be called *symboliste,* but as a symbolist poem it is much less successful than the better-organized *Four Quartets.*

The basic theme of *The Waste Land* is disintegration— on the personal and private level the psychic difficulties of its author; on the generalized level (public, mythological, symbolic) the breakdown of the culture of the Western world. On both levels the disintegration— either as symptom or as cause— is associated with sex and with religion. Sex and religion, from the fertility rites of pre-Christian times to the present, are closely linked— bound together by the Grail legend of the Fisher King, whose wound in the groin has made him impotent and has brought drought to *The Waste Land,* and by the story of Percival (derived from ancient folk material), who fails at the court of the Fisher King to do or say the right thing and therefore fails to restore the fertility of the Fisher King and lift the drought. *The Waste Land* on both levels is the story of failure—sexual, religious, and cultural. There is some indication of hope at the conclusion of the poem. There is "a damp gust bringing rain," and rain and water usually symbolize grace and renewal throughout *The Waste Land.* But the optimism (if that is what it is) is not convincing, nor is the Sanskrit benediction of the final lines. The tone of most of the poem is one of desolation and deprivation, with only fleeting glimpses of fullness of being and of psychic integration. The thousands of pages of commentary which have been devoted to this poem are ample evidence of its evocative power, but I think the evocative power will eventually fade. What Eliot was feeling about himself and his cultural milieu must have been similar to what many intellectuals were feeling in the twenties and thirties. ("It changed my life," R. P. Blackmur told me.) Nevertheless, as Eliot said of *Finnegans Wake,* one work of this kind is enough. And like *Finnegans Wake, The Waste Land* will be eventually numbered among the curiosities of literature.

V

Conversion and Integration

> *I still, after forty years, regard his [Dante's] poetry as*
> *the most persistent and deepest influence upon*
> *my own verse.*
> T. S. Eliot (1950)

Eliot paid tribute a number of times to Dante and to Dante's influence on his own poetry. From the time Eliot started during his Harvard days (with little or no knowledge of Italian) to puzzle out the meaning of the *Divina Commedia* until the end of his career, Dante was probably the poet he studied most carefully. The voice of the Italian poet echoes throughout "The Hollow Men," *Ash Wednesday,* and *Four Quartets.* The most moving poetic passage in the latter part of Eliot's career, the account of the dawn patrol in "Little Gidding," is, by Eliot's own admission, a careful imitation of Dante's style. The Dantesque voice is discernible elsewhere in *Four Quartets,* and the most vivid passages in *Ash Wednesday* have the luminous quality which Eliot ascribes to Dante's imagery. "The Hollow Men" is a twentieth-century evocation of Dante's shadowy otherworldliness. But there are problems. As one reads the poetry of Eliot's later years, one gets the impression of the Dantesque voice without Dante's meaning—and at times there appears to be no clearly defined meaning at all. "The Hollow Men" is like the ghost of a poem. And there is a looseness of structure in "The Hollow Men" and in *Ash Wednesday* that Dante would not have tolerated.

Because of his profound interest in the Italian poet, Eliot probably read

George Santayana's essay on Dante in which the philosopher said:

> As in some great symphony everything is cumulative: the movements conspire, the tension grows, the volume redoubles, the keen melody soars higher and higher; and it all ends, not with a bang, not with some casual incident, but in sustained reflection . . . a revelation and a resource for ever.[106]

As Eliot was writing his "Hollow Men" in 1924/25 during what must have been a kind of dark night of the soul preceding his conversion, he perhaps recalled this tribute to Dante's poem, "a revelation and a resource for ever," and then ironically borrowed a phrase from Santayana to conclude his own (Eliot's) "revelation," a parody of Dante's:

> This is the way the world ends
> Not with a bang but a whimper.

Modern men, including Eliot himself, without religious belief are seen as effigies. The poem is a ritual of effigies with nursery rhymes that parody church liturgy. The nursery rhyme "Here we go round the mulberry bush" is itself parodied to read "Here we go round the prickly pear." The original nursery rhyme may have implications, incidentally, that go beyond a mere child's game. According to Margaret Murray,[107] this children's song is probably a survival of the witch dance around the devil which derived from an ancient fertility dance around the horned god. The ring dance is perhaps the oldest religious ritual in the history of man. The prickly pear, like the cactus and the desert throughout "The Hollow Men" and its predecessor *The Waste Land*, suggests sterility and impotence in contrast to fertility. It is a symbol of the decadence of religion in the twentieth century.

As in the *Ur–Waste Land*, there is an epigraph from *Heart of Darkness*— "Mistah Kurtz—he dead"—indicating that Conrad's story was still much in Eliot's mind. The other epigraph, "A penny for the Old Guy," a phrase used by English children begging money to make an effigy "an old Guy" to hang or burn on Guy Fawkes Day, relates to both Kurtz and Fawkes. Fawkes, who in the Gunpowder Plot of 1605 attempted to blow up the entire English government, was, like Kurtz, one of the "lost violent souls" who ended their careers "not with a bang but a whimper." Fawkes is now memorialized as an effigy of straw—symbol of all twentieth-century men without faith. The poem, thematically, is clear enough, but line by line and section by section it is impossible to paraphrase successfully. There are references to "death's other Kingdom," to "death's dream kingdom," to "death's twilight kingdom," and to "the Kingdom" and commentators are not agreed as to the significance, if any, of these separate "kingdoms." Some lovely but frail imagery and hauntingly melancholy word music create a kind of Dantesque atmosphere suggestive of limbo or purgatory, and there is also perhaps, a glimpse of Paradise. It is an evocative mood poem but hardly more than that.

Ash Wednesday, too, has ambivalences. It has been described as a poem expressing Eliot's religious difficulties and as a triumphant affirmation of Eliot's newfound faith. It was published in parts from 1927 until 1930, when it appeared in its final form in six numbered parts. Part 2, which appeared under the title "Salutation" with the epigraph "The Hand of the Lord Was Up on me: — *e vo significando*,"[108] was published first, in 1927, the year of Eliot's conversion. "Salutation" is from Dante's *Vita Nuova* iii. "E vo significando" is from *Purgatorio* 24. 54. Part 1 was originally entitled "Perch' io No Spero" from a line by Dante's friend Guido Cavalcanti; part 3 was originally entitled "Som de L'Escalina" from *Purgatorio* 26. 146; and according to Leonard Woolf the typescript of part 4 had the title "Vestita di Color Di Fiamma" from *Purgatorio* 30. 33, and part 5 (probably Woolf meant part 6) had the title "La Sua Volontade" from Paradiso 3. 85.[109] Why Eliot removed all titles in the final version we do not know, but the Dante influence is obvious not only in the original titles but in much of the text of the poem, and that fact points to one of the major flaws of *Ash Wednesday*. There is too much borrowed material, not only from Dante but from church liturgy and elsewhere. The other major flaw is the poem's obscurity, enhanced by its formlessness, disjointedness, and lack of structure. We have a series of beautiful, sometimes powerful, phrases, images, individual lines floating as it were in ether — lines like "While jewelled unicorns draw by the gilded hearse" — and occasionally an ugly phrase or image ("an old man's mouth drivelling, beyond repair") for contrast and shock effect. There is a thinning out of texture in this poem in contrast to the controlled violence of some of Eliot's earlier work. Much of *Ash Wednesday* has the empty sweetness of Swinburne.

The Ariel Poems

Four poems, generally known as the Ariel poems — "Journey of the Magi" (1927), "A Song for Simeon" (1928), "Animula" (1929), and "Marina" (1930) — were Eliot's contribution to Faber & Faber's "Ariel Poems" by contemporary writers, a series published annually for a few years as, Eliot has told us, "a kind of Christmas card."[110] The most moving is the first, published in the year of Eliot's conversion, and the most moving passage in the entire poem is the first five lines, taken directly from Lancelot Andrewes's *Nativity Sermon* (1622). The journey of the Magi to visit the newborn Christ is derived from Matthew 2:1 – 12. Yeats's story "The Adoration of the Magi" and the striking poem "The Magi" were also probably in Eliot's mind. The memory of past pleasures during present hardship, "the silken girls bringing sherbet," is reminiscent of Pound's "Exile's Letter" in theme and style. Some of the details of the journey are biblical. "An old white horse galloped away in the meadow" may have been suggested by Revelation 6:2 where the white horse is considered a type of Christ. More likely, it is one of those personal images "charged with emotion" which Eliot mentions in his eighth Norton lecture (1933). Certainly the next line but one, "Six hands at an open door dicing for pieces of silver" (which the Magi observe after passing "a water-mill beating the darkness" is both biblical (the gambling at the foot of the cross for Christ's garments) and personal, for Eliot refers to similar images in his Norton lecture:

Why, for all of us, out of all that we have heard, seen, felt, in a lifetime, do certain images recur... six ruffians seen through an open window playing cards at night...where there was a water-mill?[111]

"The Journey of the Magi" describes the arduous journey to Bethlehem as remembered by one of the Magi years later, but the memory seems to be one of bitterness rather than hope:

> ...this Birth was
> Hard and bitter agony for us, like Death, our death.

The poem ends

> I should be glad of another death.

The conclusion is reminiscent of Yeats's "The Magi," who are also remembering, as old men, their experience of long ago. They too found it disquieting and they seem to be looking for another revelation. Yeats's poem ends with the Magi

> hoping to find once more,
> Being by Calvary's turbulence unsatisfied,
> The uncontrollable mystery on the bestial floor.

The date and tone of Eliot's poem suggest a time of crisis in Eliot's conversion to the Anglican faith.

A year later in "Song for Simeon," Eliot (through his persona) seems to be expressing the resigned attitude of a man who has found a solution to his religious problem and now waits for his dismission. Simeon (Luke 2:25 – 35), an old man, takes the infant Jesus in his arms, accepts him as the Messiah, but does not experience the kind of intense spiritual shock that, for example, Paul experiences. "Animula" derives from Dante's *Purgatorio* 16. 85ff. which Eliot quotes in his 1929 essay on Dante and which he translates "From the hands of Him who loves her before she is, there issues like a little child that plays, with weeping and laughter, the simple soul...."[112] This becomes in Eliot's first line of "Animula," "Issues from the hand of God, the simple soul." The simple soul without knowledge of God, "Fearing the warm reality, the offered good," does not live until after the death of the body, "in the silence after the viaticum." The poem ends with images of violent death brought on by modern man who is removed from God and with the prayer, "Pray for us now and at the hour of our birth," that is, at the hour of our physical death. The poem appears to be an indictment of contemporary materialistic civilization and a record of the author's journey to God. "Marina," the last of the Ariel poems, is probably the most successful poetically except for "Journey of the Magi." The lost soul, Eliot, has found a new spiritual life by the Grace of God just as his persona, Marina of Shakespeare's *Pericles,* born at sea and carried off by pirates, is eventually, after harrowing experiences, restored to her father. The sea and boat imagery recalls that of the description of a voyage in part 4 of *He Do the Police,* which Eliot derived from Dante's account of Ulysses' last voyage, and anticipates similar imagery in "Dry Salvages."

The Ariel poems, even at their best, are minor and derivative poetry, but they are of interest as a record of Eliot's conversion experience.

Four Quartets

> *It [The Divine Comedy] is therefore a constant*
> *reminder to the poet, of the obligation to explore, to*
> *find words for the inarticulate, to capture those feelings*
> *which people can hardly even feel, because they have*
> *no words for them*
> T. S. Eliot (1950)

> *Perhaps all the wisdom, and all truth, and all sincerity,*
> *are just compressed into the inappreciable moment of*
> *time in which we step over the threshold*
> *of the invisible.*
> *Joseph Conrad,* Heart of Darkness

As one goes from *Ash Wednesday* to *Four Quartets* one is immediately impressed by the fact that Eliot has made an attempt to give the latter poem a definite, formulable structure. In *Ash Wednesday* it is difficult to discern any reason for the order of the six sections, and the internal structure of each section is the loosest kind of associationism. In *Four Quartets,* we have obvious structural devices and signposts as it were. Perhaps, we have too many of them.

The title of each Quartet is a place name of personal significance to Eliot. The first, "Burnt Norton," was the name of a restored eighteenth-century manor house near the Cotswold town of Chipping Campden where Emily Hale, whose friendship with Eliot began during the poet's student days at Harvard, used to spend her summers in the 1930s. One day she took her guest to see the empty house and visit the formal garden with its dry pool, as described in the opening passage of Eliot's poem.[113] This biographical fact accounts for the strong sentiment of nostalgia and loss which pervades the opening lines of "Burnt Norton." "East Coker" is a Somerset village from which Eliot's ancestors came. His ashes are in the church there today. "The Dry Salvages" are rocks off Cape Ann, Massachusetts, where Eliot sailed as a boy and young man. "Little Gidding" refers to the church and Anglican community founded in the seventeenth century by Nicholas Ferrar. The community of saints that once lived there represents for Eliot the ideal Anglican life. Each place name is associated with mystical moments in Eliot's life reaching from his earliest memories through the present to eternity.

So far, so good. But there appear to be other structural devices, some of which may be too complicated to be significant or effective. Professor Fussell, for example, notes that each Quartet has five parts.[114] He believes that part 1 of each Quartet is concerned with time (the individual's past, the racial past, the paleontological past, and the present respectively). Part 2 of each poem deals with order vs. chaos; part 3 with action and passivity; part 4 with death and rebirth; part 5 with the word and the Word (logos). This would seem to be sufficiently complicated. But Fussell goes on to construct an elaborate diagram (with arrows going in four directions) which illustrates the structural process of the poem, that is, the interaction of six categories (Being, Time, History, Discipline, Knowledge, Language), each category having various subcategories (birth, death, etc.) for a grand total of twenty-two, all of which are carrying on a dialectical process of opposition and reconciliation by means of a dozen or so symbols. There is also a series of eleven thematic processes all going on at the same time.

Sister Cleophas finds other principles of structure. She believes that the poem can be read on four levels — the historical, allegorical, moral, and anagogical — just as the *Divine Comedy* has been explicated on these levels. On the anagogical level she discerns a major theme of each Quartet to be *purgation* as advocated by St. John of the Cross. In "Burnt Norton" there is active purgation of the senses, in "East Coker" active purgation of the rational; in "Dry Salvages" passive purgation of the senses, and in "Little Gidding" passive purgation of the rational.[115] She and Ray B. West[116] and others consider the still point (God) and the Heracliteian flux which moves around the still center to be a major motif, and they point out that Eliot seems to have designated each of the four elements of the flux of the material world (according to the ancients) to a Quartet. Thus Air is the element of "Burnt Norton"; Earth of "East Coker"; Water of "Dry Salvages"; and Fire of "Little Gidding." These four elements interact. Fire lives in the death of Air; Air lives in the death of Fire; Water lives in the death of Earth; Earth lives in the death of Water.

Harold F. Brooks, on the other hand, has found still another principle of structure.[117] He argues that each Quartet has a "regent." The regent of "Burnt Norton" is God; of "East Coker," Jesus; of "Dry Salvages," the Virgin; of "Little Gidding," the Holy Ghost. At this point one may recall the various attempts to impose an elaborate structure on Pound's *Cantos.*

The thematic imagery of the poem has received a number of complicated analyses; the most ingenious, perhaps, is that by Northrop Frye.[118] He asks the reader to draw a diagram, which I shall not attempt to construct here. It consists of two concentric circles, the outer one circumscribing a cross which represents the intersection of time and the timeless. The eight divisions within the two circles marked off by the cross correspond to various themes of the poem. Frye then proceeds with the determination and ingenuity of a first-rate chess player to interpret the thirty-six parts of the *Four Quartets* (nine parts to each Quartet because each of the five numbered parts except number 4 is divided into two sections) by means of his eight-part diagram. It is a brilliant exegesis, but one wonders how much of it represents Eliot's intention or the normal reader's response to the poem.

The most obvious structural device is suggested by the title. Each Quartet may be considered to be an imitation of a musical composition. Perhaps the Bartók quartets numbered 2–7, were in Eliot's mind; perhaps a late Beethoven quartet (number 132 most probably); perhaps Eliot is imitating the sonata form in the first "movement" of each Quartet. Critics differ.[119]

In the foregoing paragraphs I have been illustrating the kind of critical attention that has been given to *Four Quartets*. I have merely touched the surface of a vast body of hermeneutical literature that has grown up around Eliot's poem and that is increasing at an alarming rate. But I would like to argue that complication of intention on the part of the poet and complication of analysis on the part of the reader cease to be of value beyond a certain point, the point established by an intelligent use of common sense. No reader can master all of these intricate interpretations and hold them in his mind as he responds to the poem.

But to return to the musical structure of the poem, which is probably present in fact and in intention. Musical structure is not the most efficient way to organize a poem. It involves statement of a theme and variation upon the theme, the use of key words, such as *end*, and then repetition of each of those words in different contexts and with slightly different meanings, and the use of key images or symbols and then repetition of the symbols with variant phrasing and variant meanings. It involves, that is, constant repetitive circling around a subject, a method which, while it works in music, which is pure sound, produces verse which is tedious and prolix. Dame Helen Gardner comments approvingly on the method:

> The repetitive circling passage in *East Coker,* in particular, where we seem to be standing still, waiting for something to happen, for a rhythm to break, reminds one of the bridge passages and leading passages between two movements which Beethoven loved. [She is referring to the closing lines of the third movement which begin "You say I am repeating/ Something I have said before."][120]

To ask the reader to stand still in a poem and wait for something to happen might be effective if it were a narrative poem depending for its effect on suspense derived from plot, but it is merely annoying in a poem of philosophical and religious meditation.

Dame Helen comments on the repetition of the word *end* in *Four Quartets* as follows:

> Indeed, another way of describing *Four Quartets* would be to say that the poem is an exploration of the meaning of certain words. Like the images and symbols just referred to, they are common words, words we take for granted. Perhaps the words that first strike us in this way as recurring with a special and changing emphasis are the pair 'end' and 'beginning,' sometimes occurring together, sometimes apart from each other. The word 'end' occurs first, by itself, in the opening lines of *Burnt Norton:*
>
>   What might have been and what has been
>   Point to one end, which is always present.

Here 'end' has plainly some meaning beyond that of 'termination,' but we are not quite certain how much meaning to give it. Even when these two lines are repeated at the end of the first movement, the word 'end' remains vague. It is only in the fifth movement — when the word is linked with 'beginning,' in the context of ideas about form and pattern and we have apparently paradoxical statements—that we begin to think of end as meaning 'completion,' 'purpose' or even 'final cause.'

> Or say that the end precedes the beginning,
> And the end and the beginning were always there
> Before the beginning and after the end.
> And all is always now.[121]

To find out what Eliot means by the word *end* we have to read through five movements (175 lines) of "Burnt Norton." Gardner's exhaustive analysis of Eliot's play on these two words alone takes several pages. When we discover the full meaning of the word, the discovery comes with little emotional impact. The lines just quoted have about as much feeling as F. H. Bradley's precise but dry prose. Donne would have accomplished as much in two lines, and with greater force.

Eliot's musical form encourages the use of flat verse written with a relaxed mind—the excuse being that such passages are a kind of counterpoint to, or variation of, more intense passages, as in music. Thus Gardner defends the dull lines beginning "It seems as one becomes older. . ." (in the second movement of *Dry Salvages*) because "they represent a change of voice, the mind relaxing, a new approach to a theme already handled another way."[122] Now the advantage of the short poem or the poem of medium length, particularly when it is a religious and philosophical meditation, is that the author can compose every line in his best possible style. He need not lower or change his style to make it appropriate to a persona or a character as in dramatic and narrative poetry. He need not inflate his style to imitate the speech of the gods or indulge in long tiresome descriptions of battles as in the classic epic. In a poem the length of one of Eliot's Quartets, he can expect to keep the unflagging attention of the perceptive reader by thought and style and feeling alone. He need not waste lines in building up narrative suspense or by writing with a relaxed mind or engage in a series of variants on a theme, which by necessity involves tedious repetition. By adopting the musical method of composition, Eliot foregoes the advantage of the genre of the short or medium-length poem.

Dame Helen tells us that *Four Quartets* is about the four medieval elements, each with its appropriate associations—air, earth, fire, and water—and a fifth element, "the true principle of life," which is the subject of the whole poem.[123] The subject is expressed by means of recurrent images, symbols, and words, such as *sunlight* or *yew tree*, often repeated but with slightly different connotations in each context. This procedure (which Donald Davie calls *Symboliste*—the use of symbols with no referents)[124] may be occasionally effective in those passages which express the central experience of the poem, the momentary glimpse by the individual soul in time of the eternal spirit outside time, and Eliot's repetitious verbal music may create the appropriate mood for at least a partial communication of this mystical experience. But to employ this method throughout makes for a very diffuse texture. The poem becomes a tissue of half-concealed meanings and veiled suggestions. We begin to discern that only half the power of language is being used. We have no difficulty in paraphrasing the great long or medium length or short poems of the language previous to the twentieth century. It is impossible to compose a satisfactory paraphrase of much of *Four Quartets,* and this situation is of course true of other verse in the Pound-Eliot tradition

Furthermore, *Four Quartets* has no formulable meter or prosody. Dame Helen, who praises highly the "new meter" of Eliot's verse from "The Hollow Men" on, admits that she cannot scan the individual lines or formulate the prosody, although she implies there is a prosody behind this body of verse, which will eventually be formulated by future scholars.[125] Since the 1940s when she made this statement, attempts have been made by a number of scholars including Gardner herself to scan the verse of *Four Quartets.* All of these attempts are unconvincing except for the scansion of a few passages which are obviously in conventional meters. The "new meter" remains a mystery. Dame Helen also says that Eliot abandoned the conventional "heroic line" (by which she seems to mean iambic pentameter) because it is no longer possible to write original and effective verse in this line. The argument is a familiar one, going back to various attacks on the use of the iambic foot, including those by Hopkins, Whitman, and the imagists.

We have, then, a poem with an inefficient structure derived from another medium (music) and with verse written in a "new meter" which has no definable prosody except when it lapses into conventional iambic or trochaic meters, as it does in the justifiably famous account of the dawn patrol and the conversation with the compound ghost in the second part of "Little Gidding."

The poetry of *Four Quartets* is as derivative as Eliot's earlier work. The dawn patrol is a frank and successful imitation in English (without the rhyme) of Dante's *terza rima.* Less defensible is Eliot's use of literal quotations or slightly modified quotations from a wide and varied range of the world's literature, usually without quotation marks. Most of them have by now been discovered and annotated. Gardner's defense of Eliot's method strikes me as slightly blasé:

> The sources are completely unimportant. . . . The poet is speaking in words that are not his own, because these words are more expressive than anything he could say.[126]

If the sources are completely unimportant, then a great deal of scholarly research has been done in vain. I think that Eliot intended us to recognize certain sources and their contexts, such as the line from Mallarmé mentioned by Dame Helen herself in the quotation below, in which Eliot suggests he is another Mallarmé. The passage would have little significance unless one recognized its source and knew something about the French poet. The same may be said of Eliot's thefts from the mystical works of St. John of the Cross and Juliana of Norwich. These passages are used to help define the mystical experience – the major theme of the poem – and the discipline required for it. They would make little sense unless one recognized the author and context of the quotations. But in any event, I doubt that Eliot's scissors-and-paste technique, of using the language of other writers better than himself, merits the praise Dame Helen gives it. She is on sounder ground when she says of major poets that they not only write poems that are felicitous in phrase and rhythm, in which the diction seems exquisitely appropriate, but they revive the very stuff of poetry, the language and speech-rhythms of their day and country; they re-create the instrument they use, and suggest to their contemporaries and to those who come after them new capacities in the language and new possibilities of poetic expression. They are those who can

> *Donner un sens plus pur aux mots de la tribu;*
> or in Mr Eliot's rendering of Mallarmé's line:
> Purify the dialect of the tribe.[127]

But how can Eliot or any other poet "revive the very stuff of poetry, the language and speech-rhythms of their day" by quoting the language (some of it archaic) of another century or by quoting a translation from the Spanish of a seventeenth-century mystic? Or from the French of a nineteenth-century symbolist? As Dame Helen says, the major poet should use the living language of his own time, purified of course. Whenever Eliot indulges in his frequent habit of quotation, he is dodging the responsibility of any author of merit. Any poet of importance has to cope with and be aware of the work of his predecessors, but the Pound-Eliot method is not the right way to deal with the past. I shall have more to say about this in a later chapter.

There are several reasons, then, why *Four Quartets* is not a successful major poem. The structure is excessively complicated to the point of meaninglessness; the structure when it imitates that of a musical composition is inefficient and involves excessive repetitions without true development of thought and feeling; much of the verse has no formulable prosody and therefore no precise or powerful rhythm. There are stretches of flat, dull poetry. Too much of the material is derivative, with a number of direct thefts of other authors' work or close paraphrases or adaptations of their work. Much of the poem is obscure — some of it understandably so because of the difficulty of the main subject, the mystical experience, which by definition is ineffable. Any attempt to define an ineffable experience in words is bound to be somewhat unsatisfactory.

Four Quartets begins and ends with the mystical moment, the moment during which time and the timeless intersect. Now this mystical moment has some affinity with the "charged moment" of the Pre-Raphaelites and also with the "luminous detail" and the "complex in an instant of time" of Ezra Pound, but with an important difference. Pound never claimed supernatural sanction for his "charged moments," and Eliot of course did. Whether Eliot's "moment of the rose" was actually a supernatural experience or merely a psychological one is impossible to say, for certain, but the concentration on these irrational or superrational moments by both poets results in a severely limited kind of poetry in which normal human experience, the province of all or most of the major poetry in English from Chaucer on, is brushed off or made subservient to brief intense psychological or spiritual "shocks" of doubtful validity and value.

Wallace Stevens

3
Wallace Stevens
(1879–1955)

Wallace Stevens was born in Reading, Pennsylvania, October 2, 1879. His father was a successful lawyer and businessman who sent all three of his sons to college. Wallace himself, after an unsuccessful attempt to earn his living as a journalist, eventually became a lawyer and vice-president of the Hartford Insurance Company. He traced his ancestry back to the Dutch on both sides of his family. He developed an early interest in literature and in creative writing in high school. With a view to becoming an author, he enrolled as a special student at Harvard in 1897, preceding Eliot by ten years. He began keeping a journal in 1898 with a vividly written account of long walking trips — sometimes as much as thirty miles a day — in which he displayed a romantic response to nature and a healthy love of the open air. After spending three years at Harvard he went to New York to take a job on the staff of the New York *Tribune.* At Harvard he became a friend of George Santayana. He published poems under a pseudonym in the *Harvard Advocate* and became president of the *Advocate* and a member of the Signet Club.

In New York he failed to achieve success in his career as a journalist. Upon the advice of his father he entered the New York University Law School. By 1904 he had passed his bar examinations and was practicing law. In that year, while on vacation in Reading, he met Elsie Moll (born Kachel) and fell deeply in love with her. According to all accounts she was an unusually attractive person. Her profile, taken from a bust of her by Adolph Weinman (ca. 1913), appeared on the dime and fifty-cent piece of the period. The courtship was a long one; they were not married until 1909. They had one child, a daughter, Holly, born in 1924.

During his courtship Stevens wrote a number of poems to and for his future wife. He began publishing poetry for the first time since his Harvard days in 1914, in *Poetry, Trend,* and other little magazines. His first book, *Harmonium,* appeared in 1923. According to some critics, the years from 1914 to 1923 were his greatest period as a poet.

Harmonium received several perceptive reviews and was read and admired by a number of the younger poets, but few copies were sold. Stevens gave up writing poetry and turned his attention to becoming a successful businessman. By 1916 he had moved to Hartford, Connecticut, to head up a branch office of the

Hartford Insurance Company. He remained with this company for the rest of his life; he was prominent in the business community, and for many years was totally unknown as a poet among his business associates. In the early thirties, after a second edition of *Harmonium* had appeared in 1931, he began writing poetry again, usually after office hours. His double life is a comment on the state of American culture at that time. Knowledge of the fact that he was a poet would have shocked his business friends. The fact that he was a well-dressed businessman with an upper-middle-class life-style did not enhance his reputation among the poets. In 1932 he bought a house in Hartford—his first and last—within walking distance of a good rose garden. He and his wife lived in it for the rest of his life. His important book *Ideas of Order* was published in 1935, and thereafter appeared a number of volumes in beautifully printed limited editions and in trade editions. His *Collected Poems* were issued in 1954. His critical essays were collected under the title *The Necessary Angel* in 1951. He died of cancer August 2, 1955.

Stevens never owned a car, although as an insurance agent and executive he took frequent business trips and an occasional holiday in Key West, nis favorite vacation spot. His wife disliked travel, but they took one long trip together in the fall of 1923 to San Francisco via Havana and the Panama Canal, then home overland through New Mexico. The ocean part of the voyage is memorialized in his colorful poem "Sea Surface Full of Clouds." He kept up a correspondence with friends abroad in Ceylon, France, and elsewhere, and he admired French poetry and painting, but he never took a trip outside of North America.[1]

II

Wallace Stevens, like T. S. Eliot, had the habit of toying with ideas, of making use of them in his poems but of not taking them very seriously. "We have grown weary of the man who thinks," he says in "Owl's Clover." "These are tentative ideas for the purposes of poetry," he wrote in a letter commenting on "The Comedian as the Letter C."[2] Later, to Henry Church, he wrote: "I have written a small series of poems dealing with the idea of a supreme fiction, or, rather, *playing with that idea.*"[3] And a little later, in 1944, in an Emersonian mood, he said to Lila James Roney, "It might do you a world of good to spend a little time in New York after Labor Day, getting a complete change of ideas. They are so much cheaper than hats and clothes and shoes, and yet they make just as much difference."[4] I have the impression that he never took ideas seriously enough to set about constructing a coherent theory of poetry or a coherent metaphysics. Consequently even the most casual reading of his essays, letters, occasional remarks, and poems will reveal obvious inconsistencies. For example, on May 14, 1942, he wrote: "By supreme fiction, of course, I mean poetry."[5] On January 28, 1943, he said, "Supreme Fiction is not poetry."[6]

His philosophical position, which, most of the time, appears to be skeptical nominalism, contributes to the tentativeness of his poetics, for as a nominalist Stevens does not believe in the reality of universals but rather in the reality of meaningless particulars about which he writes poems. One cannot expect a clear and consistent theory of poetry to emerge from such a philosophical attitude, no matter how brilliant the poems. Nevertheless, his theorizing about poetry deserves attention for the light it casts on his poems.

Stevens considered himself to be a romantic poet. These are characteristic remarks: "It is absurd to wince at being called a romantic poet. Unless one is that, one is not a poet at all."[7] "All poets are to some extent romantic poets."[8] "What the world looks forward to is a new romanticism, a new belief."[9] As a romantic poet he wrote what he considered to be pure poetry. Referring to his book *Ideas of Order* he stated: "The book is essentially a book of pure poetry."[10] About "Owl's Clover" he said he had attempted "to emphasize the opposition between things as they are and things imagined; in short to isolate poetry."[11] In isolating poetry, "the poet should be the exponent of the imagination."[12] By means of the imagination one escapes from the drab reality of life. "The more realistic life may be, the more it needs the stimulus of the imagination."[13] There was some reason then for the Marxist critics to attack Stevens as an escapist. In fact, Stevens said in his essay "The Noble Rider and the Sound of Words" that "the poetic process is psychologically an escapist process."[14]

As a poet it was Stevens's desire "to contain the world wholly within one's perception of it."[15] He quotes Henry James with approval:

> To live in the world of creation—to get into it and stay in it—to think intensely and fruitfully—to woo combinations and inspirations into being of a depth and continuity of attention and meditation—this is the only thing.[16]

Yet it was also Stevens's lifelong contention that the imagination should maintain constant contact with the actual world and reflect it in poetry. In "The Noble Rider and the Sound of Words" he wrote: "The imagination loses vitality as it ceases to adhere to what is real. . . . [it] has the strength of reality or none at all."[17] This is the theme of "Idea of Order at Key West," "The Man with the Blue Guitar," and other poems. But the idea that one should write "pure poetry," isolated poetry, and still adhere to "the necessary angel" (that is, reality) is inconsistent and paradoxical. Stevens never did solve the problem of the proper relationship between imagination and reality. Stevens's concern with this question has been shared by many writers in the West since the 1870s. It is an aspect of the revolution against language itself so brilliantly analyzed by George Steiner in *After Babel*, and it seems to have been motivated by a deep distrust of the efficacy of language to discover reality or to describe it.[18] Stevens as a poet is not at his best in dealing with this subject. (I am thinking primarily of "The Man with the Blue Guitar.") He would have been better off to have forgotten the "problem," which, as stated in his terms, is insoluble.

Stevens considered himself a thoroughgoing experimentalist in the art of poetry, although in fact several of his greatest poems were written in conventional prosody, blank verse, rather than in the free verse of the imagists and other writers of the experimental school. "Poetry is nothing if not experimental in language,"[19] he said, and, "Experiment in form is one of the constants of the spirit."[20] He had the gift of language to a superb degree, and he enjoyed playing with it as much as he enjoyed playing with ideas. "In poetry, you must love the words, the ideas, the images, and the rhythms with all your capacity."[21] It was his love of words, images, and rhythms that produced his most beautiful poem, "Sunday Morning," and it was this same love carried to excess that produced several bizarre passages in "The Comedian as the Letter C." As a poet he "lived by perception," as Henry James, Senior, said of Emerson,[22] and his perceptions sometimes got out of control, for he had no theoretical basis for controlling them — as did, for example, Yvor Winters, for whom the morality of poetry consisted in the proper adjustment of perception to understanding, of feeling to concept. But for Stevens the only morality was "the morality of the right sensation."[23]

As he theorized about poetry, and he did so more and more as he grew older, Stevens employed certain phrases which have become famous — "the necessary angel," "major man," "the supreme fiction," etc. What did he mean by them? The most important of these is *the supreme fiction*. It is not surprising that *fiction* should be *supreme,* for, as he said in one of his aphorisms, "the truth does not matter." The concept may have been originally suggested by his reading of and conversations with Santayana, whom Stevens met in his undergraduate days at Harvard.[24]

Much of the time (in spite of his statement to Hi Simons to the contrary) Stevens appears to mean by supreme fiction simply *poetry.* The earliest use of the term in his verse occurs in "A High-Toned Old Christian Woman" (1922), the first line of which reads "Poetry is the supreme fiction, madame." The term would include all poetry, but Stevens's chief concern, when he describes and discusses it in prose and verse, is usually his own poetry, the poetry of his contemporaries, and the poetry of the future including his own poetry. The supreme fiction appears to be synonymous with "poetic truth" as defined in his essay "The Figure of the Youth As Virile Poet":

> Poetic truth is an agreement with reality brought about by the imagination of a man disposed to be strongly influenced by his imagination, which he believes, for a time, to be true, expressed in terms of his emotions or, since it is less of a restriction to say so, in terms of his personality.[25]

The phrase to note here is "which he believes for a time to be true." The implication is that it may not be true, i.e., it is a fiction. As Stevens says in a letter, "In the various predicaments of belief, it might be possible to yield, or to try to yield, ourselves to a declared fiction."[26] And to Hi Simon he said, "Logically, I ought to believe in essential imagination, but that has its difficulties. It is easier to believe in a thing created by the imagination."[27] This "thing created by the imagination" is the supreme fiction. He says in the same letter, "One's final belief must be in a fiction,"[28] and yet this "final belief" (such was Stevens's inconsistency on the subject) is that "which he believes, for a time, to be true." That is — it may change.

In his long poem *Notes toward a Supreme Fiction,* Stevens states the three main characteristics of the supreme fiction. It must be abstract, it must change, and it must give pleasure. The last two are self-evident. Poetry must change because it represents temporary beliefs of an individual or because (considered as a whole) it is being created by different personalities with differing sensibilities now and in the future. Also, perhaps, implicit in this statement is the notion that the poetry of the past has changing significance to changing generations of men. Furthermore, our concept of poetry is changing. "The conception of poetry itself has changed and is changing every day."[29] The notion that successful poetry should give pleasure goes back at least as far as Horace's *Ars Poetica* and is an aspect of Stevens's fundamental hedonism, of which more later. And it should be noted that, for Stevens, one source of pleasure is the fact that poetry changes. "The essence of poetry is change, and the essence of change is that it gives pleasure."[30]

"It must be abstract" is at first glance puzzling. One would expect a poet with Stevens's vivid imagistic style to say "It must be concrete." Stevens appears to be saying that a successful poem is the result of an abstraction — and on this point (as well as on several others) J. V. Cunningham is especially enlightening. He says that Stevens sometimes thought of the imaginative act as a process of abstraction, "a furious negative exclusion of all associations with the object, especially those of Christianity, but also of the trite and cliché, in order to intuit an inherent, a bare reality,"[31] — that is, a reality behind appearances, as he seems to be doing in "The Snow Man" and in "The Course of a Particular." In "The Noble Rider and the Sound of Words," Stevens considers the act of abstraction to be simply an act of the imagination:

> The measure of a poet is the measure of his power to abstract himself, and to withdraw with him into his abstraction the reality on which the lovers of truth insist. He must be able to abstract himself and also to abstract reality, which he does by placing it in his imagination.[32]

One is reminded here of the passage from Henry James quoted above, which Stevens so much admired. "To live in the world of creation — to get into it and stay in it . . . this the only thing." In a long letter to Hi Simons commenting on the "Notes Toward a Supreme Fiction," Stevens wrote:

> The abstract does not exist, but it is certainly as immanent, that is to say, the fictive abstract is as immanent in the mind of the poet, as the idea of God is immanent in the mind of the theologian. [I am] trying to create something as valid as the idea of God has been.[33]

Indeed, for modern man, and for Stevens especially, the supreme fiction (poetry) took the place of God, took the place, as he said in *The Man with the Blue Guitar*, "of empty heaven and its hymns."

"Major man," "central man," "super-man," "the man of glass" — all are versions of the heroic ideal that Stevens attempted to revive for the twentieth century. Usually he is considered to be the poet who provides us with the supreme fiction or in whose image the supreme fiction is created. "If we are to think of a supreme fiction, instead of creating it, as the Greeks did, for example, in the form of a mythology, we might choose to create it in the image of man: an agreed on super-man,"[34] The superman or overman (*Übermensch*) of Nietzsche immediately comes to mind. According to Stevens (writing in 1945) his major men are not "Nietzschean shadows."[35] However, as Milton J. Bates has demonstrated, Stevens went through a change of mind about Nietzsche — perhaps more than once — and in fact there are affinities between the hero of Stevens and of Nietzsche. Bates finds these similarities: Nietzsche's overman and Stevens's major man are surrogate Gods yet credible to modern men's beliefs; they may be the product of war, for war breeds heroes; they are not instruments of progress but of eternal recurrence; and they both come into being by man's creative will.[36]

What Stevens was looking for was "the well developed individual, the master of life, or the man who by his mere appearance convinces you that a mastery of life is possible," the kind of man "terribly lacking from life today."[37] He created major man to fill the need, and put him into a number of poems including "Montrachet-le-Jardin," "Examination of the Hero in a Time of War," "Chocorua to Its Neighbor," "Gigantomachia," "Paisant Chronicle," "The Pastor Caballero," and notably *Notes toward a Supreme Fiction*, and "Asides on an Oboe," which was a prelude to *Notes*. In "Asides," Stevens's hero is a "philosopher's man" who "still walks in dew," who composes poems in "immaculate imagery." He is a "central man," "without external reference," a "man of glass" who is "the transparence of the place in which/He is." In his poems and in his person he "in a million diamonds sums us up." In this poem Stevens has given us the clearest description of his major man, his ideal hero who, in his poetic function, writes poems like those of Wallace Stevens. Roy Harvey Pearce says of him that he is "the man, ourselves, whom our imagination enables us to discover 'without external reference' at the center of reality which we have made."[38]

Stevens sometimes endeavored to escape reality — the quotidian everyday world — in poems of pure fantasy. He sometimes attempted to transform it or transcend it by means of the imagination. But as a poet he was always aware of its existence. He called it the Necessary Angel:

> . . . I am the necessary angel of earth,
> Since, in my sight, you see the earth again.
> ("The Auroras of Autumn")

Throughout his career he took various attitudes toward reality. There appear to be at least three distinct "versions" of it. (1) Reality is appearances, the quotidian, the everyday actuality of normal life. (2) Reality is this world of everyday actuality transformed by the imagination, so that in reality "poetry and reality are one, or should be."[39] (3) Reality is a bare colorless void, a "nothingness" which one can intuit behind the world of appearances. This is the reality behind

> the cry of leaves that do not transcend themselves,
> In the absence of fantasia, without meaning

in "The Course of a Particular," but it is also behind (if I interpret the poem correctly) "The River of Rivers in Connecticut," where

> The mere flowing of the water is a gayety. . .
> It is not to be seen beneath the appearances
> That tell of it.

Both poems were written toward the end of Stevens's life. In the first, Stevens responds to and "accepts" the kind of reality he intuits with a kind of stoic resignation, as he did in his earlier "Snow Man." In the second, he responds to the gayety of appearances while accepting the fact that they may be illusions. The river "beneath the appearances" cannot be seen but it is there. The concept of reality transformed by the imagination to a kind of "higher reality" will be found in "The Idea of Order at Key West," in which the girl

> Knew that there never was a world for her
> Except the one she sang and, singing, made,

and in many other poems, particularly those dealing with the supreme fiction. Reality as everyday actuality appears in "The Man Whose Pharynx Was Bad" ("The Malady of the Quotidian"), in "An Ordinary Evening in New Haven," and frequently elsewhere. The quotidian reality is variously seen as something to be transformed, or endured, or enjoyed as it is. It is "the great *fond*."[40]

In closing this section on Stevens's poetic theories and on his concept of reality, imagination, and the supreme fiction, I can do no better than quote from J. Hillis Miller's *Poets of Reality:*

> For each position and for its antithesis there are fully elaborated poems or parts of poems. It is impossible to find a single systematic theory of poetry and life in Stevens. If the poet swerves this way and that seeking fixity and escape from contradiction, the critic must find a way to account for this vacillation. Stevens' poetry defines a realm in which everything "is not what it is." His poetry is not dialectical. . . . A new stage merely contradicts the first, and the first remains just as valid in its own way. . . . There is no progress, only an alternation between contradictory possibilities.[41]

III

It is obviously difficult to defend Stevens as an aesthetician or as a philosopher. However, he wrote some major poems. It is my opinion that he is at his best when there is a minimum of philosophical speculation *within the poem,* when he accepts self-evident truth — such as the fact that the old pagan religions are dead and Christianity is dead for some people, including himself — and then responds emotionally to the situation, as he did in "Sunday Morning." He appears to me to be at his weakest when he engages in many-sided speculations about philosophical matters such as the relationship between imagination and reality, as in that extremely tedious poem "The Man with the Blue Guitar." There is, of course, no general agreement among well-informed scholars and critics as to which are Stevens's best poems. In the discussion which follows I shall be chiefly concerned with those which appear to me to be his best, but I shall also consider some which have claimed considerable attention from his followers, such as *Notes toward a Supreme Fiction.*

There is almost unanimous agreement that "Sunday Morning" is one of Stevens's best poems. It is also one of his earlier successful poems. It was probably written in 1915. It made its first appearance (in mutilated form) in *Poetry* (November 1915). "Sunday Morning" is the logical place to begin a discussion of Stevens's best work.

It is primarily a meditation on death, a meditation which includes reference to past religious solutions of the question and a formulation of Stevens's own answer — the possibility of a new religion. The protagonist is a woman who on a Sunday morning is enjoying an easy, hedonistic way of life — "complacencies of the peignoir" — amid fairly luxurious surroundings, but whose enjoyment is troubled by the thought of death — first of the death of Jesus, for this is Sunday, and then of her own death.

In stanza 1 we find the protagonist lulled into a dreamlike state after

late

Coffee and oranges in a sunny chair,

when insidiously and silently her mood is darkened

As a calm darkens among water lights

by the memory of the sacrifice of Christ. In his image of the "water lights" Stevens is thinking of the surface of a lake glittering in the sun as a breeze ripples across it. The water lights "go out" when a calm suddenly occurs, smoothing out the ripples and darkening the surface of the lake.[42] The water motif is recurrent in this stanza:

The day is like wide water, without sound,

and elsewhere in the poem, and most effectively in the final stanza where the "wide water" comes to represent the vast spaces in which our island planet is floating.

In stanza 2 the poet asks why she should be concerned with

divinity if it can come
Only in silent shadows and in dreams.

She is unwisely "giving her bounty to the dead" by meditating on a sunny morning on the death of Christ. She is advised to find divinity within herself, in experiencing a full emotional life — "all pleasure and all pains." She should find her heaven in the comforts of the earth. The poet is asserting that the only divinity is the human heart; the only paradise our own earth. Immortality is implicitly denied. The poem, as Stevens said in a letter, is pagan.[43] Stanzas 3 and 4 develop further the rejection of Christianity as well as a rejection of pre-Christian pagan beliefs. (The paganism of this poem is not that of the Graeco-Roman world, the world ruled by Jove. It is rather a modern Lawrencian paganism which we shall see described later on in the poem.) Stanza 3 comments on the limitations of classical religious belief as symbolized by Jove. Jove did not believe in the brotherhood of man, as the followers of the new religion will believe:

> He moved among us, as a muttering king,
> Magnificent would move among his hinds.

The fourth stanza repeats the argument—that our only paradise is an earthly paradise—and says farewell to both pagan and Christian myths in several beautiful and nostalgic lines:

> There is not any haunt of prophecy,
> Nor any old chimera of the grave,
> Neither the golden underground, nor isle
> Melodious, where spirits gat them home,
> Nor visionary south, nor cloudy palm
> Remote on heaven's hill, that has endured
> As April's green endures. . . .

Stanza 5 continues the meditation on death and introduces a new idea: "Death is the mother of beauty," that is, an awareness of death enhances our appreciation of beauty, a notion common in romantic literature. Stevens may have been thinking of Pater's essay "Aesthetic Poetry":

> One characteristic of the pagan spirit the aesthetic poetry has, which is on the surface—the continual suggestion, pensive or passionate, of the shortness of life. This is contrasted with the bloom of the world, and gives new seduction to it—the sense of death and the desire of beauty: the desire of beauty quickened by the sense of death.[44]

Also implicit in this phrase is the notion that life is cyclic—death is followed by the birth of new generations—

> The body dies; the body's beauty lives

wrote Stevens in "Peter Quince at the Clavier." Death

> . . . causes boys to pile new plums and pears
> On disregarded plate.

The plums and pears are *new*. They are piled on *old* plate—that is, as Stevens explains in a letter,[45] silver plate which has been passed on from generation to generation as an heirloom and set aside—"disregarded." Of these new plums and pears

> . . . the maidens taste
> And stray impassioned in the littering leaves.

This striking and wholly successful image is reinforced by the establishment earlier in the stanza of the leaves "of sure obliteration" as harbingers of death. The maidens are impassioned as they taste the fruit, not only because of the presence of the boys who offer it but because the littering leaves remind them of the transitory nature of their enjoyment.

In stanza 6 there is a shift from the earthly paradise in the presence of death to the deathless paradise of Christian mythology, where there is no change and where

> . . . the boughs
> Hang always heavy in that perfect sky.

This perfect paradise is viewed with boredom. Beauty is possible only in a world of imperfection and change. The final three lines restate the theme — "Death is the mother of beauty." This stanza has the only weak phrase of the entire poem. The river shores in paradise "never touch with inarticulate pang."The notion of river shores touching (or not touching) with "inarticulate pang" is a sentimental pathetic fallacy.

In the seventh stanza Stevens presents a possible religion of the future in which men, with primitive and pagan enthusiasm, worship the sun, the source of our world and in Stevens's poetry a symbol of reality. The cardinal tenets of this revival of modified paganism are a belief in the brotherhood of man, an awareness of the transitory nature of individual human life, and an ecstatic celebration of the joy of being alive in the physical world and of being a part of the physical cosmos. In their religious chant the world of nature — the lake, the hills, the trees — is worshiped in Christian terms involving "choir" and "serafin":

> And in their chant shall enter, voice by voice,
> The windy lake wherein their lord delights,
> The trees, like serafin, and echoing hills,
> That choir among themselves long afterward.

This concept of a new post-Christian religion probably came from various sources. A comparison of the entire stanza with a passage in D. H. Lawrence's *Apocalypse* reveals striking similarity of thought and phrasing. Lawrence is talking about "The Cosmic Sense":

> For man, the vast marvel is to be alive. For man, as for flower and beast and bird, the supreme triumph is to be most vividly, most perfectly alive. Whatever the unborn and the dead may know, they cannot know the beauty, the marvel of being alive in the flesh. . . . We ought to dance with rapture that we should be alive and in the flesh, and part of the living, incarnate cosmos. I am part of the sun as my eye is part of me. That I am part of the earth my feet know perfectly, and my blood is part of the sea.[46]

Apocalypse was not published until 1932 and therefore could not be a source of Stevens's poem. It is doubtful that Lawrence used Stevens as a source. I quote Lawrence to show that the notion of a "new paganism" as described by Stevens was common among writers of the early twentieth century.

In the splendid final stanza of "Sunday Morning" we are returned to the lady in the peignoir meditating the crucifixion, and we are returned also to the water imagery of the first stanza, which performs the same function as in the first stanza but in addition comes to represent the vastness of space. A voice across the water tells her that the tomb in Palestine is "the grave of Jesus." That is, there was no resurrection, and Christianity is what Stevens would seven years later call, in "A High-Toned Christian Woman," a "supreme fiction." The last lines in magnificent language describe our planet as an "island solitude, unsponsored," in the midst of space — much as if Stevens were seeing it as the astronauts did on their trips to and from the moon:

> We live in an old chaos of the sun,
> Or old dependency of day and night,
> Or island solitude, unsponsored, free,
> Of that wide water, inescapable.
> Deer walk upon our mountains, and the quail
> Whistle about us their spontaneous cries;
> Sweet berries ripen in the wilderness;
> And in the isolation of the sky,
> At evening, casual flocks of pigeons make
> Ambiguous undulations as they sink,
> Downward to darkness, on extended wings.

The notion of life *unsponsored* by divinity is common in late Victorian and early twenieth-century thought. Here is a passage from Carl Becker's *The Heavenly City*:

> What is man that the electron should be mindful of him! Man is but a foundling in the cosmos, abandoned by the forces that created him. Unparented, unassisted and undirected by omniscient or benevolent authority, he must fend for himself, and with the aid of his own limited intelligence find his way about in an indifferent universe.[47]

The Heavenly City was published seventeen years after "Sunday Morning," but there are similar ideas in Bertrand Russell's very famous "A Free Man's Worship," first published in 1903.

Yvor Winters has discussed these lines as remarkable examples of what he calls post-symbolist imagery, that is, imagery in which the physical world is depicted in language employing the new sensitive techniques developed by the French symbolists but with an added element — the imagery, the sensory detail, is charged with significance which is not stated but clearly implied. The pigeon wings, for example, in their ambiguous undulations imply the entire nominalistic non-Christian philosophy embodied in the poem, and this significance is enforced by such words as *isolation* and *casual*. The structure of the entire poem (as Winters has pointed out) is controlled associationism. The poem does not develop in a strict logical or narrative manner — nor does it have the "uncontrolled" random associationism of Pound's *Cantos*. It progresses, repeats, and progresses again as if following the movements of a meditating, intelligent mind.[48]

The movement of the blank verse and the diction — polished and urbane — is sometimes reminiscent of Ben Jonson, more frequently of Keats and Wordsworth, occasionally of an earlier meditation on death, Bryant's "Thanatopsis."[49] There may also be echoes of *Paradise Lost*, but there is more of Milton, or of Milton parodied, in "The Comedian as the Letter C." And we may sometimes be reminded of the Shakespeare of the sonnets, although there is more Shakespeare in "Le Monocle de Mon Oncle." But these faint echoes of the style of former poets are not intrusive. The blank verse, probably the best in the twentieth century, is Stevens's own. It appears again at an equally high level in "Le Monocle de Mon Oncle," in "Of Heaven Considered as a Tomb," in "On the Manner of Addressing Clouds," and occasionally in "The Comedian as the Letter C." Then, after the publication of *Harmonium,* it was lost forever. Stevens wrote later poems in blank verse and in modified blank verse, but none of it can equal the verse in "Sunday Morning" and several other *Harmonium* poems.

"Le Monocle de Mon Oncle," Stevens's great poem on growing old, could have been subtitled "The Troubles of a Hedonist." Pleasure, including both sexual and aesthetic pleasure, is the chief good — not wisdom. Therefore the ravages of time — the beginning of the decay of the body with accompanying discomforts, the lessening of virility, the fading beauty of the loved one, the dulling of all appetites, the growing awareness of death — all these may become problems for anyone at the age of forty. Stevens was approaching his fortieth year when his poem was published in 1918.

There are immediate problems of interpretation. What does the title mean? It may have been suggested by Donald Evans's poem "En Monocle," published in 1914. Evans was a friend of Stevens. A monocle was associated with the current fad of dandyism deriving from Baudelaire and Laforgue, and Stevens was to some extent affected by this fad. Indeed, some critics considered his poetry as belonging to the "school" of dandyism.[50] In a letter Stevens says the title "means of course My Uncle's Monocle, or merely a certain point of view" and he goes on to say, "I had in mind simply a man fairly well along in life, looking back and talking in a more or less personal way about life."[51] He also indicated he was pleased with the *sound* of the title.

The lady he addresses in the first lines, the "Mother of Heaven," is according to Stevens's letter "merely somebody to swear by."[52] Very likely Stevens had Botticelli's *Birth of Venus* in mind. The lady is associated with the sea in the final lines of the first stanza. (About the same time he was composing these lines he wrote a poem inspired by Botticelli's *Birth of Venus,* entitled "The Paltry Nude Starts on a Spring Voyage," which begins, "But not on a shell, she starts. . . .") Lines 3 and 4 —

> There is not nothing, no, no, never nothing
> Like the clashed edges of two words that kill

— also present difficulties. The first of these may be simply a denial of Nothingness, of the philosophy of Nada, of the Nothingness evoked at the end of "The Snow Man." A few years after Stevens's poem was written, Hemingway, in one of his short stories, was converting the Lord's prayer into an invocation of Nada.[53] Nobody knows for sure the meaning of the next line. It has been suggested that the two words are "No More." But these words do not clash. All Stevens has to say about these two lines in his letter is: "In addition to the excitement of suave sounds, there is an excitement, an insistent provocation in the strange cacophonies of words." He had in mind such lines as

Exchequering from piebald fiscs unkeyed

in "The Comedian as the Letter C."

The "radiant bubble that she was," in the ninth line of the stanza, probably refers to the former beauty of a beloved woman, probably the one addressed in the first two lines, and/or to Venus as the archetype of female beauty. The "deep up-pouring from some saltier well" which breaks the bubble is probably the sudden realization of the present fact. The woman is losing her beauty. The stanza as a whole is a meditation on the transitory nature of the beautiful as it is manifested in any individual person, combined with the ironic wish that Stevens, the hedonist, could be a bit more of the stoical rationalist:

I wish that I might be a thinking stone.

In stanza 2 the middle-aged poet greets the spring in Shakespearian language:

I am a man of fortune greeting heirs;
For it has come that thus I greet the spring.
These choirs of welcome choir for me farewell.

The vitality and the freshness of the spring, the lover's season, has for the poet diminished. The singing red bird described in the first lines has joined the choirs of spring. The poet has not. The line

Shall I uncrumple this much crumpled thing

is obscure and Stevens himself in a letter admits he cannot explain it.[54] The original intention of the line may have simply been—shall I explain my meaning? The final two lines of the stanza appear to be addressed to the woman mentioned in the first stanza. She persists in taking a romantic view of life, pretending to have a "starry *connaissance*." Stanza three is one of the more striking passages in the poem. It is motivated by the appearance of the "woman whose hair was still down," according to Stevens's letter.[55] The final lines read:

Why, without pity on these studious ghosts,
Do you come dripping in your hair from sleep.

The hair is equated with vitality; the hair of the women in the previous lines suggests female beauty heightened by art as in the elaborate coiffures of the courtesans depicted by the Japanese artist Utamaro and as in the "mountainous coiffures of Bath." These, and the Chinese studying their beards, are "the studious ghosts." The lines

Alas! Have all the barbers lived in vain
That not one curl in nature has survived?

reinforces the notion that natural beauty and vitality are not enough. It needs to be heightened by art, particularly when the woman in question is past her prime.

Stanza 4 requires no explication. The decay of the body is compared to rotting apples, with a side glance at Eve and the apple she ate. Stanza 5 is a beautiful meditation on the transitory nature of youthful passion and on the inevitability of death. The furious star represents young, physical passion; the firefly, by contrast, represents the waning passion of middle age:

> For me, the firefly's quick, electric stroke
> Ticks tediously the time of one more year.

The stanza concludes with four magnificent lines describing the woman's first awareness of death:

> And you? Remember how the crickets came
> Out of their mother grass, like little kin,
> In the pale nights, when your first imagery
> Found inklings of your bond to all that dust.

As in Tuckerman's poem "The Cricket," and in Emily Dickinson's "Further in Summer than the Birds," the cricket is associated with death.[56]

Stanza 6, in lines less effective than those of the preceding stanza, repeats the idea that sexual love belongs to youth:

> It is a theme for Hyacinth alone.

The tone of this stanza is typical of Stevens's irony—an irony which eventually through overuse weakened his style:

> When amorists grow bald, then amours shrink
> Into the compass and curriculum
> Of introspective exiles, lecturing.

Not bad—but not great. Stanza 7 is a parable which contrasts the honey of heaven and of earth:

> The honey of heaven may or may not come,
> But that of earth both comes and goes at once.

It ends with the possibility of permanent ideal beauty, but only a possibility:

> Suppose these couriers brought amid their train
> A damsel heightened by eternal bloom.

Stanza 8 repeats the comparison of physical human decay to that of vegetable life, but this time to rotting squashes instead of to apples. The writing is not distinguished and the stanza does not develop or advance the argument. Stanza 9 presents more of Stevens's romantic irony. The poet is seeking for language fit to celebrate

> The faith of forty, ward of Cupido.

The writing is not impressive. In stanza 10 he seems to be rejecting the fruits of supernaturalism. He has no belief in the magic trees of classical myth nor the balmy boughs of Christian heaven, as he said in "Sunday Morning." But he does know a tree which is permanent. Its tip remains, to which the birds come and go. The tip is probably a symbol of a permanent reality which exists outside the individual mind. Stanza 11 is Stevens's style at its best—a meditation on sex and on aesthetic experience which springs from sex and transcends it. And yet the life of aesthetic experience also has its limitations:

> Anguishing hour!
> Last night, we sat beside a pool of pink,
> Clippered with lilies scudding the bright chromes
> Keen to the point of starlight, while a frog
> Boomed from his very belly odious chords.

The intrusion of the booming frog into this aesthete's paradise of dainty delights is a masterful touch. The twelfth and final stanza contrasts two pigeons—the blue pigeon (youth) and the white pigeon (old age). The blue pigeon circles the sky. The white pigeon flutters to the ground, but as it descends it has a "distinct shade," a value peculiarly its own.

"Le Monocle de Mon Oncle" is somewhat uneven in the quality of its blank verse, the associational structure is looser than that of "Sunday Morning," and there is some unnecessary repetition of thematic imagery, such as that of the rotting squashes and rotting apples. Nevertheless, it is one of Stevens's major poems, and in a few passages the poetry is equal or almost equal to that of "Sunday Morning."

The thought of death is a major theme in "Sunday Morning" and it is present by implication in "Le Monocle de Mon Oncle." Stevens wrote several shorter *Harmonium* pieces on death which deserve careful consideration. "Domination of Black" is one of the most unusual, a triumph of the imagist free verse movement, for only in free verse with its special rhythms and visual and sound effects could Stevens have achieved his aim, which he described as follows: "Its sole purpose is to fill the mind with images and sounds.... You are supposed to get heavens full of colors and full of sounds." He also said, "I am sorry that a poem of this sort has to contain any ideas at all."[57] And yet, it does contain an idea—the domination of black, that is the domination of the thought of death as annihilation in a vast nonhuman universe ever in relentless motion but with no "destination" or "purpose" as far as human beings are concerned. The poem builds its effect by repetition. For example, the word *turn* (in its various forms) occurs nine times. Fear is the dominant emotion as expressed in the cry of the peacocks—one of the most terrifying sounds in nature—and it too is repeated as a refrain throughout the poem:

> I heard them cry—the peacocks.
> Was it a cry against the twilight
> Or against the leaves themselves
> Turning in the wind,
> Turning as the flames
> Turned in the fire,
> Turning as the tails of the peacocks
> Turned in the loud fire,

> Loud as the hemlocks
> Full of the cry of the peacocks?
> Or was it a cry against the hemlocks?

The poem lives and moves on the page in an almost miraculous fashion. In "The Death of a Soldier" death is again seen as annihilation:

> Death is absolute and without memorial.

It is

> As in a season of autumn,
> When the wind stops,
>
> When the wind stops and, over the heavens,
> The clouds go, nevertheless,
> In their direction.

The last lines seem at first glance to be a qualification of the absoluteness of death—but the movement of the clouds, which continue to go in the same direction as the heavens, appears to have the same function as the "turning" in "Domination of Black." There is the stillness of human death: there is the continued movement of the clouds and of heaven, but there is an absolute cleavage between heaven and earth. The movement has no human meaning.

"Of Heaven Considered as a Tomb" has a similar bleak view of the possibilities of immortality. Two alternatives are suggested. After death there is nothing. Or, after death the soul, the "darkened ghost," may still walk in the icy desolation of a heaven which is like a tomb. Both alternatives are sufficiently dismal. I quote the entire poem as an example of Stevens's early style at its very best:

> What word have you, interpreters, of men
> Who in the tomb of heaven walk by night,
> The darkened ghosts of our old comedy?
> Do they believe they range the gusty cold,
> With lanterns borne aloft to light the way,
> Freemen of death, about and still about
> To find whatever it is they seek? Or does
> That burial, pillared up each day as porte
> And spiritous passage into nothingness,
> Foretell each night the one abysmal night,
> When the host shall no more wander, nor the light
> Of the steadfast lanterns creep across the dark?
> Make hue among the dark comedians,
> Halloo them in the topmost distances
> For answer from their icy Elysée.

There are other striking poems by Stevens on death, such as "The Emperor of Ice Cream," "Cortège for Rosenbloom," and "The Worms at Heaven's Gate," but the quality of the writing is less impressive than in "Of Heaven Considered as a Tomb." All three have a deliberately bizarre tone, a mocking irony which undercuts the seriousness of the theme, the kind of irony which Stevens enjoyed writing. It is flamboyant. It attracts attention on first reading. But it does not wear well.

Stevens discussed "The Emperor of Ice Cream" in several letters. It was one of his favorite poems because it

> wears a deliberately commonplace costume, and yet seems to me to contain something of the essential gaudiness of poetry.[58]

The "gaudiness," the "gaiety" of the language as he expressed it in section 11 of "Esthétique du mal" is a kind of protection against the horror of the vision of absolute death, "the horny feet" on which the lamp affixes its beam. The action of the poem itself is such an attempt. While the body is on the bed there is a party, a wake, in which the "mourners" eat ice cream whipped into "concupiscent curds" by a muscular maker of big cigars. The ice cream itself, sweet and transient, is "emperor," the pleasure principle by which the hedonist rules his life.

Stevens, in a recently discovered letter[59] to R. P. Blackmur, dated November 16, 1931, gave another reason for his own fondness for the poem:

> One of the essentials of poetry is ambiguity. I don't feel that I have touched the thing until I touch it in ambiguous form. . . . As I remember it, the ice cream poem is an instance of that.[60]

Stevens shared with his contemporaries—Eliot for instance, and Empson—the notion that ambiguity in poetry is a virtue. The notion is consonant with Eliot's repeated assertion that a poem is what it means to the individual reader. Indeed, Stevens himself says as much in the same letter:

> For the life of me, I don't, in any case, see why a poem should not mean one thing to one person and something else to another. The merest block of wood is anything that can be made out of it.[61]

We have here the principle of multiple interpretation clearly stated. A poem is anything that can be made out of it by the individual reader. The theory has given a field day to the explicators and especially, of late, to the Deconstructionists.[62] In his best *Harmonium* poems Stevens employed the principle with common sense and his ambiguity is usually controlled. In his later poems, however, the principle gives rise to deliberate obfuscation.

Stevens has more to say in his letter to Blackmur about "The Emperor of Ice Cream," and he clarifies a number of details:

> the dresses are the dresses of every day, work clothes; cast off newspapers contribute to the staleness; let be be finale, etc. —let us have a respite from the imagination (men who are not cigar makers, blondes, costumes, theology), and, in short, suppose we have ice cream. Not that I wish to exalt ice cream as an absolute good, although my little girl might. It is a symbol, obviously and ironically, of the materialism or realism proper to a refugee from the imagination. The second verse is a little closer approach to the center. That sheet, that tissue of fantails, spread it over this burly body, the blunt physical, and in that death, in the clarity and steadiness of a light affixed, let us take life as we find it, see it as it is, and in that mood, if there is an emperor, why be absurd about it, why not be quite sure of him as he manifests himself, say, in ice cream? The oddity of the association, while deliberate, is an attempt to be natural.[63]

Two more details should be mentioned. The "dresser of deal" means furniture of cheap wood. The "embroidered fantails" represent fantail pigeons.

Stevens describes ice cream as a symbol "of the materialism or realism proper to a refugee from the imagination." It is noteworthy that Stevens should equate materialism with realism and that pleasure (ice cream) becomes a substitute for the imagination. In Stevens there are two ways by which the metaphysical horror of the human situation can be alleviated—by the simple pleasures of the senses and by the aesthetic pleasures of the imagination. Both ways may properly be termed hedonistic.

"Cortège for Rosenbloom" and "The Worms at Heaven's Gate" employ the same mocking and bizarre irony, and both are successful within the limits of Stevens's intention. The heavy funeral tread of the "finical carriers" of Rosenbloom, dead in body *and* soul, on their way to his *burial* in heaven is echoed and reechoed in a triumph of repetitive rhetoric. I quote the first stanza:

> Now, the wry Rosenbloom is dead
> And his finical carriers tread,
> On a hundred legs, the tread
> Of the dead.
> Rosenbloom is dead.

It is the ground-bass of absolute death. Walton Litz calls it the ground-bass of *Harmonium.*[64] In an even more bizarre poem we have the funeral procession of "The Worms at Heaven's Gate" as they convey the body of Badroulbadour, bit by bit in their bellies, on their procession to heaven:

> Here is an eye. And here are, one by one,
> The lashes of that eye and its white lid.
> Here is the cheek on which that lid declined....

This kind of irony may be used in facing and purging the vision of death. But there is another way—to write of man's condition in a godless and indifferent universe and to suggest a more positive attitude. This is the way of "Sunday Morning," where the positive answer is found in a new kind of religion as described in stanza 7. But implicit in that great poem is another answer—the act of writing successful poetry on man's condition is in a way a kind of mastery of the condition, a temporary victory over the tragedy. This idea is beautifully stated in the fine "On the Manner of Addressing Clouds." The clouds, as in "Death of a Soldier," suggest our mortal condition; but they are also phenomena of the brute physical universe and as such have a kind of beauty of their own as, lit by the "mute bare splendors of the sun and moon," they proceed "across the stale mysterious seasons." The point of the poem is this—the mute bare splendors are all we have, unless they are magnified by the "pomps of speech," that is, poetry. I quote the entire poem:

> Gloomy grammarians in golden gowns,
> Meekly you keep the mortal rendezvous,
> Eliciting the still sustaining pomps

Of speech which are like music so profound
They seem an exaltation without sound.
Funest philosophers and ponderers,
Their evocations are the speech of clouds.
So speech of our processionals returns
In the casual evocations of your tread
Across the stale, mysterious seasons. These
Are the music of meet resignation; these
The responsive, still sustaining pomps for you
To magnify, if in that drifting waste
You are to be accompanied by more
Than mute bare splendors of the sun and moon.

The bleakness of vision appears in several poems and is unforgettably defined in two of Stevens's greatest poems, "The Snow Man" (1921), published in the same year as "On the Manner of Addressing Clouds," and "The Course of a Particular" (1950), written toward the end of Stevens's career.

Stevens made a succinct comment on "The Snow Man" in a letter to Hi Simons written over twenty years after the poem was first published. He said:

> I shall explain "The Snow Man" as an example of the necessity of identifying oneself with reality in order to understand it and enjoy it.[65]

The word that startles is *enjoy*, for this poem appears to be the obverse side of hedonism. It appears to be a poem on the necessity of stoic endurance. The snow man is modern man, Wallace Stevens, face to face with the cold reality of the universe of modern science, stripped of all consoling myths ancient or modern. The poem seems to say, "one must have a mind of winter" to face this reality "and not to think of any misery in the sound of the wind." The poem is replete with negatives. Not to think of misery is scarcely to enjoy. J. V. Cunningham writes:

> it is a poem of bleak acceptance of rejections. It takes a special kind of mind, a winter mind—and clearly, this is the experience of becoming one's environment—to look coldly on a winter landscape, and to reject the ascription of anthropomorphic feeling or monistic intimation to the sound of the wind and a few leaves.[66]

"The Snow Man" is one of the few great poems of the imagist–free-verse movement:

One must have a mind of winter
To regard the frost and the boughs
Of the pine-trees crusted with snow;

And have been cold a long time
To behold the junipers shagged with ice,
The spruces rough in the distant glitter

Of the January sun; and not to think
Of any misery in the sound of the wind,
In the sound of a few leaves

> Which is the sound of the land
> Full of the same wind
> That is blowing in the same bare place
>
> For the listener, who listens in the snow,
> And, nothing himself, beholds
> Nothing that is not there and the nothing that is.

The entire poem is one sentence. The carefully controlled cadences, the sharp sensory detail such as "junipers shagged with ice," the precise diction, the cumulative sound effect of certain repeated words—all combine to make a bleak and somber statement about the destiny of the human individual. It is Nothing. Yet it is not a poem of "sick negation," as Robinson described nihilism in "Man against the Sky," for by the quality of the language used in making his statement the poet has achieved not only an emotional and intellectual understanding of his nihilistic experience but also a kind of artistic mastery of it and victory over it.

"The Course of a Particular" has the same theme and makes use of similar materials. There is the winter landscape and the leaves in the wind which Stevens faces without "fantasia," that is, without imagination and without the creatures of his own imagination, "the puffed out heroes" which occur in his earlier poems, as in section 30 of "The Man with the Blue Guitar" in which man is described as an old "fantoche," a puppet,

> Hanging his shawl upon the wind,
> Like something on the stage, puffed out. . . .

These are the key lines in "The Course of a Particular":

> The leaves cry. It is not a cry of divine attention,
> Nor the smoke-drift of puffed-out heroes, nor human cry.
> It is the cry of leaves that do not transcend themselves,
>
> In the absence of fantasia, without meaning more
> Than they are in the final finding of the ear, in the thing
> Itself, until, at last, the cry concerns no one at all.

The leaves do not transcend themselves. Stevens does not refer to reality and man as *Nothing*—but by implication the poem is as nihilistic as "The Snow Man." The verse is quite different from the early poem with its fairly short heavily cadenced lines. Here the lines are long, giving rise to very slow movement, which is appropriate to a poem of thoughtful careful meditation.

There are several poems in which Stevens presents a common modern problem—the failure of what Yeats called "unity of being" in twentieth-century life and poetry. According to Yeats, modern man (as distinct from Renaissance man) finds it difficult to acquire a philosophic or religious belief and an artistic creed which will satisfy both his intellect and his emotions. There is a severance of the head and the heart. I have always thought that Yvor Winters was correct in interpreting "The Anecdote of the Jar" as being on this subject.[67] The jar represents the intellect, the wilderness which "sprawled up to it no longer wild" represents the emotions as well as natural beauty. The intellect fails to give order to the emotions. It merely tames them as it takes dominion over them. The poem, according to Winters, expresses "the corrupting effect of the intellect upon natural beauty."[68] Another poem, not so well known but much more interesting, "Stars at Tallapoosa," appears to be on the same subject. It presents in striking language two kinds of lines, those "straight and swift between the stars" and those of the sea and earth, "long and lax, lethargic." The poet describes pure intellect as follows:

> The lines are straight and swift between the stars.
> The night is not the cradle that they cry,
> The criers, undulating the deep-oceaned phrase.
> The lines are much too dark and much too sharp.
>
> The mind herein attains simplicity.
> There is no moon, no [69] single, silvered leaf.
> The body is no body to be seen
> But is an eye that studies its black lid.

The poet keeps his eye on the lines between the stars (intellectual activity) while "mounting the earth-lines, long and lax, lethargic" (the feelings). He mounts the earth lines and in a way conquers them. But there is no true unity of head and heart. There is at the end of the poem a kind of "enjoyment" of intellectual activity, but the intellect is not employed for understanding the emotions.

There is a similar dichotomy in "The Man Whose Pharynx Was Bad"—similar yet different. It is a division symbolized by the seasonal difference between winter and summer. One is tempted to equate winter with the intellect and summer with the emotions, and perhaps Stevens had such a dichotomy in mind. If one sticks to the text of the poem as it appears in Holly Stevens's *The Palm at the End of the Mind* (not the truncated text of *Collected Poems*), it would seem more accurate to say that each season represents a state of the soul—an extreme state, a polar state opposite to and nearly balanced against the other—which the poet would like to achieve in order to escape "the malady of the quotidian," that is, what Baudelaire called ennui, for this is a very Baudelairian poem. Yvor Winters's analysis made many years ago is still the best available:

> The poet has progressed in this poem to the point at which the intensity of emotion possible in actual human life has become insipid, and he conceives the possibility of ultimate satisfaction only in some impossible emotional finality of no matter what kind.[70]

There are interesting dichotomies also in "Bantams in Pine Woods" and "A High-Toned Old Christian Woman." "Bantams" is a triumph of gaudy rhetoric, but the rhetoric is in fact so gaudy that it obscures the meaning. There is an obvious contrast between the "universal cock," "Chieftain Iffucan of Azcan," described as a "ten foot poet among inchlings," and the "inchling," "the personal" who "bristles, and points" (defines) the "Appalachian tangs" of the pine-trees. The contrast between the cock and the inchling has been explicated

as the relationship between the imagination and reality or the difference
between the high style and the low style in poetry. According to Fred H.
Stocking, Stevens is defending his high style.[71] According to Walton Litz, he is
mocking it.[72] The symbolism is complex and Stevens may have had more than
one idea in mind. Here is my interpretation. The inchling is the small, the
personal, the particular. Iffucan is anything which threatens the survival of the
small and the particular. There is a similar theme in Frost's poem "Spring
Pools," which attacks the giant trees for drinking up the spring pools and
destroying the small spring flowers. Stevens's poem has affinities with his poems
about giants, particularly "The Plot against the Giant," in which the giant is
overcome by three girls who subdue him with "colors/As small as fish eggs" and
by subtle sounds and odors. There is, I think, behind Stevens's "Bantams" the
notion common in romantic poetry that the poet should deal with particulars,
rather than universals. Samuel Johnson's dictum that the poet should not number
the streaks of the tulip is reversed. Stevens said, "One is better satisfied by
particulars."[73] The meaning of "points the Appalachian tangs" had always
puzzled me until Walton Litz cleared it up.[74] Perhaps Stevens also had in mind
the technical meaning of the word as it is used in hymnology—"to mark the
Psalms, etc., for chanting."

"A High-Toned Old Christian Woman" is of interest because in it Stevens
employs for the first time (1922) his phrase "the supreme fiction." The
dichotomy in this poem is between Christianity and poetry; both, according to
Stevens, are supreme fictions, and both are treated ironically—the Christian
heaven and the heaven of the poet. Both have palm trees. Both are equally
imaginary. The poem is clever and amusing, but it palls after several readings.

"The Bird with the Coppery, Keen Claws" is a very obscure poem. I think
Margaret Peterson has penetrated its probable meaning.[75] Peterson points out
that Josiah Royce and William James were professors at Harvard during
Stevens's student days there. Stevens probably read books by both of them, but
he found the pragmatic relativism of James more to his taste than Royce's
absolutism. The parakeet in Stevens's poem is the Idealist Absolute of Royce as it
was parodied by James in his description of the "absolute bird." The idealist God
implies a monistic and pantheistic universe. The absolute bird is the sole ground
of being and can impart his power to every feather in the universe simply by
applying the laws of his intellect. In the words of the poem he can make "the
turbulent tinges undulate" without moving "on his coppery, keen claws."
Peterson quotes a passage from William James's *Pluralistic Universe*. Here are
the key sentences:

> We see that no smallest raindrop can come into being without a whole shower,
> no single feather without a whole bird, neck and crop, beak and tail coming
> into being simultaneously. . . . We think of ourselves as being only a few of the
> feathers so to speak, which help to constitute that absolute bird.[76]

And here is Stevens's rewriting of this passage:

> Panache upon panache, his tails deploy
> Upward and outward, in green-vented forms,

His tip a drop of water full of storms.

But though the turbulent tinges undulate
As his pure intellect applies its laws,
He moves not on his coppery, keen claws.

Stevens called "Thirteen Ways of Looking at a Blackbird" a "collection of sensations." It is like a series of Japanese prints—or rather a series of haikulike poems describing the prints. As for any further meaning—it is a case of each reader for himself. A more ambitious effort along the same lines is "Sea Surface Full of Clouds," which could have as its alternate title "Five Ways of Looking at a Sea Surface Full of Clouds." On October 18, 1923, after the publication of *Harmonium,* Stevens and his wife sailed from New York on a fifteen-day cruise to California by way of Havana and the Panama Canal. Their ship sailed by way of Tehuantepec, an isthmus of Mexico, in late October. Stevens changed the date to November, probably because he liked the sound of it better.

"Sea Surface" may be considered an exercise in pure poetry, although I think it is more than that. Of pure poetry, Stevens wrote:

when *Harmonium* was in the making there was a time when I liked the idea of images and images alone, or images and the music of verse together. I then believed in *pure poetry* as it was called.[77]

"Sea Surface" (written after the publication of *Harmonium*) exhibits a "carry over" of this interest in pure poetry; yet there are thematic innuendos. Stevens, in his letter to John Pauker, has commented on the poem:

It is very easy to say that the poem, starting with the discovery of one's own soul as the thing of primary importance in a world of flux, proceeds to the ultimate discovery of *mon esprit batard* as the final discovery. In that sense the poem has a meaning and the final section represents a summation. You appear to regard this, or some substitute for it, as giving the poem a validity that it would not possess as pure poetry.
    As a matter of fact, from my point of view, the quality called poetry is quite as precious as meaning. The truth is that, since I am far more interested in poetry than I am in philosophy, it is even more precious.[78]

Stevens seems reluctant to admit a thematic meaning, a substantial paraphrasable content, for this poem. He probably thinks of it as an exercise in linguistic virtuosity. Nevertheless, most readers find a thematic meaning in it. Walton Litz has a cogent comment. The poem progresses

from a transforming imagination which is soul to man and brother of the sky to a fancy which indulges in idle or comic transformations. The final promise of fresh transfigurings of freshest blue is never fulfilled.... [The poem] is an artificial and somewhat pretentious effort to revive the exhausted imagination, a use of language as if it were a stimulant.[79]

The "final promise of fresh transfigurings" is not fulfilled in the poem, published in 1924, nor immediately thereafter. Stevens did not start publishing poetry again until 1930, and it is probable that he wrote very little in the intervening years.

I look on the poem as a brilliantly achieved exercise in demonstrating what the imagination of the poet can do with reality. Reality is a ship at sea on a certain morning off Tehuantepec. The sea reflects the sky and clouds moving in the sky. The poet describes the deck of the ship and that part of the sea which he can observe from the deck in five scenes or pictures which range from the serenely beautiful to the comic and grotesque. According to the French refrain, each scene expresses a different mood of his soul. I think there is not much more to it than that. But the poem is memorable for its marvelous, fanciful, and ingenious language:

> An uncertain green,
> Piano-polished, held the tranced machine
> Of ocean, as a prelude holds and holds.
> Who, seeing silver petals of white blooms
> Unfolding in the water, feeling sure
> Of the milk within the saltiest spurge, heard, then,
> The sea unfolding in the sunken clouds?

In "The Comedian as the Letter C" (written 1921–22), Stevens under the guise of Crispin is surveying his own poetic career and announcing its termination—in fact as well as figuratively, for he wrote very little of consequence during the ten years following the publication of *Harmonium* in 1923.

The "Comedian," like "The Love Song of J. Alfred Prufrock," is an exercise in romantic irony in which the poet uses a persona to portray weaknesses in himself. It also has affinities with Pound's *Hugh Selwyn Mauberley*. Mauberley is in part a persona of Pound, the modern poet trying unsuccessfully to exercise his talent in an uncongenial time and country.

We now know, as the result of the publication of Stevens's letters, the meaning of the title, a meaning which Stevens kept secret for over forty years, causing considerable published speculation by various critics, all of it wrong. Stevens is simply referring to the comic sound of the letter C as it occurs throughout the poem, sometimes soft, sometimes hard as in the line

> Exchequering from piebald fiscs unkeyed.

It should not be forgotten, however, that Crispin is a comedian in his own right and that he is Wallace Stevens, the modern poet. The modern poet who tries to function in the twentieth century is a comic figure.

Crispin, the antihero,[80] goes on a journey from his native Bordeaux to Carolina with a stopover in Yucatan and (supposedly) Havana, although we see nothing of Havana in the poem. His voyage suggests the Americanizing of a European. It is also symbolic of a quest. Crispin is looking for an aesthetic and a way of life. He is bored with his provincial European existence.

In part 1, "The World without Imagination," Crispin begins his sea voyage with the conviction that man can determine his own destiny and can control his own environment. But he soon has an experience which may be called a religious conversion in reverse.[81] He comes face to face with the sea, that is, with reality, untransformed by myth, by religious ritual, by religious belief, by imagination.

Triton, the old man of the sea, is dead. It is a vision of the universe of modern science — vast, chaotic, impersonal. He is belittled by space. He is almost dissolved, just as Triton was dissolved. He has, in Cunningham's words "the intuition of a bare reality behind conventional appearance." What is left of Crispin is "some starker, barer self/ In a starker, barer world." His new view of the universe resembles that of "The Snow Man," which Stevens, apparently, had written just before starting on the "Comedian." The imagination in this situation is no help:

> The imagination here could not evade,
> In poems of plums, the strict austerity
> Of one vast, subjugating, final tone.

In part 2, "Concerning the Thunderstorms of Yucatan," Crispin, seeking to escape this vision of bare reality, lands in Yucatan. He has been made difficult and strange in all desires by his irreligious "conversion":

> He was a man made vivid by the sea. . . .
> Into a savage color he went on.

He finds for the time being a new reality in parrot squawks. He immerses himself in an exotic world of new sensations, colors, smells, sounds, etc., in an attempt to erase his vision brought about by the sea. He develops a new theory of poetry — an aesthetic which is tough, diverse, untamed, drawing its material from his immediate surroundings. In short, he escapes his vision of bare reality by an exotic way of life and by writing exotic poetry:

> Making the most of savagery of palms,
> Of moonlight on the thick, cadaverous bloom
> That yuccas breed, and of the panther's tread.

But not for long. The sea overwhelms him again, but this time in the form of a thunderstorm:

> he heard
> A rumbling, west of Mexico, it seemed,
> Approaching like a gasconade of drums.

He takes refuge in a cathedral, but only temporarily. (T. S. Eliot stayed there.) As the torrent drones on the roof he has a sudden sense of exhilaration, a feeling of freedom:

> He felt the Andean breath. His mind was free
> And more than free, elate, intent, profound
> And studious of a self possessing him.

He decides to go north.

In part 3, "Approaching Carolina," Crispin, by going north, hopes to find a new reality different from his vision of a bare reality and different from the reality of parrot squawks. He expected to find a reality of "green palmettoes in crespuscular ice/ Clipped frigidly" and "endless ledges. . .cold in a boreal mistiness of the moon." He hoped to find an environment, in short, less lush than the tropics, less stark than the sea. He still desired the "relentless contact" with reality, but he soon found that

> Moonlight was an evasion, or, if not,
> A minor meeting, facile, delicate.

He was dissatisfied, that is, with the reality of romantic subjectivism. The "moonlight fiction disappeared" and in its place

> He inhaled the rancid rosin, burly smells
> Of dampened lumber, emanations blown
> From warehouse doors, the gustiness of ropes,
> Decays of sacks, and all the arrant stinks
> That helped him round his rude aesthetic out.

He finds his material in the commonplace or the ugly. He adopts the rude aesthetic of realism or naturalism:

> He gripped more closely the essential prose

and he came to believe that poetry to be authentic should be like prose:

> That prose should wear a poem's guise at last.

Part 4, "The Idea of a Colony," opens with a reversal of the statement in part 1 that man is in control of his environment, that "man is the intelligence of his soil." Now, "his soil is man's intelligence." He becomes a naturalistic determinist. Man is controlled by his environment. Therefore

> Exit the mental moonlight, exit lex,
> Rex and principium, exit the whole
> Shebang. Exeunt omnes.

He abandons poetry altogether:

> Here was prose
> More exquisite than any tumbling verse.

Crispin's voyage was ended. He now plans to found a colony. He becomes too proud to write verse. His "appointed power" is "unwielded from disdain." His prose henceforth will be provincial—about his own back yard—like that of W. C. Williams:

> The man in Georgia waking among pines
> Should be pine-spokesman.

But even local color he now gives up as well as all theories and all romantic dreams:

> All dreams are vexing. Let them be expunged.

In part 5, "A Nice Shady Home," he has given up the idea of a colony and has settled down in a nice shady home. He becomes a true realist by giving up all writing:

> The words of things entangle and confuse.
> The plum survives its poems. . . .
> good, fat, guzzly fruit.

For him there was to be no more imagination, no more fancy:

> For realist, what is is what should be.

He lives with his blonde in a daily routine of comfortable life. He takes Voltaire's advice and cultivates his own garden.

Much of part 6, "And Daughters with Curls," is written in a parody of Miltonic blank verse as Stevens describes Crispin's domestic life with his blonde wife and his four daughters, whom he has created instead of creating personae for his poems. And so Crispin, "aspiring clown,"

> a profitless
> Philosopher, beginning with green brag,
> Concluding fadedly

comes benignly to his end. He has ended, as he began, in a more or less traditional, provincial way of life. But he has changed too. His world view is scientific, materialistic, Americanized.

The major theme of this poem, the quest for an aesthetic in the modern world, is a serious one. But Stevens treats it with an irony that is sometimes too heavy-handed. One admires the brilliance of the verbal fireworks, but there is no passage in the poem as moving as almost any passage in "Sunday Morning."

One is reminded again of *Hugh Selwyn Mauberley*, in which the persona, an aspiring poet, is also treated ironically, but with a lighter hand. It should be noted that in actual life both Pound and Stevens rose above their personae. Mauberly went off to spend the rest of his life in the indolence of the tropics, an alienated exile, whereas Pound went to Paris and Italy and continued to write and to be involved in public affairs to some extent. Stevens, like Crispin, settled down to a bourgeois way of life, but he did not give up writing permanently, although I think that the long period of poetic inactivity permanently damaged his style.

Of the poems written and published in the early thirties, "Autumn Refrain" and "The Idea of Order at Key West" have received the most favorable reception. Walton Litz has called "Autumn Refrain" "one of the great poems by a realist of the imagination."[82] The poem was written in 1931 and sent in a letter to R. P. Blackmur with this comment by Stevens:

> Here is a scrap written a few weeks ago. If it is of any interest to you, you can use it or keep it for yourself. Don't hesitate not to use it simply because you asked for it and I sent it to you. It is trivial, but you might like to put it in your own copy of Harmonium.[83]

Blackmur published the poem in the Winter 1932 issue of *Hound & Horn*, together with his essay "Examples of Wallace Stevens." Stevens himself considered the poem trivial and so did Yvor Winters.[84] I remember being enchanted by it when I first read it in 1932 in my copy of *Hound & Horn*. Here is the poem:

> The skreak and skritter of evening gone
> And grackles gone and sorrows of the sun,
> The sorrows of sun, too, gone . . . the moon and moon,
> The yellow moon of words about the nightingale
> In measureless measures, not a bird for me
> But the name of a bird and the name of a nameless air
> I have never—shall never hear. And yet beneath
> The stillness that comes to me out of this, beneath
> The stillness of everything gone, and being still,
> Being and sitting still, something resides,
> Some skreaking and skrittering residuum,
> And grates these evasions of the nightingale
> Though I have never—shall never hear that bird.
> And the stillness is in the key, all of it is,
> The stillness is all in the key of that desolate sound.[85]

I used the word *enchanted* deliberately. The poem is a marvelous incantation, an evocation of mood successfully achieved by skillful repetitive sounds. The desolation of autumn, the "stillness of everything gone," is unforgettably communicated. It is primarily a mood poem with the hint of a theme:

> something resides,
> Some skreaking and skrittering residuum

but the theme is not sufficiently developed. It remains a minor accomplishment in word music, and Stevens's and Winters's judgment of it is not far from the mark.

"Autumn Refrain" may owe something to Allen Tate's fine lines in "Ode to the Confederate Dead":

> Autumn is desolation in the plot
> Of a thousand acres where these memories grow

and something also to the leaf imagery and sound effects elsewhere in Tate's poem. But Tate attempted and to a large extent succeeded in doing something important with his desolate autumn and Stevens did not. Therein lies all the difference.

"The Idea of Order at Key West" (1934) is a much more ambitious effort than "Autumn Refrain." The poem is one of several which grew out of Stevens's many trips to Florida and especially to Key West. He wrote to Ronald Lane Latimer in 1935:

I have been going to Florida for twenty years, and all of the Florida poems have actual backgrounds. The real world seen by an imaginative man may very well seem like an imaginative construction.[86]

In the opening stanza a girl (who seems to represent Stevens's "imaginative man") is described singing by the sea ("the real world") which, simultaneously with the girl's singing, "made constant cry," which is "inhuman." In the second and third stanzas the relationship between the girl's song and the sound of the sea is considered. This relationship between imagination and reality, or between a product of the imagination (here a song) and reality, was now becoming an obsessive theme which found its most detailed expression in "The Man with the Blue Guitar." Stevens makes these points—the song of the girl and the sound of the sea are not "medleyed," that is, they are not a mixture of heterogeneous elements, a mere jumble. Nor is her song the voice of the sea; yet the sound of wind and water stirred in her phrases, and the "self" of the sea "became the self that was her song." Stevens seems to be saying that she transforms reality (the sea) into a new kind of reality (the song). The song, though somehow related to the sea, is superior to it:

> But it was she and not the sea we heard.

And he goes on to say in stanza four that

> there never was a world for her
> Except the one she sang and, singing, made.

Art, then, the supreme fiction, is superior to reality for the singing girl, a notion the direct opposite of the conclusion of "The Comedian as the Letter C," composed a dozen years earlier.

Art is also superior to reality for the listener, the narrator of the poem. "It was she and not the sea we heard." Furthermore, this act of the imagination, an act by both the narrator and the girl, gives order to reality, for it

> Mastered the night and portioned out the sea,

or as Stevens says in his letter quoted above, "The real world . . . may very well *seem* like an imaginative construction."

In this letter Stevens uses the word *seem.* In his poem he does not, and this discrepancy demonstrates the weakness of the poem as far as its philosophical content is concerned. Art *apparently* gives order to reality but in fact it does not. Stevens comments on this matter in another letter to Latimer:

> In THE IDEA OF ORDER AT KEY WEST life has ceased to be a matter of chance. It may be that every man introduces his own order into the life about him and that the idea of order in general is simply what Bishop Berkeley might have called a fortuitous concourse of personal orders. But still there is order.[87]

Again, the existence of order is asserted, but it seems to be order within the poet and not in external nature.

Another theme is implicit in the entire poem but is clearly stated only in the final lines. The contemporary poet should write

> Words of the fragrant portals, dimly starred,

> And of ourselves and of our origins,
> In ghostlier demarcations, keener sounds.

Stevens's letter to Latimer just quoted serves as a gloss on these lines:

> Possibly the unity between any man's poems is the unity of his nature. A most attractive idea to me is the idea that we are all the merest biological mechanisms. If so, the relationship of origin is what I have just referred to as unity of nature.[88]

In his perceptive remarks on this poem, Louis Martz[89] quotes from Stevens's *Opus Posthumous*:

> Men in general do not create in life and warmth alone.
> They create in darkness and coldness.

Martz points out that the narrator of the poem turns his back on the light and warmth of a Florida resort, "on a world of flame and green," and makes his poem out of

> The meaningless plunges of water and the wind.

The origin of the poem, like the origin of man, was in chaos, coldness, and darkness.

Stevens does not employ the word *imagination* in the poem, but he uses it in his letters about the poem. Stevens's concept of the imagination is well known. The imagination is the creative faculty of the poet. It gives shape to reality and to the poem. Stevens's concept of the imagination is at one with his romantic contemporaries, and on this subject Yvor Winters has made a few observations which may serve as a final comment on "The Idea of Order at Key West" and on other poems by Stevens concerning the function of the imagination.

Winters makes a sharp distinction between the *imagination* as understood by most poets from Coleridge on, and the *poetic faculty* as it was understood (implicitly if not defined) by most poets of the seventeenth century and earlier:

> the fancy (or imagination) so conceived is not the poetic faculty. That is, if I wish to write a poem about a murder, I may obtain my materials by committing a murder or by imagining a murder. But when I have done either, I do not have a poem; I have the materials for a poem. The poetic faculty must then be brought to bear upon these materials. The poetic faculty is a particular activity of the mind which takes place in language.[90]

Stevens at the end of his poem suggests that the poet of the future must write by means of the imagination about human nature and its origins in words of "ghostlier demarcations, keener sounds." But there is something vague and unsatisfactory about this phrase, as if "keener sounds" were in themselves a poetic virtue, and what is meant by "ghostlier demarcations"? A clearer concept of the poetic act would seem to be necessary if the poet of the future is to develop a fuller understanding of human nature than that of the poet of the present.

In *The Man with the Blue Guitar*, first published in 1937, Stevens attempts a definitive statement about his long-felt concern with the relationship between imagination and reality. The poem is not successful for at least two reasons — his faulty conception of the imaginative faculty, which probably derives from Coleridge and which I have mentioned above,[91] and the flatness of his style, which has undergone considerable deterioration in the twenty years that have passed since the writing of "Sunday Morning." However, the poem has received considerable critical attention. Walton Litz considers it the centerpiece of the poet's career. Stevens commented on the poem in detail in his letters, showing how seriously he himself took it. Stevens states his purpose as follows:

> The general intention of the *Blue Guitar* was to say a few things that I felt impelled to say 1. about reality; 2. about the imagination; 3. their inter-relations; and 4. principally my attitude toward each of these things. This is the general scope of the poem, which is confined to the area of poetry and makes no pretense of going beyond that area.[92]

Poem 1[93] states the problem. How can the poet-musician imitate reality exactly or present reality exactly, "play things as they are," and yet transcend reality, "play a tune beyond us"? There is no satisfactory answer to the question if we stay within Stevens's concept of the imagination:

> The man bent over his guitar,
> A shearsman of sorts. The day was green.
>
> They said, "You have a blue guitar,
> You do not play things as they are."
>
> The man replied, "Things as they are
> Are changed upon the blue guitar."
>
> And they said then, "But play, you must,
> A tune beyond us, yet ourselves,
>
> A tune upon the blue guitar
> Of things exactly as they are."

The guitar (blue) represents the imagination. The day (green) represents reality. Stevens said, "I had no particular painting of Picasso's in mind,"[94] but most readers are inclined to believe that Picasso's "The Old Guitarist" could not have been far out of his mind. (There is a parallel case in Stevens's denial that he had the critic Ramon Fernandez in mind when he used that name in "The Idea of Order at Key West." Some readers think that he did in fact have him in mind.) The phrase "a shearsman of sorts" is explicated by Stevens: "This refers to the posture of the speaker, squatting like a tailor (a shearsman) as he works on his cloth."[95] Very few readers would have formed this picture of "a shearsman" without Stevens's gloss. There are many similar difficulties of interpretation throughout the poem. One more example will suffice. Poem 10 reads:

> Raise reddest columns. Toll a bell
> And clap the hollows full of tin.
>
> Throw papers in the streets, the wills

> Of the dead, majestic in their seals.
>
> And the beautiful trombones — behold
> The approach of him whom none believes,
>
> Whom all believe that all believe,
> A pagan in a varnished car.
>
> Roll a drum upon the blue guitar.
> Lean from the steeple. Cry aloud,
>
> "Here am I, my adversary, that
> Confront you, hoo-ing the slick trombones,
>
> Yet with a petty misery
> At heart, a petty misery,
>
> Ever a prelude to your end,
> The touch that topples men and rock."

Stevens has given us a careful explication. First he explains the unusual phrase "hoo-ing the slick trombones" as "making Bing Crosby: performing in an accomplished way."[96] A few days later he rejects this explanation as nonsense, and he explains the couplet

> "Here am I, my adversary, that
> Confront you, hoo-ing the slick trombones...."

as follows:

> If we are to think of a supreme fiction, instead of creating it, as the Greeks did, for example in the form of a mythology, we might choose to create it in the image of a man, an agreed on super-man. He would not be the typical hero taking part in parades, (columns red with red-fire, bells tolling, tin cans, confetti) in whom actually no one believes as a truly great man, but in whom everybody pretends to believe, someone completely outside of the intimacies of profound faith, a politician, a soldier, Harry Truman as god. *This second-rate creature is the adversary;* I address him but with hostility, hoo-ing the slick trombones. I deride & challenge him and the words hoo-ing the slick trombones express the derision & challenge. The pejorative sense of slick is obvious. I *imagine* that when I used the word hoo-ing I intended some similar pejorative connotation (as for example, booing or hooting). The word back of it in my mind may have been hooting. Yet it may have been *hurrooing,* because the words that follow:
>
> > Yet with a petty misery
> > At heart, a petty misery
>
> mean that the cheap glory of the false hero, not a true man of the imagination, made me sick at heart. It is just that petty misery, repeated in the hearts of other men, that topples the worthless. I may have cried out Here am I and yet have stood by, unheard, hooing the slick trombones, without worrying about my English.[97]

Walton Litz has said that "one sign of Stevens's success in *The Man with the Blue Guitar* is the poem's resistance to paraphrase." [98] I cannot agree that a poem which is written primarily for its ideational content, as Stevens has stated, should resist paraphrase. In any event, Stevens, fortunately, has paraphrased parts of it and his explanations make perfect sense as in the above gloss of poem 10. But how many readers without Stevens's help would get even a small part of his intention? Stevens himself was somewhat confused about his intentions in writing the phrase "hoo-ing the slick trombones." The *Blue Guitar* is opaque and difficult to discuss; one is tempted to discuss only matters of style, but this is unfortunate for the style is inferior, as if Stevens, chiefly interested in the ideas so opaquely expressed, didn't care much about the style. Indeed this disquistion on aesthetics could have been much better presented in clear expository prose such as we find in Stevens's letters.

As Litz has pointed out, "the progression of the sequence is musical," with repetition of leitmotifs. [99] We have a situation very similar to *The Waste Land*, which has been described as a "music of ideas"; but in all fairness to Stevens, the *Blue Guitar* is more rational than *The Waste Land*. *Four Quartets*, of course, has a similar musical structure. But the musical method is not the most efficient nor the most effective way of presenting ideas in poetry or prose. Litz appears to think otherwise, as do a number of other distinguished critics, including Helen Vendler. Litz considers the poem to possess "the density of condensed thought." It "is ultimately revealed as an *ars poetica* of stunning complexity."[100]

I will endeavor to summarize briefly the ideational content of the *Blue Guitar*. Stevens appears to be making the following points about poetry in general and about reality, imagination, and their interrelationship as they occur in verse:

1. Poetry is of supreme importance in contemporary life. It takes the place of religion, of "empty heaven and its hymns."
2. Reality, things as they are, is the base of all successful poetry. Reality is the "necessary angel."
3. But reality is dull, nonhuman, flat, and depressing. It may be transformed by the imagination into poetry, which is human, vital, alive, and interesting.
4. However, this transformation must always stay close to reality. The distortion of reality in a poem must at all times be credible.
5. The poet, in transforming reality, may also transform human nature itself, the average man, into an ideal hero. The poet himself may become a hero. Stevens's concept of the hero becomes a major theme in some of his other poems. It appears as a subsidiary theme in the *Blue Guitar*.

These are the basic ideas, the themes of the poem, on which Stevens plays his many "musical" variations. For example, poem 13 gives us an example of poetry too far removed from reality—"unspotted imbecile revery"—as do several other poems. Poem 14 deals with the attempt of the poet to master brute nature (here called "the monster")—a recurrent theme, incidentally, in the poetry of Yvor Winters, but more clearly and forcefully stated by Winters than by Stevens.

Poem 19 would be incomprehensible without the authors gloss as it appears in his *Letters.* In fact, the best way to understand the *Blue Guitar* as a whole and in part is to read it in conjunction with Stevens's commentary in the *Letters.* This is what Litz does and he gives a perfectly satisfactory explanation of Stevens's intentions in his *Introspective Voyager,* unnecessary to repeat here.[101]

The bulk of the *Blue Guitar* is the poetic detail (images, tropes, etc.) used to illustrate the major themes. The significance of the detail is often obscure, although since the publication of Stevens's *Letters* we can now understand the author's intentions. But the significance is not apparent in the poem itself as it is in, for example, the final stanza of "Sunday Morning." Furthermore, the poetic detail is qualitatively unimpressive. It lacks the sparkle, the freshness, the acuteness, and the precision of the earlier poems.

Helen Vendler calls the style of several of the poems in *Blue Guitar* "flat," and indeed it is; but she excuses the flatness as being appropriate to Stevens's subject and Stevens's mood. Poem 20 is an example:

> What is there in life except one's ideas,
> Good air, good friend, what is there in life?
>
> Is it ideas that I believe?
> Good air, my only friend, believe,
>
> Believe would be a brother full
> Of love, believe would be a friend,
>
> Friendlier than my only friend,
> Good air. Poor pale, poor pale guitar. . . .

Vendler speaks, apparently with approbation, of the "unadorned" diction and of the poet's "stubborn unwillingness to progress. . . by a multitude of metaphors."[102] For some of us this kind of writing, of which there is far too much in the later Stevens, is simply dull.

One of Stevens's fundamental statements is his gloss on poem 22:

> Poetry is a passion, not a habit. This passion nourishes itself on reality. Imagination has no source except in reality, and ceases to have any value when it departs from reality. Here is a fundamental principle about the imagination: It does not create except as it transforms.[103]

The imagination appears here to be a faculty that creates by transforming reality — it is closely tied to reality; yet it changes reality. It does not transcend. It is not necessarily cognitive. The imagination seems to be identified with the poetic act itself and it seems to have affinities, as I have said, with certain aspects of Coleridge's theories, although Stevens did not like to admit the influence of Coleridge, or of anyone else for that matter!

> While, of course, I come down from the past, the past is my own and not something marked Coleridge, Wordsworth, etc. I know of no one who has been particularly important to me. My reality-imagination complex is entirely my own even though I see it in others.[104]

So wrote Stevens at the age of seventy-three.

Winters's separation of the imagination and the poetic act—the imagination furnishes the materials for the poem; the poetic act is an act of the mind in language of which the poem is the end result—seems to me a clearer statement than does any by Stevens of what actually occurs in the writing of a successful poem. If Stevens had arrived at this understanding of the imagination he never would have composed his exercise in indeterminate antitheses for the blue guitar.

We have a similar situation with *Notes toward a Supreme Fiction.* It is a poem of poetic theory—a subject which can be more clearly and more effectively presented in expository prose than in verse. There are a few basic ideas or themes, abundantly illustrated with poetic detail that is just as opaque as that of *The Man with the Blue Guitar.* The structure is not logical, but repetitive, similar to that of the *Blue Guitar.* Stevens himself called the *Notes* a miscellany "in which it would be difficult to collect the theory latent in them."[105] They are intended by the author to be unsystematic *Notes,* and there is probably a pun on the musical meaning of *Notes* that relates the poem to the earlier "Asides on an Oboe."

One of Stevens's basic subjects, the interaction of the imagination with reality, pervades this poem from beginning to end, as it does the *Blue Guitar.* Nor does Stevens progress beyond what he had to say on this subject in the earlier poem. The interaction between imagination and reality is presented in various ways including several brief "exempla" or "fables" in which some persons represent reality, others the imagination. There is the encounter of Nanzia Nunzio and Ozymandias, there is the "mystic marriage" of the great captain and the maiden Bawda, there is the poet soldier who is engaged in the war between mind and sky. There are also other symbolic personages such as Canon Aspirin, whose complex meaning cannot be fully defined, and the "fat girl" who is the earth, that is physical reality. One or two of these personages would have been enough. Their multiplicity becomes tiresome.

"Asides on an Oboe" is a prelude to *Notes toward a Supreme Fiction.* It briefly presents several ideas which were more fully developed in *Notes.* "Final belief/ Must be in fiction." This fiction will be created by and, as it were, embodied in the new hero. The old heroes, like the old gods, are dead. The new hero must be "The impossible possible philosopher's man... Who in a million diamonds sums us up." He is the poet, and "in his poems we find peace." This new hero (glass man, central man, major man) by means of his imagination evidently has the power to create a new "reality." He cries "Thou art not August unless I make thee so." (At this period in Stevens's thought "reality" and "fiction" seem to be interchangeable.) Central man is capable of finding the "central evil" as well as the "central good." In a time of war he was capable of suffering all. He became united to humanity until "we were wholly one." (The poem was first published in the *Harvard Advocate,* December 1940, a little more than a year after the outbreak of World War II.) He is "without external reference." That is, he is sufficient to himself and does not need supernatural aid.

In his numerous comments in his letters on the supreme fiction, Stevens makes it clear that it is intended to take the place "of empty heaven and its hymns." He says, "In trying to create something as valid as the idea of God has been, and for that matter remains, the first necessity seems to be breadth."[106] And again, "the fictive abstract is as immanent in the mind of the poet, as the idea of God is immanent in the mind of the theologian."[107] *Notes toward a Supreme Fiction* (1942) is composed in three parts entitled "It Must Be Abstract," "It Must Change," and "It Must Give Pleasure." Stevens says of these requirements, "I have no idea of the form that a supreme fiction would take. The *Notes* start out with the idea that it would not take any form: that it would be abstract. Of course, in the long run, poetry would be the supreme fiction; the essence of poetry is change and the essence of change is that it gives pleasure."[108] Of these three rules, the first has given the commentators the most trouble. Stevens tells us what he means by it in his essay "The Noble Rider and the Sound of Words." Speaking of the poet, he says that he must have the power to

> abstract himself, and to withdraw with him into his abstraction the reality on which the lovers of truth insist. He must be able to abstract himself and also to abstract reality, which he does by placing it in his imagination.[109]

Stevens's concept of "abstraction" as stated here and as employed in his *Notes* appears to me to be almost identical with that of Coleridge:

> The artist must first eloign himself from nature in order to return to her with full effect. Why this? Because if he were to begin by mere painful copying, he would produce masks only, not forms breathing life. He must out of his own mind create forms according to the severe laws of the intellect.... He merely absents himself a season from her [nature], that his own spirit, which has the same ground with nature, may learn her unspoken language in its main radicals, before he approaches to her endless composition of them.[110]

The first poem presents no great difficulties. The "ephebe," that is, the novitiate, the apprentice poet, is advised to demythologize reality, to divest it of all religious illusions, of all former literary associations, and see it as it is. He "must become an ignorant man again." Nothing should come between himself and the object. As for religions, "the death of one god is the death of all." As for mythology, "Phoebus is dead....The sun/ Must bear no name." The sun is often Stevens's symbol for reality.

The next nine poems are written in abstruse and elusive verse, but with the help of the prose gloss of Stevens's letters we can perceive that Stevens is advising the poet, major man, to have as his object of contemplation the first idea of the world, an idea that existed long before the human race. It is not God. "God is the center of the pathetic fallacy."[111] "There is a huge abstraction, venerable and articulate and complete, that has no reference to us [but is] accessible to poets."[112] But Stevens admits that it is not easily accessible. He says in his commentary that poem 6 is "a struggle with the inaccessibility of the abstract."[113] The poet must realize "that we live in a place/ That is not our own" (poem 10). This fact, according to Stevens, is the motivating force of all religions, but these religions, as he has repeatedly said, are now dead. In the words of poem 2 they are now merely "the celestial ennui of apartments." But the awareness that reality is not related to us is also the motivating force of all poetry, which is still viable.

Stevens's approach to his material is of course not straightforward and logical; it is rather the method of thinking around a subject, of "a thought revolved," the method of associationism — hence the difficulty of constructing a comprehensible prose paraphrase. Furthermore, there are private symbols and allusions which have been cleared up in part by Stevens's letters. For example, we now know that MacCullough "is any name, any man," and that the tanks of poem 5 are the reservoirs of Ceylon. We also know that the Arabian of poem 3 with his "damned hoobla-hoobla-how" is the moon, that is the irrational, the imaginary as opposed to the sun, which is reality. We know too that Descartes "is used as a symbol of the reason. But we live in a place that is not our own; we do not live in a land of Descartes; we have imposed the reason; Adam imposed it even in Eden."[114] It is the function of the poet, Stevens makes clear, not to impose reason on anything, but to make, by means of the imagination, "the first idea" vividly accessible to himself and to his readers:

> The poem refreshes life, so that we share
> For a moment, the first idea.....
> (Poem 3)

This notion seems to be a development of the thought at the end of "The Idea of Order at key West," written several years before *Notes*, that the poet of the future must write "Of ourselves and of our origins." Stevens seems to be urging the modern poet to get into the realms of metaphysics where, in fact, reason would be a safer guide than the imagination as conceived by Stevens. At any rate, in the forty years that have elapsed since the publication of *Notes*, no poet has given us a clear and vivid understanding of "the first idea." No one has been able

> to confect
> The final elegance, not to console
> Nor sanctify, but plainly to propound.
> (Poem 10)

The second requirement of the supreme fiction is "It must change." We have two key statements in prose by Stevens that should help us in understanding what he meant by this rule. In his essay "Two or Three Ideas" he says, "Why should a poem not change in sense when there is a fluctuation of the whole of appearance?"[115] This seems to mean that because we live in a world of changing appearances a poem which presents the world of appearances must also change. Milton's "Lycidas" meant one thing to the seventeenth century and something else to the twentieth. In "The Figure of the Youth as Virile Poet" Stevens writes:

Since philosophers do not agree in respect of what constitutes philosophic truth...even in the casual comment that truth as a static concept is to be discarded, it may not be of much use to improvise a definition of poetic truth. Nevertheless, it may be said that poetic truth is in agreement with reality, brought about by the imagination of a man disposed to be strongly influenced by his imagination, *which he believes for a time, to be true.*[116]

This statement is not crystal clear, but it appears to be one of complete relativism. Both poetic truth and philosophical truth may change from time to time. With appearances changing, with truth changing, with poetry, the supreme fiction in which we don't believe, changing, we are indeed in a world of flux! It is the world of "Domination of Black."

The poems which make up section 2 are a paean of praise to change wherever it occurs, in reality or in the supreme fiction. Static images and concepts are a "withered scene." "The great statue of the General DuPuy," which seems to represent an unchanging heroic ideal, is "rubbish in the end." "Is spring a sleep?" The answer is no. There is the "Booming and booming of the new-come bee." The exaltation of spring as a period of change and new birth is reminiscent of "Sunday Morning," in which the static concept of an un-changing paradise is viewed with boredom while that of a changing earthly paradise is enthusiastically praised. In poem 4 even the deadness of winter has its useful function as "the origin of change":

> Winter and spring, cold copulars, embrace
> And forth the particulars of rapture come.

The desire for change, the dread of monotony, is paramount. In poem 6, which echoes and reechoes with bird cries, the repetitive cries become tiresome but, says Stevens of the crying, "It will end."

If one is promoting belief in a supreme fiction, that is, belief in that which is not true, one is naturally concerned with what Stevens calls "the question of illusion as value."[117] Poem 5, a richly descriptive piece about a planter on a tropical or semitropical island, and poem 8 concerning the marriage of Nanzia Nunzio and Ozymandias deal with the question. Of the planter Stevens says, "He is . . . the laborious human who lives in illusions and who, after all the great illusions have left him, still clings to one that pierces him."[118] This is a rather ambiguous statement concerning the value of *that* particular illusion. Of Ozymandias Stevens merely says, "The poem about Ozymandias is an illustration of illusion as value." Nanzia as bride strips herself naked and says to her groom:

> Clothe me entire in the final filament,
> So that I tremble with such love so known
> And myself am precious for your perfecting.

To which Ozymandias replies:

> the bride
> Is never naked. A fictive covering
> Weaves always glistening from the heart and mind.

The meaning is not readily apparent. Perhaps it is in the contrast between the "final filament" which the bride desires and the "fictive covering" which in fact she has, the illusion woven from the mind and heart of the groom. By implication, the "fictive covering" is superior because it changes; it is not a "final filament." There is also the suggestion that direct contact with reality, the naked bride, is impossible. The fictive covering of illusion always intervenes.

Section 3, "It Must Give Pleasure," presents abundant evidence that Stevens has not forgotten the fundamental hedonism of his earlier years. Pleasure is derived from the poet's "direct engagement by the imagination with the multiplicity of reality,"[119] by the covering of bare reality with beautiful illusion, by the mere experience of change, "the merely going round." More personages from Stevens's private mythology are introduced. There is a mystic marriage between the great captain (imagination) and the maiden Bawda in Catawba (reality). After dining on lobster Bombay and drinking Meursault we meet Canon Aspirin who seems to represent the man with the adventurous mind and sensibility who, after having explored the world of thought and of sensation, comes back to his sister, to the "sensible ecstasy" of the world of fact. But his sister's life style doesn't suit him either. Eventually (it seems) he settles for

> the whole,
> The complicate, the amassing harmony,

whatever that may mean. On this complicate amassing harmony the canon attempts to impose "orders as he thinks of them." But, Stevens insists, this is a mistake. One should not impose order but attempt to find it in reality stripped of every fiction except the fictive angel of the absolute. The fictive angel of the absolute appears to be the same as "the first idea" of section 1 — or is it? Note that this angel is fictive. That is, it isn't really there.

> I can
> Do all that angels can. I enjoy like them.

That is, as a poet creating his supreme fiction, exercising his imagination, he is "Filled with expressible bliss" in contemplating "Majesty," which "is a mirror of the self." The man of imagination, the central man, like the angel, is sufficient unto himself without "external reference," enjoying the mere repetition of his existence:

> Until merely going round is a final good,
> The way wine comes at a table in the wood.

There is a final tribute to earthly delights — this time they are described as a

> Fat girl, terrestrial, my summer, my night.

She is a "soft-footed phantom," a "fragrant, . . . irrational Distortion" who is, apparently, hard to get rid of. An epilogue (the poem was composed during World War II) pays tribute to the poet as a soldier participating in the "war between the mind/ And sky."

The "argument" of *Notes toward a Supreme Fiction*, circular and tedious, is matched by the style, which is also circular and tedious. These stanzas from "It

Must Give Pleasure" are a fair sample of the quality of the writing of most of the poem. They describe the meeting between the captain and Bawda:

> This was their ceremonial hymn: Anon
> We loved but would no marriage make. Anon
> The one refused the other one to take,
>
> Foreswore the sipping of the marriage wine.
> Each must the other take not for his high,
> His puissant front nor for her subtle sound,
>
> The shoo-shoo-shoo of secret cymbals round.
> Each must the other take as sign, short sign
> To stop the whirlwind, balk the elements.
>
> The great captain loved the ever-hill Catawba
> And therefore married Bawda, whom he found there,
> And Bawda loved the captain as she loved the sun.

James Miller comments on the thematic content of the *Notes:*

> Like a frisky puppy with a bone, he grabs an idea and shakes it, he runs with it, he hides it, he guards it or buries it—only to dig it up again. . . . Stevens knew he was "playing" with ideas that many consider too weighty for poetry to comprehend. Uncertainty was part his plan.[120]

Miller approves of the method. He is "constantly surprised and enchanted by it." But some of us consider the frisky puppy approach not satisfactory for major poetry; in the long run it becomes thin and tiresome.

Stevens said of the supreme fiction: 'I don't want to say that I don't mean poetry; I don't know what I mean."[121] What we finally have is a series of miscellaneous notes composing an indeterminate open ended poem which expresses what appears to be a faulty conception of the imagination. The errors of concept and method could have been mitigated by isolated passages of eloquent stylistic grandeur—for Stevens was still capable of such writing—but there are no passages of this kind. The style is as weak as the content.

So far as I know, Roy Harvey Pearce is the only critic who has hazarded an extended analysis of "Chocorua to Its Neighbor."[122] The tenor of the poem, its primary subject, is the relationship between imagination and reality. The vehicle is Mount Chocorua, which symbolizes reality and "Its Neighbor," the "prodigious shadow" appearing in the sky above it, which symbolizes the imagination. It (the shadow) is dependent on the mountain for its existence. It is obviously different from the mountain and yet it has characteristics similar to it. The shadow is superior, in a way, to the mountain. It towers above it. It is godlike. It takes "the place of empty heaven and its hymns" to quote from the *Blue Guitar*, in which the Chocorua motif first appears. Professor Pearce describes this Chocorua *topos* as it occurs in various poems as developing towards a condition in which the poet can "be transcending without being transcendent."[123] He finds that it relates to Stevens's developing concept of the ideal hero which Stevens refers to by various names throughout his poetry—major man, the man of glass, central man, the philosopher's man, and so on. Pearce points out that in 'Chocorua" Stevens has reached the conclusion that his ideal hero may be found in a number of individuals and not just in one person or in a mere abstraction.

Of this complex of ideas I would say that the mountain and its shadow are certainly an appropriate symbol. It is, to repeat, the vehicle for commenting on:

1. The relationship between imagination (the shadow) and reality (the mountain).
2. The nature of major man, the man of imagination, the man of glass (here represented by the shadow).

In reading this poem for the first time the reader should be made aware that there is a problem of persons, pronouns, and prepositions. The title is "Chocorua [the mountain] *to* Its Neighbor" [the shadow]. But the poem opens and closes with a meditation *by* the mountain *about* its shadow. In the poem itself the mountain never speaks directly to its shadow. The mountain always refers to its shadow in the third person, never in the second person. The shadow is referred to as *he, him,* and *his.* The mountain always refers to itself in the first person, *I, my,* etc. The pronoun *its,* referring to the mountain, occurs only in the title. A better title for the poem would be "Chocorua Meditates on Its Shadow."

Stanzas 1 through 9 and the first two lines of stanza 10 are a meditation by Chocorua in which it describes its shadow. The last three lines of stanza 10 and all of stanzas 11 and 12 are a speech by the shadow in which he talks about himself. This passage is in quotes. Of himself the shadow says

> My solitaria
> Are the meditations of a central mind.

The shadow is clearly identified here with the "central man" of Stevens's other poems. In stanzas 13 to 26 (the end of the poem) Chocorua further characterizes its shadow as "rugged roy" (with reminds us of "major man") and as "a shell of dark blue glass" (which reminds us of "the man of glass").

In its general ideas there is nothing new. What of the details that "fill out" the general ideas? The first nine stanzas are a characterization of major man presented by describing the shadow of Chocorua. The poem was written during World War II. There is a reference to embattled armies and the point is made that armies are

> A swarming of number over number, not
> One foot approaching, one uplifted arm.

In attempting to envisage major man we must "perceive men without reference to their form." Major man (evidently) is collective man. At dawn the "prodigious shadow," the symbol of major man, appears over the mountain. He is "the self of selves." "To think of him destroyed the body's form." His arrival is described in effective poetic detail:

> At the end of night last night a crystal star,
> The crystal-pointed star of morning, rose
> And lit the snow to a light congenial
> To this prodigious shadow, who then came
> In an elemental freedom, sharp and cold.

The shadow is described and characterized. He has an "elemental freedom," a notion repeated in stanza 9 where the shadow inhales "a freedom out of silver shaping size." He is like the "man of glass" in "Asides on an Oboe":

> He was a shell of dark blue glass, or ice, . . .
> Blue's last transparence as it turned to black.

The shadow is further depicted in a series of typically Stevensian indeterminate antitheses and paradoxes; He was "Both substance and non-substance." "He was not man and yet he was nothing else." He was "Without existence, existing everywhere."

In stanzas 10, 11, and 12, the shadow speaks of himself without advancing the argument, but adding a tone of pathos: The soldier's cry is part of him as is the misery, the cold poverty of life. His

> solitaria
> Are the meditations of a central mind.

The rest of the poem consists of further meditations by Chocorua on the nature of its shadow, major man. He is identified also with the supreme fiction:

> He came from out of sleep.
> He rose because men wanted him to be.

He is superior to ordinary men because he is an image, not a person; he exists beyond the life of men and is yet of men, "Excluding of his largeness their defaults." He has the power

> To speak humanly from the height or from the depth
> Of human things. . . .

He has his likenesses on earth. There are individuals, as Stevens puts it, "safely under roof," who are "True transfigurers fetched out of the human mountain."

We have now reached stanza 20. There are several more stanzas which repeat what has already been said, in slightly different phrasing:

> Now, I, Chocorua, speak of this shadow as
> A human thing. It is an eminence,
> But of nothing, trash of sleep that will disappear
> With the special things of night, little by little,
> In day's constellation, and yet remain, yet be,
>
> Not father, but bare brother, megalfrere,
> Or by whatever boorish name a man
> Might call the common self, interior fons
> And fond, the total man of glubbal glub,
> Political tramp with an heraldic air, . . .

This kind of writing appears to me a bit garrulous. However, if Stevens had dealt with the relationship between imagination and reality, with the nature of major man, and with his concept of the supreme fiction in only this one poem, it would have been of considerable significance. But there is so much of the same sort of thing elsewhere in Stevens's work. As to the style, there are a few brief but effective descriptive passages—cold darkness and icy glitter are Stevens's forte. He does much better with it in "Of Heaven Considered as a Tomb," "The Snow Man," and "Domination of Black."

"Esthétique du Mal" (1944) was also written during war time. It opens with a man, probably a soldier, in Naples in a "cool café, " writing letters home while outside Vesuvius is groaning. The poem is a hedonist's meditation on evil and, because he is a hedonist, on the greatest evil, which is pain, specifically the kind of pain a soldier may suffer in battle. The poem is abstruse. It has never been adequately paraphrased; indeed adequate paraphrase is impossible, although Joseph Riddel has made an heroic attempt at it.[124]

The poem is a contrasting companion piece to "Sunday Morning." In the earlier poem all pagan and Christian myths are rejected and we are left with a world which at its best is a kind of earthly paradise in which the hedonist may cultivate his emotions and experience various kinds of pleasures available in life and art. In "Esthétique du Mal" the earthly paradise has turned into an earthly hell, the hell of war, of which groaning Vesuvius is a symbol. The hedonist is having his difficulties. The pursuit of pleasure has become a flight from pain.

In poem 1, the male protagonist (in contrast to the female protagonist of "Sunday Morning") has escaped from evil and violence momentarily. "There were roses in the cool café" where he had been reading "paragraphs/ On the sublime." But the retreat into art and the comforts of the café cannot blot out Vesuvius, which is groaning outside the window of the café. (There had been an eruption of Vesuvius shortly before the poem was written.) He is aware he is living in a world subject at any time to the eruption of evil. He is not living, to quote a later line in the poem, "at the center of a diamond." In poem 2, the protagonist is no longer in the café. He is lying in a balcony at night, listening to the last warblings of the birds, watching the moon rise in the sky, smelling the heavy scent of the acacias. He is aware (as he was in poem I as he watched Vesuvius) that the external world of the moon, the acacias, the birds is not related to his human world and that it is indifferent to pain.

In poem 3, the location and identity of the protagonist are not specified. We may assume he is the same person we met in poems 1 and 2. He may still be on the balcony at night. The poem opens with the line:

> His firm stanzas hang like hives in hell.

To whom does "his stanzas" refer? Were they written by the protagonist? Or is the reference to a book the protagonist is reading—perhaps the poetry of Dante? The poem states that today heaven and hell are one, that we are living in "terra infidel" and that Christianity has suffered from having a lord that was too human and too compassionate.

In poem 4, the protagonist seems to have disappeared. The poem begins with reference to a book entitled *"Livre de Toutes Sortes de Fleurs D'Apres Nature."* It is tempting at first glance to think Stevens had Baudelaire's *Les Fleurs du Mal* in mind, but what follows gives no support to that hypothesis. What follows is an extremely obscure commentary on this book which includes a reference to "that Spaniard of the rose," who may or may not be an actual person. The gist of the argument seems to be that the book was written by an undiscriminating sentimentalist who is interested in "all sorts of flowers." He is contrasted with the pianist who plays variations on a single theme and with the painter who specializes in the individual rose and who is (to change the figure) a specialist in love, going for the nakedest passion with the mistress instead of philandering among the maids. The notion that the artist must be a discriminating specialist is perfectly sound — but how is this thought related to the rest of "Esthétique du Mal"? These specialists are not sentimentalists, Stevens goes on to say, neither is the "genius of misfortune," which is evil, which is the genius of our wrong bodies and erring minds. This seems a roundabout way of referring to what the theologians call original sin, the primal evil of mind and body.

By the time we reach poem 5 the difficulty of "Esthétique du Mal" is apparent. The protagonist has disappeared. There seems to be no consecutive relationship between the individual poems, and the individual poems themselves become increasingly obscure. Poem 5 begins:

> Softly let all true sympathizers come.

It seems to be a paean of praise to brotherly love, to human and earthly love, to what Stevens calls "in-bar" in contrast to "ex-bar," "ex-bar" consisting of "clouds, benevolences, distant heads" — the extrahuman, mythological, supernatural world. Poem 6 presents the fable of the bird pecking the sun. The yellow sun, although he dwells in "a consummate prime," is insatiable and desires "a further consummation," which he fails to find even though he conducts "the tenderest research" for the lunar month. A big bird, insatiable as the sun, pecks at the sun for food. The symbolism is open to various interpretations. The sun may be reality (as it sometimes is in other poems by Stevens) and the big bird may be imagination feeding on reality. Imagery and symbolism in a Stevens poem are frequently made comprehensible by the context, but not here. The sun, as the source of life, may be life itself and the bird may be time — and so on. In poem 7 we return to the central theme — evil and its chief manifestation in human life as pain, with particular reference to World War II. The wound of one soldier is seen as the wound of all soldiers, and all soldiers are perceived as "The soldier of time grown deathless in great size." The wound is a red rose which "is good because life was." Here is stated the chief doctrine of the poem, which is rephrased several times. Pain is good because it is a necessary part of physical life, and physical life is assumed to be good. It is better to suffer than to be dead. The subject of poem 8 is the death of satan — a single example of the demythologizing of the modern world, which is "a tragedy/ For the imagination."

> How cold the vacancy
> When the phantoms are gone and shaken realist
> First sees reality.

We live in a world of negations. In poem 9 we are asked to contemplate this world. The moon—a symbol of the imagination—has become nothing,

> And nothing is left but comic ugliness
> Or a lustred nothingness.

The sky is divested of its fountains and the indifferent crickets chant:

> Yet we require
> Another chant, an incantation....

That is, we require another religion, or in Stevens's term another supreme fiction, although the phrase is not used here. The origin of this new religion will be "a primitive ecstasy." A similar notion occurs in stanza 7 of "Sunday Morning" and in the final lines of "The Idea of Order at Key West." Poem 10 returns to the long forgotten male protagonist of poem 1:

> He had studied the nostalgias....

That is, he had studied the lost religious beliefs and of these he preferred that represented by the "most grossly maternal," "the softest woman," "the gross, the fecund," who is reality:

> Reality explained.
> It was the last nostalgia: that he
> Should understand.

In describing understanding as "the last nostalgia" Stevens implies, although he does not state, that understanding is never to be achieved. Poem 11 begins with the famous statement of the imperfection of life:

> Life is a bitter aspic. We are not
> At the centre of a diamond.

Paratroopers fall, a vessel sinks, the village steeple tolls the funeral bell. Art, including poetry, should represent and not disguise or "prettify" bitter reality. The artist should not present

> A ship that rolls on a confected ocean,
> The weather pink....

and yet

> The gaiety of language is our seigneur.

Stevens probably had in mind Yeats's doctrine of "tragic gaiety," of the artist and the poet as defined in "Lapis Lazuli" which was published a few years before "Esthétique du Mal." At any rate, for Stevens art rather than religion was the answer to life's imperfections. Poem 12 returns us to the protagonist: "He disposes the world in categories." Three categories are defined (in very prosaic verse): the peopled worlds in which he has knowledge of humanity; the unpeopled world in which the has knowledge of himself; and a third world

> without knowledge,
> In which no one peers, in which the will makes no
> Demands. It accepts whatever is as true,
> Including pain, which otherwise, is false.
> In the third world, then, there is no pain.

This appears to be the world of stoical resignation and acceptance and of non-intellectual scrutiny ("no one peers"). But I do not understand the verbal legerdemain by which he gets rid of pain. The extremely prosaic style continues in the first part of poem 13, which develops the theme that "nature in action is the major/Tragedy" and that the lives of individuals are a "fragmentary tragedy/ Within the universal whole." Life with its evil becomes "an adventure to be endured/ With the politest helplessness." It is the philosophical position of the well mannered, the gentleman stoic.

Beginning in poem 14 with the statement that "revolution/ Is the affair of logical lunatics," a notion derived from the Marxist Victor Serge's comments on the Russian secret police, Stevens proceeds to a more general attack on the inadequacy of logic and on the lunacy of the fixed idea in a world of ideas. Implicit in this passage is the notion that ideas are interchangeable and that one idea is as good as another. The point of the poem in its general context seems to be that evil cannot be eradicated by political revolution. In these fourteen poems Stevens has demonstrated that evil is an ineradicable component of the physical world and that as a hedonist one should enjoy pleasure and as a stoic one must endure pain. Accept the universe as it is. In the final poem he states the obvious truth that

> The greatest poverty is not to live
> In the physical world

and he mentions by way of contrast the nonphysical people in paradise. But Stevens believes neither in paradise nor in nonphysical people. For him all living things live in a physical world. When they cease to live in a physical world they are dead. All Stevens is saying, then, is that it is better to be alive than dead; it is better to suffer than to die.

My synopsis of "Esthétique du Mal" is open to argument. There is little agreement among the critics as to the interpretation of its more obscure passages. However, this synopsis gives a fair idea of the uncontrolled looseness of structure, and the quotations are a fair sample of the quality of the verse, which seldom rises above mediocrity.

Helen Vendler has said "All of *Credences of Summer*. . . may be seen as a meditation on that Keatsian moment [in the ode "To Autumn"] in which the bees find that summer has o'erbrimmed their clammy cells."[125] In a later and more general discussion of the importance of Keats's poem on Stevens's work,[126] she shows the probable influence of "To Autumn" on the last stanza of "Sunday Morning." Miss Vendler doesn't say so (in fact I suspect she would disagree), but it appears to me that line for line Stevens's last stanza is superior to any stanza in "To Autumn" and that, because the ideational content of Stevens's poem is more important than that of Keats's poem, "Sunday Morning" as a whole is superior to "To Autumn"—as I believe it to be superior to any other poem by Keats. On the other hand, a line-by-line or stanza-by-stanza comparison of "Credences of Summer" with "To Autumn" shows that Keats's poem is far superior. The deterioration of Stevens's style is striking and appalling.

There are at least two reasons for the inferiority to Keats of "Credences of Summer." The style of "Credences" is somewhat mannered—through less so than that of the companion poem "Auroras of Autumn." The style is usually flat, prosaic, and occasionally pretentious. For example, in canto 9 we have a robin on a bean pole, and this is what he sees:

> The gardener's cat is dead, the gardener gone
> And last year's garden grows salacious weeds.
>
> A complex of emotions falls apart,
> In an abandoned spot. Soft, civil bird,
> The decay that you guard: of the arranged
> And of the spirit of the arranged, *douceurs,*
> *Tristesses,* the fund of life and death, suave bush
>
> And polished beast, this complex falls apart.
> And on your bean pole, it may be, you detect
> Another complex of other emotions, not
> So soft, so civil, and you make a sound,
> Which is not part of the listener's own sense.

This bilingual robin as robin is unusually perceptive, more so, even, than Hardy's darkling thrush. But the poetry is simply dead. It conveys little or no feeling.

"Credences of Summer," at first reading, may appear complex and profound, but actually there is not enough substance to justify its length—ten cantos of fifteen lines each. The poem (to return to Vendler's analysis) is a meditation on a plenary moment—that is, on what the Pre-Raphaelites would call "the charged moment;" The moment seems to have occurred during a walk Stevens took in August up Mount Penn, from which he had a view of Oley.[127] One is reminded of "Hurrahing in Harvest" by Gerard Manley Hopkins, which was written after a plenary moment of ecstasy inspired by fields of haystacks viewed against an autumnal sky on a walk from a fishing trip on the river Elwy, as well, of course, as of the first stanza of "To Autumn," and of Eliot's moment in the rose garden. Stevens describes his moment:

> One of the limits of reality
> Presents itself in Oley when the hay,
> Baked through long days, is piled in mows. It is
> A land too ripe for enigmas, too serene.
> There the distant fails the clairvoyant eye

> And the secondary senses of the ear
> Swarm, not with secondary sounds, but choirs,
> Not evocations, but last choirs, last sounds
> With nothing else compounded, carried full,
> Pure rhetoric of a language without words.

Not bad. It is probably the best passage in the poem, but it is certainly not as good as Hopkins or Keats, and perhaps not as good as Eliot, whereas Stevens at his best is superior to any of these poets. Much of Stevens's "Credences" is taken up with assertion and counter assertion, thesis and antithesis, a method frequently used in Stevens's post-*Harmonium* verse. The question Stevens asks in this poem is "whether the day in Oley, in its uniqueness, includes all others in the year, or whether it stands extrinsic to them."[128] The question is answered pro and con, "resolved," decreated, stated again and answered pro and con, "resolved," decreated and so on. Vendler describes the process in Hegelain terms. The Hegelian process of thesis, antithesis, and synthesis, combined with the Stevens doctrine of creation, decreation, and creation, becomes in Stevens's later work a mechanical means of grinding out poem after poem. As J. V. Cunningham has said, "These are the transformations of a Hartford Hegel."[129] The question at issue here is this: Is the problem of the uniqueness of the present plenary moment worth the time spent on it in "Credences of Summer"? The ideational content, in spite of the complexity of the language, is extremely thin, as thin as that of "To Autumn," and considerably thinner than that of Hopkins and Eliot, who give religious significance to their "moments." The importance of the poem, then, is determined by the style and by the poem's emotional impact, gained largely through style. But stylistically the poem cannot bear comparison with the early Stevens or with the best of Keats and Hopkins.

The quality of the verse is an even greater problem in "The Auroras of Autumn" (1947). The style is so mannered and vapid as to leave even the most devoted reader discouraged from rereading it in an attempt to ascertain the poem's significance. There is a misuse of what the rhetoricians call *ploce* and *polyptoton* — a repetition of words and word roots. Robinson, for example, uses it sparsely but effectively in "The Wandering Jew":

> That all the newness of New York
> Had nothing new in loneliness

and

> To scan once more those endless eyes
> Where all my questions ended then.

This rhetorical device was used successfully by Stevens in his earlier poems — especially in "The Snow Man" and in "Domination of Black." In his later verse it became a mechanical habit. There is a plethora of *ploce* and *polyptoton* in "Auroras of Autumn." If the device had been employed two or three times it might have been successful, but when it occurs several times in every canto it becomes exasperating. Two examples:

That pinches the pity of the pitiful man,
Like a book at evening beautiful but untrue,
Like a book on rising beautiful and true.

It is like a thing of ether that exists
Almost as predicate. But it exists,
It exists, it is visible, it is, it is. . . .

and

An unhappy people in a happy world—
Read, rabbi, the phases of this difference.
An unhappy people in an unhappy world—

Here are too many mirrors for misery.
A happy people in an unhappy world—
It cannot be.

Furthermore, there is far too much bizarre diction and other highly mannered rhetorical devices, such as facile and excessive alliteration and internal assonances:

The father fetches tellers of tales
And musicians who mute much, muse much, on the tales.

The father fetches negresses to dance,
Among the children, like curious ripenesses
Of pattern in the dance's ripening.

For these the musicians make insidious tunes,
Clawing the sing-song of their instruments.
The children laugh and jangle a tinny time.

Let me give one more example of what I have called the vapid style, where very little is being said in repetitious language:

He says no to no and yes to yes. He says yes
To no; and in saying yes he says farewell.

He measures the velocities of change.
He leaps from heaven to heaven more rapidly
Than bad angels leap from heaven to hell in flames.

But now he sits in quiet and green-a-day.
He assumes the great speeds of space and flutters them
From cloud to cloudless, cloudless to keen clear

In flights of eye and ear, the highest eye
And the lowest ear, the deep ear that discerns.

"Auroras of Autumn" is made up of ten cantos of eight three-line stanzas each. In each of the first six cantos, animals, objects, or persons are introduced, each presumably illustrating an abstract theme or themes. But now we come to the central problem of the poem. There is a fundamental ambiguity of imagery and symbol—beginning with the serpent of the first canto but including others. Donald Davie puts the matter clearly with reference to the cluster of images that end the first canto:

> We cannot tell from them whether we ought to believe that there is no principle governing the world except the principle of continual change, or that, in some way as yet unexplored, the metamorphoses of the world prove the existence of some more constant principle underlying them.[130]

We begin with a serpent. The serpent is autumn. But he may also represent time and change.[131] He may be the serpent of the Garden of Eden. He may be a symbol of complete adaptability to the environment.[132] Now symbols in modern poetry are frequently complex, as in the work of Yeats. But in most of Yeats's poetry the meaning of the symbol within a given poem is clear. Frequently it illustrates Yeats's occult system as described in *A Vision*. These occult beliefs may have no validity, but at least we can understand Yeats's intentions in his use of a given symbol. It is frequently difficult or impossible to understand Stevens's intentions in "Auroras of Autumn."

As we have seen, there is a serpent in canto 1. There is a cabin (probably Crispin's) in canto 2, a mother in the cabin (or elsewhere?) in canto 3, a father in canto 4, a mother, father, and children in canto 5, and a theater in canto 6. The theme of canto 7 appears to be the imagination (a subject introduced by the theater of canto 6). The theme of cantos 8 through 9 is probably innocence. That of canto 10 is happiness and unhappiness. As Davie has remarked, the poem begins to deteriorate with canto 6. The empty cabin and the family are apparently being used to demonstrate the unsubstantialness and impermanence of all earthly phenomena and all mythological and psychological projections from these phenomena—such as the "mother figure" and the "father figure"—in contrast to the ever-present celestial aurora. But one cannot be sure what this contrast signifies. One finds little support in the poem for the notion that the celestial lights are truly transcendent.

No one has presented a coherent prose paraphrase of the poem, although several critics, including Davie, Vendler, and Riddel, have discussed it at length. Riddel says that "The possibilities [of interpretation] are extraordinary."[133] He approves of the ambiguity. He considers the poem to be a meditation by an aging man on the self and on the passages of time which affect the self. The serpent is time, the place in which he lives is our fallen world, or Stevens's own mind. The conclusion of the poem is Stevens's search for a world of pure innocence outside time, but the search ends in unhappiness for its goal is impossible. There is no transcendence. Riddel admits he is baffled by many of the minor details.

Vendler praises the poem highly as a solemn fantasia of flux, rapidity, flickerings, and winds. The boreal serpent is perpetual motion and uncertainty. The animal serpent represents adaptability to its environment, "the presiding spiral of Stevens's wilful wish to be at home in the world."[134] She points, quite correctly I think, to the profound skepticism of the three cantos—2, 3, and 4—beginning "Farewell to an idea. . . ." Stevens is as skeptical at this time as he was forty years ago. He is here asserting the impossibility of discovering significance in the world of phenomena.

The poem remains for me hopelessly obscure and, in many passages, unsatisfactory in its style. Riddel compares it to the meditative poetry of Valéry, but if we compare it to one of Valéry's best poems, "Ebauche d'un Serpent," we will find that Stevens's poem is the inferior of the two. Valéry's serpent and its activity are a demonstrably clear development of the Garden of Eden myth.[135]

A major theme of "An Ordinary Evening in New Haven" (1949), one is not surprised to learn, is the relationship between imagination and reality. The structure of both versions of the poem is that of a number of the long poems written after the publication of *Harmonium*. It is described by Litz as "a central 'idea' with a multitude of alternate statements."[136] The method is also the same as that of many of Stevens's post-*Harmonium* poems—polar opposites, or in Hegelian terms, thesis and antithesis, are synthesized. The synthesis in this poem is referred to as a "giant" (imagined reality).[137] The giant is then "killed"—"a second giant kills the first"—and then we begin all over again (if the poet wishes) with the third giant killing the second. The giant killing can go on indefinitely. As Stevens says in "Auroras of Autumn":

> The cancellings,
> The negatives are never final.

This is the famous method of creation, decreation, creation so ably analyzed by Roy Harvey Pearce.[138] I would suggest that this method is an invitation to prolixity and facile writing. It is easy to fit in another canto, another point of view, and make a long poem longer, as Stevens does in "An Ordinary Evening in New Haven." He added twenty cantos to the original version of "An Ordinary Evening." He then kept both versions in print.[139] The method—multiple points of view commanded by a "center" and combined with creation and decreation—is not the most effective way to organize a philosophical poem. It encourages the poet to indulge in casual thinking, which irritates the attentive reader who is attempting to take all phases of the poet's ruminations seriously. The method could be justified if it produced passages of great or eloquent writing, but such passages do not occur in either version of this poem. What we have is a plethora of the rhetorical device previously analyzed—repetitious language to express repetitious themes:

> The plainness of plain things is savagery,
> As: the last plainness of a man who has fought
> Against illusion and was, in a great grinding
>
> Of growling teeth, and falls at night, snuffed out
> By the obese opiates of sleep. Plain men in plain towns
> Are not precise about the appeasement they need.
>
> They only know a savage assuagement cries
> With a savage voice; and in that cry they hear
> Themselves transposed, muted and comforted
>
> In a savage and subtle and simple harmony, . . .

It should be added in fairness that there are a few passages better than this. The poem (or at least a major part of it) is a meditation on the search for reality by a poet conscious of growing old. Stevens was approaching seventy when he wrote the poem. For him reality appears to be increasingly stark and grim. The stark stoicism in the face of desolation in canto 30 is moving:

> The wind has blown the silence of summer away.
> It buzzes beyond the horizon or in the ground:
> In mud under ponds, where the sky used to be reflected.
>
> The barrenness that appears is an exposing.
> It is not a part of what is absent, a halt
> For farewells, a sad hanging on for remembrances.
>
> It is a coming on and a coming forth.
> The pines that were fans and fragrances emerge,
> Staked solidly in a gusty grappling with rocks.

The last two lines are especially effective. There are two or three other passages of similar quality.

The central theme of both versions of "An Ordinary Evening" is defined several times. It is the search for

> The poem of pure reality, untouched
> By trope or deviation. . . .

The style should suit the subject and there are, consequently, several references to the advantages of the plain style in describing the plain sense of things — written, incidentally, in a language not totally devoid of tropes. Helen Vendler calls "An Ordinary Evening" a "resolutely impoverished poem"[140] which "over and over threatens to die of its own starvation."[141]

In his search for "the poem of pure reality" Stevens shows that impatience with words, that is, with language, which was a commonplace with our poets of the first half of this century. As T. S. Eliot said:

> Twenty years largely wasted, the years of *l'entre deux guerres* —
> Trying to learn to use words, and every attempt
> Is a wholly new start, and a different kind of failure.

For Stevens's friend William Carlos Williams the poem is not about the object but the object itself, as he wrote in book 3 of *Paterson:*

> The province of the poem is the world.
> When the sun rises, it rises in the poem
> and when it sets darkness comes down
> and the poem is dark.

Stevens expresses a similar notion:

> The poem is the cry of its occasion
> Part of the res itself and not about it.

He had expressed the same idea two years earlier in prose: "poetry is part of the structure of reality."[142] But this would appear to be a delusion similar to Archibald MacLeish's famous pronouncement: "A poem should not mean/ But be." Vendler says of "An Ordinary Evening": "it composes itself, all by itself it seems and without human intervention."[143] Her *it seems* saves the statement from being an obvious fallacy. Poems of course do not write themselves, nor are they part of the res itself. They are composed in words and they are in fact about the res, not part of it. Nor does it do to identify the words of the poem with the leaves in the gutters of New Haven and then state that both words and leaves "are the life of the world." The only significance to be gained from Stevens's long and complicated poem is not a new aesthetic but a partial realization of Stevens's simplest intention as expressed in his letter to Bernard Heringman: "My interest is to try to get as close to the ordinary, the commonplace and the ugly as it is possible to get."[144] This evocation of the commonplace from the viewpoint of an aging poet is successful in a few passages. Like the much earlier "Autumn Refrain" it is, in these passages, primarily a mood poem — the mood being one of almost unbearable desolation. But a mood of desolation cannot be maintained through thirty-one cantos. Hence the shorter version of eleven cantos is the better one. As a philosophical poem dealing with problems in aesthetics (which is what it purports to be) "An Ordinary Evening" has nothing new to offer.

"The Rock" (1950) has been widely praised. In a recent essay Roy Harvey Pearce called it a triumphant expression of "Stevens's own transcendent attitude."[145] Pearce, however, has a rather special understanding of "transcendent." For example, he calls that grim poem "The Plain Sense of Things" transcendent. I quote the last stanzas:

> Yet the absence of the imagination had
> Itself to be imagined. The great pond,
> The plain sense of it, without reflections, leaves,
> Mud, water like dirty glass, expressing silence
>
> Of a sort, silence of a rat come out to see,
> The great pond and its waste of the lilies, all this
> Had to be imagined as an inevitable knowledge,
> Required, as a necessity requires.

This

> silence of a rat come out to see,
> The great pond and its waste of the lilies

appears to be the "inevitable knowledge" of a failure of transcendence, as are the leaves in "The Course of a Particular" — these "leaves that do not transcend themselves." Pearce, however, says of "The Course of a Particular," and of several other late poems, that they reach "triumphant transcending conclusions." I believe that Pearce is mistaking an attitude of stoical resignation for an attitude of transcendence.

To return to "The Rock." There are moments in the poem when Stevens considers transcendence possible. Of the leaves which cover the rock he says:

> And yet the leaves, if they broke into bud,
> If they broke into bloom, if they bore fruit,
>
> And if we ate the incipient colorings
> Of their fresh culls might be a cure of the ground.

The *if* and the *might* suggest that this attitude is not the final one. It should be noted that the "Rock" sequence ends with a poem entitled "Not Ideas about the Thing but the Thing Itself" (1954) which is a rephrasing of William Carlos Williams's famous dictum "No ideas but in things." Both Williams's dictum and Stevens's poem appear to me to be statements of nontranscendence, as is the poem "The Rock" when considered as a whole. It is the rock which is the final reality, not the transient leaves which cover it:

> It is the rock where tranquil must adduce
> Its tranquil self, the main of things, the mind,
> The starting point of the human and the end.

The rock appears to be, finally, a symbol of the stoical acceptance of decreated reality.

In conclusion, two short poems written in Stevens's last years deserve special attention. "The River of Rivers in Connecticut" (1953) is an affirmation of the acceptance of the world of appearances for what it is and an awakening of a fresh interest in the world of particulars. The river

> is not to be seen beneath the appearances
> That tell of it. The steeple at Farmington
> Stands glistening and Haddam shines and sways.

It is the river of life this side of the final river — the river Styx, the river of death. In the River of Rivers

> The mere flowing of the water is gayety,
> Flashing and flashing in the sun.

It is to be enjoyed for itself without concern for final truth or final reality. It has no direction, purpose, or end. It is

> The river that flows nowhere, like a sea.

"The River of Rivers" is the poem of a hedonist. "The Course of a Particular" (1950) is an affirmation of a different kind. It is an affirmation of negation — a stoical acceptance of a world that is just a little more than nothingness, a minimal world. We have returned to the scene of "The Snow Man." Desolate as it is, the poet notes:

> It is still full of icy shades and shapen snow

but it is also full of crying leaves that do not transcend themselves. There is no divine attention, there are no puffed out heroes (Stevens's own creatures of the imagination), there is no imagination (fantasia). And there is, finally, the realization that this world has no human relevance. The cry of the leaves concerns no one. The last two stanzas are among the most powerful in all of Stevens:

> The leaves cry. It is not a cry of divine attention,
> Nor the smoke-drift of puffed-out heroes, nor human cry.
> It is the cry of leaves that do not transcend themselves,
>
> In the absence of fantasia, without meaning, more
> Than they are in the final finding of the ear, in the thing
> Itself, until, at last, the cry concerns no one at all.

Edwin Arlington Robinson

Edwin Arlington Robinson

(1869–1935)

"Qui pourrai-je imiter pour être original?"
François Coppée[1]

"I lean to less rebellious innovations."
Amaranth

Edwin Arlington Robinson wrote little formal criticism and published almost nothing on poetic theory. He contributed no formulations of poetic theory such as Pound's definition of the image or Eliot's objective correlative. Nor did he work out a systematic theory of poetry such as that of Yvor Winters or Cleanth Brooks. Yet he spent his life writing poetry—in fact he did little else. He was more deeply committed to his craft than any other writer discussed in this book. He thought long and deeply about his profession. He was not a learned man, but he quite naturally studied a number of poets, chiefly nineteenth-century English and American, for what he could get out of them as a practicing poet himself. To ascertain his critical position, theories of, or attitudes toward poetry as they affected his own work, one must go to his letters, to reports of his conversations with friends, and to the rare interviews he gave to journalists and critics.

Robinson was forty-five years old when *Des Imagistes* (1914) was published. By then his basic attitudes toward poetry had been formed. He was opposed to almost everything the imagists and their affiliated revolutionists were doing, and he said so in no uncertain terms. "I am pretty well satisfied that free verse, prohibition, and moving pictures are a triumvirate from hell, armed with the devil's instructions to abolish civilization" he wrote in a letter in 1921.[2] A few years earlier he had written to Amy Lowell, " 'Imagiste' work, *per se*...seems to me rather too self conscious and exclusive to stand the test of time."[3] And again in 1922 he said, "My chief objection to free verse is not that it doesn't mean anything but that it impresses me in most cases as being merely the subject matter of poetry."[4] There are many other pejorative comments by Robinson on the imagists and the other practitioners of free verse and on the entire revolutionary movement. To Louis Untermeyer he said, "Amy Lowell might make real poetry out of her material, if she were a poet. Lindsay shouts a good sermon, but poetry is not a revival meeting."[5] Nor did he have much use for the most distinguished of the revolutionists, Pound and Eliot. The character Pink in

Amaranth is an obvious caricature of Ezra Pound:

> He cuts and sets his words
> With an exotic scale so scintillating
> That no two proselytes who worship them
> Are mystified in the same way exactly.

Of Eliot he said, "I like some of his things but he seems to me to be going the wrong way."[6] And of the poetical revolution in general he said, "There is always a new movement in everything....But if you mean to ask me if this new movement implies necessarily any radical change in the structure or in the general nature of what the world has agreed thus far to call poetry, I shall have to tell you that I do not think so."[7]

In his letters Robinson frequently commented on what he himself was trying to achieve in his own verse. The statement that appears to me to be most appropriate, not only for his best poems but for his entire career, was made in 1929 to Lucius Beebe:

> I am essentially a classicist in poetic composition, and I believe that the accepted media for the masters of the past will continue to be used in the future. There is, of course, room for infinite variety, manipulation and invention within the limits of traditional forms and meters, but any violent deviation from the classic mean may be a confession of inability to do the real thing, poetically speaking.[8]

He referred to himself as a classicist several times. He approved of Charles Cestre's main thesis that his poetry is classical and that his "classic restraint is too strong...to allow him to depart from the strict principle of objectivity."[9] He wrote to his friend the classical scholar Harry de Forest Smith, "I have something of the Hellenic spirit in me....I have the spirit of wise moderation and love of classical completeness."[10] His admiration for the Latin writers, particularly Virgil, for Thomas Hardy, and for Henry James, his contempt for Thoreau, and his dislike of stereotyped and ornamental nature description ("There is very little tinkling water and there is not a red-bellied robin in the whole collection. When it comes to 'nightingales and roses' I am not 'in it,' " he said of his first book)[11] are congruent with his classical position. He spoke of his own poetry as being predominantly black and gray while occasionally "letting the white come through in places."[12] He is reported to have replied to a remark that his verse was predominantly black and gray, "Those are the colors that last,"[13] and he said he avoided crimson and purple.[14] This characteristic makes his verse an interesting contrast to that of the romantic Wallace Stevens, who admired what he called the essential gaudiness of poetry and who studded his first book, *Harmonium*, with brilliant color imagery. Robinson never denied the value of "inspiration" in achieving a successful poem, but the emphasis in remark after remark on his own verse is the care, slowness, and conscious craftsmanship of his composition. "I thought nothing when I was writing my first book of working for a week over a single line....The technical flabbiness of many writers is due to the lack in early years of just such grilling."[15] So much for the profuse strains of unpremeditated art.

However, in designating Robinson as a classical writer one has to take into account the arguments of Edwin Fussell and others that Robinson admired certain nineteenth-century romantic poets, and that his philosophical thinking was so heavily influenced by idealism, Swedenborg, and transcendentalism that he should properly be called a romantic writer with a few classical attributes. The main obstacle for those of us who see Robinson as the great twentieth-century American classicist is Emerson.

Robinson at one time expressed strong admiration for Emerson's poems,[16] and there is no doubt that certain qualities of Emerson's poetical style — epigrammatic hardness, colloquial diction, in reaction against the "pretty" diction of Poe and others, condensation, dramatic presentation of material — have affinities with Robinson and may in fact have had a direct influence on him. These characteristics Robinson and Emerson shared with their Puritan ancestors, who frequently practiced the plain style in their preaching and in their poetry. Also, in at least two stages of his career, Robinson was directly influenced by Emersonian transcendentalist ideas as well as by similar ideas in Carlyle.[17] Robinson wrote an early poem, "The Sage" (Emerson), praising that element of his poetry which Emerson derived from the Orient. Furthermore, Robinson's contempt for uniformity in American life and his admiration for strong individualism have affinities with the Emerson of "Self-reliance," but not, it should be added, with Thoreau's anarchic antisocial individualism.

All critics have agreed that Captain Craig in Robinson's poem of that name sometimes speaks the language and the philosophy of Emerson. It should be noted, however, that Craig is not necessarily the spokesman for Robinson, and in fact Robinson is somewhat ironical (albeit compassionate) in his presentation of Craig. Furthermore, there is a darkness of tone and a sense of tragedy, beginning very early in Robinson's work and lasting throughout his career, that reminds one of Hawthorne and that can be considered counter-Emersonian. The early poem "Luke Havergal" and the last long narrative poem *King Jasper,* for example. And as others have noted, Robinson's key poem, "The Man against the Sky," in spite of its brief optimistic recognition of a transcendental "life" behind the world of appearances, is largely counter-Emersonian in tone. Robinson's so-called Emersonianism is not strong enough or pervasive enough to outweigh Robinson's statement that his own poetry was classical rather than romantic.

Robinson's approach to literature and life is primarily *rational*; intuition and emotion are seldom exalted above reason. His poetry usually has substantial paraphrasable content and strives to communicate *rightness* of feeling rather than intensity of feeling, the feeling being achieved in part and controlled by the effective use of conventional prosody and conventional poetic forms. Usually he employs the traditional iambic line. His poems have unity, coherence, and a logical structure that is appropriate for the material but is not organically determined by it. The style, at its best, is impersonal, simple in diction, nonrhetorical, and without excessive ornamentation. Although there are mystical moments in some of his important poems—"The Man against the Sky," for example—the bulk of his verse is concerned with the everyday experience common to most of humanity. His poetry evaluates the experience. It is not an expression of purely personal emotion. His best poems achieve the universality we expect of the classical poet. A comparison of Eliot's "Portrait of a Lady" and Robinson's "Veteran Sirens" will point up some of the differences between a modern romanticist's and a moden classicist's approach to similar subject matter. Edwin Fussell, who, I think, overstates the case for Robinson's romantic characteristics and who mistakenly places Eliot and Robinson in the same category as "traditionalist poets," nevertheless has cogently summarized what he considers to be the classical component of Robinson's position:

> The romantic ethic also displeased Robinson in many ways, in spite of his individualism and his transcendental philosophy. Throughout his poetry emphasis on moderation and control, on self-knowledge and acceptance of limitation, on the social effects of human behavior, on retribution for moral blindness or outrage of the moral law—all these classical elements conditioned his view of the human situation.[18]

Charles Cestre, who, like myself, considers Robinson to be a modern classicist, writes:

> Robinson, as poet, deserves to be styled a modern classic, because he combines in harmonious union the old-time qualities of intellectual acumen, broad humanity, universal appeal, decorum, sense of proportion and art of composition, with powers more recently developed as means of literary expression: imaginative coloring, sensuous richness, suggestive foreshortenings and word melody. A survey of his work yields the impression of wealth of vision and felicity of technique, together with a concern for what is most human in man: preference for the general, subordination of sensation to sensibility and of sensationalism to sense, propriety and reserve—all which remind us of ancient Greece and Rome, and of the Augustan age in France and in England.[19]

This seems to me to be a fair appraisal, although I believe Robinson's "sensuous richness" to be more the exception than the rule.

Robinson's political, philosophical, religious, and sociological thinking is congruent with his poetical theory and practice. Robinson's religious beliefs are difficult to define. "Put me down as a mystic," he once said.[20] There are a number of references to a "light" which suggest mystical illumination from a Transcendental Over-soul or deity and which probably derives from Swedenborg and Emerson. There are traces of Yankee Puritan heritage in his undefined use of such terms as *grace, predestination,* and *election.* He asserts, in "The Man against the Sky" and elsewhere, a belief in immortality. He appears to have avoided church membership or attendance. A very liberal Protestant is probably as good a label for him as any, and theology appears to have been of little concern to him. Much of his poetry has serious ethical implications, but it is not religious poetry in the sense that Hopkins's or Eliot's later work is. His moral position appears to derive from a trust in reason as guide to conduct, a sense of ordinary decency, a strong belief in the sanctity of human life, and a compassionate, but at the same time skeptical, view of human nature, with an awareness of the potential depravity of some individual men, that is, a sense of original sin, inherited from his Calvinist ancestors.

Politically he was fairly conservative, with reservations about democracy which are reminiscent of James Fenimore Cooper, and like Cooper he feared the dangers of mobocracy and demagoguery in American society. He felt that America'a greatest weakness was its materialist greed, which in government might lead to plutocracy — and again one is reminded of Cooper and his attacks on the Whig party, which was composed primarily of men who gained their wealth from commerce rather than the land. He favored a strong presidency for America and wrote fine poems in praise of Lincoln and Theodore Roosevelt. He detested communism, fascism, and Nazism (which he saw only in its initial stages), and the revolutionary violence of the extreme right and left. In his political and religious beliefs he was a moderate.

Such a position lacks the brilliance, the eccentricity, and the appeal to alienated American intellectuals of that of Pound and Eliot, who spent most of their lives abroad. The poetry that came out of Robinson's way of life and way of thinking is traditionalist in what seems to me to be the right sense of the word, as distinct from the so-called traditionalism of much of the work of Pound and Eliot. Robinson's traditionalism is in the mainstream of Anglo-American poetry.

Much of Robinson's career from 1917 to 1935 was taken up with the writing of long narrative poems. ("Captain Craig," which appeared in 1902, is a character sketch and is therefore excluded from the genre of narrative poetry.) Three of these poems are on Arthurian materials; the others — there are nine of them — have modern settings. Of the Arthurian poems, *Lancelot* is probably the best, although *Tristram* achieved an astounding popularity. The other narrative poems are today generally considered as failures or, at least, unsuccessful in comparison with Robinson's best poems of short and medium length. What was the cause of these failures?

Allen Tate attributes Robinson's disappointing performance in the narrative genre to the deficiencies of the period in which the poet lived. To be successful, according to Tate, a long narrative poem must be dramatic. But, says Tate, we lost the dramatic instinct at the same time we lost the tragic hero:

> instead of the tragic hero whose downfall is deeply involved with his suprahuman relations, we get the romantic, sentimental hero whose problem is chiefly one of adjustment to society, on the one hand, and, on the other, one of futile self-assertion in the realm of the personal ego.[21]

Tate goes on to say that the dramatic approach demands the possession by the hero of a comprehensive moral scheme, a code of conduct. Our period has no such code and therefore:

> Mr. Robinson has no epos, myth, or code, no suprahuman truth, to tell him what the terminal points of human conduct are, in this age; so he goes over the same ground, again and again, writing a poem that will not be written.[22]

In a rebuttal of Tate's position, Richard P. Adams argues that the poet had access to the same mythic-symbolic material of the romantic tradition that James and Hemingway successfully employed but he failed to make proper use of it. Adams describes the aspect of the romantic tradition available to the narrative writers of our time as follows:

> the dominant "myth" is that of a transcendent relation between the individual and his environment; the dominant theme is his development, or growth, in terms of a significantly increased awareness, understanding, or appreciation of this relation; the typical structure of a narrative is the symbolic pattern of death and rebirth.... The romantic protagonist usually begins with a realization that his relation to his environment is bad, or incomplete; he then goes through a period of more or less agonizing uncertainty, puzzlement, struggle, and change; and he concludes either by achieving a more fully integral and satisfactory relation to his environment or by failing to do so.[23]

It is to be noted that both Tate and Adams believe that the hero of narratives written in our time must be "romantic," but they differ somewhat in their description of such a hero and they differ sharply in their estimate of his dramatic value in the narrative genre.

Yvor Winters is in agreement with Tate and Adams concerning the mediocrity of all of the narrative poems with modern settings, and in his book on Robinson (first edition, 1946)[24] he analyzes their weaknesses in some detail, weaknesses he seems to attribute to Robinson's lack of talent for the genre. But in a later volume, *The Function of Criticism* (1957), he argues that narrative writing, whether in verse or prose, and the epic, and the long allegorical poem, such as Spenser's *Faerie Queene,* and the poetic drama are all inferior genres when compared to the short poem which "is not essentially imitative or narrative, but expository."[25] In this form "the most powerful and the most sensitive mode of writing can be used efficiently throughout."[26] The author of the long narrative poem, on the other hand, must present in verse a good deal of material which would be more appropriately written in prose. In dialogue, especially, in order to be more or less realistic and in order to make the speeches of his characters credible, he must make them speak in verse which is not of the highest quality. Naturally, then, we would expect Robinson's expository poems such as "Hillcrest" to be superior to his long narrative poems because in the short poem he is operating in a poetic form superior to that of the long narrative poem.

In any case, by the time Robinson was writing his narrative poems the genre was almost defunct, as Robinson himself apparently realized, for in a letter to Edith Brower written in 1925 during the composition of *Tristram* he said, "a long poem nowadays is at best a getting down on one's knees to invite disaster."[27] There are of course Masefield's narratives in verse, Stephen Vincent Benét's *John Brown's Body,* and Robinson Jeffers's melodramatic narratives, but who today takes any of these seriously as literature? Indeed, with a few brilliant exceptions—Hardy's epic drama *The Dynasts*; Robert Bridges's philosophical poem, *The Testament of Beauty*; and Wallace Stevens's "The Comedian as the Letter C"—the successful long poem of any kind has almost ceased to exist. For students of the history of the genre of narrative verse, and for specialists in

Robinson, his long narratives are worth careful study. But Robinson's greater achievements, by a wide margin, are in the poems of short or medium length. In this chapter I shall consider only them, or rather a relatively small selection of what seem to me to be his best poems.

Of all Robinson's poems, "Hillcrest," written in September 1913, at the MacDowell Colony, in theme, technique, and feeling illustrates the modern classical poet at his best. The title is the name of the home of Edward MacDowell, the musical composer, and his wife at Peterborough, New Hampshire. After her husband's death in 1908, Mrs. MacDowell made her home the center of the colony, and from 1911 Robinson habitually spent his summers there.

Because of the rural surroundings so beautifully described in the first and last stanzas and because Robinson appears to be praising a life of solitude, lived close to nature, the poem at first glance seems to be Wordsworthian, but in its final implications it is not. In the first lines the colony is described as an island in a sea of trees, as a refuge from the storms of the world:

> No sound of any storm that shakes
> Old island walls with older seas
> Comes here where now September makes
> An island in a sea of trees.

Autumn is approaching and the poet (although he does not say so in the poem) will soon be leaving for the less peaceful atmosphere of urban New York City. In his retreat, far from the "roaring of a world remade" (urban America) where he has the time and the solitude necessary for contemplation, he may learn to forget his past struggles and failures, or if he still remembers them he will see them in their correct proportions. He will not exaggerate their cost ("a planet out of tune") or their importance ("great oaks" instead of "acorns"), and he will be wary of offering easy consolation to humanity:

> Between the sunlight and the shade
> A man may learn till he forgets
> The roaring of a world remade,
> And all his ruins and regrets;
>
> And if he still remembers here
> Poor fights he may have won or lost, —
> If he be ridden with the fear
> Of what some other fight may cost, —
>
> If, eager to confuse too soon,
> What he has known with what may be,
> He reads a planet out of tune
> For cause of his jarred harmony, —
>
> If here he venture to unroll
> His index of adagios,
> And he be given to console
> Humanity with what he knows, —

> He may by contemplation learn
> A little more than what he knew,
> And even see great oaks return
> To acorns out of which they grew.

The most significant words of this passage are "He may by contemplation learn." The entire poem is a statement of the value of the contemplative life as contrasted with the life of action—"roaring of a world remade."

The remainder of the poem states what the poet has learned "by contemplation" during his summers at Hillcrest. He has become aware of the dangers of vanity and the necessity for humility; he has learned that the future is precarious, and in brilliant language he states the necessity for stoical endurance:

> He may, if he but listen well,
> Through twilight and the silence here,
> Be told what there are none may tell
> To vanity's impatient ear;
>
> And he may never dare again
> Say what awaits him, or be sure
> What sunlit labyrinth of pain
> He may not enter and endure.

In the next two stanzas he proceeds from the necessity for endurance to the idealism that may be attained through endurance—or "duress" as he calls it here:

> Who knows to-day from yesterday
> May learn to count no thing too strange:
> Love builds of what Time takes away,
> Till Death itself is less than Change.
>
> Who sees enough in his duress
> May go as far as dreams have gone;
> Who sees a little may do less
> Than many who are blind have done;

Robinson used the term *idealism*, as C. P. Smith has noted, in a nontechnical sense to mean the life of the mind—that is, the life of contemplation, which, as we have seen, is the major theme of "Hillcrest."[28] The poet's idealism owes something to Swedenborg, who believed the spiritual world was ever present and that death is merely one more change of state toward complete spirituality or, as Robinson says, "Death itself is less than Change." Although Robinson claimed he was bored by Josiah Royce's lectures at Harvard, the following quotations—the first from Royce's *Spirit of Modern Philosophy* and the second from Robinson's letter to Harry de Forest Smith—could serve as a gloss on stanzas 7 to 10 of "Hillcrest." According to Royce: "It is just endurance that is the essence of spirituality. Resignation, then, is indeed part of truth—resignation, that is, of any hope of a final private happiness."[29] And Robinson wrote in a letter to Smith:

I am going to lose all those pleasures which are said to make up the happiness of this life.... I am strong enough to do without them. There is a pleasure—a joy—that is greater than all these little selfish notions and I have found the way to it through idealism.[30]

In the final three stanzas Robinson rejects the romantic view of life comparing it to that of an egocentric child, "who sees the whole/ World radiant with his own delight":

> Who sees unchastened here the soul
> Triumphant has no other sight
> Than has a child who sees the whole
> World radiant with his own delight.
>
> Far journeys and hard wandering
> Await him in whose crude surmise
> Peace, like a mask, hides everything
> That is and has been from his eyes;
>
> And all his wisdom is unfound,
> Or like a web that error weaves
> On airy looms that have a sound
> No louder now than falling leaves.

It should not escape notice that a poem that begins with what appears to be Wordsworthian praise of the delights of rural solitude ends with a repudiation of two of Wordsworth's doctrines—the "wisdom" of the child and the "peace" of mind that may be found in romantic escape to an exaltation of nature. Such "wisdom is unfound" and the imagery of the falling autumn leaves used to define this "web that error weaves" returns us to the similar imagery of the opening stanza, but with an attitude toward the rural setting of the poem considerably modified.

"Hillcrest," because of the quality of its almost flawless style and because it deals with themes basic to the poet's entire career, is probably Robinson's best philosophical poem. The more famous "The Man against the Sky" written during the spring and summer of 1915, that is, two years after "Hillcrest," is a more complex poem—that is, it is longer and deals with a greater number of themes. It too is essential to an understanding of the poet's philosophy, but unfortunately some of the writing is facile and trite. Rigorous cutting would have greatly improved it. However, because of its popularity and because it contains much that is essential Robinson, it deserves detailed discussion. The setting, like that of "Hillcrest," is the MacDowell Colony. In March 1915, a vivid recollection of a sunset blazing on the bare peak of Mt. Monadnock above the forest of the colony gave Robinson his central symbol and his opening lines:

> Between me and the sunset, like a dome
> Against the glory of a world on fire,
> Now burned a sudden hill,
> Bleak, round, and high, by flame-lit height made higher,
> With nothing on it for the flame to kill
> Save one who moved and was alone up there

> To loom before the chaos and the glare
> As if he were the last god going home
> Unto his last desire.

The figure against the sunset is Everyman in the last moments of his life before the descent to death, and the poem as a whole is a meditation on the descent of man, a subject which Robinson had discussed the year before with Lawrence Henderson, who taught biological chemistry at Harvard. The theory of evolution was the focus of their talks. Could the rise of man from matter be entirely explained by mechanistic materialism, and could the organization of the entire universe be explained on purely materialistic grounds? Robinson thought not. There are vehement rejections of deterministic philosophy throughout his correspondence. The following from a letter written in 1931 to Will Durant is typical:

> If a man is a materialist or a mechanist or whatever he likes to call himself I can
> see for him no escape from belief in a futility so prolonged and complicated and
> diabolical and preposterous as to be worse than absurd.[31]

In several letters Robinson said that "The Man against the Sky" is a denial of mechanistic materialism. In 1917 he wrote: " 'The Man Against the Sky' is a protest against a materialistic explanation of the universe."[32] He denied again and again that the poem is pessimistic. To Amy Lowell he wrote in 1916, "Nothing could have been farther from my mind when I wrote 'The Man' than any emissary of gloom or of despair. . . . I meant merely, through what I supposed to be an obvious ironic medium, to carry materialism to its logical end and to indicate its futility as explanation or a justification of existence."[33] And in another letter of the same year he said, "My purpose was to cheer people up."[34] "If materialism is true," he said in explaining the poem to Hermann Hagedorn, "then parenthood is the greatest of all crimes and the sooner the much advertised 'race' is annihilated the better."[35] In the light of these statements there is some irony in the fact that the volume *The Man against the Sky* was dedicated to Robinson's friend William E. Butler, who committeed suicide in 1912.

To return to the poem. As Robinson watches the man against the sunset, he speculates on his character — he might be heroic, mediocre, insensitive, cynical, a failure, a success. The poet reviews various types of men and their ways of living their lives and meeting their deaths, a line of thought which leads to the question of immortality and the nature of life after death, with various possible answers — including the Christian Heaven and Hell — or perhaps simple oblivion. Robinson says, if death ends everything then life is a nightmare best terminated by suicide. *If* this be true, if each individual life ends in oblivion, mass suicide would be the proper course:

> If after all that we have lived and thought,
> All comes to Nought, —
> If there be nothing after Now,
> And we be nothing anyhow,
> And we know that, — why live?
> 'Twere sure but weaklings' vain distress

> To suffer dungeons where so many doors
> Will open on the cold eternal shores
> That look sheer down
> To the dark tideless floods of Nothingness
> Where all who know may drown.

But of course this nihilistic belief is not true, Robinson states earlier in the poem as he affirms:

> But this we know, if we know anything;
> That we may laugh and fight and sing
> And of our transience here make offering
> To an orient Word that will not be erased,
> Or, save in incommunicable gleams
> Too permanent for dreams,
> Be found or known.

Nevertheless, those who have found the poem gloomy have had good cause to do so. The positive belief in the Word known only by mystical intuition is stated in a few lines. The tone of the greater part of the poem is one of darkness and despair.

The poem is organized as follows. The opening lines describe the solitary figure of a man moving against the sky down a mountain peak until he disappears. He is Everyman or more specifically modern man going down to death, and he must face his death *alone.* (The emphasis on the essential loneliness of man is characteristic of Robinson.) How did he meet death? How did he live? The answers which follow are a summary of several typical philosophical and religious attitudes taken by modern man. (1) He may have gone down to a triumphant death in great anguish like those who suffered in the fiery furnace in the Book of Daniel. This type has unshakable religious faith. (2) Or he may have gone down comfortably and easily with a complacent faith untroubled by thought. (3) Perhaps he was indifferent to his faith—his indifference might have been that of a cynic or it might have been the seeming indifference of the stoic. (4) On the other hand, he might have lived unreconciled to his fate and, like Job's wife, cursed God and died. (5) Finally, he might have been a mechanistic materialist:

> He may have built, unawed by fiery gules
> That in him no commotion stirred,
> A living reason out of molecules
> Why molecules occurred.

After depicting these various ways of living and dying, Robinson takes up the questions of life after death and of the purpose of life. As we have seen, Robinson's own position is that of the mystic. We know by intuition that God exists, and if God exists we can tentatively assume that he is beneficent, that life has a purpose, and that life does not end with our earthly existence. Robinson repeats the major theme of "The Man against the Sky" in his last poem, *King Jasper,* written in 1933–34.

> ...No God
> No Law, no purpose, could have hatched for sport
> Out of warm water and slime, a war for life
> That was unnecessary, and far better
> Had never been — if man, as we behold him,
> Is all it means.

There are a few obvious influences on the poem. It owes something to the versification and theme of Arnold's "Dover Beach" and to Wordsworth's "Ode on Intimations of Immortality," which was greatly admired by Robinson. The figure of the man against the sky was perhaps suggested by Wordsworth's description of a shepherd against the sunset in *The Prelude*:

> ...as he stepped
> Beyond the boundary line of some hill shadow,
> His form hath flashed upon me, glorified
> By the deep radiance of the setting sun;
> Or him have I descried in distant sky,
> A solitary object and sublime,
> Above all height!...

The ten human types who pass into James Thomson's "City of Dreadful Night" may have given Robinson the idea of depicting similar types.

Robinson himself thought highly of the poem. In a letter in 1932 he wrote, "Perhaps 'Man Against the Sky' comes as near as anything to representing my poetic visions."[36] Emery Neff thinks the style achieves the heroic grandeur of the Greeks and considers it to represent the height of the poet's creative powers. A number of other critics — including Wallace L. Anderson, Hermann Hagedorn, and Ellsworth Barnard — have been almost as enthusiastic. Yvor Winters, however, considers much of it to be badly written and badly structured. Louis O. Coxe thinks that in spite of its flaws it has "fine Wagnerian moments."

As a meditation on the plight of the modern man in a world which has lost much of its religious faith the poem invites comparison with Wallace Stevens's "Sunday Morning," which was written about the same time. Line for line Stevens's poem is stylistically superior to Robinson's, and as a whole it is a much greater achievement.

Of a suicide, Robinson wrote: "A suicide signifies discouragement or despair either of which is, or should be, too far beyond the scope of our piddling human censure to require of our ignorance anything less than silence."[37] The subject, much on the poet's mind throughout his career, plays a part in a number of poems, including "Richard Cory" (where it is used for cheap dramatic effect), "The Man against the Sky" (where it is suggested as the best solution to life's problems for the atheist), and the early and hauntingly moving poem "Luke Havergal" (where it is the central subject of the poem and where it is perhaps a projection of Robinson's own temptation to succumb to complete despair). The protagonist is advised by a voice from "out of the grave" to "Go to the western gate" where he may find his loved one — and this is the only way he will find her: "Yes, there is yet one way to where she is." Only in death will he be joined with her. The symbolism is obvious. West and the western gate suggest despair and death, as do the flying leaves of autumn; the dawn and the east suggest life and hope, which in the context of this poem are illusory. We have here an example of the inadequacy of paraphrase. The excellence of the poem is in the quality of the style, in the depth of feeling evoked. The flying leaves, the crimson vines, the autumnal dark, the fiery light of the lover's eyes, the marvelous rhythms and sound effects have aroused the admiration of readers as far apart in time and temperament as President Theodore Roosevelt and Allen Tate. Tate has called it "one of the great recent lyrics."[38] Roosevelt said, "I am not sure that I understand 'Luke Havergal'; but I am entirely sure that I like it."[39] (It was one of the poems which moved the president to grant Robinson a sinecure in the Treasury Department.) This brilliant tone poem must be read as a whole to be properly appreciated. I quote only the second stanza to illustrate the quality of the writing.

> No, there is not a dawn in eastern skies
> To rift the fiery night that's in your eyes;
> But there, where western glooms are gathering,
> The dark will end the dark, if anything:
> God slays Himself with every leaf that flies,
> And hell is more than half of paradise.
> No, there is not a dawn in eastern skies—
> In eastern skies.

There has been considerable speculation as to the identity of the voice which speaks the poem from "out of the grave." Some readers believe it is the voice of the beloved dead woman. However, the voice refers to the dead woman in the third person, and therefore this interpretation presents difficulties. It may be a projection from Havergal's subconscious mind—the oral hallucination of a man driven almost mad with grief. It is the same voice perhaps that Matthias (in *Matthias at the Door*) hears in a dream which tells him that he cannot die until he is born. When he asks whose voice it is, he is told:

> ". . . All voices are one voice, with many tongues
> To make it inexpressible and obscure
> To us until we hear the voice itself. . . ."

Robinson's own comments on "Luke Havergal" have not been particularly enlightening. In his letters to Edith Brower he refers to the poem as "the most rural of all the things I have done,"[40] and he also says to her "the meaning is all suggested, and is not capable of a definite working-out by anyone who doesn't happen to sympathize with the writer's fancy."[41] In a letter to Daniel Gregory Mason he calls the poem "my uncomfortable abstraction,"[42] and in writing to Harry de Forest Smith he makes what until recently has been considered the most puzzling statement of all, "I also have a piece of deliberate degeneration called 'Luke Havergal' which is not at all funny."[43] Robinson's modesty is notorious, but surely to call one of his best poems "a piece of deliberate degeneration" seems to be overdoing it a bit—until we read the convincing explanation offered by Richard P. Adams.[44] Robinson had been reading Max Nordau's *Degeneration* about the time he was writing "Luke Havergal."[45]

Nordau uses the term *degenerate* to characterize the work of the French symbolists, especially Verlaine. The word as used by Robinson is not necessarily pejorative. He is saying that he has written a symbolist poem in the manner of Verlaine—which indeed he has, for it exhibits the major characteristics of Verlaine's poetry: a melancholy tone, haunting word music, and symbolic complexity. It is probable that Robinson thought more highly of Verlaine than Nordau did; however, he sympathized with Nordau's point of view to some extent and published "A Poem for Max Nordau" in his first book, but did not subsequently reprint it. The poem is a parody of the symbolist style and begins "Dun shades quiver down the lone long fallow."[46] Another French influence on this poem has been noted by Peter Dechert, who suggests that the echo effect throughout the poem was the result of Robinson's assiduous practice with the French rondeau form early in his career.[47]

Like most symbolist poetry, "Luke Havergal" has suggested many interpretations, indeed, directly conflicting interpretations. Some readers, including myself, believe it is an invitation to suicide. However, Richard Adams, Lincoln MacVeagh, and no doubt others, hold that Havergal is advised to endure, to reject the thought of suicide. MacVeagh says, "There is no action, no story told, there is only the voice of the spirit telling a man, who has lost the woman he loves, to live out his life in patience for her sake."[48] And Adams says, "Luke Havergal is being advised against suicide. He is being urged not to die but to live, and to keep his love alive by accepting the bitter fact that his lover is dead."[49]

Compassionate irony (rather than what Ellsworth Barnard calls whimsicality) is the tone and attitude employed by Robinson in his best poems dealing with alienated or socially maladjusted characters, as evidenced by the sirens in "Veteran Sirens" and Eben Flood in "Mr. Flood's Party." "Veteran Sirens" is short enough to quote entire:

> The ghost of Ninon would be sorry now
> To laugh at them, were she to see them here,
> So brave and so alert for learning how
> To fence with reason for another year.
>
> Age offers a far comelier diadem
> Than theirs; but anguish has no eye for grace,
> When time's malicious mercy cautions them
> To think a while of number and of space.
>
> The burning hope, the worn expectancy,
> The martyred humor, and the maimed allure,
> Cry out for time to end his levity,
> And age to soften its investiture;
>
> But they, though others fade and are still fair,
> Defy their fairness and are unsubdued;
> Although they suffer, they may not forswear
> The patient ardor of the unpursued.

> Poor flesh, to fight the calendar so long;
> Poor vanity, so quaint and yet so brave;
> Poor folly, so deceived and yet so strong,
> So far from Ninon and so near the grave.

There has been some discussion concerning the title. Yvor Winters referred to the women as "old prostitutes who must continue as best they are able in their trade."[50] Ellsworth Barnard prefers to call them "superannuated flirts."[51] Laurence Perrine also objects to their being called prostitutes because, he says, Robinson never showed any sympathy for commercialized love.[52] However, Ronald Moran has demonstrated that Robinson expressed considerable sympathy for the prostitutes he visited thirty or forty times in one month when he was at Harvard in 1892.[53] Therefore, Winters's comment cannot be objected to for the reason given by Perrine. Perrine thinks of them as elderly spinsters who refuse to accept their age and their spinsterhood gracefully. Robinson's title is, let us recall, not "Old Prostitutes" or "Superannuated Flirts" or "Elderly Spinsters"—it is "Veteran Sirens." The dictionary definition of *siren* is an "alluring or dangerous woman." And when coupled with the word "veteran," the title conveys an irony and pathos identical with the entire poem. Imagine the effect if Robinson had called his poem "Ancient Whores." Yet I suspect that Winters and Louis Coxe (who twenty years later reaffirmed Winters's opinion)[54] are right in that the genesis of the poem was Robinson's experience with, and compassion for, prostitutes. Ninon de l'Enclos (1620–1705), referred to in the first and last lines, was a Parisian famous for her beauty which lasted until her seventies.

The kind of irony which Robinson achieves in this poem seems to me far superior to the facile romantic irony of Laforgue and Eliot and superior also to the rather shallow and sometimes melodramatic cynicism of some of Hardy's poems, such as those in the *Satires of Circumstance*. Robinson's irony here is used to qualify and moderate feeling in danger of becoming sentimental or falsely "tragic." The plight of the sirens who "fight the calendar so long" is movingly generalized in the final lines to apply to all humanity.

"Mr. Flood's Party," one of Robinson's most famous poems, and justifiably so, like "Veteran Sirens" comes close to sentimentality but just manages to avoid it. And once again the poet succeeds in transcending the immediate subject of his poem—a village character suggested by a Maine eccentric who proposed toasts to himself—old, lonely, alienated, and with a taste for liquor, a weakness which Robinson understood. Mr. Flood holds a one-man drinking party on a hill overlooking Tilbury Town, which he has just visited to replenish his jug. He proposes toasts to his dead friends and to himself. He raises the jug to his lips

> Alone, as if enduring to the end
> A valiant armor of scarred hopes outworn,
> He stood there in the middle of the road
> Like Roland's ghost winding a silent horn.

Roland, it will be remembered, after a long struggle raised the horn to his lips just before he died—thus admitting defeat. And

> soon amid the silver loneliness
> Of night he lifted up his voice and sang,
> Secure, with only two moons listening,
> Until the whole harmonious landscape rang—

The word *secure* is ironic. For even Flood's "security," as well as that of his jug, is like that of all of us, illusory. As Emery Neff has said, "Landscape, dramatic narrative, lyricism, irony, humor and pathos blend harmoniously in 'Mr. Flood's Party.' "[55] The poem ends

> There was not much that was ahead of him,
> And there was nothing in the town below—
> Where strangers would have shut the many doors
> That many friends had opened long ago.

Mr. Flood is an eccentric—but the experience which he endures, and in his own peculiar way defies, is common to many men. The poem is a significant and permanent contribution to the literature of alienation.

Another kind of irony, cruel and grim and reminiscent of Swift, is successfully realized in "Karma." A complacent and well-heeled businessman is walking the streets of a northern town during the Christmas holidays. As he observes

> a slowly freezing Santa Claus
> Upon the corner, with his beard and bell

he thinks of a friend whom he had ruined in a financial deal. He wishes his friend was with him now so that during this season of peace and good will he could make him some recompense. But this being impossible, he turns to the figure of Santa Claus:

> And from the fullness of his heart he fished
> A dime for Jesus who had died for men.

This travesty, this commercial degradation of the moral standards of the great religions of the West and of the East, is brilliantly suggested by the shivering Santa Claus asking for and receiving his miserably small contributions for charity and by the title of the poem. *Karma* is the doctrine, common to both Hinduism and Buddhism, that there must be compensation for harm done to others here in our present life or in future reincarnations. Karma is justice, and justice is *fated* to occur. The protagonist of the poem has done considerable harm to another man. He thinks he can square the debt by his appeal to Jesus, who according to Christian belief had squared the debt incurred by Original Sin for all mankind. But of course the ironic implication is that his gesture is hardly enough to satisfy Karmic justice.

"Miniver Cheevy" is a portrait of a romantic dreamer who considers himself to have been born too late for his talents to be recognized:

> Miniver loved the Medici,
>   Albeit he had never seen one;
> He would have sinned incessantly
>   Could he have been one.

> Miniver cursed the commonplace
> And eyed a khaki suit with loathing;
> He missed the mediaeval grace
> Of iron clothing.

He finds his escape in alcoholism and introspective fantasies. The poem is obviously a self-portrait of Robinson — or at least Miniver shares some of Robinson's weaknesses. It is an example of self-deprecatory romantic irony, which we have noted in Laforgue and in Eliot, but Robinson manages through his perfectly controlled style to stand off from his subject, to project Miniver as a character entirely separate from himself, and to see him as he is. The poem does not exhibit the facile self-indulgence of "The Love Song of J. Alfred Prufrock."

The failure of marriage and the psychological problems leading to such failure are the subjects of several of Robinson's long poems: notably *Cavender's House, Matthias at the Door,* and *Roman Bartholow.* The subject is treated incidentally in some of the poet's short poems, two of which merit especial attention — "Eros Turannos" and "The Whip."

The frequently anthologized "Eros Turannos" (Love the Tyrant) is generally considered to be the best of all of Robinson's short poems. Emery Neff calls it "high tragedy in a little room,"[56] and Yvor Winters considered it to be "universal tragedy in a Maine setting."[57] Written in 1913 (the same year in which another great poem, "Hillcrest," was composed) it presents the condensed drama of a wife betrayed by her Judas husband. Too proud to admit her mistake, fearful of a lonely old age, and unable to conquer entirely her love for him, she continues to live with him, but with traumatic psychological consequences that drive her close to madness. The poem presents the situation in a clean expository style devoid of bathos or melodrama and then defines the psychological consequences in some of the most beautiful lines of the twentieth century. Robinson was a lifelong bachelor, but he seems to have observed marital relationships carefully, particularly that of his brother Herman and his beautiful wife Emma Shepherd. Their marriage was, evidently, a failure and Herman died a poverty-stricken alcoholic. According to Chard Powers Smith, Robinson was deeply in love with Emma before, during, and after her marriage, and he considered her "betrayed" by her husband. The case for Robinson's love of Emma is not proven, although there is evidence in its favor. According to Smith, Herman often left Emma alone in their house on Capitol Island off the coast of Maine and the great lines about the sea which close the poem were suggested by this fact.[58] Smith's hypothesis, if true, would in some measure account for the power of the poem. Smith believes it was inspired by, and deals explicitly with, Herman's and Emma's marriage, but here, as in a few other poems, Robinson succeeds in transcending the specific case and universalizing the theme. "Eros Turannos" is one of the great poems on the subject of love betrayed.

In the first stanza the wife fears two things — her husband and (if she were to lose him) a lonely old age. In the second stanza the other two reasons for her acceptance of the situation are given — her pride (she will not make public her mistake) and the fact that Love (Eros the Tyrant) still has power to blur her perception of his weaknesses. The husband, aware of her acceptance of her fate, knows that he will not lose her. The third stanza defines the attitude of the complacent husband:

> A sense of ocean and old trees
> Envelopes and allures him;
> Tradition, touching all he sees,
> Beguiles and reassures him;

The fifth stanza brilliantly depicts the psychological state of the woman caught in this marital dilemma and the attitude of the townspeople toward her isolation:

> The falling leaf inaugurates
> The reign of her confusion;
> The pounding wave reverberates
> The dirge of her illusion;
> And home, where passion lived and died,
> Becomes a place where she can hide,
> While all the town and harbor side
> Vibrate with her seclusion.

The next stanza develops the attitude of the townspeople and the poet toward her situation. The phrase "tapping on our brows" suggests the woman is considered mad or close to madness. The final stanza generalizes the case. They that strive with Eros must take the consequences:

> Though like waves breaking it may be,
> Or like a changed familiar tree,
> Or like a stairway to the sea
> Where down the blind are driven.

"The Whip," one of the most obscure of the short poems, has been the subject of considerable explicatory discussion and controversy.[59] The poem obviously depicts a tragedy of love, but the relationship of the characters and the exact nature of the tragic outcome is not made clear. The following interpretation seems to me to solve most of the problems raised by the poet's maddeningly indirect approach to the action of the poem.

A husband suspecting his wife of infidelity traps her with her lover, gives chase to the fleeing lovers, probably on horseback, and all three plunge into a river, the husband "but a neck behind" his wife. She turns and strikes him across the face with her whip. He chooses "to plunge and sink" and the lovers escape. In the first stanza the narrator appears to be gazing down on the body of the husband in the coffin. There is a blue welt on the face, but it is not mentioned until the penultimate stanza. The narrator, addressing the body, says that all is over: doubt, tyranny, wrong, ruin, and "the cynic net you cast." In the second stanza we learn something of the circumstances of his death. It is "the gift the river gave." In the third stanza we learn that the wife and the lover were allowed to find "their own way to the brink," while the husband chose to drown. In the next stanza it is stated that the husband's good name has suffered as a result of the scandal and that there is something on his face, "blue, curious, like a welt." In the final stanza the welt is explained as the result of a blow by the wife. The motivation for the husband's "suicide" is probably fear of facing the ruin of his name and a realization of his wife's hatred for him. He could not bear to survive with this knowledge of the hatred of a woman whom he abjectly loved. The narrator never states that the dead man was a husband or the woman his wife. The three are referred to at the end of the second stanza as "mistress," "slave," and "lover." I have interpreted "slave" as the husband tyrannized by love just as the wife in "Eros Turannos" was tyrannized. To interpret the slave literally as a black servant does not (it seems to me) make a satisfactory explanation of the poem possible. The poem is an interesting example of Robinson's concern with the tragedy of marriage, and remarkable because although the story behind the poem is obscure and the relationship of the three characters is also obscure, the style, line by line, is crisp, clear, and dramatic.

That Robinson was obsessed with eccentrics and failures is a cliché of Robinsonian criticism, but I would like to suggest that some of his most popular poems on the subject, such as the sensational "Richard Cory" and "Flammonde" — both stereotyped in language and superficial in feeling — have undeservedly drawn attention away from several finer poems. Robinson has been the victim of anthologists who choose their poems from previous anthologies. Line for line the almost unknown poem "Doctor of Billiards" is better written than "Richard Cory." Of his "Doctor," Robinson said he was picturing "a man who seems to be throwing away a life which, for some reason known only to himself, is no longer worth living."[60] It is evident from the tone of the poem that Robinson believes there is no valid reason for the doctor, or for any man, to waste a life on mastering a trivial game such as billiards. He is revealed for what he is in severe, plain, expository verse, without compassion and even without irony:

> You click away the kingdom that is yours,
> And you click off your crown for cap and bells;
> You smile, who are still master of the feast,
> And for your smile we credit you the least;
> But when your false, unhallowed laugh occurs,
> We seem to think there may be something else.

The writing here, particularly that of the last line quoted, seems to me superior to that of the melodramatic "Richard Cory":

> So on we worked, and waited for the light,
> And went without the meat, and cursed the bread;
> And Richard Cory, one calm summer night,
> Went home and put a bullet through his head.

"Lost Anchors" is somewhat better known than "Doctor of Billiards." It is almost as obscure as "The Whip," and its meaning has been strenuously debated.[61] I quote the entire poem:

> Like a dry fish flung inland far from shore,
> There lived a sailor, warped and ocean-browned,
> Who told of an old vessel, harbor-drowned
> And out of mind a century before,
> Where divers, on descending to explore
> A legend that had lived its way around
> The world of ships, in the dark hulk had found
> Anchors, which had been seized and seen no more.
>
> Improving a dry leisure to invest
> Their misadventure with a manifest
> Analogy that he may read who runs,
> The sailor made it old as ocean grass —
> Telling of much that once had come to pass
> With him, whose mother should have had no sons.

The sailor so beautifully and precisely described in the first two lines is another of Robinson's alienated or misplaced persons. He is "Like a dry fish flung inland." He is, as the title suggests, like a lost anchor, or he is one of many who have lost their anchors. The anchors analogical of the sailor's life are introduced by memories of a story of their discovery, told by the sailor himself. This is the most obscure passage in the poem. It can be paraphrased as follows. A century ago a vessel had sunk in the harbor and been forgotten. Ships anchoring over the sunken vessel lost their anchors — they were mysteriously seized, an occurrence which gave rise to a legend of some supernatural force at work in the harbor. But divers investigating discovered the entirely natural cause of the seized anchors. They were caught in the hold of the sunken wreck. The reason for the sailor's derelict life unanchored in society is given in the final line. It too has a natural explanation as "old as ocean grass." He is of illegitimate birth. The emphasis on oldness — the word *old* occurs twice — has theological implications of original sin. Because of its obscurity, the poem has been a battleground for explicators. But it also deserves careful reading for the style, which can be described as quiet understatement with sinister undertones. The climax is in the final lines in which the reader becomes suddenly yet subtly aware of the point of the poem — the derelict, asocial life of the illegitimate victim who is not morally responsible for his predicament. And this in turn suggests the universal theme — that of the power of archaic evil in human affairs.

In "The Mill" the protagonists are tragic victims of economic forces beyond their control, and they are treated with compassion in this hauntingly beautiful poem. The action of the poem — double suicide — is melodramatic; yet the poem is not melodrama, for the motivation is completely believable. The aging miller hangs himself in his mill out of despair brought on by economic ruin, and the wife drowns herself in the mill pond out of love and grief for her dead husband. Furthermore, the suicides are described indirectly so that most readers must peruse the poem twice before understanding it. But most important is the extremely plain style, the tone of understatement, and the two concrete lines describing the interior of the mill, which suggest the warmth of a past way of life now no longer possible that contrasts with the impersonal coldness and blackness of the waters of the weir, the place of death. All of this evokes a feeling of

genuine and unsentimental pathos. I quote the widely admired passage from the
second stanza:

> And in the mill there was a warm
>   And mealy fragrance of the past.
> What else there was would only seem
>   To say again what he had meant;
> And what was hanging from a beam
>   Would not have heeded where she went.

The subject was suggested to the poet by a small abandoned mill near the
MacDowell Colony, one of the many family mills driven out of business by the
depression.[62] The poem was frequently anthologized and popular during the
depression thirties, but the quality of the writing should assure it a permanent
place in our minor literature, regardless of changing economic conditions and
politics.

Satirical harshness, on the other hand, is the tone of "Bewick Finzer," for
Finzer brought his economic disaster on himself. He is guilty of one of the sins
which Robinson considers to be capital—greed. Hence

> . . . something crumbled in his brain
> When his half million went.

He became a type and caricature of the ruined, formerly rich, whose entire
existence depends on money:

> The broken voice, the withered neck,
>   The coat worn out with care,
> The cleanliness of indigence,
>   The brilliance of despair. . . .

He is now driven to turning again and again to his friends for a loan:

> Familiar as an old mistake,
>   And futile as regret.

In "The Poor Relation" we see Robinson's style at its best and at its weakest.
Some of the diction and several of the figures of speech are trite and
sentimental—"her forehead shows/ A crinkle that had been her mother's," for
example, and the comparison of the protagonist's life to that of "the plover with
a wounded wing," and later in the poem the comparison of her seclusion to that
of a bird "safe in a comfortable cage." Yet the eighth stanza (quoted below) and
the third and fourth lines of the last stanza are among the most successful and
most powerful in all of Robinson.

The poem depicts the situation of an elderly spinster, once of good social
position, cheated (probably by death) of a husband and family, formerly
beautiful and envied by her female rivals, now living a life of poverty and
seclusion alone with her memories except for occasional duty visits by relatives
and friends. She has accepted her defeat brought about by illness, bad luck, and
the ravages of time, and she turns aside the cheerful chatter of her infrequent

visitors with their suggestions that she may yet find romance, "roses that are still to blow" in the barren wastes of her present existence. Like other Robinson characters, she is resigned to a life of stoical endurance,

> With no illusions to assuage
> The lonely changelessness of dying

while outside her retreat, by contrast, is the "roaring of a world remade," the teeming life of the big city:

> And like a giant harp that hums
> On always, and is always blending
> The coming of what never comes
> With what has past and had an ending,
> The City trembles, throbs, and pounds
> Outside, and through a thousand sounds
> The small intolerable drums
> Of Time are like slow drops descending.

It is this burst of rhetoric in which the crass vitality of the great city is brought to life that retrieves the poem. The image which concludes the stanza, successfully combining the visual and the auditory, expresses perfectly the major theme of the poem — the slow, irresistible, cumulative effects of time. It is one of the finest metaphysical conceits in twentieth-century poetry.

The dangers of irony are forcefully demonstrated when we consider the response over the years of the general reader *and* the professional critic to the sonnet "New England" first published in *The Outlook* of London in 1923 and reprinted in the newspaper of Robinson's home town in Maine, the *Gardiner Journal,* for January 31, 1924. I quote the final version of the sonnet as it appears in the *Collected Poems,* in which Robinson has changed the wording in order to make his ironical intentions clearer than in the original, but not with complete success, as will appear below.

New England

> Here where the wind is always north-north-east
> And children learn to walk on frozen toes,
> Wonder begets an envy of all those
> Who boil elsewhere with such a lyric yeast
> Of love that you will hear them at a feast
> Where demons would appeal for some repose,
> Still clamoring where the chalice overflows
> And crying wildest who have drunk the least.
>
> Passion is here a soilure of the wits,
> We're told, and Love a cross for them to bear;
> Joy shivers in the corner where she knits
> And Conscience always has the rocking-chair,
> Cheerful as when she tortured into fits
> The first cat that was ever killed by Care.

Emory Neff tells the story of what happened when one Gardiner native read the poem:

Aware that reticence had become unpopular with a younger generation of writers bent on displaying emancipation from Puritanism, Robinson included in this volume an ironic sonnet, "New England," caricaturing their disdain. When published in *The Gardiner Journal* for January 31, 1924, it wounded the local patriotism of a subscriber, who retorted with a letter and with a poem charging Robinson with infidelity to his birthplace.[63]

Robinson's reply to the outraged native, directed to the editor of the *Gardiner Journal* and published in that periodical on February 14, 1924, deserves to be quoted in full:

> 28 West Eighth Street,
> New York, February 7, 1924.
>
> *Dear Mr. Berry:*
> Having read Mr. Darling's vigorous letter and still more vigorous poem in the Journal of last week, I find myself constrained to ask for a small amount of space in which to say a few words of explanation. If Mr. Darling will be good enough to give my unfortunate sonnet one more reading, and if he will observe that Intolerance, used ironically, is the subject of the first sentence ("Intolerance born where the wind, etc.") he will see that the whole thing is a satirical attack not upon New England, but upon the same patronizing pagans whom he flays with such vehemence in his own poem. As a matter of fact, I cannot quite see how the first eight lines of my sonnet are to be regarded as even intelligible if read in any other way than as an oblique attack upon all those who are forever throwing dead cats at New England for its alleged emotional and moral frigidity. As for the last six lines, I should suppose that the deliberate insertion of "It seems" would be enough to indicate the key in which they are written. Apparently Mr. Darling has fallen into the not uncommon error of seizing upon certain words and phrases without pausing to consider just why and how they are used.
> Interpretation of one's own irony is always a little distressing, yet in this instance, it appears to be rather necessary. If this leaves Mr. Darling still in doubt, it may be assumed that I have written an unusually bad sonnet—which is quite possible.
>
> Yours very sincerely,
> E. A. Robinson.[64]

Neff goes on to say:

> In republishing the sonnet in *Dionysus in Doubt* he made his meaning obvious by removing a word of personal reference "born," and substituting "we're told" for "it seems." Such are the trials of an ironist among the literal-minded American people, who blindly ridicule other peoples for their deficiency in humor.[65]

It should be added that Robinson also changed the words "Intolerance tells" to "Wonder begets" in the third line to make his meaning still clearer. The first three lines of the sonnet originally read:

> Born where the wind is always north-north-east
> And children learn to walk on frozen toes,
> Intolerance tells an envy of all those. . . .

Robinson's ironic intention, then, would seem to have been made sufficiently clear by the poet himself in his letter of 1924 and in his revised poem in 1925, as well as by Emery Neff in his comments of 1948, but evidently doubts persisted, for an M. B. D. queried the editor of the *Explicator,* October 1951, as to "how Robinson's 'New England' can be construed as an attack not upon New England, but upon the 'patronizing pagans' referred to by Benét and Pearson" (*Oxford Anthology,* p. 127). H. H. Waggoner and Richard E. Amacher responded with a detailed line by line analysis demonstrating the success of Robinson's ironical attack upon New England's enemies.[66] It is with some surprise, then, that one reads "E. A. Robinson's Yankee Conscience" by W. R. Robinson[67] which opens with a quotation of the poem followed by an in depth analysis of several pages arguing that the poem is an attack upon the narrowness and coldness of New England life and that Robinson is demonstrating his moral and imaginative vitality by freeing himself from his New England conscience:

> Certainly Conscience, despite its authoritative zeal and its considerable success in intimidating the warm feelings, fails to squelch completely the vital urges: the poem, written in protest of its inhumanity, does defy its moral tyranny in castigating New England as a place and a community.... "New England" is anything but chauvinistic. In it a stubborn New Englander perversely turns upon his native ground the very qualities it prides itself upon, and it is this friction between the two that readily stands out as the salient fact in the imagination's relationship to its environment.[68]

Now the poet is of course doing nothing of the sort. It is stated clearly in his letter and it is implied in every line of the poem that the poet is defending New England against those who consider it unduly ascetic and conscience-ridden, and in the course of his defense he has several snide remarks to make on the pagan, hedonistic critics of the New England way, those who "boil elsewhere with such a lyric yeast." The personification of Conscience in the final lines is a caricature and is obviously not to be taken at face value.

There have been no serious problems in interpreting "Old King Cole," which is written in a style similar to that of W. M. Praed.[69] It is an amusingly ironic portrait of a village character and his two wasteful heirs:

> The world went on, their fame went on,
> And they went on—from bad to worse.

The poem has little depth, but it is a successfully executed minor performance and though it is a lesser poem deserves to be placed in the same category as "Miniver Cheevy."

"The Clerks," one of Robinson's earliest and most successful very short poems, was first published in the *Boston Evening Transcript,* June 4, 1896. The style is deceptively simple:

> I did not think that I should find them there
> When I came back again, but there they stood.

With one exception all the words in these two lines are monosyllables—just as different from what Robinson called Tennyson's polysyllabic roll as one can imagine. The sonnet marks the beginning of a reaction against the ornamental and inflated rhetoric of the late nineteenth century in favor of the plain style, of poetry of direct and serious statement unqualified by irony. In style and subject this is poetry of the seemingly commonplace. The poet, returning to Tilbury Town after a number of years, finds the shopworn brotherhood, in spite of their humdrum lives, "just as good and just as human as they ever were." He universalizes his subject at the end of the poem. We are all the clerks of Time:

> Poets and kings are but the clerks of Time,
> Tiering the same dull webs of discontent,
> Clipping the same sad alnage of the years.

In a similar vein, the sonnet to George Crabbe, published in the same year as "The Clerks," praises the work of a minor but honest poet of the commonplace lives of small-town people. Two years later Robinson began writing "Aunt Imogen," a character sketch of an old maid who visited her nephews and niece for one month every year, finding in their love compensation for the loneliness of her own life. The most touching lines of the poem are those expressing Aunt Imogen's sense of loss, her sense of what her life might have been if she had married:

>   . . . there was no sweet,
> No bitter now; nor was there anything
> To make a daily meaning for her life—
> Till truth like Harlequin, leapt out somehow
> From ambush and threw sudden savor to it—
> But the blank taste of time. There were no dreams,
> No phantoms in her future any more:
> One clinching revelation of what was
> One by-flash of irrevocable chance,
> Had acridly but honestly foretold
> The mystical fulfilment of a life
> That might have once. . . But that was all gone by:
> There was no need of reaching back for that:
> The triumph was not hers: there was no love
> Save borrowed love: there was no might have been.

The lines are probably autobiographical. Robinson's grandnephew, David Nivison,[70] thinks that Aunt Imogen is very much like Robinson himself, and Hagedorn[71] suggests that Robinson composed the poem after visits to his three nieces and that the relationship between the aunt and her nephews and niece is really Robinson's own experience. Much of this is probably true; as to the composition of the poem we have Robinson's own evidence. He wrote to D. G. Mason in 1900 that he was "wearing poetical petticoats and making a regular analysis of an old maid." He goes on to say, "I did it in the rough two years ago, when I had my eyrie over Brown's dry goods store and smoked 'Before the War' cigars. I had a good mill-pond to look out on and somehow conceived the notion of writing down this particular spinster. Maybe I thought she ought to have drowned herself; at any rate the mill-pond has something to do with it."[72] As in "The Clerks" and "George Crabbe," the style is simple in diction and restrained in feeling. The poem has frequently been referred to as Wordsworthian, and it suggests comparison with "Michael"; however, Robinson does not succeed in generalizing his subject as Wordsworth does in "Michael." W. W. Robson makes the same point in comparing "Michael" to Frost's "The Death of the Hired Man." He says:

> The significant difference between the poems—the difference in spiritual value—lies in the pastoral quality with which Wordsworth invests his simple story. He uses pastoral—normally a mode of irony for Frost—with complete seriousness; and the result is that generalizing effect which we look for in poetry of the highest order. By including this pastoral element Wordsworth has got further away from his characters than Frost; but he has also given a greater universality to his theme.[73]

The point is an important one. Because of their lack of "generalizing effect," "The Death of the Hired Man" and "Aunt Imogen" are minor poems compared to "Michael."

However, Robinson, more frequently than Frost, I think, does succeed in generalizing his particular experience in a number of his best poems, especially in "Isaac and Archibald" which also reminds us of Wordsworth in its subject matter, and the generalizing effect is achieved in part by Robinson's use of the pastoral mode. I would like to argue that Robinson's poem is equal or almost equal to Wordsworth's in its universal appeal and yet remains closer to its characters than does "Michael." Furthermore, in the authenticity and perceptiveness of its descriptive detail it is superior to Wordsworth. For Robinson here writes with his eye on the object; Wordsworth frequently does not. That is, "Isaac and Archibald" combines, in my opinion, a maximum of perceptive particularity with a maximum of universality. The poem was probably suggested by Robinson's visits when a boy to his two granduncles on his grandfather Palmer's farm.[74] The narrator looks back on a time when he was a youth of twelve living in the country. He was acquainted with two old farmers, Isaac and Archibald. The poem is á character sketch of these two slightly eccentric persons in the twilight of their lives. It defines the relationship of the two farmers to each other and to the boy, and it defines also the boy's attitude toward them at the time of the action. Furthermore, it defines the present attitude of the now mature narrator after the passage of many years. The past scenes are recalled with nostalgia, almost, but not quite, bordering on sentimentality. At the beginning of the poem the boy in the company of Isaac is on a long walk to Archibald's home. He is told by Isaac that Archibald is becoming more and more eccentric in his behavior, but he should be pardoned because of his advanced age. After they reach Archibald's house, the boy finds himself alone with his host, who tells him that Isaac is weakening fast, but that his eccentricities should be excused. The picture of the two men close to death each appraising the mental condition of the other while still maintaining their close friendship is beautifully presented in Robinson's finest style. The poem is a touching and charming evocation of rural life. For example, Isaac and Archibald go into Archibald's cellar for cider:

> Down we went,
> Out of the fiery sunshine to the gloom,
> Grateful and half sepulchral, where we found
> The barrels, like eight potent sentinels,
> Close ranged along the wall. From one of them
> A bright pine spile stuck out alluringly,
> And on the black flat stone, just under it,
> Glimmered a late-spilled proof that Archibald
> Had spoken from unfeigned experience.
> There was a fluted antique water-glass
> Close by, and in it, prisoned, or at rest,
> There was a cricket, of the brown soft sort
> That feeds on darkness. Isaac turned him out,
> And touched him with his thumb to make him jump,
> And then composedly pulled out the plug
> With such a practised hand that scarce a drop
> Did even touch his fingers. Then he drank
> And smacked his lips with a slow patronage
> And looked along the line of barrels there
> With a pride that may have been forgetfulness
> That they were Archibald's and not his own.
> "I never twist a spigot nowadays,"
> He said, and raised the glass up to the light,
> "But I thank God for orchards." And that glass
> Was filled repeatedly for the same hand
> Before I thought it worth while to discern
> Again that I was young, and that old age,
> With all his woes, had some advantages.

This quotation illustrates the poem at the level of the particular. But the poem is much more than a mere description of the pleasures of rural life. At the level of the general it is a moving meditation on the passage of time and the inevitability of death. After the scene in the cellar, Isaac goes for a walk, leaving Archibald to comment on the changes he has noticed in Isaac. After touching his forehead he says

> . . . Isaac is not quite right.
> You see it, but you don't know what it means:
> The thousand little differences — no,
> You do not know them, and it's well you don't;
> You'll know them soon enough.

The old man then advises the boy as he grows older to remember

> the light behind the stars.
> Remember that: remember that I said it.

The light in this passage and elsewhere in the poem, as one commentator has noted,[75] seems to suggest a state of natural grace in which Isaac and Archibald have been passing their lives. It appears to be Robinson's substitute for the divine and saving grace of his Calvinistic puritan ancestors. The combination of

Archibald's words and the cider puts the boy into a state of reverie in which the lives of the two farmers mingle with the lives of Homeric and biblical heroes, which are freshly in his mind from his lessons at school:

> So I lay dreaming of what things I would,
> Calm and incorrigibly satisfied
> With apples and romance and ignorance,
> And the still smoke from Archibald's clay pipe.
> There was a stillness over everything,
> As if the spirit of heat had laid its hand
> Upon the world and hushed it; and I felt
> Within the mightiness of the white sun
> That smote the land around us and wrought out
> A fragrance from the trees, a vital warmth
> And fullness for the time that was to come,
> And a glory for the world beyond the forest.
> The present and the future and the past,
> Isaac and Archibald, the burning bush,
> The Trojans and the walls of Jericho,
> Were beautifully fused.

The point of view of most of the poem is that of the boy as he grows more and more aware of old age and death. The tone of the poem is one of compassionate understanding, saved from sentimentality by a hint of detached irony. By the time we reach the end of the poem the point of view is that of the mature narrator who is able to universalize his material, whereas, if the point of view of the twelve-year-old had been maintained throughout, no such generalizing effect would have been possible. The poem concludes as follows:

> Isaac and Archibald have gone their way
> To the silence of the loved and well-forgotten.
> I knew them, and I may have laughed at them;
> But there's a laughing that has honor in it,
> And I have no regret for light words now.
> Rather I think sometimes they may have made
> Their sport of me; — but they would not do that,
> They were too old for that. They were old men,
> And I may laugh at them because I knew them.

According to Hagedorn, "For a Dead Lady," first published in 1909, is about Robinson's mother,[76] and Robinson's explanation to Edith Brower of the difficult line "The laugh that love could not forgive" indicates that the poet had a particular lady in mind. Robinson's explanation of the line is this, "I never thought of indicating anything more than her way of presuming on her attractions and 'guying' those who admire her."[77] There is one other difficult line that could refer to an incident in the life of a particular person, "The breast where roses could not live," but probably Richard Adams's explanation of this line is correct, that in death the breast had lost the color of life, of blood coursing through the veins, and thus the line could refer to any dead lady.[78] But whether the poem was inspired by a certain lady or no, the poem as a whole becomes universalized into a lament for the dead, for the loss of that which was beautiful, and the protagonist is not markedly individualized. There are no comforting thoughts about immortality, about the rewards of a life well lived. Death is caused by inexorable laws "that have creation in their keeping." Death cannot be understood. It is simply to be endured. The style is hard and brilliant:

> No more shall quiver down the days
> The flowing wonder of her ways,
> Whereof no language may requite
> The shifting and the many-shaded.
>
> The grace, divine, definitive,
> Clings only as a faint forestalling.

The last two lines quoted have that generalizing effect we noted in the discussion of "Isaac and Archibald" above.

"The Sheaves," published in 1923, is one of the most beautiful and at the same time one of the clearest and simplest poems that Robinson wrote. The theme is ancient and universal — the mystery of seasonal change, particularized in the opening lines as the change that appears in a field of ripening grain. In the final lines, by means of a simile the change is extended into the human realm so that the theme of the poem is broadened to include the mystery of growth and decay of all forms of life, together with an awareness of the essential beauty of life and the inevitable loss of that beauty as it is manifested in particular forms. Although the vehicles of the two poems differ, the tenor of "The Sheaves" is almost identical with that of "For a Dead Lady" — almost but not quite. In "For a Dead Lady" the emphasis is on the loss of that which was beautiful and on the inexorable laws that make "Time so vicious in his reaping." The same laws are operating in "The Sheaves" and yet, because *seasonal* change is the first motivating fact of the poem, there is a suggestion that the loss of beauty (the golden grain) is not permanent, for the grain will reappear next year. This fact is not plainly stated, but it is there by implication, and the awareness of it results in a tone much less bitter than that of "For a Dead Lady." The feeling evoked is one of appreciation for the mysterious force that brings so much beauty into the world even though that beauty in its individualizing forms must inevitably disappear. And so we have the astonishingly lovely lines of the sestet:

> So in a land where all days are not fair,
> Fair days went on till on another day
> A thousand golden sheaves were lying there,
> Shining and still, but not for long to stay —
> As if a thousand girls with golden hair
> Might rise from where they slept and go away.

We do not think of Robinson as a political propagandist nor as a man who was vitally concerned with political or sociological problems. His chief interests were elsewhere. Nevertheless, he had political convictions and he expressed them forcefully from time to time.[79] Among his shorter poems "The Master" (1909) and "The Revealer" (1910) are perhaps the best in this category. They are excellent character sketches of Abraham Lincoln and Theodore Roosevelt. Both poems praise strong leadership, and implicit in both poems is Robinson's conviction that democracy without strong leadership will perish. "The Master" carries the author's note "supposed to have been written not long after the Civil War," that is, shortly after Lincoln's death and about the time of Robinson's birth. However, in spite of the shift in time, the voice of the persona is that of Robinson himself, speaking in hard epigrammatic lines in a tone of bitter irony close to cynicism. The structure of the poem is not one of development but rather of constant repetition of a single point—the contrast between Lincoln's high worth as a political leader and the low estimation held of him by most Americans of the Civil War period. When Lincoln became president the majority mocked and jeered him. Only slowly, under the pressure of national tragedy and finally as a result of the martyrdom of Lincoln himself, were a few Americans educated into realizing his true worth. Here, as in his other political poems (especially "The Revealer," "Cassandra," and "Dionysus in Doubt") Robinson showed considerable impatience with the limited intelligence and culture of the common man. The best hope for democracy is to convince the common man of his own shortcomings and of the necessity of trusting in the leadership and example of "one Titan at a time" such as Lincoln:

> He knew that we must all be taught
> Like little children in a school.

The theme of the poem is summed up in the first four lines:

> A flying word from here and there
> Had sown the name at which we sneered,
> But soon the name was everywhere,
> To be reviled and then revered.

The contrast between the people and the leader who saved them is then elaborated upon for the next nine and a half stanzas. The president's fame will last forever, whereas those who jeered him will be forgotten. He was capable of seeing through deception when most men were "sore beguiled"; he ruled by mildness and good humor—"shrewd, hallowed, and harassed." There was something ancient, timeless, and tragic in his personality which has left its eternal mark on us:

> For he, to whom we had applied
> Our shopman's test of age and worth,
> Was elemental when he died,
> As he was ancient at his birth:
> The saddest among kings of earth,
> Bowed with a galling crown, this man
> Met rancor with a cryptic mirth,
> Laconic—and Olympian.

President Theodore Roosevelt, it will be remembered, praised Robinson's poetry early in the poet's career, published a favorable review of the second edition of *The Children of the Night* in the *Outlook* in 1905,[80] and gave him a sinecure in the New York Customs House, which began in 1905 and ended in 1909 when Taft became president. It is natural, then, that Robinson should be grateful to him. However, even without the favors Roosevelt had shown him, Robinson (who had a predilection for strong men — at one time in his life he admired Carlyle) would naturally have been drawn to the president's personality. Robinson dedicated *The Town Down the River* (1910) to him. The volume contained three poems on Roosevelt — "Au Revoir," "The Pilot," and "The Revealer" — of which the last named is the best and also the most obscure. It was rejected for the *Outlook* by Lyman Abbott, to whom Robinson refers in a letter to Louis Ledoux dated July 20, 1910: "By the way, did Abbott seem to know what I am driving at in T.R. or did he disagree with some degree of intelligence? I have encountered so much rotten imbecility in the way of failure to get my meaning that I am beginning to wonder myself if it may not be vague. But I won't have it anything worse than obscure, which I meant it to be — to a certain extent."[81]

In "The Revealer," Roosevelt is depicted as another Titan who showed us the necessity of rising above our crass materialism. American greed is the main object of attack from the opening lines of the poem:

> The palms of Mammon have disowned
> The gift of our complacency

to the eighth and final stanza:

> Down to our nose's very end
> We see, and are invincible, —
> Too vigilant to comprehend
> The scope of what we cannot sell.

It is the trust-busting Roosevelt who is eulogized here. The poem has as its epigraph a passage from Judges 14:

> He turned aside to see the carcase of the lion: and behold, there was a swarm of bees and honey in the carcase of the lion. . . . And the men of the city said unto him, What is sweeter than honey? and what is stronger than a lion?

Samson, it will be remembered, while on his way to arrange a feast for his marriage to a Philistine bride, was accosted by a young lion who roared at him. Samson slew it with his bare hands. A few days later on a return trip he noticed a swarm of bees in the carcass of this same lion, and honey. He ate of the honey and then at the marriage feast he taunted the Philistine groomsmen with a riddle and a wager. The riddle was, "Out of the eater came forth meat [i.e. something to eat]; out of the strong came forth sweetness." The groomsmen were unable to answer the riddle until Samson's bride betrayed him by soliciting the answer from her husband and giving it to the groomsmen, who won the bet. Robinson makes use of the biblical story of Samson in the first six stanzas of his poem. The lion is pluralized. The lions become suspicious of the hero, Roosevelt, and regard him (in stanzas 2 and 3)

> With scared, reactionary eyes. . .
> For they will never understand
> What they have never seen before.

The lions are obviously symbols of the Establishment, of the oligarchy of American capitalists who found their new leader unexpectedly liberal. (These lions, by the way, appear in a slightly altered form a few years later in "The Wandering Jew.")

In stanza 4, as a result of Roosevelt's leadership, a new light is thrown on the ills of our age and in another reference to the Samson story

> The combs of long-defended hives
> Now drip dishonored and unclean.

The poet goes on to say that we have now no Nazarite (Samson) or Nazarene (Christ)

> to prove
> The difference that is between
> Dead lions — or the sweet thereof

which appears to be one of the deliberately obscure passages to which Robinson refers in his letter quoted above. In the opening lines of the next stanza he says of Roosevelt

> But not for lions, live or dead,
> Except as we are all as one,
> Is he the world's accredited
> Revealer of what we have done;
> What You and I and Anderson
> Are still to do is his reward.

The meaning seems to be that the rewards of victory over the special interests can also be corrupting. The reforming zeal of Roosevelt must be carried on after he is gone and America must continue to purge itself of its materialism, its Tyrian heritage mentioned in the first stanza. Otherwise there may be general catastrophe (referred to in the sixth stanza) such as that which occurred when Samson destroyed Dagon's temple:

> We cannot answer for the floors
> We crowd on, or for walls that shake.

On the other hand, Robinson's phrase "walls that shake" may refer to Joshua before Jericho. The use of biblical material in this poem is not always clear or consistent in detail. However, the general intention is comprehensible and the style is hard, epigrammatic, and vigorous.

"Cassandra," first published in 1914, is another attack on American materialism written in a clear direct style with legendary material used less deviously than in "The Revealer." Cassandra, who foretold the doom of Troy, warns America of a similar fate unless it reforms. What is wrong with America? We have substituted money for religion (stanzas 1 and 2); we are not guided by reason (stanza 3); we are young, brash, pampered, and untried (stanzas 4 and 5); we think that we have had our last great wars and that the millennium is approaching, but we cannot see into the future as accurately as we think (stanzas 6 and 7); we have a new trinity of the Dollar, Dove, and Eagle, but the Eagle will devour its own children (stanzas 8 and 9); we have power but not the wisdom to be guided by the past (stanza 10):

> "The power is yours, but not the sight,
>   You see not upon what you tread;
> You have the ages for your guide,
>   But not the wisdom to be led."

We may, by treading down the old verities, pay for what we have with all we are, and few will heed this warning (stanzas 11 and 12). The poem is a memorable, but too broad, expression of moral indignation; it lacks the depth, the complexity, and the perceptive particularity of Robinson's best short poems.

"Souvenir" was first published in 1918. There is no objective evidence that I have been able to find that Robinson had read the sonnets of his fellow New Englander Frederick Goddard Tuckerman (1821–73) by that time, although of course he may have done so. Years after Robinson wrote "Souvenir," Tuckerman was rediscovered by Witter Bynner, who published his *Sonnets* in 1931 and sent a copy to Robinson inscribed "To Edwin Arlington Robinson. What do you think of him? E. A., Witter Bynner."[82] Robinson might have read the sonnets in an earlier edition; the first was published in 1860. In any event, Robinson's hauntingly beautiful poem reminds one of Tuckerman's sonnets, particularly number ten of the first series, beginning "An upper chamber in a darkened house." Both poems are meditations on death, both poems are focused on similar remembered scenes, that is, a house, and on a single figure in the house who is associated with death, both poems gain their evocative power by the use of images drawn from foliage surrounding the house, both poems employ (but with certain differences noted below) what Yvor Winters has described as "post-symbolic imagery." I quote the poems for comparison. The first is by Tuckerman.

> An upper chamber in a darkened house,
> Where, ere his footsteps reached ripe manhood's brink,
> Terror and anguish were his lot to drink;
> I cannot rid the thought nor hold it close
> But dimly dream upon that man alone:
> Now though the autumn clouds most softly pass,
> The cricket chides beneath the doorstep stone
> And greener than the season grows the grass.
> Nor can I drop my lids nor shade my brows,
> But there he stands beside the lifted sash;
> And with a swooning of the heart, I think
> Where the black shingles slope to meet the boughs
> And shattered on the roof like smallest snows,
> The tiny petals of the mountain ash.

Souvenir

A vanished house that for an hour I knew

By some forgotten chance when I was young
Had once a glimmering window overhung
With honeysuckle wet with evening dew.
Along the path tall dusky dahlias grew,
And shadowy hydrangeas reached and swung
Ferociously; and over me, among
The moths and mysteries, a blurred bat flew.

Somewhere within there were dim presences
Of days that hovered and of years gone by.
I waited, and between their silences
There was an evanescent faded noise;
And though a child, I knew it was the voice
Of one whose occupation was to die.

In a detailed analysis of Tuckerman's sonnet, Eugene England[83] argues convincingly that the figure in the house is that of Tuckerman himself grieving over the death of his wife, and of the style he says that Tuckerman has succeeded in using "natural description in the process of both creating and understanding perception and feeling."[84] He goes on to say that the "last lines are an example, probably the earliest in literary history of a new powerful technique used in modern poetry."[85] The technique is postsymbolism, as defined by Yvor Winters in his essay "Poetic Styles, Old and New" (1959).[86] Winters employs the term again in his foreword to N. Scott Momaday's edition of Tuckerman's poems.[87] He says of Tuckerman's best imagery as it occurs in "An upper chamber" and elsewhere:

> . . .theme and abstract statement charge the imagery with meaning, with the result that the imagery has the force of abstract statement.[88]

and

> . . . the thought of the poem exists in the imagery and develops through it.[89]

Postsymbolist poetry is marked by sharpness of sensory detail, but the detail is not merely descriptive; it is charged with meaning. The final lines of Tuckerman's poem have especially fine detail and are powerfully evocative, although the meaning is somewhat obscure. An abstract statement such as the final line of Robinson's poem would have helped. Probably, as England says, the tiny petals of the mountain ash shattered on the black roof suggest the juxtaposition of beauty and death. In Robinson's poem the hydrangeas which swing ferociously, the blurred bat, the moths, and the honeysuckle wet with morning dew evoke a feeling the motivation of which is clearly and powerfully stated in the final line in unequivocal, abstract language. In Tuckerman's sonnet the final line is completely imagistic. It takes the place of abstract statement, that is, "the imagery has the force of abstract statement," or at least that was probably Tuckerman's intention. There is an important difference, then, between the two poems, for Tuckerman's poem has no clear statement in abstract language of its theme. Furthermore, the imagery of Tuckerman's poem is sharper and more precise than that of Robinson's poem. Tuckerman's sensibility is closer to what we might call pure postsymbolism. Nevertheless, Robinson's sensibility in this one poem (and perhaps in "Luke Havergal" as well) reminds one of the postsymbolists and in a minor way it points to the later and more successful use of the method by Wallace Stevens and Yvor Winters.

Robinson's genius in writing the poem of medium length can best be illustrated by three important works all published in a short span of time, 1919–21. They are "The Wandering Jew," "The Three Taverns," and "Rembrandt to Rembrandt."

Edwin Arlington Robinson's "The Wandering Jew," first published in London in *Outlook,* December 24, 1919, and reprinted the next year in *The Three Taverns,* received almost no critical attention by early writers on Robinson from the twenties until the mid-forties. It is not even mentioned in the standard critical biographies of Hermann Hagedorn (1938) and Emery Neff (1948). Chard Powers Smith, in *Where the Light Falls* (1965), is equally silent. The first serious critical evaluation is by Yvor Winters, who in 1946 called it "one of the great poems not only of our time but of our language."[90] Two decades later George K. Anderson quoted the first four lines as an epigraph to his book *The Legend of the Wandering Jew* (1965) and stated, "The poem is without question the finest American treatment of the subject."[91] Louis O. Coxe (who acknowledges the influence of Winters's book on Robinson) has some perceptive things to say about the poem in his *Edwin Arlington Robinson: The Life of Poetry* (1969)[92] and in his essay "E. A. Robinson: The Lost Tradition."[93] Although there is an impressive amount of criticism extant on Robinson (even though he has never regained the popularity he had in the late twenties), there is very little in it, except for the items noted above, about "The Wandering Jew." The poem, I think, deserves a more extended treatment than it has so far received.

"The Wandering Jew" can best be appreciated through an awareness of several fields of reference—legendary, symbolic, psychological, literary, personal, etc.—all operating simultaneously as one reads the poem.

First of all, the poem derives from legendary material of great age, richness, and complexity, material that has fascinated writers whose talents range from that of the son of President Tyler to those of Shelley and Goethe. For a fairly recent survey of the astonishing number of literary (and nonliterary!) works dealing with the legend from its inception to the middle of the twentieth century, Professor Anderson's book, mentioned above, should be consulted. From it, the reader will learn that Coleridge once planned a poem on the subject, but abandoned it, although Coleridge's interest in the Jew appears in certain characteristics of the Ancient Mariner—his compulsive wandering, for example, and his glittering eye. Goethe planned and started a satiric epic on the Jew but never finished it, probably because, as Anderson points out, he discovered that after the initial confrontation between the Jew and Christ, there is little dramatic tension. The Jew's ceaseless wandering would have to be depicted in an episodic fashion with no suspense, climax, denouement, or ending. Goethe's epic would have had no more structure than a picaresque novel. The legend is most suitable for the symbolic or allegorical short story, such as Hawthorne's "Ethan Brand," or the fairly short expository and allegorical poem such as Robinson's.

In the hundreds of works about the legend, the character of the protagonist is treated in a great many different ways ranging from the incarnation of evil, the devil himself, to the Promethean hero suffering the wrath of God for the benefit of mankind. Sometimes he is even depicted as a Christ figure. Sometimes he is seen as the prototype of the suffering Jewish people. Concomitantly, the attitudes of author and reader range from loathing and hatred, to compassion, to admiration. Robinson's attitude toward his protagonist is complex for reasons which will become evident as we study the poem and its background. How much of the voluminous material on the Jew Robinson had read or heard about is difficult to say. There is no documentary evidence that he knew much of it, and his laconic letter (unpublished) to W. E. Louttit, quoted below, suggests that he had made no special study of it. However, the poem, automatically as it were, gains some depth from the very fact that it has as its frame of reference a legend with so much tradition behind it.

The legend in its barest outline is described by Anderson as follows:

> The true Legend of the Wandering Jew...is the tale of a man in Jerusalem who, when Christ was carrying his Cross to Calvary and paused to rest for a moment on this man's doorstep, drove the Saviour away (with or without physical contact, depending on the variants), crying aloud, "Walk faster!" And Christ replied, "I go, but you will walk until I come again!"[94]

What did Robinson make of this story? And what was *his* conception of the character of the protagonist, who is usually referred to as Ahasuerus? One can do no better than begin with Anderson's paraphrase of Robinson's poem:

> The poet meets Ahasuerus, whom he recognizes from an old childhood image. Old and lonely as the Jew is, he looks like an Old Testament figure, who has not been fortunate enough to have been gathered to his forefathers along with his contemporaries. As the eyes of Ahasuerus meet those of the poet, they stir in the mortal beholder a twinge of compassion. But the poet wonders if this natural twinge of compassion is welcome, for pity can sometimes be offensive, and decides to let the Wanderer talk first about what is in his mind that baffles the human observer. Ahasuerus, however, seems lost in his own thoughts and inarticulate; "a dawning on the dust of years" stimulates his memories but distorts them into supposing that the past is more to be loved than the present. Once, perhaps, he had reviled this past and seen nothing good in life, "as he had seen no good come out of Nazareth." He continues to stand silent, with only the enigmatic gaze streaming from his eyes, as if he were in the presence of One who cannot be dismissed and who never dies. His pride, however, is still with him, stiff and intractable; and he has a right to it, for in all the centuries since his curse was pronounced he has seen many second comings come and go. The poet can only surmise that there may still be defiance mixed with his pride, struggling with repentance; but of this he cannot be sure, for the old unyielding eyes may flash, but they may also flinch and turn aside to look the other way.[95]

In the first three stanzas the poet refers to his hearing of the story of the Wandering Jew when he was a child. This childhood memory is evoked when he confronts the Eternal Jew in the flesh in New York City, "still wandering," still lonely, still remembering "everything." In the final four lines of the second stanza the poet mentions a number of biblical Hebrews who were similar in appearance to the figure before him; but he rejects them all because of the certainty of his identification of this figure as the Wandering Jew himself. This passage does not advance the "argument" very much, but its reference to biblical personages successfully suggests the great age and dignity of the protagonist of the poem. I quote the first three stanzas:

> I saw by looking in his eyes
> That they remembered everything;
> And this was how I came to know
> That he was here, still wandering.
> For though the figure and the scene
> Were never to be reconciled
> I knew the man as I had known
> His image when I was a child.
>
> With evidence at every turn,
> I should have held it safe to guess
> That all the newness of New York
> Had nothing new in loneliness;
> Yet here was one who might be Noah,
> Or Nathan, or Abimelech,
> Or Lamech, out of ages lost, —
> Or, more than all, Melchizedek.
>
> Assured that he was none of these,
> I gave them back their names again,
> To scan once more those endless eyes
> Where all my questions ended then.
> I found in them what they revealed
> That I shall not live to forget,
> And wondered if they found in mine
> Compassion that I might regret.[96]

The last two lines of the quoted passage may be a bit obscure on first reading, but their meaning becomes evident as the poem progresses. They mean that the poet is inclined to pity the Jew until he, the poet, realizes that the Jew scorns compassion and would consider pity of him insulting. Here is the first indication of the protagonist's cardinal sin—pride—which is to be the major moral and psychological theme of the poem. The diction here and throughout the poem is plain, nonornamental, and for the most part abstract. It is Robinson's mature style at its best—economical and precise and entirely suitable for expository and meditative poetry. Rhetorical devices are sparingly used, but when used effective. The phonic echo in the eleventh and twelfth lines and in the nineteenth and twentieth lines, the figure the rhetoricians call *ploce* and *polyptoton*, that is, the repetition of the same phoneme or word root in different parts of speech, is very telling:

> That all the *new*ness of *New* York
> Had nothing *new* in loneliness

> To scan once more those *end*less eyes
> Where all my questions *end*ed then.

The condensed, epigrammatic style of the fourth stanza at first reading presents some difficulty. The poet is saying that just as pity is offensive to the Jew, so also is the fact that the audience of the Jew's "untempered eloquence" is confined to the "tempered ear" of Robinson alone. The protagonist is alienated and unappreciated and driven close to madness:

> Pity, I learned, was not the least
> Of time's offending benefits
> That had now for so long impugned
> The conservation of his wits:
> Rather it was that I should yield,
> Alone, the fealty that presents
> The tribute of a tempered ear
> To an untempered eloquence.

The precision of Robinson's diction is illustrated by the use of the word *fealty*, that is, "obligation to be faithful to a superior." *Fealty* is exactly what the Jew in his pride would expect. In context it is precisely the right word, denotatively, connotatively, phonically, and rhythmically. Like Flammonde, the Jew had "something royal" about him that assumed the loyal respect of his subjects, but the only subject he had in New York at this time was Robinson. The excellent use of repetition in the last two lines should be noted:

> The tribute of a tempered ear
> To an untempered eloquence.

The next stanza presents a vivid picture of spiritual pride in action. The alienated intellectual takes a perverse satisfaction in denouncing the vices of the life around him:

> Before I pondered long enough
> On whence he came and who he was,
> I trembled at his ringing wealth
> Of manifold anathemas;
> I wondered, while he seared the world,
> What new defection ailed the race,
> And if it mattered how remote
> Our fathers were from such a place.

Stanzas 6, 7, and 8 continue the depiction of a fanatic prophet of doom who can see nothing good "on this other side of death." The tone is ironic and critical, and it is clear that whatever pity or admiration the poet may have had for the man, his final evaluation is one of rejection, for the vice of spiritual pride has distorted whatever intellectual brilliance the Jew once had. There are two striking but somewhat obscure figures that require comment, but first the stanzas themselves:

> Before there was an hour for me
> To contemplate with less concern

The crumbling realm awaiting us
Than his that was beyond return,
A dawning on the dust of years
Had shaped with an elusive light
Mirages of remembered scenes
That were no longer for the sight.

For now the gloom that hid the man
Became a daylight on his wrath,
And one wherein my fancy viewed
New lions ramping in his path.
The old were dead and had no fangs,
Wherefore he loved them — seeing not
They were the same that in their time
Had eaten everything they caught.

The world around him was a gift
Of anguish to his eyes and ears,
And one that he had long reviled
As fit for devils, not for seers.
Where, then, was there a place for him
That on this other side of death
Saw nothing good, as he had seen
No good come out of Nazareth?

The beautiful line "A dawning on the dust of years" introduces a sudden change in the Jew — he is beginning to sentimentalize the past that he had once reviled. On the dust of years he begins to see *mirages*, that is, *illusions* of the past which appear to be a contrast to the sordid present. The Jew is indulging in a common form of romantic escapism. The brilliance of Robinson's figure should not pass unnoticed. The *light* of dawn on the *dust* of years would naturally produce *mirages*. The light motif is continued paradoxically in the next stanza — "the gloom that hid the man" becomes daylight wherein are seen "new lions ramping in his path," a difficult trope on first reading, but I interpret the "new lions" as present-day vices to be attacked with the same defiance with which the vices of a past age were attacked, but now because the old lions are dead he loves them, that is, he is romanticizing the past, forgetting that the lions of the past were once vicious and had "eaten everything they caught." It is appropriate here to quote from Louis O. Coxe's critique of the poem:

> What Robinson sees, notably, is the man's wholly irrelevant and outdated concern and obsession; what he anathematizes has long since ceased to plague the world, at least in the form he gives it.[97]

Coxe's interpretation of the entire poem is somewhat different from Anderson's and mine, but I think that all three readings are fairly consistent with each other. In these stanzas the legendary Wandering Jew is fading somewhat, to be replaced by the actual historical individual who inspired the poem, of whom more later.

In stanzas 9, 10, and 11, the protagonist assumes again the characteristics of the legendary figure who has denied Christ and yet is timelessly suffering with an

awareness that the good exists—"A Presence that would not be gone" which he
cannot share. He is too hardened in his sin freely to acknowledge this goodness in
speech although he may seem to be confessing his awareness of it in moments of
silence. There is nothing left for him but lonely pride:

> Yet here there was a reticence,
> And I believe his only one,
> That hushed him as if he beheld
> A Presence that would not be gone.
> In such a silence he confessed
> How much there was to be denied;
> And he would look at me and live,
> As others might have looked and died.
>
> As if at last he knew again
> That he had always known, his eyes
> Were like to those of one who gazed
> On those of One who never dies.
> For such a moment he revealed
> What life has in it to be lost;
> And I could ask if what I saw,
> Before me there, was man or ghost.
>
> He may have died so many times
> That all there was of him to see
> Was pride, that kept itself alive
> As too rebellious to be free;
> He may have told, when more than once
> Humility seemed imminent,
> How many a lonely time in vain
> The Second Coming came and went.

In the final stanza, the last four lines of which are perhaps the most powerful in
the poem, the poet seems to be thinking once more of an actual man rather than
a legendary figure. He says he does not know for certain if the protagonist is still
defiant, still refusing to admit failure, or if he is maintaining a paradoxical
attitude of stubborn pride and sudden feelings of weakness.

> Whether he still defies or not
> The failure of an angry task
> That relegates him out of time
> To chaos, I can only ask,
> But as I knew him, so he was;
> And somewhere among men to-day
> Those old, unyielding eyes may flash,
> And flinch—and look the other way.

Before leaving the legendary, psychological, philosophical, and moral aspects
of the poem, I would like to quote from Yvor Winters's succinct comments on
"The Wandering Jew." Winters says that except in "Hillcrest" Robinson never
succeeds very brilliantly with the didactic or philosophical poem but "he often
succeeds brilliantly with the poem of the particular case."[98] And he goes on to say
that the poem examines:

the vice of pride in one's own identity, a pride which will not allow one to accept a greater wisdom from without even when one recognizes that the wisdom is there and greater than one's own; the result is spiritual sickness.[99]

The poem, then, is an examination of spiritual pride as it exists in a particular case. Most poems start from the concrete—an image, or an event, or a character. "The Wandering Jew," Robinson wrote to W. E. Louttit in 1931, "was perhaps suggested by a learned old Hebrew that I knew in New York, but it is mostly fancy.—I have never made any particular study of the legend."[100] Robinson does not name the "old Hebrew" but it was undoubtedly Alfred H. Louis, and on one level the poem can be considered a character sketch of him. It is odd that all of the interest in Louis to date has been as the supposed prototype of Captain Craig, although Robinson himself denied in a talk with Edith Brower that Craig was modeled on Louis.[101] Edith Brower did not believe him and neither have most of Robinson's readers. Louis himself was sure that he was the model for Craig and he pasted his picture in a copy of the volume of *Captain Craig* which was presented by Robinson to Alice Meynell and her husband.[102]

Winters was, I believe, the first to note that there may have been a connection between Louis and Robinson's "Wandering Jew,"[103] and later several other critics have mentioned it in passing. The point is that there appear to be a number of differences between Louis and Robinson's Captain Craig whereas, as far as we can judge at this point in time, "The Wandering Jew" is an exact and precise depiction of Louis.

This remarkable character, who seems to have made an unforgettable impression on Robinson, met the poet at about the same time and perhaps in the same place that Robinson met Edith Brower, that is about 1898 in the office of Brower's employer, Titus Coan, who managed an editorial service in New York City. Louis's personality has been described in some detail in the volumes on Robinson by Hagedorn, Neff, and C. P. Smith. Most of their information comes from Algernon Blackwood's book *Episodes Before Thirty*.[104]

Alfred Hyman Louis (1829–1915),[105] the son of a well-to-do businessman of Birmingham, England, was by birth a Jew, was converted successively to the Anglican and the Roman Catholic faiths, but by his own request was buried in a Jewish cemetery with the rites. Educated at Cambridge and at Lincoln's Inn, he was for a short time coeditor of *Spectator* and was active in the early years of the Working Men's College in London, where he became acquainted with Ruskin. He was a frequent visitor at the home of George Eliot and claimed to be the model for Daniel Deronda in Eliot's *Daniel Deronda*.[106] He published a book on British foreign policy in 1861.[107] Among his friends and acquaintances were Edward Benson, archbishop of Canterbury,[108] John Stuart Mill, who praised him in a letter, Gladstone, who disliked him, Longfellow, and William Dean Howells. In 1923 Algernon Blackwood dedicated his autobiographical *Episodes before Thirty* to him and in 1930 (fifteen years after Louis's death) Robinson dedicated *The Glory of the Nightingales* to his memory.

Such are the bare facts of the life of the remarkable man who was living in New York City in dire penury at the turn of the century. Algernon Blackwood describes his first meeting and subsequent friendship with him in New York in 1894[109] in chapters 29 and 30 of *Episodes before Thirty*. His description of Louis, and even certain words and phrases, bear a strong resemblance to Robinson's "Wandering Jew." I quote a few sentences:

> Worthy of more detailed description, however, is the figure of an old, old man I met about this time, a dignified, venerable and mysterious being, a man of the world, lawyer, musician, scholar, poet, but above all, exile. Incidentally, he was madman too. What unkindly tricks fate had played with his fine brain, I never learned with accuracy. . . .He was a Jew, he was very small, his feet were tiny, his hands, I took in, were beautiful. I thought of Moses, of Abraham, some Biblical prophet come to life, of some storied being like the Wandering Jew. . . . when he rose to shake my hand, it seemed to me that some great figure of history rose to address, not me, but the nations of the world. He reached barely to my shoulder, his face upturned to mine, yet the feeling came that it was I who looked up into his eyes. The dignity and power, the frail outline conveyed were astonishing. He was a Presence. And his voice. . . increased the air of greatness, almost I had said of majesty, that he wore so naturally. It was not merely cultured, deep and musical, it vibrated with a peculiar resonance that conveyed authority beyond anything I have known in any other human voice. . . . One thing that stirred him into vehemence, when the past was mentioned, was the name of Gladstone. With flashing eyes and voice of thunder he condemned the Grand Old Man, both as to character and policy, in unmeasured terms. . . . It was in the domain of politics that I first began to notice the exaggeration and incoherence of his mind, and it was "in politics," evidently, that the deep wounds which would not heal had been received.[110]

Blackwood dwells at some length on Louis's habit of delivering long spontaneous lectures as well as his anathemas against Gladstone in "unmeasured terms" quoted above; Robinson refers to this habit as the Jew's "untempered eloquence" to which in "fealty" he gave "the tribute of a tempered ear" as if to royalty. Blackwood's Louis also suggests royalty. And there are other obvious parallels to Robinson's character including the fact that Louis reminded both Blackwood and Robinson of the Wandering Jew.

Blackwood also describes Louis in his short story "The Old Man of Visions," published in 1907.[111] The narrator of this symbolic character sketch—for it is no more than that—first sees "the bent grey figure, so slight, yet so tremendous" in the Library of the British Museum, London, and is immediately reminded "of Teufelsdrockh sitting in his watch-tower 'alone with the stars.' " Eventually the narrator makes the acquaintance of this solitary individual in a smoky Bloomsbury restaurant, goes home with him and discovers in him a spiritual guide and comforter. "The Old Man of Visions" (for so he calls himself) with his "vast-seeing eyes" appears to live "apart from the world—and above it" and yet maintains "deep sympathy with humanity," albeit he sometimes seems to be "steeped in tragedy," yet would never lift "the impenetrable veil that hung over his past"—a past that suggested a knowledge of "all the countries of the world." For the narrator, the Old Man's room, an "attic (lampless and unswept), high up under the old roofs of Bloomsbury," becomes "a little holy place out of the world, a temple" in which he finds the fulfillment of his spiritual life. He realizes, finally, that the Old Man is really "immemorial...old as the sea and coeval with the stars; and he dwelt beyond time and space." He is pure spirit. And when the narrator realizes this, he can never find the Old Man or his room again.

The sentimentality of the style is apparent in these quotations, brief as they are, for this sketch is not one of Blackwood's better performances and in literary value it is far below Robinson's poem. However, there are obvious similarities between Robinson's character and Blackwood's. They are both alienated intellectuals, cosmopolitan, eloquent, and eternal. But the Old Man also is a symbol of the perfect spiritual life, and in Robinson's poem the protagonist is hardly that.

Maude Ffoulkes was another person upon whom Louis left a lasting impression. In her autobiography *My Own Past* (1915)[112] she speaks of his "sombre and tragic personality" and says "I have never forgotten Alfred Louis," who was introduced to her in London by her friend Algernon Blackwood. Her testimony is of some worth, for Mrs. Ffoulkes was acquainted with a number of unusual personalities including the confidante of Crown Prince Rudolph and Mary Vetsera, the Countess Marie Larisch, with whom she was joint author of the countess's memoirs, *My Past* (1913).[113] Mrs. Ffoulkes published her own autobiography the year of Louis's death and included in it, in addition to a description of Louis, a picture of him together with pictures of the Countess of Cardigan, the ex–Crown Princess of Saxony, the Countess Larisch, and the Dowager Maharani of Cooch Behar. If Louis saw this book just before his death, he no doubt considered that justice had been done to him at long last by Maude Ffoulkes, who had placed him among his peers. One recalls Robinson's references to Louis's aristocratic bearing. This picture of Louis,[114] which is undated, carries the subcaption "The Original of Daniel Deronda." It shows a bearded, scholarly looking Hebrew gentleman, perhaps in his fifties or early sixties, with a slightly defiant look in his narrowed eyes. It is by far the most perceptive and intelligent portrait in Ffoulkes's volume and is in complete accord with Robinson's description of the Wandering Jew and considerably more impressive than that part of Blackwood's description which refers to him as down-at-the-heels and shabbily dressed. Robinson, of course, may have seen Ffoulkes's book before he wrote "The Wandering Jew," as well as Blackwood's story "The Old Man of Visions," but I have found no documentary evidence that he did.

"The Wandering Jew," then, has a background of broad mythological and legendary complexity as well as an historical and biographical background of interest to serious students of Robinson. It has never been a popular poem, probably becaue of its virtues and absence of defects. It lacks the chatty garrulity (so unlike Ben Jonson!) of the well-known "Ben Jonson Entertains a Man from Stratford," the slick sentimentality of "Flammonde" (which was of course in part inspired by Louis), and the cheap melodrama of "Richard Cory." It is composed in a style of great firmness and precision — the plain style at its best — and it deserves a rank equal to that of Robinson's other great "character sketches" — those of St. Paul in "The Three Taverns" and of Rembrandt in

"Rembrandt to Rembrandt."

"The Three Taverns," first published in 1919[115] is a monologue spoken by St. Paul, the greatest of the early Christians, the Apostle who founded the Christian religion and changed the world. However, Robinson does not stress unduly the religious aspects of his material. Rather, he gives us a character portrayal of a great man of steadfast purpose who is aware of the importance of what he is trying to achieve, aware also that he is probably near the end of his career, aware too that most of the world is against him. In one respect he is similar to the protagonist of "Rembrandt to Rembrandt." He asks himself the question—is his own evaluation of his work correct? Or is the world's evaluation of his work correct and he deluded? Both Paul and Rembrandt decide in favor of their own viewpoints, but Paul does so with considerably more resolution and conviction than the artist, for he has had an overwhelming spiritual experience which Rembrandt has not.

The Three Taverns is about twenty miles (or "seven leagues" as Paul says in the final lines of the poem) south of Rome. The monologue takes place in the spring of the year, approximately A.D. 60, in the reign of the emperor Nero. The circumstances are these. Paul had been imprisoned in Jerusalem on a charge of profaning the Temple and of preaching the doctrine of the Nazarene sect. He was sent to Caesarea to be tried before Felix, the procurator of Judea. He was dismissed but examined again two years later under the succeeding procurator, Festus. Paul claimed his right as a Roman citizen to be tried in Rome by the tribunal of the emperor. After the examination, Festus and Agrippa II, king of Chalcis, who was also present, came to the conclusion that Paul might have been released if he had not appealed to Caesar. But the appeal had been made, so under the guard of the centurion Julius he was sent to Rome, the voyage by ship starting in A.D. 59. After shipwreck at Malta, where he was treated kindly by the Maltese, he arrived in Puteoli on the Bay of Naples from where he traveled by foot along the Appian Way toward Rome. News of his coming had reached Rome, and a number of his Christian brethren came out to meet him at the Appii Forum. Traveling a few miles further on, he was met by more brethren at The Three Taverns (Acts 28:15). Here Robinson has him at the opening of the poem addressing several by name. The names are taken from Romans 16:7–15 where Paul sends greetings to Herodion, Apelles, Amplias, and Andronicus (the four mentioned in the first two lines of the poem), as well as other Roman Christians. There is no scriptural authority for these four being present at The Three Taverns, nor is there any scriptural authority for Paul making a speech to the Christians at this place. Robinson's monologue is purely imaginary, but the substance of it is derived from Acts and from the Epistles. As Paul speaks to the brethren, he is fully aware of the dangers ahead in submitting his case to the capricious Nero. He may be close to the end of his career. In fact, he was acquitted at his first trial (perhaps because of the influence of Nero's adviser who was then in favor, the philosopher Seneca), but he was martyred a few years later in Rome (probably A.D. 67) during the Christian persecutions which followed the burning of Rome in A.D. 64.

The poem is in eight stanzas of blank verse. In the first stanza, Paul states that he has come to Rome as he had promised, but the circumstances of his coming had not been foreseen by himself or his friends, for he comes to Rome as a prisoner and is considered by many to be a criminal. He is

> A prisoner of the Law, and of the Lord
> A voice made free.

As to what may happen to him at Nero's hands he is fatalistic and fearless:

> The cup that I shall drink
> Is mine to drink—the moment or the place
> Not mine to say. . .and if at last
> I give myself to make another crumb
> For this pernicious feast of time and men—
> Well, I have seen too much of time and men
> To fear the ravening or the wrath of either.

In stanza two Paul describes the insufficiency of his former life under the Law and then the fulfillment of his life after his conversion on the road to Damascus. Since this experience he has lived only for his faith and for the work he has begun:

> I have lived
> Because the faith within me that is life
> Endures to live, and shall, till soon or late,
> Death, like a friend unseen, shall say to me
> My toil is over and my work begun.

In the next stanza, after reminding his listeners once again that he has kept his promise and has come to Rome, he warns them that "the wolves are coming" and then gives them a long exhortation to carry on the work of Christian conversion which he has begun, and to remember that they are working in time but for eternity:

> You are to plant, and then to plant again
> Where you have gathered, gathering as you go;
> For you are in the fields that are eternal

and he encourages them by saying that although most of them will not see on earth as much as he saw on the road to Damascus, yet eventually they will see.

> The fire that smites
> A few on highways, changing all at once,
> Is not for all. . .Before we see,
> Meanwhile, we suffer; and I come to you,
> At last, through many storms and through much night.

The fourth stanza is a brief interlude, a comment on the fact that those who have the light of true faith will eventually experience more pleasure than pain; however, if their light proves to be a transitory illusion, they will suffer more than those who never thought they had experienced saving grace. The fifth stanza is an exhortation on faith and its relationship to works. Faith is primary, but the doctrine of salvation through faith should not be considered an excuse for idleness. He considers himself as a "driven agent" to communicate the Word, as a man who does not

> sit with folded hands
> Against the Coming.

Paul, or perhaps I should say at this point, Robinson's Paul goes on to defend himself against the charge of preaching inconsistently and of believing contradictory doctrines:

> I am a man of earth, who says not all
> To all alike.

There are many, he says, who

> will flourish aloft,
> Like heads of captured Pharisees on pikes,
> Our contradictions and discrepancies.

Some scholars have argued, incidentally, that Paul is not inconsistent. If one reads the Epistles in the order in which they were written (instead of in the order in which they appear in the Bible) one can demonstrate a logical development of doctrine motivated in part by Paul's growing awareness that the *parousia* would not occur in his lifetime.[116] Robinson, not aware of or not accepting this line of thought, has Paul admit the contradictions and argue that it is necessary to preach to individuals differently and that the Word transcends the mere words of logical discourse:

> And there are many more will hang themselves
> Upon the letter, seeing not in the Word
> The friend of all who fail.

Stanza 6 begins with a gloss on 1 Corinthians 13:12 — "For now we see through a glass darkly, but then face to face: now I know in part; but then shall I know even as also I am known." Robinson's Paul develops this text with an extended contrast between light and dark (a favorite motif of Robinson, as in "The Man against the Sky.") What may be darkness to some, Paul says in the poem, may be light to others. Light becomes a symbol of divine grace inscrutably imparted by God:

> You cannot say
> This woman or that man will be the next
> On whom it falls.

God's inscrutability and unpredictability in his imparting of saving grace was made much of centuries later by Calvin, who perhaps carried the idea further than Paul intended. Robinson, no Calvinist himself, was nevertheless through his New England ancestry influenced by Puritan Calvinism to some extent, as were those other distinguished writers in the New England tradition, Hawthorne and Emily Dickinson. The light-dark imagery in Robinson reminds one particularly of Hawthorne. Robinson's Paul, like Calvin's Paul, insists on the priority of faith over works, on the mysterious nature of God's grace, and, implicitly at least, on the doctrine of the elect, of which Irving Babbitt's notion of "the saving remnant" was a humanistic and non-Christian modification. However, Robinson's Paul is somewhat closer to evangelical and Arminian doctrines than is the Paul of Calvin's *Institutes*. Robinson's Paul emphasizes the necessity of the few (the elect) saving the many (the non-elect). Calvin's Paul, or rather Calvin in his interpretation of the Pauline Epistles, emphasizes the certain damnation of the many as well as the certain salvation of the few. Robinson's Paul says:

> The few at last
> Are fighting for the multitude at last.

Not all are to be saved, however, according to Robinson's Paul. He proclaims:

> Beware of stoics,
> And give your left hand to grammarians.

Grammarians here are pedants and scholars (the terms are sometimes synonymous in Robinson's poetry). One is reminded of Stevens's poem "On the Manner of Addressing Clouds," which begins

> Gloomy grammarians in golden gowns

and of Robinson's Shakespeare in "Ben Jonson Entertains a Man from Stratford," who asks

> "Ben, you're a scholar, what's the time of day?"

Snide remarks about scholars and scholarship are endemic in twentieth-century Anglo-American poetry and criticism, and Robinson did not escape the infection entirely, although he probably had more respect for scholars than Yeats, who began his poem "The Scholars" thus:

> Bald heads forgetful of their sins,
> Old learned, respectable bald heads
> Edit and annotate the lines. . . .

There is a reference to Gamaliel in stanza 6 ("Therefore remember what Gamaliel said"), as well as in stanza 3, which requires some comment. Gamaliel, in Acts 5:38–39, says, "if this counsel or this work be of men, it will come to nought: But if it be of God, ye cannot overthrow it." Gamaliel, at one time Paul's teacher, was a Pharisee, a doctor of the law, and an adviser to the Sanhedrin, the highest Jewish court. He advised leniency in the treatment of the Christian sect, pointing out that if Paul were preaching by divine sanction it would be useless to oppose him. Paul uses Gamaliel's words to encourage his brethren to continue their work with missionary zeal.

Stanza 7 is the climactic stanza of the poem. It is primarily an exhortation of comfort and consolation. Paul says that the best of life is yet to come and that one should not give way to despair because of past sins. "I was young once," Paul reminds his hearers, and he goes on to say that although he was a greater sinner than they, he was nevertheless saved by Christ. He warns them to beware of easy contempt for the world:

> The world is here
> Today, and it may not be gone tomorrow

and there are many who will yet live to experience God's grace. We have here an abandonment of Paul's earlier belief that the *parousia* would occur in his own lifetime. He warns his friends to beware of pride, which may be motivated by their awareness of being of the elect. And finally, in the emotional climax of the poem, he warns them against hate:

>   Many that hate
> Their kind are soon to know that without love
> Their faith is but the perjured name of nothing.
> I that have done some hating in my time
> See now no time for hate; I that have left,
> Fading behind me like familiar lights
> That are to shine no more for my returning,
> Home, friends, and honors, — I that have lost all else
> For wisdom, and the wealth of it, say now
> To you that out of wisdom has come love,
> That measures and is of itself the measure
> Of works and hope and faith.

The salvation of mankind will be found in love which, Paul has learned, is superior to wisdom.

The final stanza is a brief farewell in which Paul expresses his gratitude to the brethren who came so far to meet a man so dangerous. The poem ends on a note of foreboding:

> I hope that we shall meet again,
> But none may say what he shall find in Rome.

It takes a good poet to present an historical character as important as St. Paul, the eloquent author of the first Christian theological writings, the Epistles, and make him speak believably and movingly in several hundred lines of blank verse without sentimentality, bathos, or stereotyped religious diction. Consider what Browning or Tennyson would have made of this subject! Robinson, because of his ability to write in a style that is slow-moving, dignified, plain, and toward the end of the poem highly eloquent, fully succeeds in his undertaking.

"Rembrandt to Rembrandt," first printed in *Collected Poems*, 1921, was composed in the midsummer of 1920, six months after Robinson's fiftieth birthday and within a year or two of the composition of "The Wandering Jew" and "The Three Taverns." It is one of the most autobiographical (in a spiritual or psychological sense) of all of Robinson's poems. Indeed, it might have been entitled, as Emery Neff has remarked, "Robinson to Robinson,"[117] for

Rembrandt is in many ways the poet's persona. The problems, the self-questioning that tormented the painter also had tormented the poet. According to Esther Bates, Robinson at one time ranked this poem with "The Man against the Sky" as his best work.[118]

Rembrandt, born in Leyden in 1606, settled in Amsterdam in 1632 and soon became a fashionable portrait painter with many pupils. In 1634 he married Saskia van Uylenburgh, who brought him a handsome dowry. They had one son who survived infancy—Titus, born in 1641, who is mentioned by name in Robinson's poem. The happily married couple settled into a grand house which was somewhat beyond their means and there they lavishly lived and entertained until Saskia's early death in 1642. Thereafter Rembrandt's fortunes began to decline. After bankruptcy in 1658 he became the legal employee of his mistress Hendrickje Stoffels and his son Titus. He had a daughter by Hendrickje named Cornelia, born 1654. Rembrandt died in 1669, poor and forgotten.

Robinson's poem is a soliloquy addressed by the artist (now in his thirty-ninth year) to a self-portrait painted earlier in his career, when his popularity was at its height,[119] and to his image in a mirror which shows him as he now appears in 1645. At that time Rembrandt was in what art historians call his second period, with many of his now acknowledged masterpieces being painted or yet to be painted. The famous picture, the so-called *Night Watch,* had been finished in 1642, the year in which his wife Saskia died. Rembrandt in his soliloquy dates his decline in popularity from the time of this painting because of its unconventional composition, coloring, and use of light.[120]

The theme of the soliloquy is this. Is the artist correct in his estimate of himelf, or his abilities as an artist? Or is the public correct in its much lower estimate of him? The poem expresses Robinson's own former bitterness, that of the neglected artist, with occasional doubts of himself, a bitterness found also in his letters. Robinson once remarked that if the police knew his annual income from poetry he would be arrested for vagrancy. But the poem also expresses Robinson's (and Rembrandt's) victory, firm and permanent, over self-doubt. Once that victory is achieved there remains the moral choice. Should the artist, sure of his genius, defy society and take the consequences of poverty and public derision for the sake of posthumous fame? Or should he hedge his bets and occasionally paint mediocre pictures for public acclaim and money? Rembrandt (as did Robinson) overcomes all temptations which would prevent fulfillment of his highest abilities. The poem, then, defines a moral decision of the greatest importance.

Rembrandt is frequently described as a painter of the inner life of the soul. He achieved an unequaled mastery of light and shadow, and in his middle and later work his handling of light and dark textures gave to his paintings a quality which may properly be described by the overused word *poetic.* Robinson likewise is a poet of the soul and he also achieved similar effects in his poetry with his light and dark imagery. In fact, the contrast of light and dark is a major motif in Robinson. It is little wonder then that he became especially interested in the life and work of the Dutch master and that he wrote one of his finest poems with Rembrandt as his persona.

Rembrandt, of course, was preeminent in portraiture. There are frequent references to portrait painting throughout the poem, with bitter comments on the inferior work of another portrait painter, his rival Frans Hals, whose accurate and realistic but rather superficial pictures became more popular than Rembrandt's. It is natural that a poem presenting the world's greatest portrait painter should open with the protagonist addressing his self-portrait.

In the first stanza the speaker contrasts his past popularity when he was

> formerly more or less
> Distinguished in the civil scenery

with his present condition:

> In your discredited ascendency;
> Without your velvet or your feathers now.

He advises himself in a typically Robinsonian fashion to take the stoic view and

> Commend your new condition to your fate,
> And your conviction to the sieves of time.

He meditates on the reasons for his loss of public esteem. The Hollanders do not find "their fifty florins' worth" in *The Night Watch* (the picture is not named but it is described in a few phrases) because they do not understand the use of a "new golden shadow" and other color effects. He recalls his beloved Saskia's warning before she died that the Hollanders would attack him and pity themselves for the fraud he had practiced on them.

In the next stanza he compares his image in the mirror with that in the early self-portrait previously mentioned and he is momentarily tempted by the thought that all his vaunted ability was illusion, like fool's gold. He refers to his domestic losses — to the death of Saskia and three of their children:

> One, two, and three,
> The others died, and then — then Saskia died;
> And then, so men believe, the painter died.

He recovered from this indulgence in self-pity, however. He still has his son Titus left and he still has his talent, even though it is unrecognized by the Hollanders:

> Well, if God knows,
> And Rembrandt knows, it matters not so much
> What Holland knows or cares.

The belief in his own genius and in the inferiority of Dutch taste is strengthened when he considers the popularity of the wretched Frans Hals who paints

> Rat-catchers, archers, or apothecaries,
> And one as like a rabbit as another.

He is determined to struggle on alone, painting what Hollanders call the impossible while remembering the encouragement of Saskia, who foresaw his present troubles, gave him gold, and laughed.

The third stanza begins with a meditation on what might have been if Saskia had lived, and he considers various grim possibilities. She might have joined the majority of Hollanders, losing both hope and confidence in him, believing that he was

> grasping on a phantom trail
> Determining a dusky way to nowhere

and saying to him in language reminiscent of "Luke Havergal":

> That even your eyes are sick, and you see light
> Only because you dare not see the dark
> That is around you and ahead of you.

Or, remembering his past popularity, she might have excessively praised and idealized him until he was clothed over "in a shroud of dreams." On the other hand, she might have successfully encouraged him to debase his talent to satisfy popular, vulgar tastes and share with him

> The taste of death in life—which is the food
> Of art that has betrayed itself alive
> And is a food of hell.

Or she might have become angry with him for not accepting easily gained popularity, and she might have lost her natural appetite for joy and have succumbed to self-pity prompted by the pity of friends for her.

In any event, if she were alive now, Rembrandt would find it difficult to ask her to stay by him in the struggle he sees ahead, with the only reward a possible "gleam" which even if it does come will be perceived by very few.

Addressing his portrait now as a work of art, he meditates on the contrast between his image as it will appear forever in the permanent unchanging picture and his appearance now as a frail and mortal man:

> That was a fall, my friend, we had together—
> Or rather it was my house, mine alone,
> That fell, leaving you safe.

Regardless of what is happening to him now and in the future, his identity is preserved in his portrait, an identity that will outlive the decay of flesh, facile fashions, and transitory and spurious novelty. He imagines his early portrait warning him not to waste his energy in mere words; and from the memory of his past triumphs he draws his courage, in stanza 4, to defy the various devils of temptation:

> I shall not give myself
> To be the sport of any dragon-spawn
> Of Holland or elsewhere.

He shall wash away the temptations of self-doubt with

>   a golden flood
>   That with its overflow shall draw away
>   The dikes that held it —

a reference to his brilliant and successful use of light and color in *The Night Watch* and in later masterpieces.

In the fifth stanza he remarks that there are worse demons than self-doubt. One of the worst, he tells himself, is this: suppose you do achieve masterpieces? Before they are recognized as such by the public you will be dead. "You'll sleep as easy in oblivion," this demon says, as you would if you had denied the pleasures of worldly life to become posthumously famous.

>   Why not paint herrings, Rembrandt
>   Or if not herrings, why not split beef?...
>   The same God planned and made you beef and human.

Thus spoke the demon of relativism. One picture is "as good" as another. One subject for a picture is "as good" as another.

Stanza 6 is for the most part a long advisory speech by Rembrandt's "wiser spirit" who reminds him

>   You made your picture as your demon willed it;
>   That's about all of that.

Rembrandt, as he told himself in preceding passage, is

>   but a living instrument
>   Played on by powers that are invisible.

Rembrandt is reminded that he is the servant, not the master, and therefore he is advised to

>   bow your elected head
>   Under the stars tonight, and whip your devils
>   Each to his nest in hell.

In the final stanza Rembrandt, realizing he cannot escape the destiny of his genius, asks himself "Why complain?" he must not hope to regain the joys of his former life of fame and love with Saskia. He must live in a world where there are "no clocks or calendars," with a vision which cannot be understood or shared with his contemporaries. For, he tells himself, if he turns back now

>   You may as well accommodate your greatness
>   To the convenience of an easy ditch,
>   And, anchored there with all your widowed gold,
>   Forget your darkness in the dark, and hear
>   No longer the cold wash of Holland scorn.

With these powerful lines Rembrandt turns his back on all temptations that would make him other than he is. He is, finally, the ideal genius who, as Emery Neff has said, is "neither spoiled by acclaim nor daunted by unpopularity."[121]

In this chapter I have attempted to demonstrate the importance of Robinson as a modern poet by discussing what appear to me to be his best poems. Working within conventional forms he attempted less than Pound, Eliot, and Stevens, but he accomplished more. Louis O. Coxe has stated the case for Robinson clearly and cogently:

> Robinson's poetry never aims at myth-making, a symbolic and self-contained world of aesthetic or metaphysical truth. He does not, like Pound, write a personal and artistic diary, nor like Eliot a biography of modern man in his pilgrimage from atrophy through agony to rebirth, nor does he attempt the creation of a world of the imagination like Stevens. He tries to see what is set before him.[122]

Robinson's best poetry is about human experience in the world we all know, the world of everyday life. There are references to a transcendental world, but the experience of a transcendental world or the wish for this experience does not (as it does in Eliot) occupy much of his time nor does it become an appreciable part of his poetry. As a poet Robinson's quest for reality began and ended in the commonsense world of normal human life. In this respect he is similar to Hardy and he differs from Stevens, who too often escapes into a quirky and bizarre realm of romantic fancy. And he differs from Pound, whose greatest fault was that he found too much of his experience in literature — often in rather esoteric and recondite literature — and hence the champion of "Make it New" wrote the *Cantos,* which are far more derivative than Robinson's best work and much less original. Robinson's poetry is more universal than that of his three modern rivals and is likely to be of more lasting appeal. Such poems as "Hillcrest," "Eros Turannos," "Veteran Sirens," and "The Wandering Jew" are in the mainstream of poetry in English, and I think that they and a few others will become a permanent part of the literature of the English-speaking world.

Yvor Winters

Yvor Winters

(1900–1968)

"No man can hold existence in the head."

It is appropriate to conclude this volume with a study of the career of Yvor Winters, for in his poetry and in his criticism Winters began by preaching and practicing the doctrines of the revolutionary poets of our century and then, revolting against the revolutionists, he rejected their techniques and developed a mature body of poetry which made use of conventional prosody and structure. But in so doing, Winters learned to employ the iambic line with greater subtlety than did the conventional writers that immediately preceded him (such as E. A. Robinson), and he employed it to define experience more profound and complex than that of his conventional predecessors. For in the change from experimental to conventional prosody there was also a change in philosophical attitudes. Considerably more than the scansion of a line was involved in this dramatic shift. And, it should be added, Winters was the only important poet of the century to go from experimental to traditional poetic techniques. Stevens, as we have seen, used both conventional and free-verse meters, but there was no progressive development. That is, he was writing conventional blank verse and experimental free verse at the same time, "The Snow Man" and "Sunday Morning" for example. Winters's poetry as a whole presents a special "case" in which the virtues and limitations of both experimentalist and conventional twentieth-century poetry can be studied in the work of a single writer.

Winters is also the only critic of the twentieth century who formulated a coherent theory of poetry at the same time he was practicing it. Blackmur, Ransom, Tate, Eliot, Pound, and Stevens all theorized about poetry, but their theories when analyzed in their entirety appear inconsistent, haphazard, and impressionistic when compared to those developed by Winters from 1930 on. Winters was also one of the most "intellectual" of our poets. By that I mean he had a mind capable of understanding and using ideas. Also, as a professor at Stanford for many years, he became one of the most scholarly of our poets, and he always argued that sound scholarship was a help rather than a hindrance to the writing of his own poetry and that this should be true of most poets. This was a position contrary to the prevailing mood of the period, which still believed in the superiority of the inspired, untutored genius. Finally, he took poetry very seriously, more so than did the other poets studied in this volume—with the possible exception of E. A. Robinson. Winters was well read in scholastic theology, particularly in Aquinas, and he knew the difference between religion and art, between theology and poetry. Yet I think it fair to say that, as was true of so many of our intellectuals from Matthew Arnold on, poetry for him became a substitute for religion. The study of and the writing of poetry were, for him, a way of life.

Like Yeats, who made the phrase famous, Winters sought and, to a greater extent than Yeats I think, achieved "unity of being." The proper relationship between the heart and the head, between emotion and thought was a frequent theme of his poetry. It is clearly stated in "A Prayer for My Son":

> To steep the mind in sense,
> Yet never lose the aim,

and it is clearly repeated in a number of his best poems such as the allegorical "Sir Gawaine and the Green Knight"—poems which Winters described as post-symbolist in method, poems which combine suggestive sensuous richness, an awareness of and a love of the concrete world, particularly the world of nature, with a coherent structure and substantial paraphrasable denotative content. The correct relationship between thought and feeling was at the center of his theory of poetry, and his definition of this relationship, that sound feeling is motivated by understanding of rationally apprehensible subject matter, was directly contrary to some of the leading theorists of his time, for instance Housman, Ransom, and Eliot. Housman stated in *The Name and Nature of Poetry*: "Even when poetry has a meaning, as it usually has, it may be inadvisable to draw it out. 'Poetry gives most pleasure' said Coleridge 'when only generally and not perfectly understood.' "[1] And again, "Meaning is of the intellect, poetry is not." Of Blake he said, "Blake's meaning is often unimportant or virtually non-existent, so that we can listen with all our hearing to his celestial tune."[2] It is instructive to note that Housman, in defending his anti-intellectual and romantic approach to poetry, calls upon Coleridge, the patron saint of most of the theorists of our time, including Ransom, Tate, and Eliot. But Coleridge was not the patron saint of Winters.

"Meaning," in the ordinary sense of the word, became a minor component of a poem for most of our critics, who used it apologetically and put it into quotation marks to relieve their embarrassment. Eliot contributed his support to this approach with his famous figure of the dog and the burglar:

> The chief use of the "meaning" of a poem, in the ordinary sense, may be . . . to satisfy one habit of the reader, to keep his mind diverted and quiet, while the poem does its work upon him: much as the imaginary burglar is always provided with a bit of nice meat for the house-dog.[3]

Ransom described the relationship between thought and feeling in a poem as follows:

A poet is said to be distinguishable in terms of his style. It is a comprehensive word, and probably means: the general character of his irrelevances or tissues. All his technical devices contribute to it, elaborating or individualizing the universal, the core-object; likewise all his material detail. For each poem, ideally, there is distinguishable a logical object or universal, but at the same time a tissue of irrelevance from which it does not really emerge.[4]

To argue that the nonlogical components of a poem (including feeling) are *irrelevant* to the logical component is hardly a step toward unity of being in the poem or in the poet. Tate is equally obscure and unsatisfactory on this subject. Winters's position, which will be discussed in more detail later, was that a satisfactory poem should have a rationally defensible paraphrasable content—but that this paraphrasable content was by no means the total meaning of the poem. The total meaning of the poem included the effective use of rhythm and other poetic devices which qualify and convey the paraphrasable content to the reader with appropriate feeling.

It is convenient, and in accord with the facts, to divide Winters's career as a poet into two phases, the first from about 1920 to 1928 and the second from 1928 to 1968. In the first phase, Winters was writing poetry in free verse which was primarily "imagistic" and which could be claimed by the imagists as a part of their movement or, with respect to the more philosophical poems, as being derived from their movement. In the second phase, Winters employed conventional prosody and forms, including the sonnet and the heroic couplet. But there was still a marked carry-over from the early style in the use of imagery—a carry-over which resulted in what Winters was to call the post-symbolist method of writing poems.

In each of the two phases Winters formulated a body of poetic theory to explain and justify his poetic practice. The key critical documents of his first phase are *The Testament of a Stone,* written in the early twenties and published in 1924, and the introduction to his *Early Poems,* written late in his life, in 1966.

In the foreword to *The Testament of a Stone, Being Notes on the Mechanics of the Poetic Image,*[5] written let us remember when the poet was in his early twenties, Winters states his purpose, "to incite the beginnings of a scientific criticism of poetry," and he says he presupposes a knowledge in the reader of Ernest Fenollosa's *The Chinese Written Character*[6] and "scattered paragraphs" from Pound, Wyndham Lewis, Benedetto Croce, and the Hindus—thus indicating some of the influences on his own thinking at this time. Winters then defines a successful poem as one that represents "a perfect fusion of perceptions." It should be intense, original, and an end in itself. It is "a state of perfection at which a poet has arrived by whatever means...a permanent gateway to waking oblivion which is the only infinity and the only rest." The poem is or represents "a state of mind," as Winters was to define it in a poem much later than *The Testament* entitled "A Summer Commentary," which describes the aesthetic experience, theory, and practice of his youth:

> When I was young, with sharper sense,
> The farthest insect cry I heard

Could stay me; through the trees, intense,
I watched the hunter and the bird.

Where is the meaning that I found?
Or was it but a state of mind,
Some old penumbra of the ground,
In which to be but not to find?

According to Winters's early theories of writing poetry, the poet reaches a point of spiritual intensity, reproduces it in words, and thus transmits a similar spiritual intensity to others. The medium he uses is the image which combines two perceptions differing in all respects except at one point, where they fuse and cause a kind of mental vibration or aesthetic emotion—for example:

At one stride comes the dark.
                    (From Coleridge's "The Ancient Mariner")

Such an image communicates emotion directly and without thought. It is, in fact, similar to Pound's "luminous moment" and his definition of the image as a complex of thought and feeling in an instant of time. It is, in Winters's own words, "a fusion of sense-perceptions [which] *presents* the emotion."

But, Winters points out, there is another method of transmitting aesthetic emotion which does not depend on the senses; it transmits emotion through the intellect by means of what he calls the *anti-image*, where "the emotion is transmitted by intercomment rather than fusion." The anti-image is similar to the *logopeia* of Ezra Pound, the dance of the intellect among words, although Winters believes Pound's use of the term is incorrect.

Much of the above is a rephrasing in somewhat more precise terms of the current thinking of the imagists which I have noted in the chapter on Ezra Pound. It has affinities also with Eliot's concept of the objective correlative and of the notion that the mind of the poet is a catalytic agent which mysteriously and instantaneously creates a new substance out of totally different substances. Within a few years Winters was to reject or greatly modify most of this theorizing. But it is relevant to the poems he wrote in his first phase, and furthermore the kind of imagery which satisfied these criteria and which he found in the work of various poets as different as H. D. and E. A. Robinson continued to interest him. For instance, long after he had rejected imagism in his own practice, he continued to admire H. D.'s "Orchard," passages of which he quotes in *The Testament of a Stone* but also in his later criticism.

After defining the kind of perceptions which make up the successful image—sound perceptions and meaning perceptions which he divides into sense perceptions and thought perceptions—Winters takes up the various types of image and anti-image. He considers three types of images, and he finds that each kind of image has a corresponding anti-image. Within each type there may be variations. Type number one is the simple physical fact fused with a rhythm. It has one major variation—the simple physical movement fused with a rhythm. The anti-image of type one is the simple thought commented upon by a rhythm. The second type of image is the complex physical fact fused with a rhythm. The type two anti-image exists in four possible sorts: (1) two thought perceptions and one sound perception; (2) one sense perception, one thought perception, and one sound perception interfusing; (3) two sense perceptions and one sound perception that comments; (4) "two remotely separate facts, at least one of which must be physical which fuses with the rhythm and takes on an image existence of its own. . . . The unfused fact comments. This is sometimes known as the *conceit*." Winters gives as an example of this kind of anti-image the comparison of two souls to a pair of compasses in Donne's "Valediction Forbidding Mourning," in which the pair of compasses takes on a life of its own distinct from the two souls. The third type of image is composed of "two physical facts each fused with the sound" and by juxtaposition "defining each other's value." Winters gives as an example of this type Wallace Stevens's brilliant

> The maidens taste
> And stray impassioned in the littering leaves.

The straying maidens are a perfectly realized sound perception. So are the littering leaves. The two perceptions in close proximity enhance each other. The corresponding anti-image of type three consists of two separate thought perceptions juxtaposed and "acting upon each other."

The key term in Winters's analysis is *fusion*. The key term in Pound's definition of the image is *instant* or *moment*. Both Pound and Winters were attempting to define a psychological event — the response of a sensitive reader to certain kinds of verse. These psychological events do occur; yet poetry written solely to achieve them, however intense it may be, is very narrow. Hence Winters was eventually to change his methods and his theories, but in doing so he continued to make some use of the imagistic techniques he had learned early in his career. He put these techniques to the service of a kind of poetry that achieved the expression of a much wider range of human experience than did his imagistic verse. I quote another stanza from "A Summer Commentary":

> The soft voice of the nesting dove,
> And the dove in soft erratic flight
> Like a rapid hand within a glove,
> Caress the silence and the light.

The fusion of rhythm with sound and visual perceptions is similar to that of the early free verse poems and could not have been achieved without the earlier training in the construction of image and anti-image. But these lines are not expected to stand alone as a complete poem — as they would have if written in the earlier period. They are part of a longer poem in which Winters defines and contrasts his responses to the natural world, first as a young man and then years later as a more mature poet.

The theories advanced in *The Testament of a Stone* produced a poetry of very narrow range. And there was another problem. Winters was attempting to incite and to achieve himself a *scientific* criticism of poetry, an attempt quite natural to Winters, for his earliest interests were more scientific than literary, and he at one time planned to attend Stanford and train himself to be an icthyologist under Stanford's famous president William Starr Jordan. When his interest turned to literature and to the writing of poetry, his first approach was that of the scientist. His attempt to create a scientific body of criticism was wisely abandoned, but in the course of it he wrote those early free-verse poems which are of considerable interest as works of literature and which are essential to an understanding of Winters's entire career.

A poem, said Winters in *The Testament,* should be a permanent gateway to waking oblivion. There are several poems which illustrate what he meant — depictions of "a state of mind":

> yet I remain, a son
> of stone and of a
> commentary, I, an epitaph,
> astray in this
> oblivion, this
> inert labyrinth
> of sentences that
> dare not end.
>
> (From "The Cold")

> . . .
> The mind on moonlight
> And on trains
>
> Blind as a thread of water
> Stirring through a cold like dust,
> Lonely beyond all silence.
>
> (From "The Moonlight")

> . . .
> night is
> darkening in ripple
> over ripple over
> stony leaves
>   with
> happy eyes I search this
> earth of gardens dark as
> open doors
>   to what
> obliquity of nothing
> do I go
> veined cloud O pillared omen.
>
> (From "The Muezzin")

> . . .
> Scattered autumn —
> The leaves will be fainter than rain
> Ere he senses the void
> High on air
>
> And his vision
> Drifts from the place
> Where the lawn was,
> Where dew was the sea.
>
> (From "The Impalpable Void")

"Waking oblivion" is an apt phrase to describe the solipsistic experiences of
Winters's youth, experiences which approached madness:

> I screamed in sunrise
> As the mare spun
> Knee-high
> In yellow flowers.
>
> The stones
> That held the hills,
> The sun that held the
> Sky with all its
> Spreading rays, were of one
> Substance
>
>   and my God
> Lay at my feet
> And spoke from out
> My shadow, eyed me
> From the bees. . . .
>
>   What wonder, then,
> That I went mad.
>   (From "The Crystal Sun")
>
>   . . .
> he stood there
> in the streetlight
> casting a long shadow
> on the glassed begonias
> madness under
> his streaked eyelids. . . .
>
>   and he whirled off in
> Time
>   and pale and small
> children that run shrieking
> through March doorways
> burst like bubbles
> on the cold twigs
> block on block away
>   (From "Digue Dondaine, Digue Dondon")

Metaphysical terror—the mystery of time and the awareness of the human mind
confronting an inscrutable universe—and supernatural terror—"the terror in
the taste and sound of the unseen"—motivate many of these early poems:

> Can you feel through Space,
> imagine beyond Time?
>
>   The
> snow alive with moonlight
> licks about my ankles.
> Can you find this end?
>   (From "The Bitter Moon")

. . .
And in the bent heart of the seething rock
slow crystals shiver, the fine cry of Time.
                    (From "The Deep: A Service for All the Dead")

. . .
the wilderness, inveterate and
slow, a vastness one has
never seen, stings to the tongue and
ear. The terror in the taste
and sound of the unseen has
overwhelmed me.
                                        (From "The Streets")

. . .
Beyond the roof
the sky turns with an endless roaring and bears all
the stars. What could you do?
Could you climb up against the whirling
poles alone? Grind through the ghastly
twist of the sphere?
                                (From "Prayer beside a Lamp")

As a result of these experiences he decides to adopt a narrowly focused cold and
solitary stoicism:

It was the dumb decision of the
madness of my youth that left me with
this cold eye for the fact; that keeps me
quiet, walking toward a
stinging end.
                            (From "The Rows of Cold Trees")

It should be added that in this first phase Winters wrote a number of poems,
quiet in tone, without metaphysical implications, which were motivated
primarily by his observations of the natural world. For Winters had the "seeing
eye" and he wrote cleanly and precisely about what he saw. I quote "April" in its
entirety:

The little goat
crops
new grass lying down
leaps up eight inches
into air and
lands on four feet.
Not a tremor—
solid in the
spring and serious
he walks away.

This is a perfectly realized, charming minor poem and it and a half-dozen others
like it deserve to be remembered. Here is one more, entitled "Song":

Where I walk out
to meet you on the

cloth of burning
fields

the goldfinches
leap up about my
feet like angry
dandelions

quiver like a
heartbeat in the
air and are
no more

William Carlos Williams was doing this sort of thing in the twenties. Winters does it just as well.

In 1966, Winters selected those early poems he wished to see preserved and published them with an informative introduction, to which the reader is referred.[7] He gives the necessary biographical background, pointing out that the earliest poems, those published under the titles *The Immobile Wind* (1921) and *The Magpie's Shadow* (1922), were written when he was recovering from tuberculosis in a sanatorium in Santa Fe. After leaving the sanatorium he taught school in a mining camp in New Mexico for two years, then went to the University of Colorado at Boulder where he took his B.A. and M.A. in Romance languages, then to the University of Idaho at Moscow where he taught French and Spanish for two years, and then to Stanford University in 1927. He remained at Stanford for the rest of his life. While teaching in New Mexico he saw much of the brutal life of the miners who were living in semipoverty in ugly surroundings; in Moscow, Idaho, he was leading a rather solitary life with no intellectual friends to whom he could talk. The situation was alleviated somewhat by correspondence with Hart Crane and Allen Tate and other writers with interests similar to his own. The life of the solitary intellectual living in a land of great natural beauty, harsh climatic conditions, and with few of the benefits of civilized society (except his books, many of them borrowed) is the subject matter and background of many of his early poems. His marriage in 1926 to Janet Lewis and his move to the university town of Stanford inaugurated a permanent change for the better. Shortly after this move he abandoned free verse, the tone of his poetry changed considerably (according to his detractors it became "academic"), and he brought to bear on his criticism and on his new poetry a steadily accumulating knowledge of the history of English and American literature.

II

Winters's next important theoretical statement after *The Testament of a Stone* was "The Extension and Reintegration of the Human Spirit through the Poetry Mainly French and American since Poe and Baudelaire," first published in 1929, when Winters was no longer writing free verse and the second phase of his career had begun.[8] His definition of the satisfactory poem and of the function of the poet was deepened and broadened, and his philosophical position was moving away from the mystical, solipsistic determinism of his earlier years. He gets rid of the mysticism in two sentences. "The only godhead possible for man, *as man* . . . is not a mystical, but a moral godhead. The mystic achieves godhead only through self-annihilation, which is logically inconceivable."[9] Here begins the "moralism" for which Winters as poet and as critic has been so fiercely attacked and so widely misunderstood. His concept of the function of the poet too has changed. He no longer provides permanent gateways to waking oblivion. It is, rather, his function to "extend as far as possible the human consciousness and to organize the facts of life into a new and more dynamic synthesis"; as a modern man living in the twentieth century he will have to face "the metaphysical horror of modern thought, master it and leave that state of mind completed behind him for others to enter."[10]

The poet in achieving this "dynamic attitude" makes use of various technical devices of his craft, and by his skill and discipline he will achieve "the most intense moment of consciousness: the intensity of the moment of fusion is the final moral assertion of the artist."[11]

In these last statements, in his use of the word *fusion*, and in his emphasis on *intensity* as the most important achievement of the poet, Winters is retaining important aspects of the theories developed in *The Testament*. We have Pound's "luminous moment" with us once again. This terminology was to be soon dropped and his definition of the satisfactory poem was to be modified when he revised this essay and published it as chapter 2, "The Experimental School," in his book *Primitivism and Decadence* (1937).[12]

However, a substantial part of "Extension and Reintegration" anticipated Winters's final position. From very early in his career to the end of it Winters admired Baudelaire, and in this essay he presents Baudelaire's "Le Goût du Néant" as one of the great poems of modern times. He tells us why he likes it, and in so doing he tells us what he was trying to achieve in his own poetry from 1929 on. Baudelaire in this poem was "a master in relating rhymes to meaning, in relating syllable lengths, tonalities, phrase-stress, pauses, word-order, to meaning."[13] That is, all these technical devices are relevant to and contribute to the total meaning of the poem — a view diametrically opposed by Ransom when he called such devices "a tissue of irrelevancies." After a brief analysis of the rhymes in the poem, Winters says, "Every line in the poem bears not only its own weight, but the weight of all that has gone before it. It is almost never that one finds a poem so powerfully, so inseparably a unit. . . . It defines the experience in full, and refrains from obscuring it. These technical means are as definite instruments of expression as are the contents of a dictionary. It is by such means a poet produces his full effect, while having the air of understating his emotion." The qualities of style and the general theory of poetry stated here were in Winters's mind as he wrote those poems in *The Proof* (1930) which are in conventional prosody. However, he did not always live up to all of these standards. In his "Sonnet," for example, the metaphysical horror of his early verse is still there, but his definition of it does not have "the air of understating his emotion":

> Real, the writhing grain
> Means nothing, makes you nothing, and the room
> Laid bare is God, the thinning saline Doom,
> Intrinsic cringing of the shadowy brain.

This remarkable poem (which, I have been told, Winters wrote on a postcard and sent to Hart Crane) certainly does exhibit "the intensity of the moment of fusion" of his perceptions. At this time, 1928–30, we find Winters caught between two conflicting attitudes. He thought that poetry should achieve great intensity from the fusion of perceptions. Yet he admired certain poems by Baudelaire (and Robert Bridges and E. A. Robinson) in which the poet achieved "the air of understating his emotion." Hyperbole and litotes will be found side by side in certain poems in *The Proof* and in *The Journey* (1931).

About the time, then, that *The Proof* was published Winters was having second thoughts about the value of intensity in poetry, and, he tells us, in *Primitivism and Decadence* (completed in 1934 but not published until 1937), that he was discovering the key to "the ethical significance of rhetoric."[14] He was at the same time revising his analysis of the methods of the experimentalist poets (including himself) from a sympathetic elucidation to an elucidation of their shortcomings. He was coming under the influence of Irving Babbitt, especially Babbitt's critique of the romantic movement, and of William Dinsmore Briggs, whom he found helpful in attempting to reach an understanding of and a reevaluation of Elizabethan poetry.

The results of his general theories of poetry will be found in "The Morality of Poetry," the first chapter of *Primitivism and Decadence*.[15] He repeats his assertion that the poem should extend our consciousness by providing us with new perceptions of human experience and he then shows us in some detail the superiority of verse over prose for accomplishing this. He argues that the poem consists of a proper relationship between thought and feeling and that each is of equal importance and that the poem should manifest the control of the poet over his subject matter, a control which is directly related to the necessity of form. Such control he defines as a moral attitude. The good poem "represents the comprehension on a moral plane of a given experience." The proper adjustment of thought to feeling is an important aspect of a good poem, and the act of making such an adjustment Winters calls a moral act. Such was Winters's belief concerning the "morality" of poetry from this time on. Gone in this chapter are the references to fusions of perception creating momentary intensity as the necessary criteria of great poetry. Pound's "luminous moments" have become minor aspects of minor experimental poetry, an example of romantic heightening of emotion. Not intensity of feeling but soundness of feeling is the proper criterion. Nevertheless, Winters is still concerned with this matter of intensity, which he now sometimes calls "power," but he has some different things to say about it.

In the third chapter of *Primitivism and Decadence,* entitled "Poetic Convention," Winters quotes two poems he admires—"Eros" by Robert Bridges and "On the Road to the Contagious Hospital" by William Carlos Williams, the first written in conventional prosody, the second in cadenced free verse similar to

Winters's early experimental style and characteristic of Williams's style throughout his career. He finds a climactic passage in each poem, which he calls powerful and intense; he points out that the greater parts of both poems are written in language of low intensity—in what he calls conventional language, "in which the perceptual content is slight or negligible" and in which the claims to strong feeling are not justified until the climactic passage of the poem is reached. This is Winters's final rejection of the doctrines of the luminous moment and the objective correlative. A certain amount of conventional language is necessary in almost every great poem which is longer than a few lines. The notion that the greatest poetry must be achieved by the juxtaposition of luminous moments, with the conventional language of low intensity omitted (as in *The Waste Land*), is shown to be a fallacy. Bridges, in "Eros," achieves unity, coherence, and cumulative power by using traditional structure, prosody, and conventional language, and his poem is superior to most of the poetry of the experimentalists. As for Williams, he must be considered as belonging to the experimentalists by virtue of his meter, but "in other qualities of his language" he is "one of the most richly traditional poets of the past hundred and fifty years." And in "On the Road to the Contagious Hospital" he employs conventional and perceptual language successfully enough to merit comparison with Hardy and Bridges. Winters was to lower his estimate of Williams somewhat in later years, but this was his opinion in the mid-thirties.

As I mentioned above, Winters's critical theory of poetry, like his poetic practice, is in two phases—the first, already discussed, he developed from about 1920 to 1928; the second he developed during the thirties and early forties, although he did not state in print his formulation of the postsymbolic method until the late fifties.

The formulation of his basic theory is most completely and most clearly stated in "A Foreword" to *In Defense of Reason*, first published in 1947, and again in essays published in *The Function of Criticism,* 1957. His first formulation of the postsymbolic method was in his lecture "Poetic Styles, Old and New," delivered at the Johns Hopkins Poetry Festival in the fall of 1958 and published in *Four Poets on Poetry,* 1959.[16] However, in practice, all of these theories were operating in his poetry from 1930 on, and he refers to his basic theories a number of times in critical writings at various dates after 1930.

In "A Foreword" to *In Defense of Reason* Winters defines the principal theories of literature—all of which he finds inadequate and rejects. According to the *didactic* theory, literature should offer moral instruction. But this view is too narrow, particularly with reference to poetry. It does not account for the nonparaphrasable value of poetry. Furthermore, moral instruction can be better given in expository prose than in poetry. The *hedonistic* theory of literature states that literature should give pleasure. There are two kinds of hedonists. First there are those who believe that the end of life is pleasure and that pleasure consists of intensity of feeling, in the cultivation of the emotions for their own sake. Winters argues that this view leads to a search for more and more violent experience and for more and more subtle nuances of feeling, ending eventually in disillusionment with art and with life. Second, there are hedonists who believe that literature, and particularly poetry, should give aesthetic pleasure which is quite different from every other pleasure. Literary experience is thus divorced from life. The French symbolists carried this to extremes. The symbolist poem gives intense pleasure of a very special sort that has nothing to do with life. Winters thinks that this theory degrades literature to a trivial esoteric indulgence.

The *Horatian formula* (*prodesse et delectare*) that states that literature should teach and delight combines the didactic and hedonistic views. It is dismissed by Winters as having the disadvantages mentioned above of both theories.

The *romantic* theory of literature takes into account the great power that literature can exert over the minds of men, but the romantics have fallacious notions about literature and about life. They believe that literature is primarily an emotional experience, that men are naturally good, and that the rational faculty is unreliable. They preach surrender to impulse, to the emotions, and this leads to automatism and determinism. Emerson is one of the chief sinners. Winters thinks that romantic doctrine has prevailed in the literature and the life of Western civilization for the last two hundred and fifty years and that it is dangerous to both. Besides being deterministic, romanticism tends to be relativistic.

The theory of literature that Winters defends is *absolutist*. Literature approximates a real apprehension and communication of a particular kind of objective truth. He is primarily concerned with poetry. For him, a poem is a statement in words about a human experience. The poem is good when it makes a defensible rational statement about a given experience and at the same time communicates the emotion which ought to be motivated by a rational understanding of that experience. A successful poem, then, communicates both thought and feeling by means of language in which both conceptual and connotative contents of words are efficiently used, and in English, as he explains later, they are most efficiently used in verse written in the accentual-syllabic line, usually iambic.

In 1948, in a lecture on Hopkins delivered at Princeton University,[17] Winters restated and clarified aspects of his basic theory. He said:

> Words are primarily conceptual; the words *grief, tree, poetry, God,* represent concepts; they may communicate some feeling and remembered sensory impression as well, and they may be made to communicate a great deal of these, but they will do it by virtue of their conceptual identity, and in so far as this identity is impaired they will communicate less of these and communicate them with less force and precision. It is the business of the poet, then, to make a statement in words about an experience; the statement must be in some sense and in a fair measure acceptable rationally; and the feeling communicated should be proper to the rational understanding of the experience.[18]

According to this doctrine, words communicate feeling primarily by means of their "conceptual identity." Words are not things and ideas are not things, as William Carlos Williams and others seemed to believe, nor are poems things, as Archibald MacLeish implied in his famous "Ars Poetica" — "a poem should not mean/But be." Furthermore, Winters argued, when we read a poem, which is composed of words, our feelings are primarily motivated by an understanding of the conceptual content of the words, what the words are "saying." He regarded Eliot's "auditory imagination" — the notion that feeling can be communicated by images, archetypes, sounds, and rhythms from the racial memory via the subconscious — with suspicion, as he also did the idea of Mallarmé and other French symbolists that the "inscrutable image," the image which has no meaning, can effectively communicate feeling.

In a lecture on "The Audible Reading of Poetry" delivered at Kenyon College in 1949,[19] Winters explained why in his opinion the accentual syllabic line is the most efficient way of using words in English. After making a distinction between *meter*, "the arithmetical norm, the purely theoretic structure of the line," and *rhythm*, "the controlled departure from the norm," Winters goes on to describe the advantages of metrical language and of rhythm over nonmetrical language and nonrhythmical expression:

> Now rhythm is in a measure expressive of emotion. If the poet, then, is endeavoring to make a statement in which rational understanding and emotion are properly related to each other, metrical language will be of the greatest advantage to him, for it will provide him with a means of qualifying his notion more precisely than he could otherwise do, of adjusting it more finely to the rational understanding which gives rise to it. The rational and emotional contents of the poem thus exist simultaneously, from moment to moment, in the poem; they are not distinct, but are separable only by analysis; the poet is not writing in language which was first conceptual and then emotionalized, nor in prose which has been metered; he is writing in poetical language. And the rhythm of the poem permeates the entire poem as pervasively as blood permeates the human body: remove it and you have a corpse.[20]

He then goes into some detail concerning the prosody of the accentual syllabic line, giving examples of its use and misuse. I quote an essential passage from his observations on English scansion:

> the basic rule of English scansion is this: that the accented syllable can be determined only in relationship to the other syllable or syllables within the same foot. The accented syllable of a given foot, as we shall eventually see, may be one of the lightest syllables in its line. But with this rule as a reservation, we may go on to say that poetic meter must be constructed out of the inherent (or mechanical) accentual materials of the language, so that the accented syllable of a foot will naturally be heavier than the unaccented; and if the poet desires to indicate a rhetorical stress he should do it by a metrical stress.[21]

He points out the fact that most of the distinguished verse in English is written in the iambic line:

> English verse is predominantly iambic in structure, and although this fact has irritated certain poets and stirred them to curious experiments, the fact that so vast a number of eminent poets have found the iambic movement more useful than any other must have some kind of explanation. . . . it is far more flexible and perceptive than any other kind of English verse thus far devised.[22]

He warns us again that

> the accented syllable can be recognized as such only with reference to the other syllable or syllables within the same foot, for no two syllables bear exactly the same degree of accent: it is this fact which gives the rhythm of the best English verse its extreme sensitivity. But rhythm, in poetry as in music, is controlled variation from an arithmetical norm; and the rhythm ceases to be rhythm, and becomes merely movement, whenever the norm itself is no longer discernible.[23]

He now demonstrates the subtlety and the proper scansion of an iambic pentameter line by quoting Shakespeare's Sonnet 30 and analyzing the first line thus:

When tŏ thĕ sessĭŏns óf swĕet silĕnt thóught.

This line is composed of a trochee followed by four iambs and is correctly scanned above. (Such substitution of a trochee for an iamb in the first place is common practice in English poetry.) In the third foot, *of* both theoretically and actually receives the accent when the line is properly read, for it should be pronounced with slightly more force than-*sions*, the other syllable in the same foot. In the fourth place the syllable *si*-properly receives the accent rather than *sweet*, which is the other syllable in the same foot. Of course, *si*- is more heavily accented than *of*, and this is one of the facts of English meter—that one may have a number of accented syllables in the same line with each one having a different degree of emphasis. Furthermore, it should be noted that *sweet*, though unaccented, is pronounced with greater emphasis than *of*, which is accented, and rightly so because they are in different feet. With respect to the third and fourth feet "we have in effect four degrees of accent within two successive feet."[24] That is, we have a rising rhythm. Such considerations make for a fluid, sensitive medium for the expression of thought and feeling. If we scan and read the line as some do:

When tŏ thĕ sessĭŏns ŏf swéet silĕnt thóught,

making a spondee of the fourth foot, we have destroyed the subtlety of the rhythm.

In this essay Winters gives more analyses of the effective use of the accentual syllabic line in English verse. I have presented enough to demonstrate the carefully thought out theoretical and practical considerations which governed the writing of his own poetry from 1928 on.

Although Winters was making use from 1928 on of a style and method he was eventually to call *postsymbolist*, and although he describes the method in detail in his analysis of Paul Valéry's "Ebauche d'un Serpent" which Winters first published in 1956,[25] I believe that his first use of the term was in his lecture "Poetic Styles, Old and New," delivered at the Johns Hopkins Poetry Festival in November 1958.[26] After commenting on the poetic styles in English poetry of the medieval and Renaissance periods and on the theories of the symbol developed by Mallarmé in the nineteenth century and of the image developed by Pound in the twentieth century, Winters turns his attention to Wallace Stevens's famous poem "Sunday Morning." He points out that the structure of this poem is neither rational nor narrative but "controlled associationism"—as distinct from the uncontrolled associationism of Pound's *Cantos.* "The imagery," he says, "is post associationistic. Let us call the total method *post-symbolist.*"[27]

He then analyzes certain passages of "Sunday Morning" to illustrate what he means by postsymbolist (or postassociationistic) imagery. In commenting on four lines from the last stanza

> We live in an old chaos of the sun,
> Or old dependency of day and night,
> Or island solitude, unsponsored, free,
> Of that wide water, inescapable

he says, "Every phrase in this last passage is beautiful at the descriptive level, but the descriptive and the philosophical cannot be separated; *chaos, solitude, unsponsored, free, inescapable* work at both levels. The sensory detail is not ornament; it is a part of the essential theme."[28] He also considers the imagery of Valéry's "Ebauche d'un Serpent" to be postsymbolic. In this poem "we get the sharp sensory detail contained in a poem or passage of such nature that the detail is charged with meaning without ever being told of the meaning explicitly, or is described in language indicating such meaning indirectly but clearly."[29] Furthermore, Winters points out that in both these poems the significance of the sensory detail is cumulative within the poem. In "Sunday Morning," for example, water as it is described in the last stanza carries the weight of meanings ascribed to it in the preceding stanzas.

What Winters means by "controlled associationism" is most clearly stated in his discussion of "Ebauche d'un Serpent," where we have "nothing resembling the free association of Pound's *Cantos*; but we have rather an imitation of the psychological movement of a great mind back and forth among closely related topics, the shifts occurring as the passion aroused by one topic suggests an aspect of another topic."[30] Furthermore, the associational structure has a controlling theme, Valéry's "metaphysical concept of the creation."[31]

When a poet uses the total postsymbolist method, then, he employs a structure of controlled associationism and a style with sensory detail that is not only fresh and beautiful on the descriptive level but is also charged with meaning—the sensory detail embodies as it were the essential theme or themes of the poem. Winters considers the "post-symbolist sensibility" to be "potentially the greatest achievement in occidental poetry."[32] The postsymbolist method is a way of looking and of writing about the world and about one's experience in it, and it may be at work in poets earlier than the French symbolists, poets such as Emily Dickinson and F. G. Tuckerman. Winters has found examples of the method in both these poets, and he analyzes Tuckerman's postsymbolic method in some detail in his Foreword to the edition of Tuckerman's poems edited by N. Scott Momaday.[33] But he thinks the greatest achievements in the method may be found in the work of Stevens and of Paul Valéry.

Finally, in chapter five entitled "Post-Symbolist Methods" of his last book,

Forms of Discovery (1967), Winters expands his discussion of the subject, analyzes in some detail what he considers to be the finest examples of post-symbolist writing, and states: "The method, I believe, is potentially the richest method to appear. In fact, I will go farther; I believe that the greatest poems employing this method are the greatest poems that we have."[34]

As I have mentioned, the method may also be found in Winters's own poetry. I shall point out a few instances of its occurrence in my discussion of Winters's individual poems.

III

These ideas about poetry, then, were beginning to take form in Winters's mind as he composed the poems which appeared in *The Journey* (1931)[35] and *Before Disaster* (1934).[36] The publication of *The Journey*, a pamphlet of eight poems, was a remarkable and important event although it was not widely noticed at the time.[37] All of the poems are in heroic couplets—and by an author who had become known as an experimentalist writer of imagistic free verse. The poems in *The Journey*, together with a few rhymed poems in *The Proof* and all of the poems in *Before Disaster* (there are twenty-three, all short), marked the beginning of the "reactionary" movement of the thirties and a rejection of much of the experimentalist poetry of the 1910s and 1920s. In the foreword to *Before Disaster* Winters states his newly adopted prosodic principles clearly:

> I believe accentual-syllabic verse superior in principle to accentual, since it provides a norm which accounts for the conformity or deviation of every syllable, renders it possible to perceive every detail in relationship to a perfect norm, and hence makes for the greatest precision of movement, the most sensitive shades of perception, that is, of variation. The finest sensitivity is the product of the clearest form; the abandonment or weakening of form in the interests of greater fluidity can lead only in the direction of imperception. Accentual verse, on the other hand, as distinct from accentual-syllabic, tends to substitute perpetual variety for exact variation; change exists for its own sake and is only imperfectly a form of perception.[38]

This statement was followed by what became Winters's famous critique of "expressive form":

> I cannot grasp the contemporary notion that the traditional virtues of style are incompatible with a poetry of modern subject matter; it appears to rest on the fallacy of expressive form, the notion that the form of the poem should express the *matter*. This fallacy results in the writing of chaotic poetry about the traffic; of loose poetry about our sprawling nation; of semi-conscious poetry about semi-conscious states. But the matter of poetry is and always has been chaotic; it is raw nature. To let the form of the poem succumb to its matter is and will always be the destruction of poetry and may be the destruction of intelligence. Poetry is form; its constituents are thought and feeling as they are embodied in language; and though form cannot be wholly reduced to principles, there are certain principles which it cannot violate.[39]

Those poems collected in *The Journey* are the results of Winters's experiments in a verse form dramatically different from the "free verse" of *The Bare Hills* — the heroic couplet, brought to perfection by Pope two centuries earlier, a fact which according to T. S. Eliot should discourage its use in the twentieth century. Few if any poets have (with the exception of Winters) used it successfully in the twentieth century. In the nineteenth century it was employed with some success by Keats in *Endymion,* by Byron, by Browning in "My Last Duchess," and notably by Bridges in one of his finest poems, "The Summer House on the Mound," which had a direct influence upon the writing of "On a View of Pasadena from the Hills," the fourth poem in *The Journey.*

The California landscape (like the New Mexico and Montana landscapes of his earlier verse) is the primary inspiration of this poem, and the scene he views at dawn from the hills as he looks down on the city of Pasadena is described with great beauty and power. But of course the poem is more than mere description. The time is about 1930, when the poet is thirty years old. Pasadena is the home of his now aging father, as it was of the poet's childhood, and a good deal of the poem is taken up with a recollection of his childhood days and the changes that have occurred in the last twenty years. Bridges does somewhat the same thing in his recollection of childhood days in his "Summer House on the Mound"; there are rhythms reminiscent of Bridges's poem and a few slight verbal echoes. From 1910 to 1930 parts of California were becoming rapidly urbanized. The urban explosion was not as great as that which occurred after World War II, but the way we were going was clear enough in 1930 and therefore there are comments in the poem on the change near the turn of the century from the primitive landscape to the urban one. In 1930 we were still in the pre-smog era and for that reason the poem is not an attack on the despoilers of the environment, as it might have been forty years later. On the contrary, suburban developments are seen as having a kind of beauty of their own; in fact, they are considered an ecological improvement. Where once there was a dust bowl there are now lawns, acacias, eucalypti, and a pool alive with fish:

> Slow air, slow fire! O deep delay of Time!
> That summer crater smoked like slaking lime,
> The hills so dry, so dense the underbrush,
> That where I pushed my way the giant hush
> Was changed to soft explosion as the sage
> Broke down to powdered ash, the sift of age,
> And fell along my path in shadowy rift.
> On these rocks now no burning ashes drift,
> Mowed lawn has crept along the granite bench,
> The yellow blossoms of acacia drench
> The dawn with pollen; and, with waxen green,
> The long leaves of the eucalypti screen
> The closer hills from view — lithe, tall, and fine,
> And elegant with youth, they bend and shine.
> The small dark pool, jutting with living rock,
> Trembles at every atmospheric shock,
> Blurred to its depth with the cold living ooze.
> From cloudy caves, heavy with summer dews,
> The shyest and most tremulous beings stir,

> The pulsing of their fins a lucent blur,
> That, like illusion, glances off the eyes.
> The pulsing mouths are metronomes, precise.

This passage I believe deserves careful study for its masterly handling of the couplets (some run over, some closed), for its incidental rhythmical and sound effects, for its beautiful and precise imagery, and for its overall rhetorical power. It is formal writing at its best and in my opinion superior to what Frost had been doing with his conversational blank verse or the young Auden was just beginning to do with his rather facile imitations of various conventional verse forms. The poem as a whole is a meditation on the passage of time, which has brought change for better and for worse. It ends with a description of his father's house, which the poet treats with considerable irony; it is no homestead that he can inherit and live in

>   but a shining sphere
> Of glass and glassy moments, frail surprise,
> My father's phantasy of Paradise;
> Which melts upon his death, which he attained
> With loss of heart for every step he gained.

The father and his friends are seen as old and broken men who have misspent their lives in the attainment of superficial, material pleasures and comfort, and now

> They spend astutely their depleted breath,
> With tired ironic visage wait for death.

The poem draws to a conclusion with two great stanzas in which the poet contemplates the power of the modern city—

> The city, on the tremendous valley floor,
> Draws its dream deeper for one passion more,
> Superb on solid loam, and breathing deep,
> Poised for a moment at the verge of sleep.

He then closes with a comment on the encroachment of the motor car and on urbanization of the natural environment:

> Cement roads mark the hills, wide, bending free
> Of cliff and headland. Dropping toward the sea,
> Through suburb after suburb, vast ravines
> Swell to the summer drone of fine machines.
> The driver, melting down the distance here,
> May cast in flight the faint hoof of a deer
> Or pass the faint head set perplexedly.
> And man-made stone outgrows the living tree,
> And at its rising, air is shaken, men
> Are shattered, and the tremor swells again,
> Extending to the naked salty shore,
> Rank with the sea, which crumbles evermore.

"The Slow Pacific Swell" is written in a similar style and, like "A View of

Pasadena," begins with a California landscape and with a childhood recollection of the same landscape twenty years earlier. In this poem, however, we see the landscape as unchanged with the passage of time, for the poet is viewing the sea which is eternal and the spring flowers of the coast which return year after year:

> Far out of sight, forever stands the sea,
> Bounding the land with pale tranquillity.
> When a small child, I watched it from a hill
> At thirty miles or more. The vision still
> Lies in the eye, soft blue and far away:
> The rain has washed the dust from April day;
> Paint-brush and lupine lie against the ground;
> The wind above the hill-top has the sound
> Of distant water in unbroken sky;
> Dark and precise, the little steamers ply—
> Firm in direction, they seem not to stir.

Winters has described in prose the circumstances of the poem:

> I used to get to the hilltop occasionally at about four in the afternoon; the sun was still high and was toward the west. There was a discernible reflection from the surface of the water (without the reflection the water would have been invisible) and the boats were visible in silhouette—although actually only the two large liners, the Yale and the Harvard, could be seen, and they looked about an inch long, and for the rest we had to be satisfied with the plumes of smoke.[40]

"The Slow Pacific Swell" is thematic as well as descriptive. The theme is the confrontation of the human mind with the natural world—here represented by the land and by the sea and its inhabitants—and the land-sea dichotomy has a symbolic significance similar to that summarized in chapters 23 and 58 of Melville's *Moby-Dick*. The land represents the knowable, the relatively secure; the sea represents the terror and danger of the unknowable, not necessarily hostile to man but at least indifferent to him. Both land and sea have at times a beauty to which the human mind can respond:

> The vision still
> Lies in the eye, soft blue and far away:
> The rain has washed the dust from April day;
> Paint-brush and lupine lie against the ground

and

> The whale stood shining, and then sunk in spray.

The poet states that he prefers the land to the sea but nevertheless "would be near" the sea. Again we have the symbolism of *Moby-Dick* and one of Winters's recurrent themes, the proper relationship between character and experience, between mind and sensation:

> A landsman, I. The sea is but a sound.
> I would be near it on a sandy mound,

> And hear the steady rushing of the deep
> While I lay stinging in the sand with sleep.

A gloss on these lines is this passage from Winters's essay on Melville:

> The symbolism of *Moby Dick* is based on the antithesis of the sea and the land: the land represents the known, the mastered, in human experience; the sea, the half-known, the obscure region of instinct, uncritical feeling, danger, and terror.... The relationship of man to the half known, however, is not a simple and static one; he cannot merely stay on land, or he will perish of imperception, but must venture on the sea, without losing his relationship to the land; we have, in brief, the relationship of principle to perception, or, in other words, the problem of judgment.[41]

The essay on Melville was written several years after "The Slow Pacific Swell," when Winters's critical ideas had become more clearly formulated than they were in 1929–30. However, the symbolic relationship between land and sea which Winters finds in *Moby-Dick* is similar to that of the poem. The successful poet must be a man of principle *and* perception. In terms of Melville's romantic epic the man of principle must venture into the sea of perception if he is to live fully; in terms of the poem, the poet once ventured onto the sea and suffered near-death "half drenched in dissolution"—a clear reference to "the madness of my youth." Now he "would be near it" (but in a safe position "on a sandy mound"!) in order to experience the enriching perceptions it provides.

The poem ends with a powerful passage depicting the sea as symbolic of the blind, brute, inscrutable physical universe:

> By night a chaos of commingling power,
> The whole Pacific hovers hour by hour.
> The slow Pacific swell stirs on the sand,
> Sleeping to sink away, withdrawing land,
> Heaving and wrinkled in the moon, and blind,
> Or gathers seaward, ebbing out of mind.

This magnificent poem is a very early example of what, as we have seen, Winters was later to call "post-symbolism." Howard Kaye, defining postsymbolism as "a way of charging sensory details with abstract meaning," comments as follows on the final lines:

> The physical description of the moonlit sea, the abstract ideas of the sea's eternity, destructiveness, and mindlessness, and the emotional effect of terror are inseparable. The verb "hovers," applied to the whole Pacific Ocean, creates a stunning suggestion of an immense looming mass of water. The image is also a link to the looming whale. "Stirs" and "sleeping" suggest a metaphor of the sea as animal, and the line "Heaving and wrinkled in the moon, and blind" sounds like a description of an ancient beast: perhaps a whale. "Ebbing out of mind" means ebbing eternally (time out of mind); ebbing mindlessly; or, more subtly and horribly, the sea seems by association with the image of "withdrawing land" to be drawing the poet's mind out with it as it ebbs.[42]

There are other important poems in *The Journey*. "The Marriage" celebrates with feeling and delicacy the poet's own courtship and marriage:

> Wild spring in dream escaping, the debate
> Of flesh and spirit on those vernal nights,
> Its resolution in naive delights,
> The young kids bleating softly in the rain —
> All this to pass, not to return again.
> And when I found your flesh did not resist,
> It was the living spirit that I kissed,
> It was the spirit's change in which I lay.

The pastoral note is introduced with Winters's characteristic felicity:

> The young kids bleating softly in the rain —

as well as the medieval theme of the debate of flesh vs. spirit, together with the beautifully phrased comment on the temporary nature of youthful love:

> All this to pass, not to return again.

"The Marriage" is one of the few satisfactory poems written by an American in the twentieth century on the subject. The title poem, "The Journey," is a description of a journey by train through the Snake River Country, where the lives of the inhabitants are frequently as violent and appalling as the landscape:

> At night the turbulence of drink and mud,
> Blue glare of gas, the dances dripping blood . . .

but, as we would expect, the poem is far more than mere description. Almost every line is charged with detail of symbolic significance. The theme of the poem, implicit throughout, is clearly evident in these lines:

> Once when the train paused in an empty place,
> I met the unmoved landscape face to face.

The theme is the relationship of the human mind to raw, brute nature and in this poem it is stated, or rather, movingly presented, but left unresolved. It *is* resolved in the last poem in the book, "December Eclogue," which also opens with strikingly descriptive writing of the landscape:

> Frost burns the air till noon. The dogs, quick-eyed,
> Start pheasants on my walks. The countryside
> Lies slightly fevered in a gathering dream.
> Through distant fields a running child may scream,
> A lone horse, shaggy in the salt-marsh, neigh.
> These are not signals, and I go my way.

Winters is a dualist in these poems. There is an uncrossable gap between man and nature, between mind and matter, between human consciousness and the outside world. There is no true communication between man and nature:

> These are not signals, and I go my way.

The pantheistic, solipsistic mysticism of Winters's youth is firmly and finally rejected. (One remembers Winters's high praise of Robert Frost's poem "The Most of It," which is on the same theme and represents Frost's rejection of Emersonian pantheistic mysticism.) Winters's own resolution of the theme as expressed in the rest of "December Eclogue" is to turn to the life of the civilized mind, of the poet and scholar, even though this life is beset with difficulties — the stupidity and malice of the academic establishment and of much of the literary establishment, the deadly routine of teaching elementary classes in order to earn a living, and the dangers of his own violent, emotional temperament. "A Vision" is a nightmare tale of Gothic horror written in dense and ponderous couplets, involving a Widow, a Lover, a severed head, and the poet who becomes identified with the lover. The symbolism is difficult to penetrate, but fortunately Winters has left us his own gloss on the poem:

> The Widow is Evil, half sensual, half spiritual; the head, her beloved and coadjutor, is Death; the lover is one beguiled and overcome. The observer, at first distant from the lover, becomes one with him: as one might form one's character, personal or poetic, on a dangerous model, and so be possessed and destroyed.[43]

The particular temptation that might destroy the lover and the observer appears to be the immersion in pure sensation and the surrender to complete irrationality. Most readers feel the poem to be overwritten, although there is some felicitous imagery, for example:

> The midnight wind poured steadily through pines.
> I saw the trees flame thin, in watery lines.

"The Grave" is a meditation on death. The poet comments on the urn and its ashes:

> Under a little plaque he waits alone.
> There is no faintest tremor in that urn.
> Each flake of ash is sure in its return —
> Never to alter, a pure quality,
> A shadow cast against Eternity.

The phrase "pure quality" was undoubtedly suggested by Allen Tate's distinction between quality and quantity, which Tate defined in his essay "The Fallacy of Humanism," published in *Hound & Horn* in 1930, an essay which had considerable influence on Winters's own thinking at that time.[44] In setting up the dichotomy of "quality" and "quantity," Tate defined quantity as "abstract, timeless, rootless" ideas. Of "quality" Tate said, "The source of quality is nature itself because it is the source of experience." "Pure Quality would be pure evil...pure quality is pure disintegration."[45] Tate's definition of "pure quality" was certainly in Winters's mind as he wrote "The Grave" and probably as he wrote "A Vision," where the male protagonist is in danger of succumbing to pure quality. In the same essay Tate wrote: "But if you never have Quality...you have no experience either." Tate goes on to argue that it is the poet's task to keep a precarious balance on the brink of pure quality. The theme of the relationship between what Tate called quality and quantity has of course affinities with a major recurrent theme in Winters's poetry from about 1929 on—but expressed in various terms, such as the relationship between intellect and sensibility. The proper relationship for the poet in the modern world is one of precarious balance, as in "The Grave":

> To stand, precarious, near the utter end

and in a number of Winters's other poems.

One other poem in *The Journey* deserves comment. Entitled "The Critiad: a Poetical Survey of Recent Criticism," it is Winters's response to the criticisms of his own poetry and also a stinging satire on the literary establishment of the late twenties. It is written in heroic couplets, with overtones of Alexander Pope and Charles Churchill:

> What can I learn here? If they'd read me twice
> And then collaborate on their advice,
> They might reform me. As the matter stands,
> I rest a monster in their fumbling hands.

These critics are guilty of

> Creating definitions right and left,
> Deft because empty, empty because deft,
> Dissembling with fine academic smirk
> The faint stupidity of all their work.

There follows a series of concise ironic characterizations of a number of the leading critics and poets of the day—for example:

> Zabel and Wilson next! Both circumspect,
> Evasive when examined for defect,
> Substantial men, destined to sound careers,
> With weather eye out for the coming years.

Perhaps the most amusing portrait is this little sketch of the indefatigable founding editor of *Poetry,* Harriet Monroe:

> Our Aunt Maria! With disheveled hair,
> With classic features drooping in despair,
> With voice inaudible, with coat awry,
> With some faint imprecision in her eye,
> But with determination in her tread,
> She moves to judge the living and the dead.
> Let any rival but suggest a name
> That he has published, she's a prior claim.
> But read her paper and you know the worst:
> Her method's to print everybody first.

Very few escape the lash. "The Critiad," which was the lead poem in *The*

Journey, probably turned off most potential reviewers. Whether or not this was the reason, the fact is that this important volume received scant attention in the press.

Before Disaster, which was published as one of the Tryon Pamphlets in 1934 at a price of twenty-five cents, was probably the best bargain in poetry in this century — even in the depths of the depression! It contains twenty-one poems written in Winters's then new formalism and in a style so hard (to use Frost's favorite pun) they will be hard to get rid of. The defense of this new formalism is given in the introduction to the pamphlet. The essential passages, as quoted above, are two important contributions to the poetic theory of this century — the argument for the superiority of the accentual syllabic line (for poems written in English) and the exposure of the fallacy of expressive form.

Two major interrelated themes pervade the poems in this volume — the personal struggles of the poet to achieve integration in what he considered to be an age of intellectual and aesthetic chaos, and the public social, economic, and political disasters which he feared were imminent and which indeed reached a crisis five years after the publication of the book, with the outbreak of World War II.

The personal theme is clearly stated in the first poem, "The Dedication," written to his wife. I quote the first stanza:

> Confusion, cold and still,
> Impeding act and thought,
> And the inchoate will:
> With these at last I wrought.

The public theme is in the title poem "Before Disaster: Written Early in the Winter of 1932–33" which begins:

> Evening traffic homeward burns,
> Swift and even on the turns,
> Drifting weight in triple rows,
> Fixed relation and repose.
> This one edges out and by,
> Inch by inch with steady eye.
> But should error be increased,
> Mass and moment are released;
> Matter loosens, flooding blind,
> Levels drivers to its kind.
> Ranks of nations thus descend,
> Watchful, to a stormy end.

And it is related to the personal theme in the final lines:

> By a moment's calm beguiled,
> I have got a wife and child.
> Fool and scoundrel guide the State
> Peace is whore to Greed and Hate.
> Nowhere may I turn to flee:
> Action is security.

> Treading change with savage heel,
> We must live or die by steel.

The verse is hard, lucid, and unambiguous. One cannot spend an hour in the classroom explicating its potentially suggestive meanings. It doesn't require explication but it is nonetheless a powerful performance. Its style is somewhat influenced, I think, by Winters's immersion in Elizabethan poetry during which he developed an admiration for the poetry of plain, blunt statement as he found it in some of the poems of Sir Thomas Wyatt, George Gascoigne, Thomas Nashe, Sir Walter Raleigh, and others. Winters's lines

> By a moment's calm beguiled
> I have got a wife and child

remind me of the poetry of "the school of Gascoigne."

Winters's reevaluation of sixteenth-century lyric poetry in England appeared in *Poetry* early in 1939, about five years after the publication of *Before Disaster*, but we know that he had begun reading this body of poetry years before that date.[46] In the first essay he refers to "about fifteen years of fairly constant immersion in the poetry under consideration."[47] His main thesis is that the poetry of the period has not yet been properly evaluated, that much of the better-known poetry that appears in the anthologies is inferior and that what he calls the "school of Gascoigne"—those writers who employed a plain style in the manner of Gascoigne in contrast to those who employed the ornamental style of the Petrarchans—has been unjustly neglected. He describes the chief characteristics of the poetry of the school of Gascoigne as follows:

> a theme usually broad, simple, and obvious . . . but usually a theme of some importance, humanly speaking; a feeling restrained to the minimum required by the subject; a rhetoric restrained to a similar minimum . . . [and a] strong tendency towards aphoristic statement.[48]

He praises in particular certain poems by Gascoigne, Nashe, Raleigh, and Wyatt (who preceded Gascoigne) and also poems by Ben Jonson, Fulke Greville, and others who came after Gascoigne, who sometimes wrote in the plain style and who probably derived much of it from Gascoigne. Winters called Ben Jonson "a classicist in the best sense," a phrase which is descriptive of much of his own poetry written from 1930 on. But Winters quite rightly resented being referred to as a twentieth-century Tudor or Elizabethan poet, and I do not want to overstate the case of the influence of the Elizabethans on him. Nevertheless he did, in fact, when he chose to write in the plain style, benefit from his study of those sixteenth-century poets whom he especially admired. An example of the plain style in *Before Disaster* is the "Dedication for a Book of Criticism," which begins:

> He who learns may feed on lies:
> He who understands is wise.
> He who understands the great
> Joins them in their own estate:

Throughout the poem the language is denotative and abstract, with little if any attempt at rendering sensory experience. It is a style which is the opposite of that of most of the poetry in *The Bare Hills*. It has all of the characteristics which Winters attributed to the poets of the school of Gascoigne in the quotation above from his essay. In my own opinion this style is somewhat limited, and I think that this poem does not represent Winters at his best. He is at his best as a post-symbolist poet, when he is employing his great talent at rendering sensory experience concomitantly with his ability to express precisely the conceptual material of his poetry. Nevertheless the plain style as it is used in *Before Disaster* and in his later work has a directness and force which I find admirable, and I would not want to see any of the poetry written in it forgotten. The other poems in *Before Disaster* that are wholly or almost wholly written in the plain style, with little concrete, connotative diction, are "A Post-Card to the Social Muse," "On the Death of Senator Thomas J. Walsh," "The Prince" (with the exception of the last two lines), "To a Young Writer" (with the exception of the fifth line), and "For My Father's Grave" which reads:

> Here lies one sweet of heart.
> Stay! thou too must depart.
> In silence set thy store —
> These ashes speak no more.

But we are not done with the plain style in citing these poems which, as I have said, are written almost entirely in abstract language without figures of speech. The last line of "The Prince" states that the successful leader of his people must become immortal and

> Stare publicly from death through marble eyes.

Here the identification of the bust or statue with death reminds us of Donne more than it does of Jonson or Gascoigne. But in many of the other poems in *Before Disaster*, concrete language and figures of speech are carefully used not in the manner of post-symbolism or of Donne but in the manner of the restrained rhetoric of Jonson and Fulke Greville. The tone of the plain direct statement is there, the diction is still largely denotative and unambiguous, and the figures of speech are rather simple. For example, consider the last stanza of "Orpheus," written in memory of Hart Crane:

> Yet the fingers on the lyre
> Spread like an avenging fire.
> Crying loud, the immortal tongue,
> From the empty body wrung,
> Broken in a bloody dream,
> Sang unmeaning down the stream.

There are here two simple comparisons (one stated, the other implied) between Crane and Orpheus. The diction is concrete and vivid, indeed in the next to last line violent, but the complexities of the postsymbolist style are not present. A quiet example of the poetry of direct statement is "Anacreontic," which has an effective minimum of concrete diction:

> Peace! there is peace at last.
> Deep in the Tuscan shade,
> Swathed in the Grecian past,
> Old Landor's bones are laid.
>
> How many years have fled!
> But o'er the sunken clay
> Of the auguster dead
> The centuries delay.
>
> Come, write good verses then!
> That still, from age to age,
> The eyes of able men
> may settle on our page.

"The Werwolf," on the other hand, is dense with concrete language and somewhat obscured by hidden meanings. Winters did not include it in his *Collected Poems*. The two poems to his infant daughter are among the most moving in the book. The last two stanzas of the second poem illustrate the aphoristic style at its best:

> Take few men to your heart!
> Unstable, fierce, unkind,
> The ways that men impart.
> True love is slow to find.
>
> True art is slow to grow.
> Like a belated friend,
> It comes to let one know
> Of what has had an end.

Perhaps the best poem in *Before Disaster* and one of the finest in the entire Winters canon is "On the Road to the Sunnyvale Air-Base." Douglas Peterson has published a brilliant analysis of "On the Road," to which the reader is referred and to which I am indebted in the following brief discussion.[49] Peterson considers the poem to be a triumphant example of the postsymbolist method by means of which freshly perceived sensory detail is rendered intelligible by a governing idea—the Darwinian concept of the persistence of life and at the same time an awareness of the superior value of human life at its best:

> Here scholars pause to speak.

These concepts are "the means which enable him to see himself and other men as essentially agents within the process that concerns him," and here, as in other postsymbolist poems by Winters, "brilliant descriptive details simultaneously illuminate and are in turn illuminated by the conceptual structures of which they are a part." This is the poem:

> The calloused grass lies hard
> Against the cracking plain:

Life is a grayish stain;
The salt-marsh hems my yard.

Dry dikes rise hill on hill:
In sloughs of tidal slime
Shell-fish deposit lime,
Wild sea-fowl creep at will.

The highway, like a beach,
Turns whiter, shadowy, dry:
Loud, pale against the sky,
The bombing planes hold speech.

Yet fruit grows on the trees;
Here scholars pause to speak;
Through gardens bare and Greek,
I hear my neighbor's bees.

The first two stanzas describe the harsh salt marsh which surrounds the poet's home and the forms of lower life which inhabit the marsh. In the third stanza we see the marsh traversed by a human construct, the highway (which is also described in harsh terms) which leads to what (in the thirties when the poem was written) was considered a triumph of human technology, the Sunnyvale Air-Base built to house the enormous dirigibles of that time, including the famous *Macon*.[50] Over the road hover the most advanced agents of human destruction, the bombing planes. The final stanza, introduced by "Yet," presents the resolution of the theme — the twentieth-century Darwinian universe in which we live and from which we human beings evolved after millenia of struggle for survival, a struggle which still persists even at the human level, *yet* has a place, however limited, for the communion of the civilized minds of the scholar and the poet. Every sensory detail in a subtle and carefully controlled way contributes to the poetic realization of the theme. The reader should consider carefully, for example, the cadenced sound effects of the last two lines and the connotations of "bare" and "Greek."

The beautifully written "Midas" and "Sonnet to the Moon" are somewhat obscure if one comes upon them without having read Winters's previous poetry and criticism. Fortunately, they can here be considered in context and with the help of Winters's own explanatory comment which appeared in the Notes to his *Poems* that he printed himself in 1940.[51] "Midas" is an allegorical poem derived from the famous tale of the man to whom the wish was granted that everything he touched would turn to gold. His end is described in the final lines of the poem:

Ere he knew that he must die,
Ore had veinëd lip and eye:
Caught him scarcely looking back,
Startled at his golden track,
Immortalized the quickened shade
Of meaning by a moment made.

In his "Notes," Winters defines the literary results of his early solipsism and mystical pantheism — "the literary discipline becomes largely a technique of inducing and fixing a kind of verbal hallucination of which the comprehensible motive is seriously imperfect" — and cites his free-verse "The Goatherds" and "Nocturne" as examples of the use of this technique. In "Midas," written in controlled and polished couplets, we have (allegorically) defined the solipsistic, mystical poet in action and his inevitable end. Winters describes the poem as one "which deals with the progress of illusion," and it should be noted that here, as in the later poem "John Sutter," gold also becomes the symbol for pure evil. Similarly in "Sonnet to the Moon," we have unforgettably presented "the de-intellectualized sensibility":

> O triple goddess! Contemplate my plight!
> Opacity, my fate! Change, my delight!
> The yellow tom-cat, sunk in shifting fur,
> Changes and dreams, a phosphorescent blur.

The triple goddess whom Winters addresses is the very ancient Hecate described as follows by Jung and Kerényi:

> One such characteristic, and the chief among them, is the *triple form* which appears relatively late in artistic representations of the goddess, but is indirectly confirmed by Hesiod. The Poet of the Theogony acclaims her as the mighty Mistress of the *three* realms — earth, heaven, and sea. He also says that the goddess already had this dominion in the time of the Titans, before Zeus and his order.[52]

They also point out that the epithet *Phosphoros* is frequently applied to her — hence Winters's "phosphorescent blur." They associate her with Demeter and Persephone, hence she is a triple goddess in another sense — as maiden, mother, and moon. Charles Anthon describes Hecate as follows:

> She was the moon, and hence were connected with her all those accessory ideas which are grouped around that of the moon: she "is the goddess that troubles the reason of men, the goddess that presides over nocturnal ceremonies, and, consequently over magic; hence her identity with Diana for the Grecian mythology, with Isis for the Egyptians."[53]

Anthon also refers to "the *three formed* goddess, ruling as Selene in the sky, as Artemis or Diana on earth, as Hecate or Proserpina in the underworld."[54] Thus the triple goddess's three realms were sometimes considered to be heaven, earth, and hell.

As has been pointed out by several critics, the moon becomes a complex symbol in Winters's poetry. It suggests darkness (the dark of the moon), the occult, the mysterious, the border areas of perception. It stands for the full complexity of the dark sides of life and religion. Moonlight sometimes stands for that which is shifting, indefinable, and at times alluringly beautiful. As we shall see, Artemis, as a moon goddess, plays an important part in Winters's poem "Theseus." She represents the essential existential mystery of experience.

"Midas" and "Sonnet to the Moon" point up the difference between the earlier and the later poems. In the earlier free-verse poems Winters was, in a way, the victim of his mystical solipsism. In the later poems he understands and defines it.

"Phasellus Ille" was suggested by R. P. Blackmur's poem of the same title, which was inspired by Catullus's charming and nostalgic praise of his pinnace "Phasellus ille quem videtis, hospites...", which had successfully weathered many a violent storm and was now retired to a quiet lake. Blackmur contrasts his small unseaworthy and leaky boat to the fast and tight sailing ship Catullus boasted of and then says:

> I do not need the bluster and the wail
> in this small boat, of perilous high seas
> nor the blown salt smarting in my teeth;
> if the tide lift and weigh me in his scale
> I know, and feel in me the knowledge freeze,
> how smooth the utter sea is, underneath.[55]

Blackmur's poem is more serious and profound than that of Catullus. It is convincing in its detail—we feel that the poem arises from actual experience with the boat and the sea as well as from the metaphysical awareness expressed in the last two lines. Winters considered it to be one of Blackmur's best poems. In his own poem Winters transforms the boat into his own small home which, like a ship, is withstanding the shock of a storm. In the final lines the threat is more precisely stated than in Blackmur's poem:

> The hazards of insane inheritance,
> Lave our smooth hull with what we little know.

In describing by contrast the interior of his house, Winters writes one line containing three true spondees:

> Wárm mind, wárm heárt, beám, bolt, and lóck,
> You hold the love you took....

The accents are Winters's own and appear in the poem. A successful spondaic line in an otherwise iambic poem is unusual in English verse.

All of the other poems in *Before Disaster* not here discussed are worth a careful reading, but it is necessary to move on to the poet's later work. Characteristic of the style and content of the entire pamphlet are the last three lines of "On Teaching the Young":

> The poet's only bliss
> Is in cold certitude—
> Laurel, archaic, rude.

The next few years were discouraging ones for Winters. He was attempting to weather out the depression on an instructor's salary; the department long delayed his promotion to an assistant professorship, as he memorably states in his "Song from an Academic Bower." It has never been reprinted and therefore I quote the entire poem.

These walls are brown and faded,
And during eighteen years
I have sat here unshaded,
Not wholly with my peers.
I have considered long
The reasons for my song.

Such thought as I have mastered
Has been my own for pay,
While each persuasive bastard
Who came has had his day:
The rough hide of the ass,
If curried well, will pass.

Although in my indenture
I have worn out my youth,
Yet in the slow adventure
I have observed a truth—
Truth that is bare and old,
Worn plain with being told:

Those men who seek for learning,
Driven by the airy lash,
If they are undiscerning
Find gritty salt and ash—
Then turn like fiery snakes
To battle for the stakes.

While those whose minds are living
Grow hard and cool and gay,
Elude the unforgiving,
And somehow have their say
In words no fool can touch
Because they mean too much.[56]

He was having trouble getting a book of poems published, although he was writing some of his best poetry at this time. Finally he bought a hand press and printed his *Poems* himself in 1940. The Notes carry this statement: "The kind of political maneuvering which appears to be a prerequisite at present to the publication of a book of poems is impossible from Los Altos, even if one possess, as I do not, the taste or the talent for it."

The volume is a selection from his earliest published work to 1940 and it includes "all of my verse which I care to preserve." There are twenty-five poems which appear after those selected from the *Before Disaster* group. With the exception of "Theseus," which was in *Hound & Horn* in 1933, all of them were published in 1934 or later, most of them later than 1934. However, several may have been finished by 1933 or even earlier, as I can remember Winters reading "Heracles" to a class in the spring of that year. Of this group, the most important are "Theseus," "Heracles," "Socrates," "John Sutter," "The California Oaks," "Sir Gawaine and the Green Knight," "Time and the Garden," "A Prayer for My Son," and "A Summer Commentary."

"Theseus" was a major undertaking. It is a poem that deserves much more attention than it has so far received. Winters's only published comment on the poem (as far as I know) is "Theseus is the man of action"[57] — in contrast, that is, to the protagonists of three other poems by Winters—Socrates, the man of principle; Alcmena, the ethical will; and Heracles, the artist.

Theseus, warrior, lover, and statesman, is presented in his relationship with experience—here is the usual romantic and postromantic epistemological concern with subject and object—but the experience Theseus undergoes is of a rather special sort—occult and semidivine—here symbolized by the moon, the major and pervasive symbol in the poem, as it has been throughout Winters's entire career. (See "Nocturne" in *The Bare Hills* [1929]; "Sonnet to the Moon" in *Before Disaster* [1934]; "To the Moon" in *Collected Poems* [1952].) Experience in this poem is, as Grosvenor Powell has pointed out,[58] mysterious and ambiguous, but there is nothing ambiguous about Winters's poetic presentation of it.

In the poem, the moon-experience is embodied in various personages, including the three women with whom Theseus has sexual relations: Hippolyta (the Amazonian priestess of the moon-goddess, Artemis); Ariadne, daughter of Pasiphaë, another moon-goddess who is referred to in the poem as "daughter of the moon"; and Phaedra, another daughter of Pasiphaë. (According to Anthon, Pasiphaë herself is the moon and her story rests on an astronomical basis. The Cretans worshiped her as a lunar deity.) Hippolytus, son of Theseus and Hippolyta, is also "a man of moonlight." The sexual relationship between Theseus and the three women symbolizes the fusion between the human protagonist and the outer world, which, like the moon, is seen in terms of darkness and light.

Those familiar with the mythic story of Theseus will be aware that Winters has made some changes in it for thematic and poetic reasons.[59] The main action of Winters's poem is as follows. In part 1, "The Wrath of Artemis," Theseus, in the company of Heracles, engages in battle with the Amazons. Hippolyta, a priestess of Artemis, is seized by Heracles and subsquently raped by Theseus. She will eventually give birth to his son Hippolytus. In Part 2, "Theseus and Ariadne," Theseus, with the help of Ariadne, kills the Minotaur (the bestial offspring of Pasiphaë and a bull and therefore half-brother to Ariadne) and then carries off Ariadne. After sexual relations with her he kills her and takes as his next mate Phaedra, the sister of Ariadne. In Part 3, "The Old Age of Theseus," the hero is seen meditating on his past experiences. After the death of Ariadne and his marriage with Phaedra, he became head of the state and, now a statesman preoccupied with political affairs, lived through the deaths of Phaedra and of Hippolytus, brought about by the incestuous love of Phaedra for the son of Theseus. In the final lines of the poem we see him betrayed by the state and by the treacherous Lycomedes, who causes his death.

Such a bare summary of action does no justice at all to the poetic beauty and profundity of "Theseus," but it may help the reader follow the complicated story and the many mythological allusions. The poem begins with a stunningly beautiful presentation of the battle with the Amazons and the abduction of Hippolyta:

On the wet sand the queen emerged from forest,
Tall as a man, half naked, and at ease,
Leaned on her bow and eyed them. This, the priestess,
Who, with her savages, had harried Greece
From south to east, and now fought down from Thrace,
Her arrows cold as moonlight, and her flesh
Bright as her arrows, and her hatred still.
Heracles eyed the ground, and Theseus watched her.
Remote and thin as a bird-call over ice
From deep in the forest came the cry of her warriors,
Defiance from Artemis, the evasive daemon:
Hippolyta smiled, but Heracles moved softly
And seized her suddenly, bore her to the ship,
Bound her and left her vibrating like a deer,
Astounded beyond terror. And her women
Fell as they came, like water to dry earth,
An inundation of the living moon.

The passage may owe something to T. Sturge Moore's fascinating poem "The Rout of the Amazons," which Winters admired. The blank verse is in my judgment equal to the best of Robinson and Stevens, and the postsymbolist sensory detail is more effectively handled than in most of Stevens. There are passages of somewhat lower intensity as we proceed through the poem, but nowhere is there a serious let-down. Powell praises especially these lines from part 3:

>   — the Orphic music
>   That swelled the measure of the Argo's oars
>   To a golden stride coëval with the Sun —

pointing out that the sun's "movements are outside of time and are eternally repeated, like the actions in myth.... This is the fullest use of poetic language."[60]

The poem ends with the death of "the man of action":

>   So cast him from the rock to solitude,
>   To the cold perfection of unending peace.

The implication is that the man of action will find perfection only in the peace of death.

Perfection for the artist, however, may be found elsewhere. Winters writes of the hero of his poem "Heracles": "Allegorically, he is the artist, in hand to hand, or intuitive, combat with experience. The apotheosis at the end represents, for me, the moral, or formal apotheosis of the artist in the finished work."[61]

A primary source of "Heracles" is the account of the hero given by Charles Anthon in his *Classical Dictionary*.[62] Anthon begins with a summary of Heracles' life, the main episodes of which are well known. He was the son of Zeus and Alcmena of whom Hera, Zeus's wife, was naturally jealous. Hera vowed destruction of the infant mothered by her rival and she was his effective enemy throughout his remarkable career, which began with his strangling in his cradle two serpents sent by Hera to devour him. Upon reaching manhood he performed various public services including the slaying of the lion of Mount Cithaeron. Then, in a fit of madness brought on by Hera, he killed his own children. As penance he was forced by Eurystheus (in whose power he had been placed by a rash vow of Zeus) to undertake twelve labors, all seemingly impossible. Heracles successfully accomplished the first labor by strangling the Nemean lion with his bare hands, clothing himself in its skin, and carrying the carcass on his shoulders to Eurystheus, who then in fear and trembling retired to a brazen vault—"Eurystheus vibrant in his den of brass," as Winters describes him. Heracles' second labor was to kill the many headed Hydra of Lerna. When he accomplished this, he dipped his arrows into its poisonous blood, thus making the wounds they inflicted incurable. After finishing his twelve labors and performing other exploits, he married Deïanira. On a journey with her he came to a river; Nessus the centaur by divine decree was the ferryman. Heracles forded the river himself. Deïanira got into the boat with Nessus and was assaulted by him. Heracles shot him through the heart as he landed. The centaur managed to take Deïanira aside and convince her that his poisoned blood was in fact a love philtre which could be used to maintain the love of Heracles for his wife if it was ever in danger of wavering. Sometime later, Deïanira, fearing that her husband was falling in love with his captive Iole, tinged a tunic with the centaur's blood and sent it to Heracles. When Heracles put it on, he suffered unbearable torment. Thus Winters:

> And yet the Centaur stung me from afar,
> His blood envenomed with the Hydra's blood;
> Thence was I outcast from the earthy war.
>
> Nessus the Centaur, with his wineskin full,
> His branch and thyrsus, and his fleshy grip—
> Her whom he could not force he yet could gull.
> And she drank poison from his bearded lip.

Deïanira, when she heard what she had done, hanged herself. Heracles mounted his funeral pyre and ordered his body to be burnt. As the flames ascended the pyre, he was carried to heaven and endowed with immortality.

After describing the end of Heracles, Anthon in a long, detailed, and eloquent passage sets out to prove that Heracles was a sun god, that the twelve labors are analogous to the twelve signs of the zodiac through which the sun passes. To quote Winters again:

> Compelled down ways obscure with analogue
> To force the Symbols of the Zodiac—

Furthermore, Anthon argues, the story of Heracles did not originate with the Greeks. It came from the East, and Heracles was a sun god in Egypt long before he was adopted by the Greeks. Anthon argues his case with fervor, and I suspect the passage had considerable impact on Winters. I quote a few key sentences from Anthon's account:

There is in it [the mythology of Hercules] identification of one or more

Grecian heroes with Melcarth, the sun-god of the Phoenicians. Hence we find Hercules so frequently represented as the sun-god, and his twelve labours regarded as the passage of the sun through the twelve signs of the zodiac. He is the powerful planet which animates and imparts fecundity to the universe, whose divinity has been honoured in every quarter by temples and altars, and consecrated in the religious strains of all nations. . . . If we fix from this point [the summer solstice, at which time Heracles founded the Olympic games] the departure of the sun on his annual career and compare the progress of the luminary through the signs of the zodiac with that of the twelve labours of Hercules, altering somewhat the order in which they are handed down to us, a very striking coincidence is instantly observed. . . . In the first month the sun passes into the sign *Leo*; and in his first labour Hercules slew the Nemean lion. . . . In the second month the sun enters the sign *Virgo*, when the constellation of the Hydra sets; and in his second labour Hercules destroyed the Lernaean hydra.

Anthon proceeds in like manner through the other ten labors and then comments:

If Hercules be regarded as having actually existed, nothing can be more monstrous, nothing more at variance with every principle of chronology, nothing more replete with contradictions, than the adventures of such an individual as poetry makes him to have been. But, considered as the luminary that gives light and life to the world, as the god who impregnates all nature with his fertilizing rays, every part of the legend teems with animation and beauty, and is marked by a pleasing and perfect harmony.

The protagonist of Winters's poem, then, is considerably more than the giant Roman Hercules with a big club. He is a solar deity, the principle of life itself, in eternal conflict with the forces of darkness, and this fact accounts for much of the feeling of the poem.

But Heracles is also, allegorically considered, as we have seen, "the artist in hand-to-hand or semi-intuitive combat with experience." The poem is a moving statement of the difficulties to be overcome by a poet of this time or of any time.

One should not leave the poem without noting the triumphant fusion of the major themes in the last two stanzas:

> This was my grief, that out of grief I grew —
> Translated as I was from earth at last,
> From the sad pain that Deïanira knew.
> Transmuted slowly in a fiery blast,
>
> Perfect, and moving perfectly, I raid
> Eternal silence to eternal ends:
> And Deïanira, an imperfect shade,
> Retreats in silence as my arc descends.

The "fiery blast" which transmuted Heracles refers to the effect of the poisoned garment which consumed his flesh as with fire, to the flames of his funeral pyre, and to the burning rays of the sun god. The lines

> Perfect, and moving perfectly, I raid
> Eternal silence to eternal ends

refer to Heracles as a solar deity moving through space. But these lines also, as we have seen, express the formal perfection (on the allegorical level) which the poet finds in his completed work. Thus all three levels—literal, mythical, and allegorical are successfully brought together at the end of the poem.

"Heracles" is written in dense, ponderous, slow-moving iambic pentameter lines grouped in quatrains. The style is entirely appropriate for the subject. The texture and movement of the lines owe something, I believe, to T. Sturge Moore, whom Winters was rereading in the early thirties at the very time he was writing his mythological poems. The publication of Moore's collected poems in four volumes in 1931–33 was the occasion for Winters's close study of a poet he had admired for some years. Winters reviewed the collection in *Hound & Horn* in the spring of 1933 and scandalized the establishment by claiming that at his best Moore was a better poet than Yeats. (It should be noticed, incidentally, that in Moore's collection are poems on Theseus, the Amazons, the centaurs, Artemis, Chiron, and Heracles—all subjects of Winters's poems.) If one compares the last stanza of Moore's "Tragic Fates I" with almost any quatrain of "Heracles," one will notice a similarity of rhythm and texture. It reads:

> Though circumstances sleek as robes of ermine,
> With sword, with crown, with jewelled, poisoned cup,
> With blood poured out our tragic moods determine,
> Thy naked corpse shall fill their measure up.[63]

Compare this stanza from "Heracles":

> Compelled down ways obscure with analogue
> To force the Symbols of the Zodiac—
> Bright Lion, Boundless Hydra, Fiery Dog—
> I spread them on my arms as on a rack.

For his brief poem "Alcmena," stating his admiration for the mother of Heracles—here called Alcides—Winters employed a similar packed line, but this time arranged in iambic couplets. The primary source is probably Anthon's *Classical Dictionary*. Alcmena, before yielding to her lover Amphitryon, insisted that he punish the Teleboans who had slain her brothers. He went on a successful expedition against them and on returning to Thebes discovered that Alcmena had been united with Zeus, an act which resulted in the birth of Heracles. After the death of her son, she lived to see his son Hyllus slay the tyrant Eurystheus, who had by a trick of Hera gained ascendancy over Heracles and had imposed the twelve labors on him. The head of Eurystheus was sent to Alcmena. She dug out the eyes with a weaving shuttle. Out of respect for her courage and pride Zeus made her immortal and espoused her to Rhadamanthus who according to Pindar was a judge in the island of the blessed but according to Latin poets was a judge in the lower world. Winters follows the Latin version of the story. He intended this poem to be allegorical, for in his note to *Poems*, 1940, he says, "Alcmena is the ethical will, verging on barbarity, in itself, but when impregnated with genius, producing the artist." The intention to present "the ethical will, verging on barbarity" is obviously successful, but I think the second part of Winters's intention is not realized in the poem. Nevertheless its stony hard style makes it memorable within its limits. The poem ends thus:

> But Zeus remembered the unbending dame,
> Her giant maidenhood, the tireless frame,
> That long had honored and had served him well,
> And made her Rhadamanthus' queen in Hell.

"Chiron" is even shorter than "Alcmena" and at the same time a more difficult and profound poem. Again turning to Anthon's *Dictionary* we see that Chiron was an immortal centaur, with a body half man and half horse, the offspring of Saturn and the nymph Philyra. Fearing the jealousy of his wife, Rhea, Saturn changed himself into a stallion and the nymph into a mare before completing the seduction. Chiron was a scholar, especially versed in music and surgery, and he numbered among his pupils Achilles and Heracles. In the fight between Heracles and the centaurs, Chiron was accidentally wounded by one of Heracles' arrows, which had been poisoned with the blood of the Lernaean Hydra. He suffered unbearable pain—"By the stallion body racked." He longed to die. He was allowed by Jove to impart his immortality to Prometheus and thus by dying was released from misery.

The crux of the poem is in the second stanza:

> Dying scholar, dim with fact,
> By the stallion body racked,
> Studying my long defeat,
> I have mastered Jove's deceit.

What is Jove's deceit? As I read the poem it means this: Chiron on being granted immortality, a seeming good, finds that the seeming good is negated by the fact that he still must live in a physical body which can suffer pain. He masters the deceit by finding a way to die. The poem, then, expresses an old man's longing for death. The mind, no matter how fully developed, is tied to the body, must suffer its ills, and must die with it. This theme will also be found in one of Winters's best later poems, "To the Holy Spirit." Once the scholar has accepted the fact of mortality he will be like Chiron:

> On the edge of naught I wait
> Magnitude inviolate.[64]

In "Socrates" Winters describes the man of principle, in contrast to Theseus, the man of action, and Heracles, the artist. The poem is forcefully written. Socrates emerges as an appealing and admirable figure. Anthon in his summary of Socrates' life emphasizes that Socrates was a *moral* philosopher, intent on correcting the envy of the young who had been led astray by the sophists and other unsound teachers. Hence Winters's line

> Tired in the noon-day by the badly taught.

Winters did not consider himself a reincarnation of Socrates; nevertheless, there is a good deal of Winters in this poem—the contempt for superficial thinking, the insistence on absolute values, the importance of definition. Socrates' enemies, on the other hand,

> Judge definition the most fierce of crimes.

The poem is a tribute to the power of intellect, and Socrates did in fact become

> The vast foundation of a Western World

for Plato and Aristotle followed him. Especially characteristic of Winters are the final two lines:

> And him whom I have changed, I call my friend.
> The mind is formed. Dissuade it, he who can.

Winters lived for over fifty years in California — most of the time in Los Altos, which was once a small rural town near Stanford University and about thirty or forty miles southeast of San Francisco, on the fringes of the Bay area. This area has one of the best climates in the United States — hot in midsummer, but with air so dry that one is quickly cooled in the shade. There is little if any rain in the summer. There is moderate rainfall in the winter months which turns the bare golden-brown foothills to sudden green. Fruit trees, olive trees, and vineyards abound. It is natural that Winters should write descriptively about the California landscape and that he should put many of his thematic poems in a California setting. Two of the best of these — "On the Road to the Air Base" and "Summer Commentary" — have already been discussed. "The California Oaks" is also one of the finest of this group. It is elegiac in tone, for it is, in part at least, a lament for the passing of these ancient giant trees — "the archaic race" — a destruction brought about by the encroachment of American settlers from the East, beginning with the gold rush of 1849. "The California Oaks" is an ecological poem written many years before the current fashionable emphasis on ecology. The passing of old trees — whether by the woodman's axe or otherwise — is a dangerous subject, which has led more than one good poet into sentimental clichés. Hopkins's famous "Binsey Poplars," for instance, is a bit of romantic fluff when compared to Winters's poem, which is written in the same slow-moving and stately style of "Heracles" — though less ponderous and less complexly allusive. Winters employed an interesting stanza form which, I believe, he never used again. It consists of eight lines of iambic pentameter, with the seventh line broken between the sixth and seventh syllables to give an extra rhyme. The result is a rhythm and a sound effect quite different from that of the iambic pentameter quatrain. A quotation is better than a description. Here is the first stanza:

> Spreading and low, unwatered, concentrate
> Of years of growth that thickens, not expands,
> With leaves like mica and with roots that grate
> Upon the deep foundations of these lands,
> In your brown shadow, on your heavy loam
> — Leaves shrinking to the whisper of decay —
> What feet have come to roam,

what eyes to stay?
Your motion has o'ertaken what calm hands?

It should be noted that the final line rhymes with the second line and this fact, together with the internal rhyme of the broken line, gives a very satisfactory and complex "binding" effect. Each stanza is a complete unit and the movement of the lines within the stanza is slow and dignified. The poem is to me a perfect example of classic form and beauty.

Winters's intention is to give a sense of great antiquity to the trees — he uses the word *archaic* twice — and to reinforce this he describes the arrival of human beings beneath the trees from three historical episodes — Hwui-Shan in A.D. 499 who is met by the Indians already there, Drake in the sixteenth century, and then the Spaniards. The early presence of Hwui-Shan raised some eyebrows in academia when the poem was first published in the *Southern Review* in 1936, but now the notion that ancient man may have crossed both the Atlantic and the Pacific long before Columbus has become commonplace. The stanza describing Hwui-Shan is, I think, the most beautiful in the poem:

Quick as a sunbeam, when a bird divides
The lesser branches, on impassive ground,
Hwui-Shan, the ancient, for a moment glides,
Demure with wisdom, and without a sound;
Brown feet that come to meet him, quick and shy,
Move in the flesh, then, browner, dry to bone;
The brook-like shadows lie
                    where sun had shone;
Ceaseless, the dead leaves gather, mound on mound.

"The California Oaks" ends with the invasion of the miners, followed by the permanent settlers. As a result:

The archaic race —
Black oak, live oak, and valley oak — ere long
Must crumble on the place
            which they made strong
And in the calm they guarded now abide.

Winters in the thirties was doing considerable reading in the history of California and of the West; the most significant poetic result was "John Sutter," which surveys the life of this famous patriarch of the West.[65] The pioneer adventurer and founding father of California was born in Germany of Swiss parentage. He abandoned his family and fled to the States to escape a debtors' prison. By 1839 he had made his way via New York, St. Louis, the Oregon Trail, and Hawaii to the confluence of the Sacramento and American rivers (near the site of the present city of Sacramento) where with a few loyal native Hawaiian followers and several whites he built, with Indian labor, Fort Sutter, which commanded the entire area of upper California. By the end of 1845 he was in possession of 4,000 head of cattle, 3,000 sheep, other livestock, vast wheat fields, a lumbering industry, a salmon fishery, a distillery, and a beaver fur trade that competed with that of the Hudson's Bay Company. Compulsively generous, he never turned from his door any of the increasing number of immigrants, and he spent considerable sums on the entertainment of his friends—$2,000 on one famous Fourth of July banquet when he entertained the governor of California and William Tecumseh Sherman. His good fortune came to an end with the discovery of gold in January 1848, on the American River about thirty miles from Fort Sutter. By 1849 the garden empire was engulfed by a horde of lawless miners who pillaged and stole his property. In disgust, he retreated to the comparative quiet of his Hock Farm on the Feather River, which was burned to the ground by an arsonist in 1865. Sutter, now virtually penniless, left California forever.[66]

Winters's poem presents the tragedy of a man of considerable stature brought down by the greed of lesser men. Sutter sought wealth and power and his methods of attaining them were not always scrupulous, but he was a man of vision, who developed a waste land into a flourishing empire and prepared the way for what has become the state of California. Those who destroyed him were motivated by the lust for gold, which Winters sees as pure evil:

> Metal, intrinsic value, deep and dense,
> Preanimate, inimitable, still,
> Real, but an evil with no human sense,
> Dispersed the mind to concentrate the will.

In this powerful poem Winters catches the spirit of a man and of a pioneer nation:

> I was the patriarch of the shining land,
> Of the blond summer and metallic grain;
> Men vanished at the motion of my hand,
> And when I beckoned they would come again.
>
> The earth grew dense with grain at my desire;
> The shade was deepened at the springs and streams;
> Moving in dust that clung like pillared fire,
> The gathering herds grew heavy in my dreams.

And then he describes the end:

> With knives they dug the metal out of stone;
> Turned rivers back, for gold through ages piled,
> Drove knives to hearts, and faced the gold alone;
> Valley and river ruined and reviled;[67]
>
> Reviled and ruined me, my servant slew,
> Strangled him from the figtree by my door.
> When they had done what fury bade them do,
> I was a cursing beggar, stripped and sore.

"John Day, Frontiersman" also pays tribute to the pioneer spirit. John Day (1770?–1820), the so-called Kentucky hunter, was actually born in Virginia. Little is known about his early life. By 1798 he was in Missouri engaged in farming, trapping, hunting, and mining. In November 1810, he met the Wilson

Price Hunt party of Astorians at the Nodaway River and signed to go on their expedition to the mouth of the Columbia River. Hunt was one of John Jacob Astor's agents in the overland expedition, commissioned to explore the country and the trail from St. Louis to the newly founded settlement of Astoria at the mouth of the Columbia with a view to the eventual establishment of fur trading posts in that area. On this trip, in December 1811, he became so ill that he was left behind at Weiser, Idaho, on the Snake River, his friend Ramsay Crooks staying with him. The following spring the two men made their way across the Blue Mountains to the Columbia River. There they met the friendly Walla Walla Indians, but when they reached the confluence of the Columbia and the mouth of a river known today as the John Day River they were assaulted by hostile Indians, robbed, and stripped naked. They started back toward Walla Walla territory but were rescued by another party of Astorians whom they accompained to Astoria, Day arriving there in May 1812. The next month he started on a return trip to New York with other Astorians, went insane, and had to be returned to Astoria. He recovered, entered the service of the rival North West Company, died in 1820, and is buried, probably, where he is reported to have died, in the Salmon River Mountains of Idaho.[68] He is mentioned several times in Washington Irving's *Astoria* (1836), which is an account of John Jacob Astor's attempt to control the fur trade of the Pacific Northwest and the Columbia River. This book is probably one of Winters's sources for his poem. Irving describes Day as follows:

> Another recruit that joined the camp at Nodawa deserves equal mention. This was John Day, a hunter from the backwoods of Virginia, who had been several years on the Missouri in the service of Mr. Crooks, and of other traders. He was about forty years of age, six feet two inches high, straight as an Indian; with an elastic step as if he trod on springs, and a handsome open manly countenance. It was his boast that, in his younger days, nothing could hurt or daunt him; but he had "lived too fast," and injured his constitution by his excesses. Still he was strong to hand, bold of heart, a prime woodman and an almost unerring shot. He had the frank spirit of a Virginian, and the rough heroism of a pioneer of the west.[69]

According to Irving, Day did not recover from his insanity but died within the year. Modern research has proved that this is a mistake and that Day did not die until 1820. Winters repeats Irving's mistake, saying that Day "died a madman." Winters accurately describes the John Day River in Oregon as "a gentle river in a fertile land." The river draws a large area with little rainfall and therefore does not deliver much water.

Day was a man very different in temperament from Sutter. Less gregarious than the founder of California, his goal was not wealth or political power but the desire to discover and see new lands. He sometimes faced the perils of hunting and of exploration alone. In his sympathetic portrait of him Winters succeeds in universalizing and commending the adventurous individual who penetrates any frontier—physical, aesthetic, intellectual, spiritual—at the risk of loneliness, madness, and death:

> Amid the stony winter, gray with care,
> Hunted by savages from sleep to sleep
> —Those patriots of darkness and despair!—
> You climbed in solitude what rigid steep!

There are probably implicit subjective elements in most of the poems about persons Winters admired—such as the desire for the intellectual power and influence of Socrates, the symbolic aesthetic prowess of Heracles, the courage of the solitary John Day. But let us not call these persons *personae*—an overused and badly used word. In poetry, as in drama and fiction, there is likely to be something of the creator in the created beings of any author. (There is a bit of Melville, for example, in the blasphemous Ahab—but Ahab is by no means the persona of Melville, nor his spokesman.) In "On Rereading a Passage from John Muir," however, the subjective element is obviously there and is beautifully and movingly explicit. Winters's desire to be a naturalist, at home in nature, like John Muir, was, he says, a "childhood's revery," and yet it is clear that in writing the poem he is admitting that a good deal of that desire is still with him:

> This was my childhood's revery: to be
> Not one who seeks in nature his release
> But one forever by the dripping tree,
> Paradisaïc in his pristine peace.
> I might have been this man. . . .

"An Elegy," which also has a California setting (the same as the poem "On the Road to the Air Base"), deserves careful attention. Dedicated to the U.S.N. dirigible *Macon,* which was destroyed by a storm in 1935, it establishes, in the first stanzas, the dirigible as a symbol of Western man's technological power— establishes it and criticizes it. The object created by this power has a kind of beauty—but it is a temporary beauty, "thoughtless" and "deceptive":

> There was one symbol in especial, one
> Great form of thoughtless beauty that arose
> Above the mountains, to foretell the close
> Of this deception, at meridian.

This object, this *thing,* the result of man's misuse of his intellect meets its inevitable fate:

> Wind in the wind! O form more light than cloud!
> Storm amid storms! And by the storms dispersed!
> The brain-drawn metal rose until accursed
> By its extension and the sky was loud!

And in the last lines the senseless plundering in the twentieth century of our natural resources ends in final disaster. Our age

> Crowded the world with strong ingenious things,
> Used the provision it could not replace,
> To leave but Cretan myths, a sandy trace
> Through the last stone age, for the pastoral kings.

Winters frequently made use of natural life—birds, trees, shrubs, snakes, etc.—for explicitly philosophical statements, but when he did so the eye was still on the material object so that it had an importance of its own although it was being used to illustrate a theme. For example, in "The Manzanita" we have a beautiful description of the "old arbutus":

> The skin is rose: yet infinitely thin,
> It is a color only. What one tells
> Of ancient wood and softly glinting skin
> Is less than are the tiny waxen bells.

And then we have the statement that expresses Winters's fundamental dualism—that there is an unbridgeable gap between the human world and the natural world—a dualism which he also found in Emily Dickinson, expressed in several poems Winters particularly admired, such as "Further in Summer Than the Birds." He is, of course, reacting against the pantheistic monism of Wordsworth, who found moral instruction in the vernal woods, and of Emerson, who communicated with his cabbages. This is the final stanza of "The Manzanita":

> This life is not our life; nor for our wit
> The sweetness of these shades; these are alone.
> There is no wisdom here; seek not for it!
> This is the shadow of the vast madrone.

The world of nature is used in a similar fashion in the beautiful "Time and the Garden." He describes the spring activity in his garden and the excitement it causes:

> I long to crowd the little garden, gain
> Its sweetness in my hand and crush it small
> And taste it in a moment, time and all!

And he then compares this to his desire to gain quickly the fruits of scholarship, of his study of the

> Poets who wrote great poems, one by one.

It is

> The passion to condense from book to book
> Unbroken wisdom in a single look.

Nature, the garden, is fully appreciated and described for itself; but wisdom is found in books. Wisdom, unlike sensual experiences, comes late—the title of this poem is "Time and the Garden"—and when it finally comes,

> The mind's immortal, but the man is dead.

"A Spring Serpent" is on its superficial level an apt description of a little garden snake in a garden. It begins:

> The little snake now grieves
> With whispering pause, and slow,
> Uncertain where to go
> Among the glassy leaves. . . .

It is a real snake as it moves through the rest of the poem; it exists in its own right as a snake and we can consider the poem merely descriptive if we want to. But the intention of the poet is to make the snake a vehicle for a somewhat complex tenor. Fortunately we have Winters's own explication of the poem to go on, an exception to Winters's usual rule to remain silent in print about his poems.[70] The snake is being used to illustrate Winters's critique of romantic poetry, particularly as it appears in Mallarmé's theory of pure poetry, The characteristics of the snake—its grief and uncertainty, its hedonistic sensuousness, its shifting, deceptive nature, and its remoteness from human intelligence—are all characteristics of romantic poetry and romantic doctrine, according to Winters.

Winters kept goats for several years in his back yard, and for a number of years he bred prizewinning Airedales. His love of dogs, or I should say his love of those dogs he owned and bred (Winters was not very ecumenical when it came to dogs), is best expressed in his "Elegy on a Young Airedale Bitch Lost Some Years Since in the Salt Marsh" and especially in the last two stanzas:

> The old dogs now are dead,
> Tired with the hunt and cold,
> Sunk in the earth and old.
> But your bewildered head,
>
> Led by what heron cry,
> Lies by what tidal stream?—
> Drenched with ancestral dream,
> And cast ashore to dry.

In "A Winter Evening," set near Alviso, California, a very doggy dog (not Winters's own) is presented in the last stanza to contrast with the picture of defeated human diligence in the preceding stanzas:

> And by a swollen ditch, a dog,
> Mud-soaked and happy, in a daze
> Works into rain as dark as fog,
> And moves down coldly solvent ways.

To round off this discussion of the California group there is "In Praise of California Wines," a minor poem but a charming one on a charming subject. After a passing reference to the ancient culture of the vine ("pre-Socratic"), the poet praises his native wine:

> It yields the pleasure of the eye,
> It charms the skin, it warms the heart

and then pays tribute to its therapeutic effects:

When worn for sleep the head is dull,
When art has failed us, far behind,
Its sweet corruption fills the skull
Till we are happy to be blind.

The native wine, in the thirties, when Winters wrote this poem, sold in Palo Alto for fifty cents a gallon. "In Praise of California Wines" deserves to be ranked with those other classic tributes to the vine: Rochester's "Upon Drinking in a Bowl" and Herrick's "To live merrily, and to trust to Good Verses."

Winters wrote a few topical poems when he felt the occasion deeply or thought it important. There are two main groups: the poems on the Lamson "murder" case and those on World War II.

On Memorial Day, 1933, the wife of David Lamson, sales manager of the Stanford University Press, was found dead in the bathtub of the Lamson house on the campus of Stanford University. Lamson was tried for murder, was sentenced to death, and spent about a year on death row, where he wrote his book *We Who Are About to Die*.[71] The case caused a sensation and was widely covered by the media. The faculty and staff of Stanford University and the residents of the town of Palo Alto split into strongly opposed factions—those who thought Lamson guilty and those who thought him innocent. Winters became involved in the case through his daughter, then a child, who knew the Lamson daughter, also a child. He took the trouble to read the report of the first trial (few did!) and helped the defense lawyer Edwin V. McKenzie prepare his brief in the second trial. Winters became convinced that Lamson was innocent and that he had been convicted as a result of the prejudice of the judge, the stupidity of the jury, and the conniving of a corrupt police force egged on by public opinion which had been inflamed by inaccurate and sensationalist reports in the press. He wrote and published a brilliant pamphlet defending Lamson,[72] refuting much of the evidence used against him, and demonstrating that the death of Mrs. Lamson was an accident and that no murder had been committed, a view held by most of those who considered Lamson innocent. The California supreme court reversed the decision of the first trial on the ground that the judge had ruled out the possibility of an accident and that Lamson had not been given a fair trial. Three more trials resulted in mistrials, and Lamson was allowed to go free.

Winters became deeply involved in the affair and it took much of his time and energy for two or three years. It is not surprising, therefore, that he wrote several poems about the case. Those which appear in the *Collected Poems* are "To Edwin V. McKenzie," "To a Woman on Her Defense of Her Brother Unjustly Convicted of Murder," and "To David Lamson." However just the cause for which they were written and however strong their motivation—a man's life was at stake—the three poems are not among Winters's best. The poet was too close to his material and he tended to overwrite. The style is not postsymbolist. It is direct, plain, and abstract with highly rhetorical diction. Perhaps the best of the three poems is "To David Lamson," which is quieter in tone than the other two. After castigating those scholars on the Stanford faculty who, Winters believes, lost their ability to discriminate truth from fiction, Winters recalls:

> How I found a quiet friend,
> Working at the evening's end,
> Far beyond the tongues that rail,
> Hidden in the county jail.

The poem is dedicated to Lamson "Awaiting retrial, in the jail at San Jose." The jail was about a half hour's drive from the Stanford campus. Winters, after his classes, frequently visited Lamson there—sometimes taking with him two or three students. They talked about the current economic situation (we were then in the depths of the depression) and politics, but chiefly about poetry; and Winters, seated on the cell floor with his back to the wall, would read poems to Lamson—once in a while an unpublished poem of his own which he had just written.

The other group of occasional poems is about World War II. "In Summer Noon: 1941" expresses, in the pastoral setting of his garden, the poet's awareness of the growing conflict.

> Past summer bough and cry,
> The sky, distended, bare,
> Now whispers like a shell
> Of the increase of war.

Winters didn't know it, but we were only a few months from Pearl Harbor. In diction that reminds one of Hardy, Winters states what he believes may be the final outcome:

> The fieldmouse and the hare,
> The small snake of the garden
> Whose little muscles harden,
> Whose eyes now quickened stare,
> Though driven by the sound
> —Too small and free to pardon!—
> Will repossess this ground.

In another Hardyesque poem, the beautifully written "Night of Battle," Winters defines the impersonal leveling effect of war which blots out the individuating characteristics of human beings:

> In the long path of lead
> That changes place like light
> No shape of hand or head
> Means anything tonight.

For some time after Pearl Harbor, residents of California, particularly those who lived near the coast, considered an invasion by the Japanese to be a distinct possibility. Winters kept a rifle in his study with a cache of shells behind his books. I suspect that this is the gun he addresses in "To a Military Rifle, 1942." Winters was neither isolationist nor pacifist. He considered the Nazis barbarians who had to be destroyed, and he considered the Japanese stupid for allying themselves with the Nazis. He addresses the rifle:

> When other concepts end,
> This concept, hard and pure,
> Shapes every mind therefor.
> The time is yours, be sure,
> Old Hammerheel of War.

"Moonlight Alert," dated June 1943, is written in iambic pentameter couplets and the style, the imagery and texture of the verse, reminds one of the poems written a dozen years earlier and published in *The Journey*. The air raid sirens wake him to a world of icy nightmare, of hallucination:

> The siren scream
> Took on the fixity of shallow dream.
> In the dread sweetness I could see the fall,
> Like petals sifting from a quiet wall,
> Of yellow soldiers through indifferent air,
> Falling to die in solitude.

The opening lines of "Defense of Empire" describe the roar of the planes which shake the blossoms about the poet's door. He thinks of the young men who have learned "to control the earth and air" but, he goes on to say, have not yet learned the true meaning of what they are doing or the perils which will confront the state they are guarding, nor can they define the worth of the state, for, in the present age, thought has become dissociated from sense. These things

> I traced in quiet; and the shrift
> Of wrath was all my recompense.

"Sir Gawaine and the Green Knight" is deservedly one of Winters's most famous poems. It is explicitly allegorical. On the literal level the poem uses as its frame of reference the medieval story of Sir Gawaine's adventures with the Green Knight. The story as told in the well-known alliterative poem of the fourteenth century is this. At Camelot, while Arthur and his knights are feasting on New Year's Day, a giant knight clothed in green enters and challenges any knight to exchange one stroke of the axe with him. Gawaine accepts and cuts off the knight's head, whereupon the knight picks up his head and rides off saying that Gawaine must meet him in one year at the Green Chapel in Wales. True to his word, Gawaine the next Christmas Eve journeys to Wales, enters a dense forest, finds the castle, and is welcomed by the lord and lady of the castle. Gawaine and the lord agree to exchange whatever each gets by hunting or otherwise. The lady tempts Gawaine on three successive nights, giving him kisses and a girdle which makes him invulnerable. Gawaine gives the kisses to the lord, but not the girdle. At the appointed hour on New Year's day Gawaine goes to the Green Chapel, meets the Green Knight, and bows his head for the blow of the axe. The Green Knight lets him off with a slight scratch on the neck. The knight then explains that he is the lord of the castle and because Gawaine had kept all his promises save one he is allowed to escape the ordeal with only a scratch.

Winters has left us an account of the composition of the poem. The poem was first published in the *New Republic,* June 2, 1937. In the same issue a note by the editor states that he had requested an explanation of the poem. Winters's answer follows. I quote the most relevant part of the letter:

> I was recently reading to my five-year-old daughter a version of the Green Knight story which occurs in the Everyman volume of fairy tales by Ernest Rhys. Thinking it over, and thinking over the similar tales in the Cuchulain cycle, I observed the elements that would lead one to identify the knight as some kind of vegetation demon: the greenness, his indestructibility, the remote and wild region in which he lived, etc. Taking him thus for the sake of the experiment, I proceeded to see what I could extract from him poetically; I took it for granted, incidentally, that a good deal more occurred in the castle than Gawayne later reported explicitly. Thus we get a vegetation demon, a demon of growth (physical growth), sense, nature in all its non-human significations, tempting and trying a human, the human surviving more through habitual balance than through perfect control at the height of temptation, but gradually recovering himself. If you like, at a more general level, it is the relationship of the artist toward sensibility: [Hart] Crane was a Gawayne who succumbed.[73]

The poem begins with a memorable description of the knight:

> Reptilian green the wrinkled throat,
> Green as a bough of yew the beard;
> He bent his head, and so I smote;
> Then for a thought my vision cleared.

Gawaine, after cutting off the knight's head, seeks out the knight's castle as he had promised to do and is entertained by the lord and lady:

> He beat the woods to bring me meat.
> His lady, like a forest vine,
> Grew in my arms; the growth was sweet;
> And yet what thoughtless force was mine!

The lady's temptations now become more dangerous:

> Her beauty, lithe, unholy, pure,
> Took shapes that I had never known;
> And had I once been insecure,
> Had grafted laurel in my bone.

After undergoing the trial in the Green Chapel, Gawaine leaves forever his "forest experience":

> I left the green bark and the shade,
> Where growth was rapid, thick, and still;
> I found a road that men had made
> And rested on a drying hill.

On the allegorical level, then, the poem says that the poet (Gawaine) must deal with the dangerous alluring beauty of the nonhuman world which threatens his very identity as a rational human being. Note that the lady—lithe, unholy, pure—represents something else than human love. She grew in his arms "like a forest vine." The word *pure* does not mean innocent. It means deprivation of being, that is, of human being. It means what Allen Tate called "pure quality," and Gawaine's temporary union with the lady, mindless physical lust, is equivalent to an immersion in pure and evil quality, to use Tate's phrase, that is, an immersion in pure sensation.[74]

The sixth stanza of this poem as it appears in the collected edition was not in the original version. It states the major theme of the poem clearly and unequivocally. Winters added it after the objection of obscurity by the editor of the *New Republic* and after Allen Tate's remark that the lady ran away with the poem.

The striking sensory detail of this poem is not mere description. In the post-symbolist manner, the sensory detail is charged with significance. *Reptilian* and *lithe* suggest the evil traditionally ascribed to the serpent, and *yew* has connotations of death.

"Gawaine and the Green Knight" and "Heracles" are perhaps Winters's best poems dealing with the artist and his relation to his own sensibility and to the outer world—to experience. Both protagonists act intuitively; both engage in combat, in symbolic war; both recover from the immersion in sensation—Heracles by apotheosis, Gawaine by retreating to "a drying hill."

Winters was a man with a strongly religious temperament who, like many intellectuals of the early twentieth century, under the tremendous impact of modern science—especially astronomy—began life as a materialist and (I believe) as an atheist—or at least as an agnostic. And, like many of his contemporaries, he found this religious and this philosophical position unsatisfactory—both from an intellectual and an emotional point of view. But unlike some of the famous poets of our time—I am thinking especially of Eliot, Tate, and Auden—he did not convert to any specific church, nor even to Christianity. As he wrote in a late poem "A Fragment":

> I cannot find my way to Nazareth.
> I have had enough of this.

However, he did find his way to theism. He states his final position in "A Foreword" to *In Defense of Reason*:

> Finally, I am aware that my absolutism implies a theistic position, unfortunate as this admission may be. If experience appears to indicate that absolute truths exist, that we are able to work toward an approximate apprehension of them, but that they are antecedent to our apprehension and that our apprehension is seldom and perhaps never perfect, then there is only one place in which those truths may be located, and I see no way to escape this conclusion. I merely wish to point out that my critical and moral notions are derived from the observation of literature and of life, and that my theism is derived from my critical and moral notions. I did not proceed from the opposite direction.[75]

Winters arrived at his theism slowly, reluctantly, and as a direct result of his philosophical conviction that absolute truths exist and that a philosophy of relativism is false and not in accord with the facts of experience.

Theism implies belief in the "supernatural." The possibility that supernatural beings, both good and evil, may exist and affect human life was in Winters's mind long before he published his formal statement, quoted above, concerning theism. He had considerable interest in the long history of demonic possession and in the possibility that some cases could not be explained entirely on psychological grounds. And then there was his own experience. In the poem "A Petition" the lines

> It was not I that spoke:
> The wild fiend moved my tongue

are not necessarily merely figurative. A beautiful example of Winters's concern with the supernatural is to be found in "An October Nocturne," date October 31 [Halloween], 1936. There is a fine description in the first two stanzas of a plane moving past the moon and then suddenly, before our eyes as it were, the plane is transformed into a demon:

> Pure in each proven line!
> The balance and the aim,
> Half empty, half divine!
> I saw how true you came.

> Dissevered from your cause,
> Your function was your goal.
> Oblivious of my laws,
> You made your calm patrol.

"Half empty, half divine" is an exact definition of a demon. "A Song in Passing" states succinctly Winters's views on immortality and on God:

> Eternity is here.
> There is no other place.
> The only thing I fear
> Is the Almighty Face.

This is certainly not a very comforting poem nor a Christian one. Yet the possibility of communication between a human being and God is suggested in "A Prayer for My Son" and "To the Holy Spirit." "A Prayer for My Son" begins with a definition of the relationship between God ("Eternal Spirit") and the world:

> Eternal Spirit, you
> Whose will maintains the world,
> Who thought and made it true

and ends with a prayer that God have compassion on his young son:

> Eternal Spirit, you
> Who guided Socrates,

> Pity this small and new
> Bright soul on hands and knees.

"To the Holy Spirit," one of Winters's four or five best poems, is set in a deserted graveyard in the Salinas Valley. It is a meditation on the nature of God and man and on death. As in the previous poems, there is little hope of individual immortality:

> And I, alas, am bound
> Pure mind to flesh and bone,
> And flesh and bone to ground.

However, there is the possibility of communication between God and man and the possibility of man's understanding of God, at least partially, for God is pure mind and the poet, who is in part mind, can reach an intellectual understanding of God:

> Yet when I go from sense
> And trace thee down in thought,
> I meet thee, then, intense,
> And know thee as I ought.

(It appears to me that God and the Holy Spirit are one in this poem, although there is a difference of opinion about this.) As to the question of death and immortality — there is only one certainty, that of the physical death of the individual. Implicit in this poem and "Prayer for My Son" is a fundamental dualism, a dichotomy between mind and matter, that is, between spirit and body. Also implicit in the poem is the notion that the physical everyday world in which we live may be an illusion, but it is an illusion that we have to live with, an idea which Winters has expressed more than once. In the description of the hills at the beginning of the poem we have:

> We see them, for we must;
> Calm in deceit, they stay.

The hills may be an illusion: nevertheless, for us, they exist.

His final comment on the "fallen sons" of the Holy Spirit, that is, those whose bodies are in the graveyard, is:

> All of this stir of age,
> Though it elude my sense
> Into what heritage
> I know not, seems to fall,
> Quiet beyond recall,
> Into irrelevance.

Does "this stir of age" refer only to those in the graveyard? I think not. In my reading of the poem, it refers to all human history, which falls into irrelevance because, finally, it is separated from that which is real, true, and eternal — the Holy Spirit. The individual can by considerable intellectual effort communicate with and partially understand the Holy Spirit, but only temporarily, because his mind perishes with his body. Winters doesn't state it this baldly or explicitly, but that seems to me to be the implied meaning of the entire poem.

"To the Moon" is Winters's farewell to the Muse whom, after a lifetime of service, the poet addresses as a supernatural being:

> Goddess of poetry
> Maiden of icy stone
> With no anatomy.

The poem ends with a question addressed to the Muse:

> What is your pleasure now?

Her pleasure turned out to be at least one more very important poem — "At the San Francisco Airport," written in 1954 and addressed to his daughter, who was then in her early twenties and about to take a long journey and settle into her own independent life. In saying farewell to his daughter the poet sums up his own career:

> But you and I in part are one:
> The frightened brain, the nervous will,
> The knowledge of what must be done,
> The passion to acquire the skill
> To face that which you dare not shun.
>
> The rain of matter upon sense
> Destroys me momently. The score:
> There comes what will come. The expense
> Is what one thought, and something more —
> One's being and intelligence.

The lines

> The rain of matter upon sense
> Destroys me momently

may refer to an actual rain falling at the airport. They refer also perhaps to the deluge of noise assaulting the ears from the engines and perhaps also to the blazing lights assaulting the eyes. Symbolically they carry us back a quarter of a century to the line in "Slow Pacific Swell":

> Half drenched in dissolution, I lay bare

that is, to the poet's early immersion in sensation, which almost destroyed him and which he, as a poet, still experiences "momently." The expense of his own career has been "One's being and intelligence," as, by implication, it may be for his daughter, or for anyone who lives his life fully, sensitively, and intelligently. The word *terminal* occurs in the first and last stanzas with reference, of course, to the air terminal but also with reference to the parting between himself and his daughter and with reference to the end of his career as a poet. The central symbolic word is *light* and by implication its opposite, *night* or darkness. The light of the airport "Gives perfect vision, false and hard." And at the end of the poem the poet is "In light, and nothing else, awake." I think we have a dichotomy here between *light* and *night* analogous to that between the land and the sea in "Slow Pacific Swell" (and in *Moby-Dick*). The light represents that which is known and understandable, at least in human terms. Hence it gives "perfect vision." Yet it is also false, because this vision leaves out of account the mysterious and the unknown, the *night*, in which the planes and the individuals in them must travel. We have the same light in "To the Holy Spirit":

> High noon returns the mind
> Upon its local fact:
> Dry grass and sand; we find
> No vision to distract.

The light of "high noon" shows us the "local fact" as well as the hills "calm in deceit," but what it shows us is not the totality of experience and therefore it is an illusion, it is "false."

In this chapter I have discussed those poems of Winters which seem to me of greatest importance from a literary point of view as well as a few of lesser importance but which aid us in understanding his career. He lived for a little less than fourteen years after completing "At the San Francisco Airport" but wrote very few poems during this period, as far as we know. I have seen only three in print that can be dated after 1954 — "Two Old-Fashioned Songs" and a poem written upon the retirement of his friend and colleague Herbert Dean Meritt, professor of English and philology at Stanford University.[76] Of these three, I prefer the second of the "Old-Fashioned Songs" entitled "A Dream Vision." In the last two stanzas Winters appears to be taking leave of some of his critics who, in his dream, appear as bullfinches, wrens, and mockingbirds

> Screaming with a pointed tongue
> Objurgation without word.

Notes

Chapter 1   Ezra Pound

1. N. Christoph de Nagy, *The Poetry of Ezra Pound: The Pre-Imagist Stage* (Bern, Switzerland: Francke: 1960), pp. 176–77.

2. Ibid., p. 176.

3. And, it should be added, in Joyce. See Archie K. Loss, "The Pre-Raphaelite Woman, the Symbolist Femme-Enfant, and the Girl with Long Flowing Hair in the Earlier Work of Joyce," *Journal of Modern Literature* 3 (February 1973): 3–23; Kenneth Fields, "Postures of the Nerves: Reflections of the Nineteenth Century in the Poems of Wallace Stevens," *Southern Review*, n.s. 7 (July 1971):778–824.

4. De Nagy, *Pre-Imagist Stage*, p. 177.

5. *Personae* (1909), *Exultations* (1909), *Provença* (1910), and *Canzoni* (1911). Also much of his two chapters on Provençal poetry in his critical book *The Spirit of Romance* (1910) is taken up by verse and prose of the troubadours.

6. Stuart McDougal, *Ezra Pound and the Troubadour Tradition* (Princeton, N.J.: Princeton University Press,1972), pp. 12ff.

7. Ezra Pound, *The Spirit of Romance* (London: J. M. Dent & Sons, Ltd., 1910), pp. 27–28.

8. I use the text as it appears in Ezra Pound, *Instigations* (New York: Boni and Liveright, 1920), p. 312. An earlier poetic version entitled "Bird-Latin" appeared in the *New Age*, February 22, 1912, under the title "Three Canzoni of Arnaut Daniel," pp. 392–93.

9. *Spirit of Romance* (1910), pp. 41–43.

10. The poem is discussed by McDougal, *Troubadour Tradition*, pp. 45ff.; de Nagy, *Pre-Imagist Stage*, pp. 121ff.; and Hugh Witemeyer, *The Poetry of Ezra Pound: Forms and Renewal, 1908–1920* (Berkeley and Los Angeles: University of California Press 1969), pp. 70 ff.

11. De Nagy, *Pre-Imagist Stage*, pp. 30ff.

12. *New Age*, December 7, 1911, p. 130.

13. Ibid.

14. Ibid., p. 178.

15. Thomas H. Jackson, *The Early Poetry of Ezra Pound* (Cambridge, Mass.: Harvard University Press, 1968), pp. 28–29; 155–56.

16. In *Stephen Hero* (Joyce's first draft for *A Portrait of the Artist as a Young Man*), Stephen considers collecting "many such moments together in a book of epiphanies. By an epiphany he meant a sudden spiritual manifestation. . . ." See *Stephen Hero*, edited by Theodore Spencer (New York: New Directions, 1944), p. 211. Joyce deleted this passage from *A Portrait*, but he refers to this theory again in *Ulysses*, (New York: Random House, 1934), p. 41. See Spencer's introduction to *Stephen Hero*, pp. 16ff., for an illuminating discussion of this theory.

17. "I Gather the Limbs of Osiris, III. Guido Cavalcanti," *New Age*, December 14, 1911, p. 155.

18. "I Gather the Limbs of Osiris, VI. On Virtue," *New Age*, January 4, 1912, p. 224.

19. N. Christoph de Nagy, *Ezra Pound's Poetics and Literary Tradition* (Bern: Francke Verlag 1966), p. 29.

20. Glenn Hughes, *Imagism and the Imagists* (Stanford, Calif.: Stanford University Press, 1931); Stanley K. Coffman, *Imagism: A Chapter for the History of Modern Poetry* (Norman, Okla.: University of Oklahoma Press, 1951); J. B. Harmer, *Victory in Limbo: A History of Imagism 1908–1917* (New York: St. Martin's Press, 1975).

21. Donald E. Stanford, "Classicism and the Modern Poet," *Southern Review*, n.s.5 (Spring 1969): 475–500.

22. "A Lecture on Modern Poetry," in *Further Speculations by T. E. Hulme*, edited by Sam Hynes (Minneapolis, Minn.: University of Minnesota Press, 1955), pp. 68–69.

23. Ibid., p. 73.

24. For the early date of the delivery of "A Lecture on Modern Poetry," see Hynes, *Further Speculations*, p. xviii: Pound's comparison of the *Cantos* to a Bach fugue is in W. B. Yeats, "A Packet for Ezra Pound," *A Vision* (London: The Macmillan Co., 1937), p. 4.

25. See Stanford, "Classicism and the Modern Poet," pp. 478–79; Michael Roberts, *T. E. Hulme* (London: Faber and Faber, 1938), pp. 58ff.

26. Pound, *Instigations*, p. 357.

27. Ernest Fenollosa, "The Chinese Written Character as a Medium for Poetry," in Pound's *Instigations*, p. 367.

28. Ibid., p. 370.

29. K. K. Ruthven, *A Guide to Ezra Pound's Personae* (Berkeley and Los Angeles: University of California Press, 1969), p. 204.

30. Ezra Pound, "Affirmations . . . II. Vorticism, " *New Age*, January 14, 1915, pp. 277–78.

31. Yeats, *A Vision* (London: The Macmillan Co., 1937), p. 4.

32. The *Cantos* are numbered 1–109; however, two—72 and 73—were never published.'

33. Hugh Kenner, *The Pound Era* (Berkeley, Calif.: University of California Press, 1971), p. 429.

34. Daniel D. Pearlman, *The Barb of Time: On the Unity of Ezra Pound's Cantos* (New York: Oxford University Press, 1969), p. 260.

35. Ibid., p. 250.

36. Ibid., p. 284.

37. Ibid., p. 285.

38. Ibid., p. 284.

Chapter 2   T. S. Eliot

1. In "To Criticize the Critic" (1961) Eliot comments on his influence as a critic, with especial reference to Donne. "The critic . . . cannot create a taste." A few lines later he admits that he created an increased taste for Donne through his own poetry, which was influenced by Donne. "As the taste for my own poetry spread, so did the taste for the poets to whom I owed the greatest debt." I believe it to be a fact, however, that many of my own generation were sent to reading Donne as much by Eliot's essays as by his poems. Furthermore, the direct influence of Donne on Eliot's own style was almost nonexistent.

2. "A Note on Richard Crashaw," *For Lancelot Andrewes* (Garden City, N.Y.: Doubleday, Doran and Co., 1929, pp. 132–36. We did not realize as we read with admiration Eliot's scathing comments on Shelley that much of it was "warmed over Robertson," as was Eliot's essay "Hamlet and His Problems" (1919). See Leo Storm, "J. M. Robertson and T. S. Eliot," *Journal of Modern Literature* 5(April 1976): 315–21.

3. "Byron" (1937), *On Poetry and Poets* (New York: Noonday Press, 1961), p. 224.

4. "To Criticize the Critic," *To Criticize the Critic* (New York: Farrar, Straus and Giroux, 1965), p.20.

5. *Kenyon Review* 3(Winter 1941): 7–30; 3(Spring 1941):221–39. Reprinted in *In Defense of Reason*, (New York: The Swallow Press and William Morrow and Co., 1947), pp. 460–501.

6. See Donald E. Stanford, "Classicism and the Modern Poet," *Southern Review*, n.s.5 (Spring 1969): 475–500; Austin Warren, "Continuity in T. S. Eliot's Literary Criticism," *T. S. Eliot: The Man and His Work*, edited by Allen Tate (New York: Delacorte Press, 1966), pp. 278–98; Mario Praz, "T. S. Eliot as a Critic," ibid., pp. 262–77; Stephen Spender, *T. S. Eliot* (New York: Viking Press, 1976), chapter 8. See particularly p. 139: "His [Eliot's] remarks about writing poetry sometimes appear inconsistent, if not self-contradictory. Perhaps, though, Eliot does not so much contradict himself as submit to self-correction, an operation which sometimes seems to be performed under an anesthetic."

7. "The Music of Poetry," *On Poetry and Poets*, p. 17.

8. *Selected Essays 1917–1932* (New York: Harcourt, Brace and Co., 1932), p. 7.

9. "Yeats," *Selected Prose of T. S. Eliot,* edited by Frank Kermode (New York: Harcourt Brace Jovanovich and Farrar, Straus and Giroux, 1975), p. 251.

10. "Cyril Tourneur." *Selected Essays,* p. 159.

11. "John Ford," ibid. p. 176.

12. Ibid., p. 179.

13. *On Poetry and Poets,* p. 33.

14. "Philip Massinger," *The Sacred Wood: Essays on Poetry and Criticism* (London: Methuen, 1920), p. 139.

15. Stanford, "Classicism and the Modern Poet."

16. Both essays appeared in *The Sacred Wood.*

17. In *The Frontiers of Criticism* (Minneapolis: University of Minnesota Press, 1956).

18. "Hamlet and His Problems," *Sacred Wood,* p. 96.

19. "Introduction," *The Use of Poetry and the Use of Criticism* (Cambridge, Mass.: Harvard University Press, 1933), p. 8.

20. *Selected Essays,* p. 19.

21. "Reflections on Contemporary Poetry," *Egoist* 4 (October 1917): 133.

22. "Shakespeare and the Stoicism of Seneca," *Selected Essays,* pp. 117–18.

23. "Religion and Literature," *Selected Prose of T. S. Eliot,* p. 97.

24. "The Social Function of Poetry," *On Poetry and Poets,* p. 4.

25. "The Music of Poetry," ibid., p. 17.

26. "The Frontiers of Criticism," ibid., p. 117.

27. See particularly *Ezra Pound His Metric and Poetry* (New York: Alfred A. Knopf, 1917 [i.e. 1918]); "The Method of Mr. Pound," *Athenaeum* (London), no. 4669 (October 24, 1919):1065–66; *Ezra Pound Selected Poems,* edited with an introduction by T. S. Eliot (London: Faber & Gwyer, 1928); *Literary Essays of Ezra Pound,* edited with an introduction by T. S. Eliot (London: Faber and Faber, 1954).

28. *After Strange Gods: A Primer of Modern Heresy* (London: Faber and Faber, 1934), p. 42.

29. See Donald Gallup, *T. S. Eliot and Ezra Pound* (New Haven, Conn.: Henry W. Wenning/C. A. Stonehill, Inc., 1970), for a detailed factual account of the Pound-Eliot relationship.

30. See especially ibid., pp. 5ff.

31. Ibid., pp. 16ff.

32. Winters, *In Defense of Reason,* pp. 466ff.; Allan Mowbray, *T. S. Eliot's Impersonal Theory of Poetry* (Lewisburg, Pa.: Bucknell University Press, 1974), pp. 25ff.

33. *Selected Essays,* 124–25.

34. *Sacred Wood,* pp. 64–65.

35. *Selected Essays,* p. 299.

36. First pointed out by Yvor Winters, *In Defense of Reason,* p. 469.

37. "Tuckerman's Sonnet I:10: The First Post-Symbolist Poem," *Southern Review,* n.s.12 (Spring 1976):331.

38. Valerie Eliot, ed., *T.S. Eliot The Waste Land: A Facsimile and Transcript of the Original Drafts Including The Annotations of Ezra Pound* (New York: Harcourt Brace Jovanovich, 1971). p. 129; Kermode, *Selected Prose,* pp. 20–22, 135, 207.

39. "Swinburne as Poet," (1920), *Sacred Wood,* p. 149.

40. "Conclusion" (1933), *Use of Poetry and Use of Criticism,* p. 146.

41. " 'Ulysses', Order, and Myth," *Selected Prose,* pp. 177–78.

42. *Selected Prose,* pp. 13ff.

43. "Dante," *Selected Essays,* p. 212.

44. "Shakespeare and the Stoicism of Seneca," *Selected Essays,* pp. 117–18. On the other hand he seems to be reversing himself when in *The Use of Poetry* he *attacks* the notion that poetry should be representative of its age. He says that we now have "a criticism which seems to demand of poetry not that it shall be well written, but that it shall be 'representative of its age.' " *Use of Poetry,* p. 15. However, Eliot himself did much to foster the notion that poetry should be representative of its age.

45. "Dante," *Selected Essays,* p. 204.

46. "The Possibility of a Poetic Drama," *Sacred Wood,* p. 68.

47. A. E. Housman, *The Name and Nature of Poetry* (New York: The Macmillan Company, 1933).

p. 46. The passage which Eliot cites occurs just after the quotation.

48. "Isolated Superiority," *Dial* 84 (January 1928): 6. A review of Pound's *Personae*.

49. Kermode, *Selected Prose*, pp. 13, 15.

50. *After Strange Gods*, p. 42.

51. "Tradition and the Individual Talent," *Selected Essays*, p.7.

52. *Portrait of the Artist as a Young Man* (New York: Viking Critical Library Edition, 1968), p. 215.

53. In his preface to the 1928 edition of *The Sacred Wood*. And yet after formulating an aesthetics of superior amusement Eliot had the effrontery to criticize Paul Valéry as follows: "The one complaint which I am tempted to lodge against Valéry's poetics, is that it provides us with no criterion of *seriousness*." Italics Eliot's ! "Introduction," Paul Valéry, *The Art of Poetry*, Bollingen Series 45 (New York: Pantheon Books, 1958), p. xxiii.

54. "Yeats," *Selected Prose*, p. 250.

55. "Matthew Arnold," *Use of Poetry*, p. 111.

56. *Instigations* (New York: Boni and Liveright, 1920), p. 378.

57. *On Poetry and Poets*, pp. 126, 128.

58. *Time*, November 13, 1950, p. 53.

59. *On Poetry and Poets*, p. 23.

60. "The Aims of Poetic Drama," *Adam International Review* 17(November 1949):16.

61. "Dante," *Selected Essays*, p. 200.

62. "Conclusion," *Use of Poetry*, p. 148.

63. Ibid., 149.

64. "The Three Voices of Poetry" (1953), *On Poetry and Poets*, p. 107.

65. "Conclusion," *Use of Poetry*, p. 144.

66. "A Brief Introduction to the Method of Paul Valéry," in *Le Serpent par Paul Valéry with a Translation into English by Mark Wardle and an Introduction by T. S. Eliot* (London: R. Cobden-Sanderson, 1924), p. 13.

67. "A Sceptical Patrician," *Athenaeum*, no. 4647 (May 23, 1919):362. A review of *The Education of Henry Adams*.

68. "Preface," *Bubu of Montparnasse*, by Charles-Louis Philippe (New York: Avalon Press, 1945), p. 11. The "Preface" was first published in 1932 for the Black Sun Press edition of that year.

69. C. P. Snow, "Challenge to the Intellect," *Times Literary Supplement*, August 15, 1958, p. 3.

70. See especially René Taupin, *L'influence du Symbolisme français sur la poésie Américaine* (Paris: Librairie Ancienne Honoré Champion, 1929), pp. 211–40; 257–64; Warren Ramsey, *Jules Laforgue and the Ironic Inheritance* (New York: Oxford Unviersity Press, 1953), passim; Thomas R. Rees, *The Technique of T. S. Eliot* (The Hague: Mouton, 1974), chapter 2. In his Introduction to the *Selected Poems* of Ezra Pound (London: Faber & Faber, 1928), p. viii, Eliot wrote: "The form in which I began to write, in 1908 or '09 was directly drawn from the study of Laforgue together with the later Elizabethan drama."

71. T. S. Eliot, *Poems Written in Early Youth* (London: Faber & Faber, 1967), p. 30.

72. Ibid., p. 41.

73. Ramsey, *Laforgue*, p. 135.

74. Ibid., pp. 118–19.

75. Arthur Symons, *The Symbolist Movement in Literature*, rev. ed. (New York: E. P. Dutton & Co., 1919), p. 303.

76. George Watson has almost destroyed this myth by proving that Verdenal died on the field of battle while caring for the wounded. See his "Quest for a Frenchman," *Sewanee Review* 84 (Summer 1976):465–75. It has not yet been proved, however, whether or not Eliot knew for certain the manner of his friend's death at the time he wrote "Dans le Restaurant" (1916/17), composed when World War I was still raging. In any event, Verdenal, as well as Eliot's Parisian tutor Alain-Fournier, admired Laforgue and probably strengthened Eliot's interest in him.

77. See Ramsey, *Laforgue*, p. 38; Laforgue's letter is in *Oeuvres complètes de Jules Laforgue* (Paris: Edition du Mercure de France, 1901–25), 4:6–8.

78. "Jules Laforgue, and Tristan Corbière in many of his poems, are nearer to the 'school of Donne' than any modern English Poet." ("The Metaphysical Poets," *Selectred Essays* p. 249.)

79. Taupin, *L'influence du Symbolisme*, p. 228.

80. Rees, *Technique of T. S. Eliot*, p. 49.

81. See especially Laforgue's "Complainte des pianos qu'on entend dans les quartiers aisés."

82. Spender, *T. S. Eliot*, pp. 42–44.

83. The first two lines of Théophile Gautier's "Carmen" inspired Eliot's lines:

> Carmen est maigre, — un trait de bistre
> Cerne son oeil de gitana.

84. For Eliot's comments on Jean de Bosschère see "Reflections on Contemporary Poetry," *Egoist* 4 (October 1917):133.

85. See especially William Arrowsmith, "Daedal Harmonies," *Southern Review*, n.s. 13 (January 1977):1–47 to which I am indebted; D. J. Lake, "T. S. Eliot's 'Vita Nuova' and 'Mi Chemin': The Sensus Historicus," *Ariel* (English) 2(1971):43–57.

86. "Wordsworth and Coleridge," *Use of Poetry*, p. 60.

87. "The Literature of Politics," *To Criticize the Critic* (New York: Farrar, Straus & Giroux, 1965), p. 138.

88. Lake, "Eliot's 'Vita Nuora,' " p. 45.

89. See Christopher Clausen, "Tintern Abbey to Little Gidding," *Sewanee Review* 84(Summer 1976:405–24.

90. Allen Tate, "Poetry Modern and Unmodern," *Essays of Four Decades*, (Chicago: Swallow Press, 1968), 230–33.

91. Winters, *In Defense of Reason* pp. 46–47.

92. *After Strange Gods*, p. 55.

93. Ibid., p. 56.

94. Valerie Eliot, ed., *The Waste Land*, p. 1.

95. "The Three Voices of Poetry," *On Poetry and Poets*, p. 107.

96. Ibid., p. 111.

97. "Conclusion," *Use of Poetry*, p. 137.

98. "From the Pensées of Pascal," *Selected Prose*, p. 237.

99. "Virgil and the Christian World," *On Poetry and Poets*, p. 137.

100. Valerie Eliot, ed., *The Waste Land*, p. 125.

101. "Introduction," *Nightwood* by Djuna Barnes (New York: Harcourt, Brace and Co., 1937), pp. [x, xiii].

102. Although Dante may have been influenced in his characterization of Ulysses and in his motives for the voyage by various classical sources. See Ernest Barker, "Dante and the Last Voyage of Ulysses," *Traditions of Civility* (Cambridge: at the University Press, 1948), pp. 53–73.

103. "Dante," *Sacred Wood*, p. 166.

104. "Dante," *Selected Essays*, p. 211.

105. " 'In Memoriam,' " *Selected Prose*, p. 241.

106. George Santayana, *Three Philosophical Poets: Lucretius, Dante, Goethe* (Cambridge, Mass.: Harvard University Press, 1910), p. 133.

107. See her *The Witch-Cult in Western Europe* (Oxford: Clarendon Press, 1921), pp. 130–33. The book was published shortly before Eliot wrote "The Hollow Men," and Eliot, with his considerable interest in the occult and in anthropology, had probably read it. See also Donald E. Stanford, "Two Notes on T. S. Eliot," *Twentieth Century Literature* 1(1955):133–34.

108. In the *Saturday Review of Literature* 4(December 10, 1927):429.

109. B. C. Southam, *A Guide to the Selected Poems of T. S. Eliot*, (New York. Harcourt, Brace & World, 1968), pp. 135–36.

110. Grover Smith, *T. S. Eliot's Poetry and Plays: A Study in Sources and Meaning*, 2nd ed. (Chicago: University of Chicago Press, 1974), p. 122. "The Cultivation of Christmas Trees," a very slight poem, is usually not considered as belonging to the Ariel group.

111. "Conclusion," *Use of Poetry*, p. 141.

112. "Dante," *Selected Essays*, p. 220.

113. T. S. Matthews, *Great Tom* (New York: Harper & Row, 1974), p. 130.

114. B. H. Fussell, "Structural Methods in *Four Quartets*," *Journal of English Literary History*

22(1955):212–41.

115. Sister M. Cleophas, "Notes on Levels of Meaning in *Four Quartets*," *Renascence* 2(1950):102–16.

116. Ray B. West, Jr., "Personal History and the *Four Quartets*," *New Mexico Quarterly* 23(1953):269–82.

117. Harold F. Brooks, "*Four Quartets:* the Structure in Relation to the Themes," in *Eliot in Perspective, A Symposium,* ed. by Graham Martin (New York: Humanities Press, 1970), pp. 132–47.

118. Northrop Frye, *T. S. Eliot* (New York: Grove Press, 1963), pp. 77ff.

119. See especially Herbert Howarth, "Eliot, Beethoven, J. W. N. Sullivan," *Comparative Literature* 9(Fall 1957):322–32.

120. Helen Gardner, *The Art of T. S. Eliot* (London: The Cresset Press, 1949), p. 41.

121. Ibid., pp. 51–52.

122. Ibid., p. 76.

123. Ibid., pp. 44–45.

124. Donald Davie, "Pound and Eliot: "A Distinction" in *Eliot in Perspective,* edited by Graham Martin, pp. 62–82.

125. Gardner, *Art of T. S. Eliot,* p. 16.

126. Ibid., pp. 54–55.

127. Ibid., p. 4

Chapter 3   Wallace Stevens

1. See Holly Stevens, *Souvenirs and Prophecies: The Young Wallace Stevens* (New York: Alfred A. Knopf, 1977), for an account of the poet's early years. *Letters of Wallace Stevens,* edited by Holly Stevens (New York: Alfred A. Knopf, 1966), contains much biographical information. Peter Brazeau's biography of Stevens will cover the years 1915 to 1955.

2. *Letters of Wallace Stevens* (hereafter referred to as L), pp. 293–94.

3. L, 409. Italics mine.

4. L, 472.

5. L, 407.

6. L, 438.

7. "A Poet That Matters," *Life and Letters Today* 13 (December 1935): 64. (A review of Marianne Moore's *Selected Poems.*)

8. "Preface," *William Carlos Williams, Collected Poems* (New York: The Objectivist Press, 1934), p. 3.

9. L, 350.

10. Dust jacket, *Ideas of Order* (New York: Alfred A. Knopf, 1936).

11. Dust jacket, *The Man with the Blue Guitar* (New York: Alfred A. Knopf, 1937).

12. Dust jacket, *Ideas of Order.*

13. Ibid.

14. *The Necessary Angel: Essays on Reality and the Imagination* (New York: Alfred A. Knopf, 1951) [hereafter referred to as NA], p. 30.

15. L, 501.

16. L, 506, Stevens found the sentence by James quoted in F. O. Matthiessen, *Henry James: The Major Phase* New York: Oxford University Press 1944), p. 10. The sentence also appears in F. O. Matthiessen and Kenneth B. Murdock, eds., *The Notebooks of Henry James* (New York: Oxford University Press, 1947), p. 112, dated October 23, 1891.

17. NA, 6–7.

18. George Steiner, *After Babel* (New York: Oxford University Press, 1975), pp. 176ff. "The concept of 'the lacking word' marks modern literature. The principal division in the history of Western literature occurs between the early 1870s and the turn of the century. It divides a literature essentially housed in language from one for which language has become a prison. . . . Goethe and Victor Hugo were probably the last major poets to find that language was sufficient to their needs."

19. L, 589.

20. L, 590.

21. "Adagia," *Opus Posthumous* (New York: Alfred A. Knopf, 1959) [hereafter referred to as OP], p. 161. And on the same page Stevens wrote: "All poetry is experimental poetry."

22. As quoted in Henry Bamford Parkes, *The Pragmatic Test* (San Francisco: The Colt Press, 1941), p. 43.

23. As quoted in Oscar Williams, ed., *A Little Treasury of Modern Poetry,* Third College Edition (New York: Charles Scribner's Sons, 1970), p. xxx.

24. See Willard E. Arnett, *George Santayana* (New York: Washington Square Press, Inc. 1968), pp. 140–41. "The thought of George Santayana must ... be characterized finally as *a philosophy of ultimate disillusion.* In the last analysis, he claimed, neither the senses, nor art, nor religion, nor philosophy can provide any trustworthy clues to the ultimate character of existence." (Italics are Arnett's) This statement appears to me to be an accurate description of Wallace Stevens's position. Arnett goes on to say of Santayana, "he did not know or care much about causes and existences as such; he was interested rather in appearances—the ideas, images, ideals, or beauties—that existence may arouse in the minds of men." This is the theme of one of Stevens's last poems, "The River of Rivers in Connecticut." It should be remembered that Stevens was a young man in his twenties (an impressionable age) when he met Santayana.

25. NA, 54.

26. L, 443.

27. L, 370.

28. Ibid.

29. L, 414.

30. L, 430.

31. J. V. Cunningham, "The Styles and Procedures of Wallace Stevens," *Denver Quarterly* (Spring 1966):15.

32. NA, 23.

33. L, 434–35.

34. L, 789.

35. L, 485.

36. Milton J. Bates, "Major Man and Overman: Wallace Stevens' Use of Nietzsche,' *Southern Review* 15(October 1979):832ff.

37. L, 518.

38. Roy Harvey Pearce, "Wallace Stevens: The Life of the Imagination" *PMLA* 66(September 1951):570.

39. NA, 81.

40. L, 505.

41. J. Hillis Miller, *Poets of Reality* (Cambridge, Mass.: Harvard University Press, 1965), p. 259.

42. I am indebted to Yvor Winters for his explanation of this commonly misunderstood line. See his "Poetic Styles, Old and New," in *Four Poets on Poetry,* edited by Don Cameron Allen (Baltimore, Md: Johns Hopkins Press, 1959), p. 73.

43. L, 250.

44. Walter Pater, "Aesthetic Poetry," in *Victorian Poetry and Poetics,* edited by Walter E. Houghton and C. Robert Stange), (Boston: Houghton Mifflin Co., 1959), p. 721.

45. L, 183.

46. D. H. Lawrence, *Apocalypse* (London: Martin Secker, 1932), pp. 222–23.

47. Carl L. Becker, *The Heavenly City of the Eighteenth Century Philosophers,* (New Haven, Conn.: Yale University Press 1932), p. 15.

48. See Winters, "Poetic Styles, Old and New," pp. 72–75.

49. See Yvor Winters, "Wallace Stevens, or the Hedonist's Progress," *In Defense of Reason* (New York: The Swallow Press and William Morrow and Co., 1947), pp. 431–59; J. V. Cunningham, "The Poetry of Wallace Stevens," *Poetry* 75 (December 1949): 149–65.

50. According to David Perkins, *A History of Modern Poetry* (Cambridge, Mass.: Harvard University Press, 1976), p. 538, "Donald Evans ... read his Laforguian 'En Monocle' at a party Stevens attended." The poem begins "Born with a monocle he stares at life,/And sends his soul on pensive promenades." The poem was also available to Stevens in Donald Evans, *Sonnets from the Patagonian*

(New York: Claire Marie, 1914). The title of another poem in this volume, "Failure at Forty," may have been suggestive to Stevens at this time. For a critical analysis of Evans's poetry see Kenneth Fields, "Past Masters: Walter Conrad Arensberg and Donald Evans," *Southern Review* 6(Spring 1970):317–39. On Stevens as a dandy, see Gorham Munson, "The Dandyism of Wallace Stevens," *Dial,* 79 (November 1925):413–17.

51. L, 250–51.

52. L, 251.

53. Ernest Hemingway, "A Clean Well Lighted Place," written about 1932 or 1933.

54. L, 251.

55. L, 251.

56. Helen Vendler states categorically that Stevens took his crickets from Keats's "To Autumn" — "Hedge-crickets sing." ("Stevens and Keats' 'To Autumn,'" in *Wallace Stevens: A Celebration,* edited by Frank Doggett and Robert Buttel [Princeton, N. J.: Princeton University Press, 1980], p. 180.) Keats's crickets have been overrated, I think. They are unremarkable. Dickinson does much better with her crickets. So does Tuckerman. So does Stevens. Stevens could not have read Tuckerman's poem by 1918 when he wrote "Le Monocle." He may have known Dickinson's poem and he must have known "To Autumn," although it is not mentioned in his published journal or letters. I suspect Stevens got his crickets from Mother Nature.

57. L, 251.

58. L, 263.

59. See Holly Stevens, "Flux^2," *Southern Review* 15 (Autumn 1979):771–74.

60. Ibid., p. 773.

61. Ibid., p. 774.

62. See especially J. Hillis Miller's far-fetched and elaborate explication of Wordsworth's "A Slumber Did My Spirit Seal," in "On Edge: The Crossways of Contemporary Criticism," *Bulletin of the American Academy of Arts and Sciences* 32 (January 1979):13–32.

63. Stevens, "Flux^2," pp. 773–74.

64. A. Walton Litz, *Introspective Voyager: The Poetic Development of Wallace Stevens* (New York: Oxford University Press, 1972), p. 97.

65. L, 464.

66. Cunningham, "The Style and Procedures of Wallace Stevens," p. 26.

67. Winters, "Wallace Stevens," pp. 435–37.

68. Ibid., p. 437.

69. This line was misprinted in *Collected Poems* as "There is no moon, on single, silvered leaf." It is correctly printed in Holly Stevens, *Palm at the End of the Mind* (New York: Random House, 1972), second printing, not the first printing.

70. Winters, "Wallace Stevens," p. 438.

71. Fred H. Stocking, "Stevens' 'Bantams in Pine-Woods,' " *Explicator* 3 (April 1945), item 45.

72. Litz, *Introspective Voyager,* p. 116.

73. "The Relation between Poetry and Painting," *The Necessary Angel,* p. 160.

74. *Introspective Voyager,* p. 116. According to Litz "points" means "defines."

75. Peterson, "*Harmonium* and William James," *Southern Review* 7 (July 1971):664–67.

76. Ibid., p. 665.

77. L, 288.

78. L, 389–90.

79. Litz, *Introspective Voyager,* p. 150.

80. The valet Crispin was a stock burlesque figure of seventeenth- and eighteenth-century French comedy. His origin is probably in the *commedia dell'arte.* He has affinities with Horace's bad poet Crispinus, with the Crispinus of Jonson's *The Poetaster,* and with various harlequin figures. How much of this possible source material Stevens had read is anybody's guess. Guy Davenport has pointed out that the description of Crispin in such standard reference works as the *Nouveau Larousse Illustré* would have supplied much of the information. See his "Spinoza's Tulips: A Commentary on 'The Comedian as the Letter C,' " *Perspectives,* 7(Autumn 1954):149–50.

81. J. V. Cunningham calls it "a religious experience without the content of a traditional religion." See his "The Poetry of Wallace Stevens," first published in *Poetry* 75 (December 1949):149–65.

Revised and reprinted in *Tradition and Poetic Structure* (Denver, Colo: Alan Swallow, 1960).

82. Litz, *Introspective Voyager* p. 171.

83. Stevens, "Flux^2," p. 774.

84. As stated in a conversation in 1932 with me.

85. I am quoting the text as it was first published in the *Hound & Horn*. Line eight was deleted in subsequent reprintings, but it was restored in the text as it appears in Holly Stevens, *The Palm at the End of the Mind*.

86. L, 289.

87. L, 293.

88. L, 294.

89. "The World as Meditation," *Yale Review* 47 (1958):517–36.

90. Yvor Winters, *Forms of Discovery* (Chicago: Alan Swallow, 1967), pp. 148–49.

91. There is disagreement among critics concerning the extent of the influence of Coleridge's concept of the imagination on Stevens's thinking and (regardless of the influence) the similarities or dissimilarities of Coleridge's and Stevens's concepts. According to Frank Lentricchia, Stevens was not a Coleridgean: "The simple point that needs to be made is that Stevens is not a Coleridgean." (*The Gaiety of Language* [Berkeley, Calif.: University of California Press, 1968], p. 120.) On the other hand Frank Kermode (*Wallace Stevens*, [London: Oliver and Boyd, 1960], pp. 37, 57–58) and Marius Bewley ("Romanticism Reconsidered," *Hudson Review* 17 [Spring 1964]: p. 127) both consider Stevens to be Coleridgean. Diane Middlebrook (*Walt Whitman and Wallace Stevens* [Ithaca, N. Y., and London: Cornell University Press, 1974], pp. 17–19; pp. 30ff.) concurs with Bewley and Kermode: "Stevens' resemblance to Whitman lies deeper, in the area of a shared theory of poetry which derives ultimately from Coleridge." She finds evidence of Coleridge's theories in *Notes toward a Supreme Fiction, Auroras of Autumn,* and elsewhere. Both Stevens and Coleridge believed that truth was mental, the product of cognition. Both believed that the imagination was a shaping force. Furthermore, Stevens's theory of "abstraction" appears to owe much to Coleridge's notion that "The artist must first eloign himself from nature in order to return to her with full effect." She agrees, however, with Lentricchia that Stevens did not believe, as Coleridge did, in the immanence of spirit in nature. (Middlebrook's opinions on this subject were augmented by correspondence with the author.) Walton Litz in *The Introspective Voyager* pp. 245–46, is about midway between Kermode and Lentricchia: "Although accepting the Coleridgean belief that 'pure poetry' is the balance or reconciliation of opposite or discordant qualities, Stevens refuses to give primacy to either the imagination or its materials preferring to locate the soul of poetry in a 'universal intercourse.' " That is, Stevens did not accept Coleridge's notion that something can exist exclusively by reason of the imagination. Stevens himself denied any strong influence of Coleridge (L. 792). It was, of course, Stevens's habit to deny the strong influence of anyone. The foregoing is a very brief example of how confusing modern concepts of the imagination have become. A good deal of the confusion, I suspect, must be laid to Coleridge.

92. L, 788.

93. Stevens in his letters referred to these numbered sections as poems.

94. L, 786.

95. L, 783.

96. Ibid.

97. L, 789.

98. L. 234.

99. Litz, *Introspective Voyager* p. 234.

100. Ibid., p. 235.

101. Ibid., pp. 229ff.

102. Helen Hennessy Vendler, *On Extended Wings: Wallace Stevens' Longer Poems* (Cambridge, Mass.: Harvard University Press, 1969), p. 125.

103. L, 364.

104. L, 792.

105. L. 430–31.

106. L, 435.

107. L. 434.

108. L, 430.

109. NA, 33.

110. Coleridge, "On Poesy or Art," *Biographia Literaria*, ed. J. Shawcross (London: Clarendon Press, 1907), 2:258. Diane Middlebrook, who first drew my attention to this passage with reference to Stevens, also finds similar ideas in Whitman. See her *Walt Whitman and Wallace Stevens* (Ithaca, N.Y. and London: Cornell University Press, 1974).

111. L, 444.

112. Ibid.

113. L, 434.

114. L, 433.

115. OP, 213.

116. NA, 54. Italics mine.

117. L, 431.

118. L, 435.

119. James E. Miller, Jr., *The American Quest for a Supreme Fiction* (Chicago: University of Chicago Press, 1979), p. 61.

120. Ibid., p. 56.

121. L, 435.

122. "Chocorua to Its Neighbor," *Southern Review* 15 (October 1979):777–91. In the remarks which follow I am not attempting to impugn the brilliance and learning of this essay. Pearce traces the Chocorua *topos* to Henry James's *The American Scene*. He pursues it through Stevens's poetry until its final statement in "The Poem that Took the Place of a Mountain" and he presents historical background about Mount Chocorua of interest to any serious reader of Stevens's poem. Pearce and I, however, disagree as to the poem's literary merits.

123. Ibid., p. 779.

124. Joseph N. Riddel, *The Clairvoyant Eye: The Poetry and Poetics of Wallace Stevens* (Baton Rouge, La.: Louisiana State University Press, 1965), pp. 202–16.

125. *On Extended Wings*, p. 242.

126. Vendler, "Stevens and Keats' 'To Autumn,' " pp. 171–95.

127. *On Extended Wings*, p. 331.

128. Ibid., p. 234.

129. "Style and Procedures of Wallace Stevens," p. 13.

130. "The Auroras of Autumn," first published in *Perspectives* 7 (Autumn 1954), reprinted in *The Achievement of Wallace Stevens*, edited by Ashley Brown and Robert S. Haller (New York: J. B. Lippincott Co., 1962), pp. 166–78. This quotation is on p. 167.

131. He is so interpreted by Riddel, *Clairvoyant Eye*, p. 236.

132. See Vendler, *On Extended Wings*, p. 250.

133. *Clairvoyant Eye*, p. 237.

134. *On Extended Wings*, pp. 246–50.

135. See Yvor Winters, *The Function of Criticism: Problems and Exercises* (Denver: Alan Swallow, 1957), pp. 70–74; Helen P. Trimpi, "Contexts for 'Being,' 'Divinity,' and 'Self' in Valéry and Edgar Bowers," *Southern Review* 13 (Winter 1977):pp. 56–65.

136. Litz, *Introspective Voyager*, p. 287.

137. Or so the giant appears to be here. Stevens is not consistent in his use of the giant as symbol. In "A Primitive Like an Orb" Stevens refers to

the giant of nothingness, each one
and the giant ever changing, living in change.

Roy Harvey Pearce says this giant "is at once lover, believer, poet, painter, altogether decreated." See "Towards Decreation: Stevens and the 'Theory of Poetry,' " *Wallace Stevens: a Celebration*, p. 301.

138. Ibid., pp. 286–307. See also Roy Harvey Pearce, *The Continuity of American Poetry* (Princeton, N. J.: Princeton University Press, 1961), pp. 404–19.

139. The shorter version appeared in *Transactions of the Connecticut Academy of Arts and Sciences*

38(December 1949), pp. 161–72, and in *Selected Poems* (London, 1953). This Faber and Faber selection was reprinted once in Stevens's lifetime. The longer version appeared in *The Auroras of Autumn* (New York, 1950), and in the *Collected Poems* (New York, 1954).
140. *On Extended Wings*, p. 269.
141. Ibid., p. 270.
142. "Three Academic Pieces," NA, p. 81.
143. *On Extended Wings*, p. 270.
144. L, 636.
145. "Towards Decreation," p. 303.

Chapter 4 Edwin Arlington Robinson

1. This quotation from François Coppée's comedy *Le Trésor* is on the title page of Robinson's first book, *The Torrent and the Night Before* (1896).
2. Ridgely Torrence, ed., *Selected Letters of Edwin Arlington Robinson* (New York: Macmillan, 1940), p. 128. In a letter to Witter Bynner dated October 14, 1921.
3. Ibid., p. 93. In a letter dated March 18, 1916.
4. Richard Cary, ed., *Edwin Arlington Robinson's Letters to Edith Brower* (Cambridge, Mass.: Harvard University Press, 1968), pp. 180–81. Letter dated October 31, 1922.
5. Louis Untermeyer, "E.A.R.: A Remembrance," *Saturday Review*, April 10, 1965, p. 33.
6. Quoted in Edwin Fussell, *Edwin Arlington Robinson: The Literary Background of a Traditional Poet* (Berkeley and Los Angeles: University of California Press, 1954), p. 180. The quotation is from an unpublished letter to Mrs. Laura E. Richards, April 9, 1933.
7. Quoted in Fussell, *Robinson*, p. 176, from Lloyd R. Morris, ed., *The Young Idea: An Anthology of Opinion Concerning the Spirit and Aims of Contemporary American Literature* (New York, 1917), pp. 193–94.
8. Lucius Beebe, "Robinson Sees Romantic Strain in Future Verse," *New York Herald Tribune*, December 22, 1929, pt. I, p. 19.
9. Charles Cestre, *An Introduction to Edwin Arlington Robinson* (New York: The Macmillan Company, 1930), p. 22. Of Cestre, Robinson said, "The Frenchman knows what I am up to. And somehow he always has." See Rollo Walter Brown, *Next Door to a Poet* (New York: D. Appleton-Century Co.), p. 25.
10. Denham Sutcliffe, ed., *Untriangulated Stars: Letters of Edwin Arlington Robinson to Harry de Forest Smith 1890–1905* (Cambridge, Mass.: Harvard University Press, 1947) p. 141. In a letter dated March 18, 1894.
11. Torrence, *Selected Letters*, pp. 12–13. In a letter to Arthur R. Gledhill, dated October 28, 1896.
12. Ibid., p. 49. In a letter to Mrs. Laura E. Richards dated January 18, 1902.
13. Ibid., p. 186.
14. Cary, *Letters to Edith Brower*, p. 140. In a letter dated April 1, 1901.
15. Torrence, *Selected Letters*, p. 103. In a letter to L. N. Chase dated July 11, 1917.
16. Fussell, *Robinson*, pp. 25ff.
17. Ibid.
18. Ibid., pp. 137–38.
19. Cestre, *Robinson*, p. 5.
20. Torrence, *Selected Letters*, p. 160. In a letter to Helen Grace Adams dated January 1, 1930.
21. Allen Tate, *Essays of Four Decades* (Chicago: Swallow Press, 1968), p. 345. From an essay entitled "Edwin Arlington Robinson," first published in 1933.
22. Ibid., p. 347.
23. Richard P. Adams, "The Failure of Edwin Arlington Robinson," *Tulane Studies in English* 11(1961):119.
24. Yvor Winters, *Edwin Arlington Robinson* (Norfolk, Conn.: New Directions, 1946). Because of copyright restrictions this first edition contains no quotations from Robinson's poems. The reader is referred in each instance to the appropriate page number in the *Collected Poems* of Robinson. Reprinted in 1971 with the quotations included. Page numbers in this chapter are those of the 1971

edition.

25. Yvor Winters, *The Function of Criticism* (Denver, Colo.: Alan Swallow, 1957), p. 60.

26. Ibid., p. 59.

27. Cary, *Letters to Edith Brower*, p. 186.

28. Chard Powers Smith, *Where the Light Falls: A Portrait of Edwin Arlington Robinson* (New York: The Macmillan Company, 1965), pp. 285, 290.

29. Josiah Royce, *The Spirit of Modern Philosophy* (Boston and New York: Houghton Mifflin Co. [1892]), p. 264.

30. Sutcliffe, *Untriangulated Stars*, pp. 279–80. In a letter dated March 15, 1897.

31. Torrence, *Selected Letters*, p. 164. In a letter to Will Durant dated September 18, 1931.

32. Ibid., p. 104. In a letter to L. N. Chase dated July 11, 1917.

33. Ibid., p. 93. In a letter to Amy Lowell dated March 18, 1916.

34. Ibid., p. 92. In a letter to Albert R. Ledoux dated March 2, 1916.

35. Emery Neff, *Edwin Arlington Robinson* (New York: William Sloane Associates, 1948), p. 175.

36. Quoted in Edna Davis Romig, "Tilbury Town and Camelot," *University of Colorado Studies* 19, no. 3(1932):318.

37. Torrence, *Selected Letters*, p. 127. In a letter to Arthur Davison Ficke dated June 23, 1921.

38. Tate, *Essays of Four Decades*, p. 345.

39. Theodore Roosevelt, "The Children of the Night," *Outlook* (New York) 80 (August 12, 1905):913–14. Reprinted in Richard Cary, *Early Reception of Edwin Arlington Robinson: The First Twenty Years* (Waterville, Maine: Colby College Press), pp. 170–71.

40. Cary, *Letters to Edith Brower*, p. 141. In a letter dated April 28, 1901.

41. Ibid., p. 39. In a letter dated April 21, 1897.

42. Daniel Gregory Mason, ed., "Early Letters of Edwin Arlington Robinson," *Virginia Quarterly Review* 13(1937):64. In a letter to D. G. Mason dated May 18, 1900.

43. Sutcliffe. *Untriangulated Stars*, p. 238. In a letter to Harry de Forest Smith dated December 14, 1895.

44. Adams, "Failure of Robinson," pp. 131–32.

45. Max Simon Nordau, *Degeneration* (New York: D. Appleton and Co., 1896).

46. The poem has been reprinted in Richard Cary, *Uncollected Poems and Prose of Edwin Arlington Robinson*, (Waterville, Maine: Colby College Press, 1975), p. 32.

47. Peter Dechert, "He Shouts to See Them Scamper So: E. A. Robinson and the French Forms," in Richard Cary, ed., *Appreciation of Edwin Arlington Robinson: 28 Interpretive Essays* (Waterville, Maine: Colby College Press, 1969), p. 340.

48. Lincoln MacVeagh, "Edwin Arlington Robinson," *New Republic* 2(April 10, 1915):267–68. Reprinted in Cary, *Early Reception of Robinson*, pp. 281–83.

49. Adams, "Failure of Robinson," p. 133.

50. Winters, *Robinson* p. 33.

51. Ellsworth Barnard, *Edwin Arlington Robinson: A Critical Study* (New York: The Macmillan Company, 1952), p. 295.

52. Laurence Perrine, "Robinson's 'Veteran Sirens,' " *Explicator* 6(November 1947), Item 13.

53. In an unpublished essay "The Sirens in 'Veteran Sirens.' " And see Smith, *Where the Light Falls*, pp. 116, 395. See also Ronald Moran, "With Firm Address: A Critical Study of 26 Shorter Poems of E. A. Robinson," Ph. D. diss. Louisiana State University, pp. 122–25.

54. Louis O. Coxe, *Edwin Arlington Robinson: The Life of Poetry* (New York: Pegasus, 1969), p. 112.

55. Neff, *Robinson*, p. 198.

56. Ibid., p. 181

57. Winters, *Robinson*, p. 32.

58. Smith, *Where the Light Falls*, p. 90. Robinson's alleged love for Emma Shepherd is a major theme of this book.

59. See especially Cestre, *Robinson*, pp. 51–52; Henry Pettit, "Robinson's *The Whip*," *Explicator* 1 (April 1943); Robinson's letter to Carl J. Weber dated Jan. 28, 1923, in the *Saturday Review of Literature* 26(April 17, 1943): 54. In this letter Robinson says, "I hardly know what to say about 'The Whip' except that it is supposed to be a literal and not a figurative instrument"; Ben Ray Redman,

Saturday Review of Literature 26(April 17, 1943):18–19 — a parody; Yvor Winters, *Robinson*, pp. 49–51; an exchange of letters between William Rose Benét and Yvor Winters in the *Saturday Review of Literature* 30 (January 18, 1947): 32, and 30(March 8, 1947):48; Barnard, *Robinson*, pp. 46, 99, 137–38, 207, 228, 251, 290; Lawrance Thompson, ed., *Tilbury Town: Selected Poems of Edwin Arlington Robinson* (New York: The Macmillan Company, 1953), pp. xi–xiii and 139; Wallace L. Anderson, *Edwin Arlington Robinson: A Critical Introduction* (Cambridge, Mass.: Harvard University Press 1969), pp. 104–5; Ronald Moran, *With Firm Address*, pp. 54–64.

60. Torrence, *Selected Letters*, p. 104. In a letter to L. N. Chase dated July 11, 1917.

61. See especially Winters, *Robinson*, pp. 42–43; Celeste Turner Wright, "Robinson's 'Lost Anchors,' " *Explicator* 11(1953), Item 57; Ronald Moran, *With Firm Address*, pp. 155–62; S. A. Cowan, "Robinson's 'Lost Anchors,' " *Explicator* 23(1965), Item 64; James Grimshaw, "Robinson's 'Lost Anchors,' " *Explicator* 30(1971), Item 36; Richard Tuerk, "Robinson's 'Lost Anchors,' " *Explicator* 32 (1974), Item 37.

62. Neff, *Robinson*, p. 197.

63. Ibid., p. 221.

64. Reprinted in Charles Beecher Hogan, *A Bibliography of Edwin Arlington Robinson* (New Haven, Conn.: Yale University Press, 1936), pp. 179–80, and in Cary, *Uncollected Poems and Prose*, pp. 83–84; see also ibid., pp. 189–91. Errors, chiefly typographical, in the text of the Gardiner version have been silently corrected.

65. Neff, *Robinson*, p. 221.

66. *Explicator* 10 (1952), Item 33.

67. First published in the *Colby Library Quarterly* 8(September 1969): 371–85. Reprinted in Cary's *Appreciation*, pp. 322–34. Page references are to the Cary reprint.

68. Cary, *Appreciation*, pp. 323–24.

69. See Winters, *Robinson*, p. 24; Hoyt H. Hudson, "Robinson and Praed," *Poetry* 61(February 1943):612–20.

70. David S. Nivison, "Does It Matter How Annandale Went Out?" *Colby Library Quarterly*, series 5 (December 1960):173. "In 'Aunt Imogen,' for example, after assembling his character he had to imagine what it would be like to be such a person. And he found that to a surprising degree he *was* such a person. To this extent the poem is self-explorative." Nivison, a grandnephew of Robinson, is the son of Ruth (Mrs. William Nivison), one of Robinson's three nieces. For another account of Robinson's relationship with his nieces and grandnephews see Richard Cary, "Robinson's Notes to His Nieces," *Colby Library Quarterly*, series 5 (December 1960):195–203.

71. Hermann Hagedorn, *Edwin Arlington Robinson: A Biography* (New York: The Macmillan Company, 1938), p. 145.

72. Mason, "Early Letters," p. 67. In a letter to D. G. Mason dated July 31, 1900.

73. W. W. Robson, "The Achievement of Robert Frost," *Southern Review*, n.s.4 (1966):753.

74. Smith, *Where the Light Falls*, p. 359, Hagedorn suggests it was his cousin Seth Palmer's farm that furnished the setting for the poem (Hagedorn, *Robinson*, p. 19). See also Laura E. Richards, *E.A.R.* (New York: Princeton University Press, 1921), reissued by Russell & Russell, 1967, p. 17 "One fancies he [E.A.R.] was always ready, at any age, for a drive to Alna, and a visit to his cousins there.... One thinks that Isaac and Archibald lived in that region too." Robinson's birthplace, "Head of Tide," was in the township of Alna, Maine. Robinson told Laura Richards that the idea of two old men each thinking the other was crazy came from his friendship with Alfred H. Louis and William Henry Thorne,who published a quarterly called the *Globe*. Each had confided to Robinson that he was convinced the other was crazy and both, according to Robinson, were not far wrong (Hagedorn, *Robinson* p. 168).

75. Smith, *Where the Light Falls*, pp. 311, 327. For further discussion of this poem see J. C. Levenson, "Robinson's Modernity," *The Virginia Quarterly Review* 44(Autumn 1968): 590–610.

76. Hagedorn, *Robinson*, p. 238.

77. Cary, *Letters to Edith Brower*, p. 155.

78. Adams, "Failure of Robinson," p. 143. For a more complicated analysis of this difficult line see Clyde L. Grimm, "Robinson's 'For a Dead Lady': An Exercise in Evaluation," *Colby Library Quarterly* 7(December 1967):535–47.

79. See Yvor Winters, "Religious and Social Ideas in the Didactic Works of E. A. Robinson," *Arizona*

Quarterly 1(Spring 1945):70–85.

80. Theodore Roosevelt, "The Children of the Night," *Outlook* (New York) 80 (August 12, 1905):913–14. For a discussion of the relationship between Roosevelt and Robinson see C. J. Weber, "Poet and President," *New England Quarterly* 16(December 1943):615–26.

81. Torrence, *Selected Letters*, p. 67. In a letter to Louis V. Ledoux dated July 20, 1910.

82. Richard Cary, "The Library of Edwin Arlington Robinson: Addenda," *Colby Library Quarterly* series 7 (March 1967): 414.

83. Eugene England, "Tuckerman's Sonnet I:10: The First Post-Symbolist Poem," *Southern Review* n.s. 12 (Spring 1976)323–47.

84. Ibid., p. 329.

85. Ibid., p. 341.

86. Yvor Winters, "Poetic Styles, Old and New," in *Four Poets on Poetry*, edited with an introduction by Don Cameron Allen (Baltimore, Md.: Johns Hopkins Press, 1959), pp. 44–75.

87. N. Scott Momaday, ed., *The Complete Poems of Frederick Goddard Tuckerman*, with a critical foreword by Yvor Winters (New York: Oxford University Press, 1965).

88. Ibid., p. xiii.

89. Ibid., pp. xv–xvi.

90. Winters, *Robinson*, p. 38.

91. George K. Anderson, *The Legend of the Wandering Jew* (Providence, R. I.: Brown University Press, 1965), p. 318.

92. Coxe, *Robinson*, pp. 130–32, 159–60.

93. Louis O. Coxe, "E. A. Robinson: The Lost Tradition," in *Appreciation of Edwin Arlington Robinson: 28 Interpretive Essays* (Waterville, Maine: Colby College Press, 1969), pp. 164–77.

94. Anderson, *Wandering Jew*, p. 11.

95. Ibid., p. 318.

96. The poem is in *Collected Poems of Edwin Arlington Robinson* (New York: The Macmillan Company, 1942), pp. 456–59.

97. Coxe, *Robinson*, p. 130.

98. Winters, *Robinson*, p. 37.

99. Ibid., p. 42.

100. The unpublished letter is in the W. Easton Louttit Collection of the Brown University Library. I quote by the kind permission of the Brown University Library.

101. Cary, *Letters to Edith Brower*, pp. 211–12.

102. W. Denham Sutcliffe, "The Original of Robinson's Captain Craig," *New England Quarterly* 16 (Sept. 1943): 407–31. The reference to the Meynell volume is on p. 430.

103. Winters, *Robinson*, p. 7.

104. Algernon Blackwood, *Episodes before Thirty* (New York: E. P. Dutton & Co., 1923), pp. 299ff. For further information on Louis see Sutcliffe's article cited above, and Robert W. Hill, "More Light on a Shadowy Figure: A. H. Louis, the Original of E. A. Robinson's 'Captain Craig,' " *Bulletin of the New York Public Library* 60(August 1956): 373–77.

105. His obituary is in the *Times* (London), Oct. 20, 1915, p. 11.

106. According to Maude Ffoulkes. See below. According to Hagedorn, *Robinson*, p. 134, Louis claimed he was the original of Mordecai in *Daniel Deronda*.

107. *England and Europe: A Discussion of National Policy* (London: R. Bentley, 1861).

108. This is the archbishop who gave Henry James his donnée for *The Turn of the Screw.*

109. Maud M. C. Ffoulkes, *My Own Past* (London: Cassell and Co., 1915), p. 194. Mrs. Ffoulkes, who knew both Blackwood and Louis, gives 1894 as the date of their first meeting. I have been unable to confirm this date elsewhere.

110. *Episodes before Thirty*, pp. 299–307.

111. Algernon Blackwood, *The Listener and Other Stories* (London: Eveleigh Nash, 1907). Reprinted by Books for Libraries Press, Freeport, New York, 1971. The story is on pages 261–75 of the reprint edition.

112. Pp. 193–99.

113. *My Past* (London: Eveleigh Nash, 1913). The countess was responsible for Eliot's famous line in *The Waste Land*, "Marie, Marie hold on tight." See Valerie Eliot, ed., *The Waste Land* (New York:

Harcourt Brace, Jovanovich, 1971), pp. 125–26.

114. Opposite p. 198.

115. In *The Lyric,* May–June, 1919.

116. For a recent discussion of this subject see Charles Buck and Greer Taylor, *Saint Paul: A Study of the Development of His Thought* (New York: Charles Scribner's Sons, 1969).

117. Neff, *Robinson,* p. 202.

118. Esther Willard Bates, *Edwin Arlington Robinson and His Manuscripts* (Waterville, Maine: Colby College Library, 1944), p. 23.

119. There are over a hundred self-portraits by Rembrandt of which about seventy are paintings. (Bredius entitles about sixty paintings as self-portraits, but in addition to these Rembrandt painted himself into a number of group pictures.) Arranged chronologically from 1629 until 1669 they show Rembrandt as a very young man, later (in the 1630s) at the height of his fame and happiness, and then, as the years pass, with a face increasingly ravaged by anxiety and age. His earlier portraits show him frequently well, even lavishly attired, sometimes in officer's dress with feathered cap and gorget. The portrait addressed by Rembrandt in Robinson's poem may well be Bredius number 25, painted in 1635, which shows the artist wearing a cap with two huge feathers and a sumptuous velvet cape or coat. "Where are your velvet and your feathers now?"

120. Emery Neff, *Robinson.*, pp. 200–202, in discussing this poem identifies the painting mentioned in the first stanza as *The Night Watch,* a painting which because of its "new golden shadow" drew the "bewildered and unhappy scorn" of the Hollanders. I see no reason to doubt this identification. However, in the interest of historical accuracy, a few comments are necessary. The picture was originally called *The Civic Guard,* according to some authorities. According to them it portrays a portion of the civic guard issuing forth in broad daylight and not at night. On the other hand, according to Ludwig Goldscheider in *Rembrandt* (London: Phaidon Press, 1960, p. 170) a shooting company rather than the civic guard is depicted. A. Bredius, in *Rembrandt: The Complete Edition of the Paintings* (3rd ed.; London: Phaidon, 1969, p. 584), entitled it "The Militia Company of Frans Banning Cocq," after the name of the central figure, and states that the group is being portrayed as it is about to form a parade. The erroneous title *The Night Watch* was probably given to the picture in the early nineteenth century. Goldscheider claims that the painting was in fact very popular with the Hollanders, and that those who had paid a considerable amount of money to have their portraits depicted in it were completely satisfied with the painting. The legend that they were indignant and that the picture was unpopular and marked the beginning of Rembrandt's decline in fashion was started, says Goldscheider, by the romantic movement. However, Robinson obviously believed the legend to be the truth, and in fact Rembrandt did suffer a decline in his popularity beginning about 1645, during the period in which he was painting some of his masterpieces. Therefore the power of Robinson's psychological portrayal of an alienated and unpopular genius is true to historical fact even though the picture in question did not (in all probability) play a part in Rembrandt's loss of public esteem.

121. Neff, *Robinson,* p. 257.

122. Coxe, *Robinson,* p. 160.

Chapter 5   Yvor Winters

1. A. E. Housman, *The Name and Nature of Poetry* (New York: The Macmillan Company, 1933), p. 36.

2. Ibid., p. 39.

3. T. S. Eliot, *The Use of Poetry and the Use of Criticism* (Cambridge, Mass.: Harvard University Press, 1933), p. 144.

4. John Crowe Ransom, *The World's Body* (New York: Charles Scribner's Sons, 1938), p. 348.

5. First published in *Secession* 8 (April 1924), 20 pages; reprinted in Francis Murphy, ed., *Yvor Winters: Uncollected Essays and Reviews* (Chicago: Swallow Press, 1973), pp. 194–215.

6. *Instigations of Ezra Pound Together with an Essay on the Chinese Written Character by Ernest Fenollosa* (New York: Boni and Liveright, 1920).

7. *The Early Poems of Yvor Winters* (Denver, Colo.: Alan Swallow, 1966). Winters's *Collected*

Poems are published by Swallow Press (Revised Edition, Chicago, 1960), and by Carcanet Press (Manchester, England, 1978). The Carcanet edition, with an introduction by Donald Davie, is more nearly definitive than earlier collections. It was also published by Swallow press in 1980.

8. In *The New American Caravan,* III (1929), pp. 361–402. Reprinted in *Uncollected Essays*, pp. 225–70. Page numbers refer to this reprint.

9. Ibid., p. 226.

10. Ibid.

11. Ibid., p. 227.

12. *Primitivism and Decadence: A Study of American Experimental Poetry* (New York: Arrow Editions, 1937).

13. *Uncollected Essays*, p. 229.

14. P. xi.

15. An earlier draft of this essay was published under the title "Poetry, Morality, and Criticism" in *The Critique of Humanism,* edited by C. Hartley Grattan (New York: Brewer and Warren, 1930), pp. 301–33.

16. Don Cameron Allen, ed., *Four Poets on Poetry* (Baltimore, Md.: Johns Hopkins Press, 1959), pp. 44–75.

17. It was published as an essay in "The Poetry of Gerard Manley Hopkins" in two parts in the winter and spring 1949 issues of *The Hudson Review* and was reprinted in *The Function of Criticism* (Denver, Colo.: Alan Swallow, 1957), pp. 103–56.

18. *Function of Criticism*, pp. 103–4.

19. Reprinted in *The Function of Criticism.*

20. Ibid., p. 83.

21. Ibid., p. 88.

22. Ibid., pp. 91–92.

23. Ibid., p. 94.

24. Ibid.

25. In "Problems for the Modern Critic of Literature," *Hudson Review* 9 (Autumn 1956): 325–86; reprinted in *The Function of Criticism*, pp. 9–78.

26. Reprinted in *Four Poets.* See note 16 above.

27. *Four Poets,* p. 72.

28. Ibid., p. 73.

29. *Function of Criticism*, p. 69.

30. Ibid., p. 66.

31. Ibid.

32. Ibid., p. 75.

33. N. Scott Momaday, ed., *The Complete Poems of Frederick Goddard Tuckerman, with a Critical Foreword by Yvor Winters* (New York: Oxford University Press, 1965).

34. *Forms of Discovery* (Chicago: Alan Swallow, 1967), p. 253.

35. *The Journey and Other Poems* (Ithaca, N. Y.: Dragon Press, 1931).

36. *Before Disaster,* The Tryon Pamphlets (Tryon, N. C., 1934).

37. It was, however, reviewed by J. V. Cunningham under the title "Obscurity and Dust," *Poetry* 40 (June 1932):163–65.

38. *Before Disaster,* p. iv.

39. Ibid., pp. v–vi.

40. "By Way of Clarification," *Twentieth Century Literature* 10 (October 1964):132.

41. "Herman Melville and the Problems of Moral Navigation," in *In Defense of Reason* (New York: Swallow Press and William Morrow and Co., 1947), pp. 200, 202.

42. Howard Kaye, "The Post-Symbolist Poetry of Yvor Winters," *Southern Review* n.s. 7(Winter 1971): 187.

43. Yvor Winters, *Poems* (Los Altos, Calif.: Gyroscope Press, 1940), in "Notes" [unnumbered page].

44. Reprinted in Grattan, *Critique of Humanism*, pp. 131–66. Page references are to this reprint.

45. Ibid., p. 163.

46. "The 16th Century Lyric in England," Part I, *Poetry* 53 (February 1939):258–72; Part II, ibid., 53 (March 1939):320–35; Part III, ibid., 54 (April 1939):35–51. This essay was revised and reprinted

in *Forms of Discovery,* chapter 1. See also Raymond Oliver, "Yvor Winters and the English Renaissance," *Southern Review* n.s. 17(Autumn 1981): 758–80.

47. *Poetry* 53(February 1939): 260.

48. Ibid., p. 262.

49. Douglas L. Peterson, "Yvor Winters' 'By the Road to the Air base,' " *Southern Review,* n.s. 15 (Summer 1979):567–74. The original title as it appeared in *Before Disaster* was shortened to "By the Road to the Air-Base" in all subsequent reprintings.

50. Ibid., p. 568.

51. *Poems* (Los Altos, Calif.: Gyroscope Press, 1940).

52. C. J. Jung and C. Kerényi, *Essays on a Science of Mythology,* Bollingen Series XII (New York: Pantheon Books, 1949), p. 156.

53. *Classical Dictionary* (New York: Harper's, 1843), p. 579.

54. Ibid., p. 434.

55. The poem is most readily available in *Poems of R. P. Blackmur* (Princeton, N. J.: Princeton University Press, 1977), p. 43.

56. The poem appeared in *Poetry* 69 (December 1946):140–41. According to campus gossip it was read before the Stanford University Board of Supervisors at the time of Winters's promotion.

57. *Poems,* 1940, note on unnumbered page.

58. Grosvenor E. Powell, "Yvor Winters' Greek allegories," *Southern Review* n.s. 14 (Spring 1978):262–80.

59. See ibid. for an analysis of these changes.

60. Ibid., p. 279.

61. Note in *Poems,* 1940.

62. "Heracles is treated as a Sun-god, the particular statement used being that of Anthon's *Classical Dictionary,*" Note in *Poems* 1940. See Charles Anthon, *A Classical Dictionary* (New York: Harper Brothers), in various editions. I have used that of 1843 for the quotations below.

63. *The Poems of T. Sturge Moore,* Collected Edition, vol.3 (London: Macmillan and Co., 1932), p. 246.

64. Powell develops a similar thesis in his article previously cited. He compares the poem to Ben Jonson's "To Heaven," which is about a scholar poet who wishes to die.

65. According to Kenneth Fields, who had a number of conversations with Winters in his last years, a source book for the Gold Rush material in "John Sutter" was Robert Glass Cleland, *A History of California: The American Period* (New York: The Macmillan Company, 1922). See especially chapters 17, "The Gold Rush," and 19, "Mines and Miners." Fields also mentions as a source book for some of the California poems Charles E. Chapman, *A History of California: The Spanish Period* (New York: The Macmillan Company, 1921). Winters himself cites this volume in his note to "The California Oaks," in *Collected Poems.* See Kenneth Wayne Fields, *The Rhetoric of Artifice* (Ann Arbor, Mich.: University Microfilms, 1967), p. 292. Another possible source for "John Sutter" is *The Diary of Johann August Sutter* (San Francisco: Grabhorn Press, 1932). Winters was personally acquainted with the owner of the Grabhorn Press.

66. For further details see Richard Dillon, *Fool's Gold* (New York: Coward-McCann, 1967) and James Peter Zollinger, *Sutter: The Man and His Empire* (New York: Oxford University Press, 1939).

67. The source for this stanza, the seventh of the poem, is Cleland, *California,* pp. 266–68, 276: "Where the streams were small, the miner easily turned them aside, and dug out the virgin gold thus exposed with his butcher knife.... [For large streams the] measures were reasonably successful and the arduous and unproductive labor of the preceding months would find its reward, many times over, when the gold deposited year after year for untold centuries ...was dug out of the pot holes.... Hydraulic mining...soon came to supersede all other forms...but the land so treated was ruined eternally.... Society was reckless, drunkenness common, and everyone went around with knife or pistol. Murder was therefore the commonest of crimes."

68. See Edgeley W. Todd's edition of Washington Irving's *Astoria* (Norman, Okla.: University of Oklahoma Press, 1964), pp. 138–39 (note) for a fairly recent biographical sketch of Day.

69. Ibid.

70. See Yvor Winters, "By Way of Clarification," *Twentieth Century Literature* 10 (October 1964):132–34.

71. New York: Charles Scribner's Sons, 1935.

72. Frances Theresa Russell and Yvor Winters, *The Case of David Lamson* (San Francisco, 1934). Winters told me that he wrote most of this pamphlet himself and I believe him.

73. *New Republic* 91 (2 June 1937):104–5.

74. See Howard Kaye, "The Post-Symbolist Poetry of Yvor Winters," *Southern Review* 7 (Winter 1971): 176–97. I am indebted to this essay.

75. *In Defense of Reason,* p. 14.

76. "To Herbert Dean Meritt," in *Philological Essays in Honour of Herbert Dean Meritt,* edited by James L. Rosier (The Hague: Mouton, 1970), p.[7].

Bibliography

The following bibliography is highly selective. For more comprehensive bibliographies the following may be consulted: Donald Gallup, *A Bibliography of Ezra Pound* (London: Rupert Hart-Davis, 1963); Donald Gallup, *T. S. Eliot: A Bibliography* (London: Faber & Faber, 1969); J. M. Edelstein, *Wallace Stevens: A Descriptive Bibliography* (Pittsburgh: University of Pittsburgh Press, 1973); Charles Hogan, *A Bibliography of Edwin Arlington Robinson* (New Haven, Conn.: Yale University Press, 1936), and William White, *Edwin Arlington Robinson: A Supplementary Bibliography* (Kent, Ohio: Kent State University Press, 1971); Kenneth A. Lohf and Eugene P. Sheehy, *Yvor Winters: A Bibliography* (Denver: Alan Swallow, 1959). Grosvenor Powell is compiling a comprehensive bibliography of Yvor Winters for the Garland Bibliographies of Literary Critics to be published by the Garland Press.

Chapter 1   Ezra Pound

Poetry of Ezra Pound

Separate Works

A Lume Spento. Venice: Printed for the author by A. Antonini, 1908.

A Quinzaine for This Yule. London: Pollock & Co., 1908.

Personae of Ezra Pound. London: Elkin Mathews, 1909.

Exultations of Ezra Pound. London: Elkin Mathews, 1909.

Provença: Poems Selected from Personae, Exultations, and Canzoniere of Ezra Pound. Boston: Small, Maynard and Co., 1910.

Canzoni of Ezra Pound. London: Elkin Mathews, 1911.

Ripostes of Ezra Pound Whereto Are Appended the Complete Poetical Works of T. E. Hulme with Prefatory Note. London: Stephen Swift and Co., 1912.

Lustra of Ezra Pound. London: Elkin Mathews, 1916.

Umbra: The Early Poems of Ezra Pound. London: Elkin Mathews, 1920.

The Cantos, 1–95. New York: New Directions, 1965.

Selected and Collected Editions

Personae: The Collected Poems of Ezra Pound. New York: New Directions, 1926.

Selected Poems. Edited and with an introduction by T. S. Eliot. London: Faber and Gwyer, 1928.

Collected Early Poems of Ezra Pound. Edited by Michael John King. New York: New Directions, 1976.

Translations

Cathay Translations by Ezra Pound for the Most Part from the Chinese of Rihaku, from the Notes of the Late Ernest Fenollosa, and the Decipherings of the Professors Mori and Ariga. London: Elkin Mathews, 1915.
Certain Noble Plays of Japan: From the Manuscripts of Ernest Fenollosa. Chosen and finished by Ezra Pound, with an introduction by William Butler Yeats. Churchtown, Ireland: Cuala Press, 1916.
Ezra Pound: Translations. With an introduction by Hugh Kenner. New York: New Directions, 1963.

Prose of Ezra Pound

Separate Works

The Spirit of Romance. London: J. M. Dent & Sons, 1910.
Gaudier-Brzeska: A Memoir by Ezra Pound. London: John Lane, The Bodley Head. New York: John Lane Co., 1916.
'Noh,' or, Accomplishment: A Study of the Classical Stage of Japan, by Ernest Fenollosa and Ezra Pound. New York: Alfred A. Knopf, 1917.
Pavannes and Divisions. New York: Alfred A. Knopf, 1918.
Instigations. New York: Boni and Liveright, 1920.
Make It New. London: Faber and Faber, 1934.

Selected and Collected Editions

Literary Essays. Edited with an introduction by T. S. Eliot. Norfolk, Conn.: New Directions, 1918.
The Letters of Ezra Pound 1907–1941. Edited by D. D. Paige. New York: Harcourt, Brace and Co., 1950.
Pound/Joyce: The Letters of Ezra Pound to James Joyce, with Pound's Essays on Joyce. Edited by Forrest Reid.
New York: New Directions, 1967.
Ezra Pound: Selected Prose 1909–1965. Edited by William Cookson. New York: New Directions, 1973.

Translation

Fenollosa, Ernest Francisco. *The Chinese Written Character as a Medium for Poetry.* Edited by Ezra Pound. San Francisco: City Light Books, 1936. [First published 1919]

Books on Ezra Pound

Baumann, Walter. *The Rose in the Steel Dust: An Examination of the Cantos of Ezra Pound.* Coral Gables, Fla.: University of Miami Press, 1970.
Bush, Ronald. *The Genesis of Ezra Pound's Cantos.* Princeton, N.J.: Princeton University Press, 1976.
Chace, William M. *The Political Identities of Ezra Pound and T. S. Eliot.* Stanford, Calif.: Stanford University Press, 1973.
Dekker, George. *Sailing after Knowledge: The Cantos of Ezra Pound.* London: Routledge & Kegan Paul, 1963.
Dembo, Laurence Sanford. *The Confucian Odes of Ezra Pound: A Critical Appraisal.* Berkeley: University of California Press, 1963.

Edwards, John Hamilton, and Vasse, William H. *Annotated Index to the Cantos of Ezra Pound: Cantos I–LXXXIV.* Berkeley: University of California Press, 1957.

Espey, J. J. *Ezra Pound's 'Mauberley': A Study in Composition.* Berkeley: University of California Press, 1955.

Fraser, George Sutherland. *Ezra Pound.* Edinburgh: Oliver and Boyd, 1960.

Hutchins, Patricia. *Ezra Pound's Kensington: An Exploration, 1885–1913.* London: Faber and Faber, 1965.

Jackson, Thomas H. *The Early Poetry of Ezra Pound.* Cambridge, Mass.: Harvard University Press, 1968.

Kenner, Hugh. *The Poetry of Ezra Pound.* Norfolk, Conn.: New Directions, 1951.

———. *The Pound Era.* Berkeley: University of California Press, 1971.

McDougal, Stuart. *Ezra Pound and the Troubadour Tradition.* Princeton, N.J.: Princeton University Press, 1972.

Nagy, N. Christoph de. *Ezra Pound's Poetics and Literary Tradition.* Bern: Francke, 1966.

———. *The Poetry of Ezra Pound: The Pre-Imagist Stage.* Bern: Francke, 1960.

Norman, Charles. *Ezra Pound.* New York: Macmillan, 1960.

Pearlman, Daniel D. *The Barb of Time: On the Unity of Ezra Pound's Cantos.* New York: Oxford University Press, 1969.

Pearson, Norman Holmes, and King, Michael, eds. *End to Torment: A Memoir of Ezra Pound by H. D.* New York: New Directions, 1979.

Russell, Peter. *An Examination of Ezra Pound.* Norfolk, Conn.: New Directions, 1950.

Ruthven, K. K. *A Guide to Ezra Pound's Personae.* Berkeley and Los Angeles: University of California Press, 1969.

Schneidau, Herbert N. *Ezra Pound: The Image and the Real.* Baton Rouge: Louisiana State University Press, 1969.

Stock, Noel. *The Life of Ezra Pound.* New York: Pantheon Books, 1970.

Sullivan, J. P. *Ezra Pound and Sextus Propertius: A Study in Creative Translation.* Austin: University of Texas Press, 1964.

Terrell, Carroll F. *A Companion to the Cantos of Ezra Pound.* Berkeley: University of California Press, 1980.

Witemeyer, Hugh. *The Poetry of Ezra Pound: Forms and Renewal, 1908–1920.* Berkeley and Los Angeles: University of California Press, 1969.

Yip, Wai-lim. *Ezra Pound's Cathay.* Princeton, N.J.: Princeton University Press, 1969.

General

Coffman, Stanley K. *Imagism: A Chapter for the History of Modern Poetry.* Norman, Okla.: University of Oklahoma Press, 1951.

Harmer, J. B. *Victory in Limbo: A History of Imagism 1908–1917.* New York: St. Martin's Press, 1975.

Hughes, Glenn. *Imagism and Imagists.* Stanford, Calif.: Stanford University Press, 1931.

Hulme, T. E. *Speculations: Essays on Humanism and the Philosophy of Art.* Edited by Herbert Read. New York: Harcourt Brace & Co., 1924.

Hynes, Sam, ed. *Further Speculations by T. E. Hulme.* Minneapolis, Minn.: University of Minnesota Press, 1955.

Roberts, Michael. *T. E. Hulme.* London: Faber and Faber, 1938.

Chapter 2   T. S. Eliot

Poetry of T.S. Eliot

Separate Works

Prufrock and Other Observations. London: The Egoist, 1917.
Poems. New York: Alfred A. Knopf, 1920.
The Waste Land. New York: Boni and Liveright, 1922.
Ash Wednesday. London: Faber and Faber, 1930.
Sweeney Agonistes. London: Faber and Faber, 1932.
The Rock. London: Faber and Faber, 1934.
Four Quartets. New York: Harcourt, Brace, 1943.

Selected and Collected Editions

Poems 1909–1925. London: Faber and Gwyer, 1925.
Collected Poems 1909–1935. London: Faber and Faber, 1936.
The Complete Poems and Plays. New York: Harcourt, Brace, 1952.
Poems Written in Early Youth. London: Faber and Faber, 1967.
T. S. Eliot, The Waste Land: A Facsimile and Transcript of the Original Drafts Including the Annotations of Ezra Pound. Edited by Valerie Eliot. New York: Harcourt Brace Jovanovich, 1971.

Prose of T. S. Eliot

Separate Works

Ezra Pound: His Metric and Poetry. New York: Alfred A. Knopf, 1918.
The Sacred Wood: Essays on Poetry and Criticism London: Methuen, 1920.
Homage to John Dryden. London: L. and V. Woolf, 1924.
For Lancelot Andrewes. Garden City, N.Y.: Doubleday, Doran and Co., 1929.
The Use of Poetry and the Use of Criticism. Cambridge, Mass.: Harvard University Press, 1933.
After Strange Gods: A Primer of Modern Heresy. London: Faber and Faber, 1934.
Elizabethan Essays. London: Faber and Faber, 1934.
The Frontiers of Criticism. Minneapolis: University of Minnesota Press, 1956.
To Criticize the Critic. New York: Farrar, Straus & Giroux, 1965.

Selected and Collected Editions

Essays Ancient and Modern. New York: Harcourt, Brace and Co., 1936.
Selected Essays 1917–1932. New York: Harcourt, Brace and Co., 1932.
On Poetry and Poets. New York: Noonday Press, 1961.
Selected Prose of T. S. Eliot. Edited by Frank Kermode. New York: Harcourt Brace Jovanovich and Farrar, Straus and Giroux, 1975.

Books on T. S. Eliot

Bradbrook, C. M. *T. S. Eliot: The Making of The Waste Land.* London: Longman, 1972.

Drew, Elizabeth. *T. S. Eliot: The Design of His Poetry*. New York: Charles Scribner's Sons, 1949.

Freed, Lewis, *T. S. Eliot: The Critic as Philosopher*. West Lafayette, Ind.: Purdue University Press, 1979.

Frye, Northrop. *T. S. Eliot*. New York: Grove Press, 1963.

Gallup, Donald. *T. S. Eliot and Ezra Pound*. New Haven, Conn.: Henry W. Wenning/C.A. Stonehill, Inc., 1970.

Gardner, Helen. *The Art of T. S. Eliot*. London: The Cresset Press, 1949.

——. *The Composition of Four Quartets*. New York: Oxford University Press, 1978.

Gordon, Lyndale. *Eliot's Early Years*. New York: Oxford University Press, 1977.

Hargrove, Nancy Duvall. *Landscape as Symbol in the Poetry of T. S. Eliot*. Jackson, Miss.: University of Mississippi Press, 1978.

Kenner, Hugh. *The Invisible Poet: T. S. Eliot*. New York: McDowell, Obolensky, 1959.

Martin, Graham. *Eliot in Perspective*. New York: Humanities Press, 1970.

Matthews, T. S. *Great Tom*. New York: Harper & Row, 1974.

Matthiessen, F. O. *The Achievement of T. S. Eliot: An Essay on the Nature of Poetry*. New York: Oxford University Press, 1935. Second edition, enlarged, 1947. Third edition, with additional chapter by C. L. Barber, 1958.

Maxwell, D. E. S. *The Poetry of T. S. Eliot*. London: Routledge and Kegan Paul, 1952.

Miller, James E. *T. S. Eliot's Personal Waste Land*. University Park, Pa.: Pennsylvania State University Press, 1977.

Moody, A. D. *Thomas Stearns Eliot, Poet*. Cambridge: Cambridge University Press, 1979.

Mowbray, Allan. *T. S. Eliot's Impersonal Theory of Poetry*. Lewisburg, Pa.: Bucknell University Press, 1974.

Preston, Raymond. *Four Quartets Rehearsed*. New York: Sheed and Ward, 1946.

Ramsey, Warren. *Jules Laforgue and the Ironic Inheritance*. New York: Oxford University Press, 1953.

Rees, Thomas R. *The Technique of T. S. Eliot*. The Hague: Mouton, 1974.

Sencourt, Robert. *T. S. Eliot: A Memoir*. New York: Dodd, Mead & Co., 1971.

Smith, Grover. *T. S. Eliot's Poetry and Plays: A Study in Sources and Meaning*. Chicago: University of Chicago Press, 1974.

Southam, B. C. *A Guide to the Selected Poems of T. S. Eliot*. New York: Harcourt, Brace & World, 1968.

Spender, Stephen. *T. S. Eliot*. New York: Viking Press, 1976.

Tate, Allen, ed. *T. S. Eliot: The Man and His Work*. New York: Delacorte Press, 1966.

Unger, Leonard, ed. *T. S. Eliot: A Selected Critique*. New York: Rinehart, 1948.

Articles on T. S. Eliot Referred to in Text

Arrowsmith, William. "Daedal Harmonies." *Southern Review*, n.s. 13 (January 1977):1–47.

Clausen, Christopher. "Tintern Abbey to Little Gidding." *Sewanee Review* 84 (Summer 1976):405–24.

Cleophas, Sister M. "Notes on Levels of Meaning in *Four Quartets*." *Renascence* 2 (1950):102–16.

Fussell, B. H. "Structural Methods in *Four Quartets*." *Journal of English Literary History* 22 (1955):212–41.

Howarth, Herbert. "Eliot, Beethoven, J. W. N. Sullivan." *Comparative Literature* 9 (Fall

1957):322–32.

Lake, D. J. "T. S. Eliot's 'Vita Nuova' and 'Mi Chemin': The Sensus Historicus." *Ariel* (English) 2 (1971):43–57.

Stanford, Donald E. "Classicism and the Modern Poet." *Southern Review,* n.s. 5 (Spring 1969):475–500.

———. "Two Notes on T. S. Eliot." *Twentieth Century Literature* 1 (1955):133–34.

Storm, Leo. "J. M. Robertson and T. S. Eliot." *Journal of Modern Literature* 5 (April 1976):315–21.

West, Roy B., Jr. "Personal History and the *Four Quartets.*" *New Mexico Quarterly* 23 (1953):269–82.

Winters, Yvor. "T. S. Eliot: The Illusion of Reaction." *Kenyon Review* 3 (Winter 1941):7–30; 3 (Spring 1941):221–39.

General

Books with Introductions by T. S. Eliot

Barnes, Djuna. *Nightwood.* With an introduction by T. S. Eliot. New York: Harcourt, Brace & Co., 1937.

Literary Essays of Ezra Pound. Edited with an introduction by T. S. Eliot. London: Faber and Faber, 1934.

Philippe, Charles-Louis. *Bubu of Montparnasse.* With a preface by T. S. Eliot. New York: Avalon Press, 1945.

Valéry, Paul. *The Art of Poetry.* With an introduction by T. S. Eliot. New York: Pantheon Books, 1958.

———. *Le Serpent.* Translated by Mark Wardle, with an introduction by T. S. Eliot. London: R. Cobden-Sanderson, 1924.

Other

Barker, Ernest. *Traditions of Civility.* Cambridge: At the University Press, 1948.

Santayana, George. *Three Philosophical Poets: Lucretius, Dante, Goethe.* Cambridge, Mass.: Harvard University Press, 1910.

Symons, Arthur. *The Symbolist Movement in Literature.* New York: E. P. Dutton, 1919.

Tate, Allen. *Essays of Four Decades.* Chicago: Swallow Press, 1968.

Taupin, René. *L'influence du symbolisme français sur la poesie americaine.* Paris: Librairie Ancienne Honoré Champion, 1929.

Chapter 3   Wallace Stevens

Poetry of Wallace Stevens

Separate Works

Harmonium. New York: Alfred A. Knopf, 1923.

Harmonium. 2d ed. New York: Alfred A. Knopf, 1931.

Ideas of Order. New York: Alfred A. Knopf 1936.

Owl's Clover. New York. Alcestis Press, 1936.

The Man with the Blue Guitar. New York: Alfred A. Knopf, 1937.

Parts of a World. New York: Alfred A. Knopf, 1942.

Notes toward a Supreme Fiction. Cummington, Mass.: Cummington Press, 1942.

Esthétique du Mal. Cummington, Mass.: Cummington Press, 1945.

Transport to Summer. New York: Alfred A. Knopf, 1947.

Three Academic Pieces. Cummington, Mass.: Cummington Press, 1947.

A Primitive like an Orb. New York: Banyan Press, 1948.

The Auroras of Autumn. New York: Alfred A. Knopf, 1950.

Selected and Collected Editions

The Collected Poems of Wallace Stevens. New York: Alfred A. Knopf, 1954.

The Palm at the End of the Mind: Selected Poems and a Play by Wallace Stevens. Edited by Holly Stevens. New York: Alfred A. Knopf, 1971.

Prose of Wallace Stevens

Separate Works

The Necessary Angel: Essays on Reality and the Imagination. New York: Alfred A. Knopf, 1951.

Selected and Collected Editions

Opus Posthumous. Edited, and with an introduction by Samuel French Morse. New York: Alfred A. Knopf, 1957.

Letters of Wallace Stevens. Edited by Holly Stevens. New York: Alfred A. Knopf, 1966.

Books on Wallace Stevens

Beckett, Lucy. *Wallace Stevens.* Cambridge: Cambridge University Press, 1974.

Benamou, Michel. *Wallace Stevens and the Symbolist Imagination.* Princeton, N.J.: Princeton University Press, 1972.

Blessing, Richard Allen. *Wallace Stevens' "Whole Harmonium."* Syracuse, N.Y.: Syracuse University Press, 1970.

Brown, Ashley, and Haller, Robert S. *The Achievement of Wallace Stevens.* New York: J. B. Lippincott Co., 1962.

Brown, Merle E. *Wallace Stevens: The Poem as Act.* Detroit: Wayne State University Press, 1970.

Doggett, Frank. *Wallace Stevens: The Making of the Poem.* Baltimore, Md., and London: Johns Hopkins University Press, 1980.

——, and Buttel, Robert. *Wallace Stevens: A Celebration.* Princeton, N.J.: Princeton University Press, 1980.

Kermode, Frank. *Wallace Stevens.* London: Oliver and Boyd, 1960.

Kessler, Edward. *Images of Wallace Stevens.* New Brunswick, N.J.: Rutgers University Press, 1972.

Lentricchia, Frank. *The Gaiety of Language.* Berkeley: University of California Press, 1968.

Litz, Walton A. *Introspective Voyager: The Poetic Development of Wallace Stevens.* New York: Oxford University Press, 1972.

Middlebrook, Diane. *Walt Whitman and Wallace Stevens.* Ithaca, N.Y., and London: Cornell University Press, 1974.

Morris, Adelaide Kirby. *Wallace Stevens: Imagination and Faith.* Princeton, N.J.: Princeton University Press, 1974.

Morse, Samuel French. *Wallace Stevens: Poetry as Life.* New York: Pegasus, 1970.

Pearce, Roy Harvey, and Miller, J. Hillis, eds. *The Act of the Mind: Essays on the Poetry of Wallace Stevens.* Baltimore, Md.: Johns Hopkins University Press,1965.

Perlis, Alan. *Wallace Stevens: A World of Transforming Shapes.* Lewisburg, Pa.: Bucknell University Press, 1976.

Riddel, Joseph N. *The Clairvoyant Eye: The Poetry and Poetics of Wallace Stevens.* Baton Rouge, La.: Louisiana State University Press, 1965.

Stevens, Holly. *Souvenirs and Prophecies: The Young Wallace Stevens.* New York: Alfred A. Knopf, 1977.

Vendler, Helen Hennessy. *On Extended Wings: Wallace Stevens' Longer Poems.* Cambridge, Mass.: Harvard University Press, 1969.

Articles on Stevens Referred to in Text

Bates, Milton J., "Major Man and Overman: Wallace Stevens' Use of Nietzsche." *Southern Review* 15 (Autumn 1979):811–39.

Cunningham, J. V. "The Poetry of Wallace Stevens." *Poetry* 75 (December 1949):149–65.

——. "The Styles and Procedures of Wallace Stevens." *Denver Quarterly* 1 (Spring 1966):8–28.

Martz, Louis. "The World as Meditation." *Yale Review* 47 (1958):517–36.

Munson, Gorham. "The Dandyism of Wallace Stevens." *The Dial* 79 (November 1925):413–17.

Pearce, Roy Harvey. "Wallace Stevens: The Life of the Imagination" *PMLA* 66 (September 1951):561–82.

——. "Chocorua to Its Neighbor." *Southern Review* 15 (October 1979):777–91.

Peterson, Margaret. "*Harmonium* and William James." *Southern Review* 7 (July 1971):658–82.

Stevens, Holly. "Flux^2." *Southern Review* 15 (Autumn 1979):771–74.

Stocking, Fred H. "Stevens' 'Bantams in Pine-Woods'." *Explicator* 3 (April 1945), Item 45.

Winters, Yvor. "Wallace Stevens, or the Hedonist's Progress" in *In Defense of Reason* (New York, 1947):431–59.

General

Arnett, Willard A. *George Santayana.* New York: Washington Square Press, 1968.

Miller, J. Hillis. *Poets of Reality.* Cambridge, Mass.: Harvard University Press, 1965.

Miller, James E., Jr. *The American Quest for a Supreme Fiction.* Chicago: University of Chicago Press, 1979.

Perkins, David. *A History of Modern Poetry.* Cambridge, Mass.: Harvard University Press, 1976.

Steiner, George. *After Babel.* New York.: Oxford University Press, 1975.

Wallace Stevens Centennial Issue. Southern Review 15 (Autumn 1979). Eleven essays on Stevens.

Wallace Stevens and the Romantic Heritage. Southern Review 7 (Summer 1971). Eight essays on Stevens.

Chapter 4   Edwin Arlington Robinson

Poetry of Edwin Arlington Robinson

Separate Works

The Torrent and the Night Before. Cambridge, Mass.: Privately printed, 1896.
The Children of the Night. Boston: Badger, 1897.
Captain Craig. Boston and New York: Houghton Mifflin, 1902.
The Town down the River. New York: Scribner's, 1910.
The Man against the Sky. New York: The Macmillan Company, 1916.
Merlin. New York: The Macmillan Company, 1917.
Lancelot. New York: Seltzer, 1920.
The Three Taverns. New York: The Macmillan Company, 1920.
Avon's Harvest. New York: The Macmillan Company, 1921.
Roman Bartholow. New York: The Macmillan Company, 1923.
The Man Who Died Twice. New York: The Macmillan Company, 1924.
Dionysus in Doubt. New York: The Macmillan Company, 1925.
Tristram. New York: The Macmillan Company, 1927.
Sonnets 1889–1927. New York: Gaige, 1928.
Cavender's House. New York: The Macmillan Company, 1929.
The Glory of the Nightingales. New York: The Macmillan Company, 1930.
Matthias at the Door. New York: The Macmillan Company, 1931.
Nicodemus. New York: The Macmillan Company, 1932.
Talifer. New York: The Macmillan Company, 1933.
Amaranth. New York: The Macmillan Company, 1934.
King Jasper. New York: The Macmillan Company, 1935.

Selected and Collected Editions

Tilbury Town: Selected Poems of Edwin Arlington Robinson. Edited by Laurance
   Thompson. New York: The Macmillan Company, 1953.
Selected Poems of Edwin Arlington Robinson. Edited by Morton D. Zabel. New York:
   The Macmillan Company, 1965.
Selected Early Poems and Letters of E. A. Robinson. Edited by Charles T. Davis. New
   York: Holt, Rinehart and Winston, 1960.
Collected Poems. New York: The Macmillan Company, 1921.
Collected Poems. New York: The Macmillan Company, 1929.
Selected Poems. New York: The Macmillan Company, 1931.
Collected Poems. New York: The Macmillan Company, 1937.
Uncollected Poems and Prose of Edwin Arlington Robinson. Edited by Richard Cary.
   Waterville, Maine: Colby College Press, 1975.

Prose of Edwin Arlington Robinson

Letters

"Early Letters of Edwin Arlington Robinson." Edited by Daniel Gregory Mason. *Virginia
   Quarterly Review* 13 (1937):52–69.

Selected Letters of Edwin Arlington Robinson. Edited by Ridgely Torrence. New York: The Macmillan Company, 1940.

Untriangulated Stars: Letters of Edwin Arlington Robinson to Harry de Forest Smith 1890–1905. Edited by Denham Sutcliffe. Cambridge, Mass.: Harvard University Press, 1947.

Edwin Arlington Robinson's Letters to Edith Brower. Edited by Richard Cary. Cambridge, Mass.: Harvard University Press, 1968.

Books on Edwin Arlington Robinson

Anderson, Wallace L. *Edwin Arlington Robinson: A Critical Introduction.* Cambridge, Mass.: Harvard University Press, 1969.

Barnard, Ellsworth. *Edwin Arlington Robinson: A Critical Study.* New York: The Macmillan Company, 1952.

——, ed. *Edwin Arlington Robinson: Centenary Essays.* Athens, Ga.: University of Georgia Press, 1969.

Bates, Esther Willard. *Edwin Arlington Robinson and His Manuscripts.* Waterville, Maine: Colby College Library, 1944.

Brown, Rollo Walter. *Next Door to a Poet.* New York: Appleton-Century, 1937.

Cary, Richard. *Appreciation of Edwin Arlington Robinson: 28 Interpretive Essays.* Waterville, Maine: Colby College Press, 1969.

——. *Early Reception of Edwin Arlington Robinson: The First Twenty Years.* Waterville, Maine: Colby College Press, 1974.

Cestre, Charles. *An Introduction to Edwin Arlington Robinson.* New York: The Macmillan Company, 1930.

Coffin, R. P. T. *New Poetry of New England: Frost and Robinson.* Baltimore, Md.: Johns Hopkins Press, 1938.

Coxe, Louis O. *Edwin Arlington Robinson: The Life of Poetry.* New York: Pegasus, 1969.

Fussell, Edwin. *Edwin Arlington Robinson: The Literary Background of a Traditional Poet.* Berkeley and Los Angeles: University of California Press, 1954.

Hagedorn, Hermann. *Edwin Arlington Robinson: A Biography.* New York: The Macmillan Company, 1938.

Kaplan, Estelle. *Philosophy in the Poetry of Edwin Arlington Robinson.* New York: Columbia University Press, 1940.

Morris, Lloyd. *The Poetry of Edwin Arlington Robinson.* New York: Doran, 1923.

Murphy, Francis, ed. *Edwin Arlington Robinson: A Collection of Critical Essays.* Englewood Cliffs, N.J.: Prentice-Hall, 1970.

Neff, Emery. *Edwin Arlington Robinson.* New York: William Sloane Associates, 1948.

Redman, Ben Ray. *Edwin Arlington Robinson.* New York: McBride, 1926

Richards, Laura E. *E.A.R.* New York: Princeton University Press, 1921.

Robinson, W. R. *Edwin Arlington Robinson: A Poetry of the Act.* Cleveland, Ohio: Western Reserve University Press, 1967.

Smith, Chard Powers. *Where the Light Falls: A Portrait of Edwin Arlington Robinson.* New York: The Macmillan Company, 1965.

Van Doren, Mark. *Edwin Arlington Robinson.* New York: Literary Guild of America, 1927.

Winters, Yvor. *Edwin Arlington Robinson.* Norfolk, Conn.: New Directions, 1971.

Articles on Robinson Referred to in Text

Adams, Richard P. "The Failure of Edwin Arlington Robinson." *Tulane Studies in English* 11 (1961):97–151.

Cary, Richard. "The Library of Edwin Arlington Robinson: Addenda." *Colby Library Quarterly,* series 7 (March 1967):398–415.

Cary, Richard. "Robinson's Notes to His Nieces." *Colby Library Quarterly,* series 5 (December 1960):195–203.

Grimm, Clyde L. "Robinson's 'For a Dead Lady': An Exercise in Evaluation." *Colby Library Quarterly* 7 (December 1967):535–47.

Hill, Robert H. "More Light on a Shadowy Figure: A. H. Louis, the Original of E. A. Robinson's 'Captain Craig'." *Bulletin of the New York Public Library* 60 (August 1956):373–77.

Hudson, Hoyt H. "Robinson and Praed." *Poetry* 61 (February 1943):612–20.

Levenson, J. C. "Robinson's Modernity." *The Virginia Quarterly Review* 44 (Autumn 1968):590–610.

MacVeagh, Lincoln. "Edwin Arlington Robinson." *New Republic* 2 (10 April 1915):267–68.

Nivison, David S. "Does It Matter How Annandale Went Out?" *Colby Library Quarterly,* series 5 (December 1960):170–75.

Perrine, Laurence. "Robinson's 'Veteran Sirens'." *Explicator* 6 (November 1947), Item 13.

Pettit, Henry. "Robinson's *The Whip.*" *Explicator* 1 (April 1943).

Robinson, W. R. "E. A. Robinson's Yankee Conscience." *Colby Library Quarterly* 8 (September 1969):371–85.

Romig, Edna Davis. "Tilbury Town and Camelot." *University of Colorado Studies* 19, no. 3 (1932):303–26.

Roosevelt, Theodore. "The Children of the Night." *Outlook* (New York) 80 (August 12, 1905):913–14.

Sutcliffe, W. Denham. "The Original of Robinson's Captain Craig." *New England Quarterly* 16 (September 1943):407–31.

Untermeyer, Louis. "E.A.R.: a Remembrance," *Saturday Review* (April 10, 1965):33–34.

Weber, C. J. "Poet and President." *New England Quarterly* 16 (December 1943):615–26.

Winters, Yvor. "Religious and Social Ideas in the Didactic Works of E. A. Robinson." *Arizona Quarterly* 1 (Spring 1945):70–85.

General

Anderson, George K. *The Legend of the Wandering Jew.* Providence, R.I.: Brown University Press, 1965.

Blackwood, Algernon. *Episodes before Thirty.* New York: E. P. Dutton & Co., 1923.

Nordau, Max Simon. *Degeneration.* New York: D. Appleton and Co., 1896.

Royce, Josiah. *The Spirit of Modern Philosophy.* Boston and New York: Houghton Mifflin Co., 1892.

Tate, Allen. *Essays of Four Decades.* Chicago: Swallow Press, 1968.

Winters, Yvor. *The Function of Criticism.* Denver, Colo.: Alan Swallow, 1957.

Chapter 5   Yvor Winters

Poetry of Yvor Winters

Separate Works

The Immobile Wind. Evanston, Ill.: Monroe Wheeler, 1921.

The Magpie's Shadow. Chicago: Musterbrookhouse, 1922.

The Bare Hills: A Book of Poems. Boston: The Four Seas Co., 1927.

The Proof. New York: Coward McCann, 1930.

The Journey and Other Poems. Ithaca, N.Y.: The Dragon Press, 1931.

Before Disaster. Tryon, N.C.: The Tryon Pamphlets, 1934.

Poems. Los Altos, Calif.: The Gyroscope Press, 1940.

The Giant Weapon. [Norfolk, Conn.]: New Directions, 1943.

To the Holy Spirit: A Poem. [San Francisco]: The Club of California, 1947.

Three Poems. Cummington, Mass.: The Cummington Press, 1950.

Selected and Collected Editions

Collected Poems. Denver, Colo.: Alan Swallow, 1952. Enlarged edition, 1960.

The Collected Poems of Yvor Winters. With an introduction by Donald Davie. Manchester, England: Carcanet New Press, 1978; Chicago: The Swallow Press [1980].

The Early Poems of Yvor Winters 1920–28. With an introduction by Yvor Winters. Denver: Alan Swallow, 1966.

Prose of Yvor Winters

Separate Works

Notes on the Mechanics of the Poetic Image: The Testament of a Stone. Secession no. 8, April 1924. Reprinted in *Uncollected Essays and Reviews.*

The Case of David Lamson: A Summary. In collaboration with Frances Theresa Russell. San Francisco: Lamson Defense Committee, 1934.

Primitivism and Decadence: A Study of American Experimental Poetry. New York: Arrow Editions, 1937.

Maule's Curse: Seven Studies in the History of American Obscurantism. Norfolk, Conn.: New Directions, 1938.

The Anatomy of Nonsense. Norfolk, Conn.: New Directions, 1943.

Edwin Arlington Robinson. Norfolk, Conn.: New Directions, 1946. Revised edition, 1971.

In Defense of Reason. New York: Swallow Press and William Morrow and Co., 1947.

The Function of Criticism: Problems and Exercises. Denver, Colo.: Alan Swallow, 1957.

The Poetry of W. B. Yeats. The Swallow Pamphlets no. 10. Denver, Colo.: Alan Swallow, 1960.

Forms of Discovery: Critical and Historical Essays on the Forms of the Short Poem in English. Denver, Colo.: Alan Swallow, 1967.

Selected and Collected Editions

Yvor Winters on Modern Poets. With an introduction by Keith McKean. New York: Meridian Books, 1959.

Yvor Winters: Uncollected Essays and Reviews. Edited and introduced by Francis Murphy. Chicago: The Swallow Press, 1973.

Books on Yvor Winters

Isaacs, Elizabeth. *An Introduction to the Poetry of Yvor Winters.* Chicago: Swallow Press and Ohio University Press, 1981.

Johnson, Carol. *Reason's Double Agents.* Chapel Hill: University of North Carolina Press, 1966. [A chapter on Yvor Winters.]

Kaye, Howard. *The Poetry of Yvor Winters.* Ann Arbor, Mich.: University Microfilms, 1969.

McKean, Keith F. *The Moral Measure of Literature.* Denver, Colo.: Alan Swallow, 1961. [A chapter on Winters.]

Powell, Grosvenor. *Language as Being in the Poetry of Yvor Winters.* Baton Rouge: Louisiana State University Press, 1980.

Sexton, Richard J. *The Complex of Yvor Winters' Criticism.* The Hague: Mouton, 1973.

Articles on Winters Referred to in Text

Cunningham, J. V. "Obscurity and Dust." *Poetry* 40 (June 1932):163–65.

Kaye, Howard. "The Post-Symbolist Poetry of Yvor Winters." *Southern Review,* n.s. 7 (Winter 1971):176–97.

Oliver, Raymond. "Yvor Winters and the English Renaissance." *Southern Review,* n.s. 17 (Autumn 1981):

Peterson, Douglas L. "Yvor Winters' 'By the Road to the Air Base'." *Southern Review,* n.s. 15 (Summer 1979):567–74.

Powell, Grosvenor. "Yvor Winters' Greek Allegories." *Southern Review,* n.s. 14 (Spring 1978):262–80.

General

Chapman, Charles E. *A History of California: The Spanish Period.* New York: The Macmillan Company, 1921.

Cleland, Robert Glass. *A History of California: The American Period.* New York: The Macmillian Company, 1922.

The Diary of Johann August Sutter. San Francisco: Grabhorn Press, 1932.

Dillon, Richard. *Fool's Gold.* New York: Coward-McCann, 1967.

Fields, Kenneth Wayne. *The Rhetoric of Artifice.* Ann Arbor, Mich.: University Microfilms, 1967.

Housman, A. E. *The Name and Nature of Poetry.* New York: The Macmillan Company, 1933.

Jung, C. J., and Kerényi, C. *Essays on a Science of Mythology.* Bollingen Series 12. New York: Pantheon Books, 1949.

Momaday, N. Scott, ed. *The Complete Poems of Frederick Goddard Tuckerman, with a Critical Foreword by Yvor Winters.* New York: Oxford University Press, 1965.

The Poems of T. Sturge Moore. Collected Edition, 4 vols. London: Macmillan and Co., 1932.

Ransom, John Crowe. *The World's Body.* New York: Charles Scribner's Sons, 1938.

Todd, Edgeley W., ed. *Astoria.* Norman, Okla.: University of Oklahoma Press, 1964.

Zollinger, Peter. *Sutter: The Man and His Empire.* New York: Oxford University Press, 1939.

Index